GOSPELS *of* WEALTH

GOSPELS *of* WEALTH

How the Rich Portray Their Lives

Paul G. Schervish,
Platon E. Coutsoukis, and
Ethan Lewis

PRAEGER

Westport, Connecticut
London

Library of Congress Cataloging-in-Publication Data

Schervish, Paul G.
    Gospels of wealth : how the rich portray their lives / Paul G.
Schervish, Platon E. Coutsoukis, and Ethan Lewis.
       p. cm.
    Includes bibliographical references and index.
    ISBN 0–275–94643–6.—ISBN 0–275–95094–8 (pbk.)
    1. Wealth—United States—Moral and ethical aspects.
2. Millionaires—United States—Interviews. 3. Sociology—
Biographical methods. I. Coutsoukis, Platon E. II. Lewis, Ethan.
III. Title.
HC110.W4S34 1994
332'.092'273—dc20   94–33272

British Library Cataloguing in Publication Data is available.

Library of Congress Catalog Card Number: 94–33272
ISBN: 0–275–94643–6
ISBN: 0–275–95094–8 (pbk.)

First published in 1994

Praeger Publishers, 88 Post Road West, Westport, CT 06881
An imprint of Greenwood Publishing Group, Inc.

Printed in the United States of America

The paper used in this book complies with the
Permanent Paper Standard issued by the National
Information Standards Organization (Z39.48–1984).

10 9 8 7 6 5 4 3 2 1

This book is dedicated to

Julia, Gabriel, and Alexander
—PGS

Sandy, my wife, and my son, Christopher
—PEC

My mother, with love
—EL

Contents

Preface

Over the past eight years I have been engaged with several graduate students in studying the biographical narratives of wealthy individuals. These narratives were obtained from interviews conducted with 130 millionaires from 1985 to 1987 in connection with the Study on Wealth and Philanthropy,[1] funded by the T. B. Murphy Foundation Charitable Trust and carried out under my direction at Boston College. Two of the students who worked on this project, Platon Coutsoukis and Ethan Lewis, now join me as authors of this book.

In the course of our interviews with 130 millionaires we learned much about the meaning of wealth and the lives of the wealthy. We have also taken the opportunity to listen to what others have to say in support or in reproof of those with riches. Perhaps the most important lesson I learned turned out to be more about myself than about the rich. It is that when it comes to such a highly charged issue as wealth, we need to cultivate the sober posture of neither adulation nor attack, of being neither at the feet nor at the throat of the wealthy.

In a culture that so highly values industriousness, we are easily tempted to let our predispositions about a group's economic virtue sway our judgments about its moral stature. As curious as it may seem at first, it is not by chance that defenders of the rich are frequently the most vociferous detractors of the poor and vice versa. In both cases the basis for criticism is the same, namely that someone has accrued a level of advantage without exercising a corresponding level of responsibility. We hear that the wealthy are powerful but reckless in their lifestyles and financial dealings. Similarly, the complaint against the poor, especially the welfare poor, is that they are beneficiaries of the liberal state but derelict in regard to family, education, and work.

The major effect of these considerations on our thinking has been to suggest a novel approach to the narratives we heard during the interviews. We would speak neither for nor against the wealthy without first letting them speak for themselves. This required a fresh point of departure. That starting point, it turns out, is to examine the biographical accounts of the wealthy first and foremost as moral biographies. That is, before setting out on a course of criticism or praise we must first listen to what the wealthy recount as the set of moral obligations to which they respond in charting their daily lives. This does not mean that we must abandon all critical evaluation of what we hear. It does mean, however, that before we can make any case for or against the rich, we must first understand the cases they make on their own behalf.

What I have to say about the moral biographies of the wealthy has appeared in several publications.[2] In this book we offer readers the opportunity to listen to and evaluate these moral biographies. We have selected twelve articulate narratives which are highly representative of the female and male inheritors and entrepreneurs we interviewed. By providing extended excerpts from the transcripts, we enable others to make their own sense of the world of wealth and the wealthy. An introductory essay, "The Wealthy and the World of Wealth," outlines the general conceptual framework we have developed to interpret the biographical narratives of the wealthy. In addition, we introduce each transcript with a thematic summary in which we highlight the motifs we found most salient in that narrative. Naturally we hope that our approach proves useful. But our primary concern in this book is to encourage other complementary and even contradictory interpretations.

From the outset of the Study on Wealth and Philanthropy, we insured respondents anonymity but advised them that material from their interviews would be used in publications. Therefore, throughout the book we have taken steps to conceal the true identity of the individuals we interviewed. In addition to providing pseudonyms for the respondents, we have substituted fictitious names for those individuals, institutions, businesses, and locations to which respondents make reference. For instance, we would refer to a real estate developer from Detroit who tells about making a contribution to the University of Michigan medical school as a fast-food franchiser from Chicago who made a contribution to the Northwestern University business school. In assembling our narratives, we have extracted the most relevant passages from each interview. Where appropriate we have reordered passages to form more coherent story lines and edited grammar to make accounts more readable. In all instances we have eschewed the practice of constructing composite narratives whereby a researcher pieces together statements from numerous respondents in order to fashion a typical account.

Many people have contributed to making this book possible. My greatest debt of gratitude is to Thomas B. Murphy, who intellectually inspired and financially supported our examination of the financial and spiritual biographies of the wealthy. I am also grateful to Donald J. White, Dean of the Graduate School of Arts and Sciences at Boston College, and Paul Slaggart, at that time an officer in the Boston College Development Office, who brought me together with Tom Murphy at the inception of the research. I am also grateful to Andrew Herman and Lynn Rhenisch, who helped conduct interviews and manage the Study on Wealth and Philanthropy. Andrew Herman, who was my co-author on the study's final report and on several presentations and articles, will always be valued as a kind and intelligent colleague to whom I owe so much of my thinking on the meaning and practice of wealth. Study advisory board members Anne Bartley, Norbert Fruehauf, Virginia A. Hodgkinson, John Lowell, and J. Donald Monan, S.J., along with Lillian H. Bauder, Jeanne Johnson, and Thomas B. Murphy were only for reasons of personal generosity repeatedly instrumental in helping us secure access to respondents. Finally, I want to make what is anything but a perfunctory expression of appreciation to all the respondents, and especially to those whose stories are contained anonymously in this book. In every instance they were generous with their time and forthcoming about their lives.

NOTES

1. For a discussion of the research methodology and a description of the sample, see Paul G. Schervish and Andrew Herman, *Empowerment and Beneficence: Strategies of Living and Giving Among the Wealthy*, Final Report of the Study on Wealth and Philanthropy (Social Welfare Research Institute, Boston College, 1988).

2. In addition to *Empowerment and Beneficence*, publications based on the Study of Wealth and Philanthropy include Paul G. Schervish, "Wealth and the Spiritual Secret of Money," in Robert Wuthnow and Virginia A. Hodgkinson , editors, *Faith and Philanthropy in America: Exploring the Role of Religion in America's Voluntary Sector*, (San Francisco: Jossey-Bass, 1990); "The Moral Biographies of the Wealthy and the Cultural Scripture of Wealth," in Paul G. Schervish, editor, *Wealth in Western Thought: The Case for and Against the Rich* (Westport, Conn.: Praeger, 1994); and Paul G. Schervish with Obie Benz, Peggy Dulany, Thomas B. Murphy, and Stanley Salett, *Taking Giving Seriously* (Indianapolis: Indiana University Center on Philanthropy, 1993).

Paul G. Schervish

GOSPELS *of* WEALTH

Introduction: The Wealthy and the World of Wealth

Paul G. Schervish

ELEMENTS OF A SOCIOLOGY OF WEALTH

David Frisby remarks that in writing *The Philosophy of Money* Georg Simmel "extracted the totality of the spirit of the age from his analysis of money."[1] The twelve first-person accounts contained in this book enable us to extract at least part of the spirit of our age. The conceptual scheme that follows outlines the framework which my associates and I have developed to analyze the biographical narratives we gathered in the course of our interviews with 130 millionaires between 1985 and 1987. Some of what we have to say about each transcript is briefly stated in our short introduction to each transcript. So that readers may understand the conceptual language we use there and have at least a rudimentary starting point for their own interpretations, we outline the core themes and associated concepts we have developed over the past few years to make sense of the lives of the wealthy. We fully expect that with the transcripts before them, readers will develop many additional and even more insightful interpretations of what the wealthy have to say.

The broad theoretical framework with which we analyze the wealthy and the world of wealth is what I call the *sociology of wealth*. The sociology of wealth focuses our attention upon the central role of riches in the dual processes of socialization and social construction, that is, the daily routines of learning about and shaping the world. The sociology of wealth examines those particular processes by which the rich learn the privileges and responsibilities of wealth and exercise those privileges and responsibilities in fashioning the world around them.

Technically, to be considered wealthy in our research, an individual had to have at least $1 million in net worth in 1985 dollars. In reality, only five of our respondents enjoyed a net worth less than $5 million—and those were all young inheritors who had not yet received the bulk of their legacy. But from the point of view of sociology, the wealthy are those individuals who are financially secure. These are the individuals in the top 1% of the wealth distribution who in their own lives are in little or no danger of having their fortune decimated even by grave illness. The financially secure are those who in their own lifetime are unlikely to backslide into the middle class. Being wealthy is a matter of possessing "fortunes," says Andrew Carnegie, "not moderate sums saved by many years of effort, the returns from which are required for the comfortable maintenance and education of families." This latter condition "is not wealth, but only competence, which it should be the aim of all to acquire, and which it is for the best interests of society should be acquired."[2]

The research agenda of a sociology of wealth is to explore how money in general, and wealth in particular, is a resource of social life that is both constraining and enabling, a matter, as I said, of socialization and social construction. This is the twofold interplay or dialectic of alignment: an alignment of the wealthy to the rules of wealth and an alignment of the world to the will of the wealthy. On the one hand, wealth provides a set of rules that must be internalized if it is to be mobilized as a means of self-expression and power. The wealthy become aligned to the objective rules of money, or the way money works in the world. Through such alignment the wealthy obtain their earliest financial identity, an identity that provides initial conceptions about themselves and money. Entrepreneurs must learn the rules of wealth accumulation. They must learn how to find a niche in the market and then successfully administer a company in a competitive environment. Inheritors must learn the personal and social responsibilities commensurate to their status, including what it means to be philanthropic, how to inculcate the values of wealth in their children, and how to apportion the family trust to subsequent generations. On the other hand, this alignment to the rules of money imbues the rich with both the conscious desire and the objective means to mobilize wealth as an efficacious resource to reconstitute themselves and the world. Although there are rules to learn and obligations to follow, there are also horizons to pursue and expectations to fulfill. Wealth enables the wealthy to fulfill their wills. Yes, the rules of entrepreneurship and inheritance must be honored, but with money in hand, whole new opportunities for business, investment, politics, philanthropy, self-development, and leisure arise.

In this chapter, I will speak about three general aspects of the sociology of wealth that are relevant for analyzing the biographical accounts of the wealthy. The first is the distinctive attributes of *freedom* that accompany wealth and endow the wealthy with temporal, spatial, and psychological empowerment. The second aspect of the sociology of wealth is the particular social capacity of the rich to create rather than simply work within given institutions. This capacity, which I term *hyperagency*, enables the wealthy to build a worldly domain of *principality* and an inner domain of self-confident *individuality*. Hyperagency is the fundamental class trait of the rich and is the common thread running through power-elite, capitalist class, cultural-leadership, and moral-stewardship theories of the wealthy. The third element in a sociology of wealth concerns the self-presentation of the wealthy in the genre of *moral biography*. The wealthy tell their stories as morality-plays. They present their lives as dramatic narratives organized under three rubrics: the *dialectic of fortune and virtue, liminality*, and *nomos*. The dialectic of fortune and virtue is the dynamic interplay between the circumstances given by fate and the dedicated efforts of an individual to improve one's fate. Liminality is the experience of undergoing a process of self-transformation whereby the wealthy move from being disposed over by their wealth to disposing over it. The nomos is the symbolic discourse within which the wealthy frame their narratives of fortune, virtue, and liminality, for example, as stories of rebirth, insight, healing, forgiveness, or reunion.

I discuss a fourth element of a sociology of wealth in the Afterword to this book where I explore the rules for interpreting the "truth" of moral biographies and for undertaking a critical assessment of these narratives. The starting point for assessing the "truth" of what the wealthy have to say is to recognize that what they say is itself a "truth." As I will argue, any critique of the wealthy must begin not with a litany of their irresponsibilities but with an assessment of inadequacies in their array of responsibilities.

WEALTH, FREEDOM AND EMPOWERMENT

Freedom

Freedom is the most frequently cited material resource of wealth. Being rich confers a twofold set of freedoms. The first is *freedom from* necessity—freedom from having to earn one's daily bread. The second dimension of empowerment for wealthy individuals is *freedom to* choose among alternative realms of involvement, to exercise their talents, to pursue their desires, and, most importantly, to become effective actors in the world. Although most respondents use the word "freedom" to summarize these fundamental empowering capacities of wealth, their actual practice of this freedom reveals three intersecting forms of empowerment: temporal, spatial, and psychological.

Temporal Empowerment

Temporal empowerment refers to the capacity of the wealthy to overcome the usual constraints of time. Riches enable them to reconstitute the consequences of the past, extend their interests into the future even beyond their mortality, and free themselves from the inexorable march of time in the present. The wealthy do not have to remain passive receivers of what has been bequeathed to them by fortune. Rather, they are able to accentuate those aspects of their personal and social past that they deem beneficial, deflect the negative consequences of previous events, and redeem aspects of their lives they have come to regret. For instance, numerous inheritors strive diligently to recast the meaning of their family's wealth by mobilizing their money to engage in what they consider to be more socially responsible investment portfolios, career paths, and philanthropic strategies than their forebears.

In addition to reshaping the past, the wealthy also activate the future. The empowerment of money enables them not simply to await the future but to initiate it by intervening in the present to shape the contours of coming events. By founding family businesses, endowing foundations, funding political causes, and establishing a structure of trust funds, the wealthy set in motion an active agenda that meets their desires and shapes how others will operate.

It is in the present, of course, that the wealthy redeem the past and initiate the future. But the wealthy exercise temporal empowerment in regard to the present simply by substituting money for time. By hiring accountants, housekeepers, gardeners, and personal secretaries to perform various mundane tasks, the wealthy expand the portion of the day they can devote to doing what they want or what they deem important. Moreover, being well-to-do frees up time that would otherwise be spent in the marketplace shopping around for the best prices on clothing, cars, home furnishings, and vacations. None of this means, however, that the wealthy sit around doing nothing. Indeed, they feel the same pressures as the rest of us to remain industrious. But when they choose, they have the money and can make the time to play golf, take a trip, participate in therapy, or support philanthropic causes.

Spatial Empowerment

Spatial empowerment is the geographical counterpart to temporal empowerment. It refers to how the wealthy extend themselves territorially into the world and create a social space over which they exercise control. This spatial domain of empowerment is much like a castle. It simultaneously provides a fortress of independence, a citadel of command, and a visible outpost that secures their dominion in more than one place at the same time.

The first manifestation of spatial empowerment is living within a fortress of independence. The wealthy enjoy a form of sovereign autonomy that enables them to physically move about the world as they wish while, at the same time, insulating themselves from the movements or intrusions of others. On the one hand, autonomous sovereignty entails the ability to move freely through the physical world and, therefore, through the social world in pursuit of sites of self-expression and control. This means not just that the wealthy can travel widely or avoid the travels of others, but also that they can gain social access even to those people and activities that like themselves are spatially protected. The wealthy travel to the meetings and vacation spots of their choice; they move freely in and out of business, political, and philanthropic involvements; and they gain personal access to government officials, celebrities, and other luminaries. On the other hand, the wealthy can carefully insulate themselves in sanctuaries of independence that shield them from the unwanted intrusions or demands of others. They often build a physical, and thus social, barrier around themselves through such accoutrements as limousines with heavily tinted glass, exclusive residences with security guards, and aides-de-camp to screen funding requests and appointments.

The second aspect of spatial empowerment entails the construction of a far-reaching *base of command*. A base of command is the array of positions and organizations through which an individual exercises control over the way others act and think. Such power is rooted not just in the legally supported property rights associated with the ownership of businesses, financial investments, and real estate, or with the holding of executive positions, board memberships, and public offices. It derives equally from informal expressions of influences such as deciding whether to fund certain causes, candidates, or endeavors. The ability to establish bases of command extends to many areas of life and to a wide territory. As family heads, investors, business owners, philanthropists, political contributors, and board members, the rich command the organizational and economic resources to mobilize even at a distance the time, skills, and consciousness of others. In this way, spatial empowerment can be understood as a series of material "outposts" of the wealthy, reflections and bearers of their will that have an effective influence even in their physical absence.

The final dimension of spatial empowerment is the creation of visible outposts that physically embody the personal presence of the wealthy individual simultaneously in more than one place. Whether in the form of an art collection, home, business operation, real estate empire, or personal foundation, such artifactual re-presentations are not simply lifeless physical objects, but active expressions of who they are and what they want to accomplish. If the notion of base of command emphasizes the organizational capacities of the wealthy influence over a broad territory from a central location, the complementary notion of visible outposts emphasizes the capacity of the wealthy to make their interests, values, aspirations—indeed their very selves—physically present in many places at once through specific organizations and social activities. Such visible outposts can in fact be considered franchises of one's self. The most obvious forms of such outposts are the factories, offices, and retail locations of one's business as well as retail franchises that dot a geographical territory. Other examples of artifactual representation include the creation of foundations, institutes, museum collections, and hospital wings that even when they do not bear a family name are nevertheless spatial extensions of the wealthy person's presence. In addition, many extend their spatial empowerment by self-promotion through advertising, press releases, and other forms of publicity. Finally, there is a not-so-obvious yet common way the wealthy create franchises of the self. This is through the way they lend their "character" or imprint their "personality" on both the general directions and everyday workings of their companies, estate planning, consumption patterns, and philanthropy. For instance, the couple who were most concerned about concealing their family background, possession of wealth, control over a personal foundation, and extensive philanthropic giving were also among the respondents most intent upon ensuring that the activities they engaged in—including living in a modest home—closely mirrored their stringent personal values about living a simple lifestyle.

Psychological Empowerment

Whereas temporal and spatial empowerment are the capacities whereby the wealthy extend and imprint a self upon the world, psychological empowerment refers to their corresponding consciousness whereby they perceive themselves as possessing an important destiny and the wherewithal to accomplish it. Psychological empowerment is the combination of great expectations and confidence. In contrast to temporal and spatial empowerment, psychological empowerment is less exclusively the preserve of the wealthy, and can be seen as characterizing the personal disposition of all people with confident egos. We all know people who command a particularly self-assured understanding of the relation of self to world, people we describe in such divergent phrases as "being in, but not of the world," "strength of character," and "powerful personality." Yet wealth is a potent ingredient for generating psychological empowerment because it depends in such large measure upon the ability to insulate oneself from the pressures of the mundane. Clearly, material wealth promotes the attitude that one's self-determined goals are more important than an agenda imposed from the outside, and that one has the right and ability to pursue such self-determined goals.

In our research we discovered two distinct—even contrary—stages of psychological empowerment. The first, and usually earlier, phase centers around the development of a resolute worldview wherein the wealthy are at the controlling center of their social involvements. At this stage, psychological empowerment is the combination of knowing their interests and sensing their ability and entitlement to pursue these interests. Such psychological empowerment is apparent in the determined vision of many entrepreneurs who confidently discount the element of risk in their transition from the safe harbor of salaried employment to the uncharted waters of independent and self-directed enterprise. This same determination leads many inheritors to assertively claim positions of authority and stewardship in progressive community foundations or in more conventional cultural institutions. For inheritors and entrepreneurs alike, then, psychological empowerment invariably gets set in motion as the "great expectation" that one may forthrightly pursue private interests as a public contribution.

If the first phase of psychological empowerment revolves around feeling entitled and efficacious in regard to one's interests, the second entails self-reflective attention to the source and quality of those interests. At this second level psychological empowerment becomes characterized by a set of orientations related to what psychologists call self-actualization and what spiritual traditions refer to as holiness or wisdom. In this phase, psychological empowerment becomes the capacity of the wealthy to turn their attention inward in an effort to evaluate the spiritual or moral quality of their interests and propose to themselves a less self-centered set of priorities. Those who do so may be described as having learned the *spiritual secret* of money. The scope of their self-interest increasingly broadens and deepens to include a greater diversity of people and needs. If in the first phase of psychological empowerment the wealthy base their public behavior on their private interests, in the second they base their personal concerns on public needs.

For some of our respondents, these two phases of psychological empowerment turn out to be sequential. This is most clearly exemplified by respondents who recount a radical conversion from trying to accumulate or consume as much material wealth as possible to trying to spend more time with their families or become more involved in religious or philanthropic endeavors. But the distinction between the two phases of psychological empowerment cannot be reduced to a distinction between economic enterprise and philanthropy. Indeed, one of our major findings is that philanthropy may reflect the first level of psychological empowerment just as business activity may reflect the second. In fact, many of our respondents bring the second level of psychological empowerment to bear equally on their economic and philanthropic activities so as to eliminate the separation between them as two distinct moral fields of practice. For instance, one high-tech entrepreneur recounts mobilizing his business aspirations only after coming to recognize that business success was the condition for making a social contribution. The most effective way to improve the lives of the needy, he reasoned, was to go into a lucrative venture whose profitability would fund philanthropic endeavors and offer the opportunity for him to institute participatory and humanistic worker-management relations. Thus, the second level of psychological empowerment is not a question of the type of action but of the dispositions that couch that action, namely how thoroughly one is motivated by an empathetic care for others.

HYPERAGENCY, PRINCIPALITY, AND INDIVIDUALITY

Hyperagency

In broadest terms the empowerment of the wealthy can be described as the capacity to exercise *hyperagency*. This is the ability to determine the conditions and circumstances of life instead of merely living within them. As *agents*, most people search out the most suitable place for themselves in a world constructed by others. As *hyperagents*, the wealthy construct a world that suits their desires and values. If agency means ferreting out the best possible path within the institutionally given constraints imposed by others, hyperagency means being able to construct a self and a world that transcend the established institutional limits and, in fact, create the limits for others. As one real estate magnate declares, wealth grants him the "power to get through time and red-tape barriers. I can pick up the phone and call a congressman who's heard my name and I can have the impact of one million votes on the issue with a phone call. You always have the upper hand in negotiating, and it allows you to do in one-tenth the time what it would take somebody else ten times the time [to do] because of the credibility they'd have to develop."

Agents *find*, hyperagents *found*; that is, where agency means finding one's place in the world, hyperagency means founding the world. Hyperagency is a form of expanded freedom. "I'm free, you know. I'm free of financial restrictions. It's wonderful. What more could I want?" declares a woman with inherited wealth who recognizes her potential to shape her destiny. "I have money that I can do things with—for myself and for the causes I feel are important. My next career could be anything. I have that freedom and I'm not afraid to sort of think, 'well, maybe you *could* do that.' "

Principality

Hyperagency is not some abstract capacity. On the contrary, it is always concretely manifested through the two interrelated activities of world-building and self-construction, that is, through the interrelated domains of *principality* and *individuality*. Principality is the embodiment of hyper-agency in the spheres of time and space; individuality the embodiment of hyperagency in the sphere of self and identity.

Principality is the sum total of social activities, organizations, and property through which individuals concretely exhibit the spatial and temporal empowerment spoken of above. In some way, all people have a modest principality just as they have at least a modest individuality. The most obvious difference is the extensive size and duration of the principalities of the wealthy, which for some includes the capacity to enlarge their realm of command by gaining influence over government, economic, and cultural institutions. Put simply, the wealthy are distinctive in the extent to which they are able to align institutions to their wills rather than simply jockey for advantage within the given domains.

Principalities take a variety of forms. These include self-directed organizations such as businesses or foundations; personal property such as clothing, automobiles, yachts, and homes; involvement in organizations controlled by others, such as board memberships, named hospital wings, and university chairs; and leadership and fund-raising positions in public and cultural affairs. Whatever form it takes, every principality is essentially an extended material presence expanding the horizons of spatial and temporal empowerment. For example, entrepreneurs initially incarnate their aspirations and ideas in the form of a business. As their enterprises succeed, the territory, scope, and durability of their principality expands. They open new facilities, expand markets, venture into new product areas, diversify investments, plan for their retirement, and establish vehicles for passing on their money. The world-constructing potential of wealth emerges as well in the entrepreneurs' personal lives—as indeed, it does for inheritors. The wealthy increase the comfort, size, and geographical dispersion of their homes. They travel more broadly. And they otherwise accrue material possessions such as clothing, jewelry, art, boats, and automobiles that publicly enlarge the range of their self-expression. The wealthy expand the boundaries of their principality even further by establishing outposts or satellites of influence as they support cultural institutions, sponsor medical research, contribute to political campaigns, and revitalize their cities.

Individuality

Where principality involves world-building, individuality revolves around self-construction. For most people, identity derives in large measure from how they accommodate themselves to the world. For the wealthy, however, accommodation to the world is complemented, and in extreme cases virtually eliminated, by accommodating the world to themselves. Individuality, then, is the distinctive psychological attribute of identity characterized both by a sense of entitlement to shape the world in accord with one's desires and by the confident drive to do so. Individuality is the effect of a conscious and successful effort to enhance one's worldly presence as a hyperagent. It is the outcome of being able to forge a tight link between what one wants to be and what one is capable of becoming. It is the concrete manifestation of psychological empowerment.

In many instances, individuality derives from an explicit project of self-construction directed at building a centered, fulfilled, and assured personality. Counseling, religious practice, and various other paths of spiritual growth provide the insight, inspiration, and support to develop a fortified—though not necessarily enlightened—personality. But even those who do not actively pursue such psychological renovation are never content for long with passively coping with the world. The wealthy rarely accede to institutional forces that threaten to circumscribe their sense of psychological sovereignty. Almost to a person, our respondents articulate not just a desire, but a moral obligation to take charge of their lives and govern their fortune. Rather than serving their riches, they make their riches serve them in the realms of business, family, consumption, and philanthropy. For instance, inheritors who at first experience wealth as imposing an alien identity wrestle with their fate until they arrive at a more propitious self-understanding. Wealthy entrepreneurs derive their sense of individuality from their business success. But even before such success occurs, entrepreneurs often manifest an embryonic individuality. Often from childhood prospective entrepreneurs harbor the aspirations for autonomy, wealth, and self-expression that inspire that critical transition from employee to employer and set in motion an entrepreneurial career. No matter the origins of wealth, the essence of individuality is that enhanced sense of self or strength of character that Machiavelli called *virtù*, and which we know as virtue. As such, individuality is that inner domain of self-knowledge, self-assurance, and self-dedication by which the wealthy aspire to great expectations of principality and from which they receive the emotional wherewithal to brave the challenge of these expectations.

DRAMATIC NARRATIVES OF MORAL BIOGRAPHY

In addition to being about empowerment and hyperagency, the twelve narratives presented in this book are also about morality. Morality is the normatively directed use of power. To tell one's story as a moral biography requires an account of *both* power and normative bearings. In this section we discuss how in content and style the autobiographical accounts enunciated by our respondents are morality tales. In addition to telling about their lives of freedom and empowerment, they highlight the array of struggles they face, the responsibilities they feel, and the sacrifices they make in order to improve their own lives and the lives of those around them. Like all of us, the wealthy attempt to present their stories in a good light. This does not mean that their stories are exceptionally self-righteous or self-serving. In fact we hear much about failures and unmerited breaks and advantages. Yet, as important as these are, such episodes of failure and luck always remain part of a larger moral narrative. In such a narrative the wealthy individual is the central dramatic character not only in overcoming failure but in making use of fortuitous circumstances. To present one's biography in a good light, then, does not require the telling of a perfect life—but the telling of a meaningful life, a life with a general upward trajectory of betterment for which the narrator is always partly responsible.

Dialectic of Fortune and Virtue

The wealthy routinely employ three narrative techniques that turn their accounts of principality and individuality into moral biographies of world-building and self-construction. The first technique is to describe their life as a dialectical process of *fortune and virtue* whereby individuals recount their dedicated and sometimes arduous efforts to better the hand dealt by fate.

In recounting their biographies, both those who earned or inherited their wealth continually emphasize their efforts to utilize advantages and overcome obstacles in every aspect of their daily lives. We interpret this common phenomenon as representing an underlying dialectic of fortune and virtue by which the wealthy move from being disposed over, or socialized by the world, to disposing over, or socially constructing it. By means of disciplined effort and strength of character—*virtue*—the wealthy repeatedly attempt to transform the circumstances they face—*fortune*—into something better or more satisfying. This establishes a new fortune that in turn requires the attention of virtue. The wealthy are not particularly self-righteous about their devotion to virtue. Rather, they see virtue as the necessary and, indeed, quite unexceptional dedication to actively amending their fate.

Liminality

The second technique is to highlight those especially important periods of transition or transformation which anthropologists refer to as *liminality*.[3] Respondents describe such episodes as periods in their lives when they endure and eventually overcome various forms of suffering as they advance along their moral journeys. During these relatively extensive transition periods, the wealthy undergo often profound transformations of identity and social position. Drawing on anthropological and literary studies, we refer to such phases as periods of *liminality*, from the Latin word meaning *threshold* or passageway. As such, liminality denotes the boundaries between and passage through different stages of life and identity that occur at important turning points, such as becoming an entrepreneur or receiving the first installment of a substantial inheritance. In times of liminality, virtue is especially significant. For it is at the crossroads of life that it becomes especially important to transform those aspects of fate that fortune imposes as obstacles, sufferings, or challenges. By focusing on these periods of liminality, respondents highlight the intricate process of change by which they move from one stage of their relation to money to the next and hence from one stage of identity to another. For instance, we often hear of the changes in self-conception and behavior that occur when successful entrepreneurs search for other ave-

nues of self-expression outside of their business life, or when disen-
chanted inheritors explore vocations in business, politics, or philanthropy separate from the traditional expectations and responsibilities
they feel their families have obliged them to assume.

The Nomos

The third narrative technique is to relate the foregoing implementations
of virtue and passages through liminality within a framework of literary
imagery or *nomos*.[4] Each narrative nomos is a dramatic story of life, death,
and rebirth told through the symbolic motifs of initiation, healing, learning,
and forgiveness. *Nomos* is the Greek word meaning law, ordering principle,
or pattern, and here denotes a dramatic progression through identifiable
phases of self-development. As such, a nomos is the coherent thematic
pattern that organizes the story line of a narrative and shapes the particular
language, tone, and imagery by which the respondents express their virtuous encounters with fortune and liminality.

There are as many nomos patterns as there are symbolic motifs. But at
its core, each nomos expresses the journey from an initial condition
through a phase of transformation (liminality) to a new plateau of identity. This plateau then constitutes the starting point for the next phase of
world-building and self-construction where the dialectic of fortune and
virtue begins anew. The most encompassing formulation of the progression is at the *archetypal* level where it takes the form of the ontological
progression from life, to death, to rebirth. Although some respondents
adequately capture their biographies with this basic imagery, most further portray their nomos by adding imagery at the *mythic* and even more
specific *figurative* levels. The four mythic patterns bridging the archetypal
and figurative levels are *gnosis* (learning insights), *purgation* (obtaining
reconciliation), *healing* (restoring health), and *initiation* (becoming incorporated). Table 1 schematically describes the nomos patterns at the archetypal, mythic, and figurative levels of abstraction.

For example, where an individual biography is couched in terms of an
iterative quest for understanding or insight we designate it as an instance
of the mythic pattern of gnosis. This gnosis pattern often becomes specified at the figurative level as "the Odyssey" or an "awakening." The
dominant theme of Odyssey is one of a continual testing and trial that
generates an upward spiral of wisdom and inspiration. The dramatic
nomos of awakening entails the progression from an initial personal
dilemma inducing a period of painful self-scrutiny and eventuating in a
self-revelation establishing a fortified identity. By designating the leading
or combined nomos patterns for each individual, we interpret biographies not as a series of discrete events but as integrated and thematically
coherent totalities with spiritual purpose and moral consequence. The

Table 1
Archetypal, Mythic, and Figurative Patterns of Dramatic Progression

Level of Analysis	Nomos Pattern	Dramatic Structure		
		Initial Condition	*Liminality*	*Denouement*
Archetypal	*Calendrical-Cosmogonic*	life	death	rebirth
Mythic	*Initiation*	union	separation	reunion
	Forgiveness	sin	purgation	reconciliation
	Gnosis	experience	questioning	insight
	Healing	health	illness	restoration
Figurative (examples)	*Courtship*	attraction	tribulation	marriage
	Vocation	being lost	call/transformation	mission
	Horatio Alger	arrival	trial	success
	Journey/Odyssey	home	adventure/test	establishment of new home
	Agricultural	planting	growth	harvest
	Sport/War	engagement	combat	victory
	Business	investment	risk/failure	profit
	Awakening	confusion	self-scrutiny	revelation

upshot is a description of the personal histories of our respondents within an analytical framework that goes beyond how the respondents spontaneously characterize themselves but which remains congruent with the fertile imagery and meanings they attribute to their lives.

Every narrative in our research incorporates all three of the foregoing techniques simultaneously. We distinguish among them here only for the sake of description. For instance, a narrative of healing (nomos) entails the overcoming of mental or physical distress (liminality) by the exercise of dedicated effort (virtue). Taken in concert, the three narrative techniques establish one's life story as a moral biography. Applying virtue to improve one's lot in the normal course of daily affairs, the dutiful exertion of virtue during especially difficult liminal transitions, and the symbolic framing of one's life as initiation, healing, learning, and forgiveness—all contribute to authenticating the implicit claim that the empowerment of wealth is married to normative bearing and, thereby, that one's story is a moral drama.

THE SOCIOLOGY OF WEALTH AND
THE GOSPEL OF WEALTH

In describing the major lines of a sociology of wealth, we have emphasized two issues: empowerment and responsibility. As we have indicated, accounts of both power and responsibility are necessary for the wealthy to cast their life stories as moral biographies. In regard to power, we emphasize the specially privileged agency by which the wealthy (1) possess freedom from constraint and freedom of choice; (2) embody a confident inner disposition of psychological empowerment or *individuality*; and (3) actualize that individuality in their efforts of world-construction or principality. The empowerment of wealth grants the rich that extraordinary attribute of hyperagency. Rather than simply wending their way through institutional constraints, the wealthy are institution builders.

We contend that this hyperagency or institution building is the chief attribute or class trait of the wealthy. Heretofore, theories of the wealthy in modern capitalist society have stressed the organizational or social conditions that enable the rich to forge, defend, and legitimate their privilege. *Marxist theory*, for example, argues that the class power of the wealthy derives from their ownership of the means of production. By controlling economic production, capitalists are able to exploit workers, accumulate wealth, and shape the contours of the political and cultural spheres.[5] Alternatively, various *consumption theories*, which draw much of their intellectual heritage from Thorstein Veblen, view the wealthy as driven by consumerism, as objects of popular emulation, and as the leading purveyors of fashion and high culture.[6] A third strain of research on the wealthy is the variety of *power elite theories* that highlight the processes by which the wealthy and their sponsored representatives obtain decision-making power by gaining control of the upper reaches of political, cultural, religious, medical, leisure, entertainment, educational, and other leading institutions.[7] Finally there is the moral stewardship model of the wealthy. This approach views the wealthy as especially dedicated to employing resources in the sphere of production and sometimes in the sphere of philanthropy in a manner that advances social welfare. Far from being hedonistic consumers, the wealthy are the indispensable agents in the socially necessary process of capital accumulation and investment.[8]

Despite the numerous important insights generated by these predominant theories, they all suffer from a common defect. Each of these theoretical approaches makes the mistake of generalizing about the wealthy as a class from an attribute that characterizes only a subgroup of the class. As important as they may be, ownership of the means of production, lifestyle and prestige, control over social, political, and economic policy, and moral stewardship pertain to only certain segments of the wealthy. In contrast, the foregoing sociology of wealth suggests a more fundamental formulation of the distinctive class trait of the wealthy. This general class trait is hyperagency. The advantage of this characterization is that in addition to retaining empowerment as a key element, hyperagency is a capacity shared by all members of the class, both those who exercise principality and individuality in the public realm as well as those who choose to pursue their world building and self-construction only in the more localized private spheres of their lives. The ability of the rich to create the institutional environment in which they choose to live, and in which others must live, is the distinctive class trait of the wealthy. It is also the elemental starting point for reframing existing theories.

If the major insight in regard to empowerment revolves around the notion of hyperagency, the major insight in regard to responsibility concerns the notion of moral biography. We have examined three narrative techniques by which the wealthy recount their life stories as morality tales. These techniques, in part because the wealthy are not directly aware of using them, reflect the underlying emotional predispositions of the wealthy toward feeling and responding to what they perceive as the array of moral obligations enveloping their daily round. Just as the notion of empowerment describes the outer world of wealth and the wealthy, the notion of moral biography describes the inner world. The daily supervision of fate by virtue, the dutiful suffering through liminal transitions, and the symbolic composition of autobiographical narratives are all implicit strategies for presenting lives as moral tales. The wealthy are not just world builders. Rightly or wrongly they view themselves as disciples. From their perspective, they are followers of an ethical path both in how they perform in the face of obstacles and in what they feel as obligating duties.

By no means does their, or our, charting of their lives as moral biographies exempt the wealthy from ethical scrutiny. Indeed, as I will discuss in the Afterword to this book, important issues of interpretation and evaluation must be attended to in order to hold such empowered agents to principles of accountability beyond what they themselves contemplate. Nevertheless, the wealthy and the world of wealth must first and foremost be examined for what they are, namely, a self-acknowledged conjoining of power and responsibility. As such, we can justifiably call their life stories, including the narratives that follow, *contemporary gospels of wealth.*

In two famous essays Andrew Carnegie charts a practical course of philanthropy for the wealthy who wish to fulfill their civic and religious duties.[9] Carnegie's essays did not originally bear the title "Gospel of Wealth," which was provided by the editor who compiled the two essays for publication. Fortunately, the title is apt. For what we hear from Carnegie is a report of his personal economic discipleship in which he links the socially productive accumulation and distribution of wealth to the moral dictates of Providence. The wealthy whose stories are told here have not sought to apply the appellation of "gospel" to their lives any more than Carnegie and Jesus did. Nevertheless, insofar as the wealthy tell a moral tale of empowerment linked to responsibility, their stories are gospels. That is, the wealthy tender stories in which the central protagonist is offered as a model for emulation.

In every story we hear about the dramatic progression of financial success and spiritual growth in which it is crucial to state how *both* empowerment and normative direction are operative. Whenever either power or responsibility is missing, there is no possibility of an active morality. On the one hand, power without normative direction excludes morality because hyperagency ends up being at best, capricious, and at worst, arbitrary. On the other hand, normative direction without a domain of empowerment also excludes the possibility of morality, in this case because even the noblest normative purpose turns out to be materially ineffectual and inconsequential. In the end, unraveling the ubiquitous *interplay* of empowerment and morality as it takes form in contemporary gospels of wealth is our strategy for making sociological sense of the wealthy and the world of wealth. We present the following narratives with the intention of providing an opportunity for others to evaluate whether our interpretation makes sense and to improve upon it.

NOTES

1. David Frisby, "Introduction to the Translation" in *Georg Simmel on Individuality and Social Forms*, edited by Donald N. Levine (Chicago: University of Chicago Press, 1971), p. 7.

2. Andrew Carnegie, *The Gospel of Wealth and Other Timely Essays*, Edward C. Kirkland (ed.) (Cambridge, Mass.: Harvard University Press, 1962), p. 19.

3. See, for instance, Victor W. Turner, *The Ritual Process: Structure and Anti-Structure* (Chicago: Aldine, 1969).

4. I have worked with this notion of nomos for so long that it is hard for me to know exactly which aspects of this framework I have developed and which I have learned from others. It is clear, however, that I owe my greatest debt to Thomas E. Porter who, as my teacher and in his writing, introduced me to this framework in the study of drama. See Thomas E. Porter, *Myth and Modern American Drama* (Detroit: Wayne State University Press, 1969). In addition to Porter and Turner I am indebted to the anthropological and philosophical writings of Van Gennep, Huizinga, and Lonergan. See Arnold Van Gennep, *The Rites of Passage*, Monika B. Vizedom and Gabrielle L. Caffee, trans. (Chicago: University of Chicago Press, 1961); Johan Huizinga, *Homo Ludens: A Study of the Play Element in Culture* (Boston: Beacon Press, 1969); Bernard F. Lonergan, *Insight: A Study of Human Understanding* (New York: Philosophical Library, 1958).

5. Just two examples are Karl Marx, *Capital: A Critique of Political Economy, Volume I: The Process of Capitalist Production*, edited by Frederick Engels (New York: International Publishers, 1967, originally published in 1867; and Karl Marx and Frederick Engels, *Manifesto of the Communist Party*, in *Karl Marx and Frederick Engels, Selected Works*, Volume One (Moscow: Progress Publishers, 1969, originally published in 1848).

6. See Thorstein Veblen, *The Theory of the Leisure Class* (New Brunswick, N.J.: Transaction Publishers, 1992, reprint of 1889 edition). In the footsteps of Veblen are Stuart Ewen, *Captains of Consciousness: Advertising and the Social Roots of the Consumer Culture* (New York: McGraw-Hill, 1976); Stuart Ewen and Elizabeth Ewen, *Channels of Desire: Mass Images and the Shaping of American Consciousness* (Minneapolis: University of Minnesota Press, 1992); and G. William Domhoff, *The Higher Circles: The Governing Class in America* (New York: Vintage Books, 1971) and *The Bohemian Grove and Other Retreats: A Study in Ruling-Class Cohesiveness* (New York: Harper & Row, 1974).

7. The power elite tradition is represented by C. Wright Mills, *The Power Elite* (Oxford: Oxford University Press, 1956); and G. William Domhoff, *Who Rules America Now?: A View for the 80s* (Englewood Cliffs, N.J.: Prentice-Hall, 1983) and *The Power Elite and the State: How Policy Is Made in America* (New York: Aldine DeGruyter, 1990).

8. The moral stewardship model is espoused by Max Weber, *The Protestant Ethic and the Spirit of Capitalism*, translated by Talcott Parsons (New York: Macmillan, 1958, originally published 1904–05); Peter L. Berger, *The Capitalist Revolution: Fifty Propositions about Prosperity, Equality, and Liberty* (New York: Basic Books, 1968; Peter L. Berger, editor, *The Capitalist Spirit: Toward a Religious Ethic of Wealth Creation* (San Francisco, Calif.: ICS Press, 1990); Andrew Carnegie, *Gospel of Wealth*; and Michael Novak, *This Hemisphere of Liberty: A Philosophy of the Americas* (Washington, D.C.: The AEI Press, 1990) and *The Catholic Ethic and the Spirit of Capitalism* (New York: Free Press, 1993).

9. Andrew Carnegie, *The Gospel of Wealth*.

1

Brendan Dwyer:
The Primacy of Ideas

Dwyer embodies his own belief that ideas are the nation's prime resource. The fifty-seven-year-old entrepreneur made his first fortune from his innovative insurance plan, his second from an innovative publishing house that specializes in Bibles. Wealth, and the thinking that goes into making wealth, he has turned to religious concerns.

In all the realms of his life—financial, philanthropic, and principally, spiritual—what matters most to Brendan Dwyer is obtaining the proper insight. "I'm not sure there's anything more to my secret than attempting to find some worthwhile idea." Material capital, as Dwyer puts it, is "subsidiary"; "intellectual capital" keys success. After all, "you can take a flawed idea and execute it perfectly and you've got a boondoggle."

There have been few "boondoggles" among the 57-year-old Detroiter's ventures. His own "peculiar combination of learning and data" combined his math skills with the insight that he could sell these skills in a competitive market. He parlays them first into a special electronics post in the Navy and a college education courtesy of the GI Bill, then in the insurance world, where the demand for actuaries always exceeds the supply. His stake in ideas eventually gives Dwyer command of his own time when, having patented a new technique for calculating actuarial tables, he goes into business for himself. "Time is the ultimate resource." When one has more time, one has more time for ideas. Dwyer expands his entrepreneurial ventures from being a self-made man simply to making others: "There's a great deal of intellectual capital resident and I'd like to find a way to tap that." One idea leading to the growth of more is the steady but incessant conviction to spur the economy. "Business growth [is] the magic, the golden goose. . . . Economic growth can meet needs on a broader scale." The ideas most worth "searching out [are] ideas that are directed at growth on a larger scale."

But growth and the intellectual capital that fuels it leads, most importantly, to a spiritual end. Dwyer demonstrates this personally through an intertwining of Roman Catholicism, business, and philanthropic involvement. The crowning achievement of his intellectual investment occurs when he backs a religious publishing house. The spiritual aims of the company are united with keen business sense: Dwyer makes Green Meadows lucrative by cornering the American Bible market; it becomes a unique supplier of Good Books just as Summit alone could offer Dwyer's actuarial calculations. In traditional charitable affairs, Dwyer remains the entrepreneur, investing his funds in charities toward which he feels "a personal conviction" and the ability "to make a difference." Philanthropic gifts not so motivated (of which Dwyer gives many) he equates with "utility bill[s]; their payment is essential but for maintenance purposes, not for genuine, spiritual growth."

And as business works in a spiritual sphere, it is imperative for Dwyer that the converse be the case. What drew him to Green Meadows was its philosophy that the operation be run according to Christian principles. Green Meadows promotes a Christian environment in the workplace. Likewise in commerce, it practices Christian ethics. Dwyer points to the example of the firm turning the other cheek—losing a significant sum because the purchaser "made an honest mistake" and Green Meadows had "a long-term relationship with them." Yet according to Dwyer, Christian principles contribute to the success of business. In the long term, "there is no inherent conflict" between temporal and spiritual imperatives.

This is true as well for an individual, in whom spirituality and *principality*, *fortune* and *virtue*, are plotted jointly. Dwyer's keenest insight is perhaps his greater "concern about my vertical relationship than horizontal." The spiritual axis, more important in itself, governs the temporal. When vertically attuned to God, one keeps horizontally oriented in the material world. "My role is to attempt, insofar as I can, to harmonize my activity with the roles that the Creator would like to have born. . . . To the extent my activity harmonizes with the role He sees for me, I'm going to have a peace and tranquillity you can't get in any other way. And when I'm in conflict with that, then I'm going to have a certain tension and disunity." Fortune and virtue are thus complementary; spirituality and individuality virtually synonymous. According to Dwyer, it is no accident that the various strands of his cosmos (business, philanthropy, spirituality) coincide to form one strand. When one "harmonizes" his role with the Maker, this internal harmony is a matter of course; to use Dwyer's terms, the union "evolves" over time.

BIOGRAPHICAL NARRATIVE

Child of the Depression
"At the time you are going through it, you don't think it is particularly bad, but in retrospect . . ."

I was born in Worcester, Massachusetts in 1927. So I grew up during the depths of the Depression. And there was no question that we were poor, but we didn't really know it so it didn't make that much of a difference. Our family suffered during the Depression, and had to deal with unemployment. My mother and father both graduated from high school but they worked in a shoe factory; they both met there. And then, my father left the shoe factory, and worked a little bit for one of the utilities and got involved in politics. And so, he was gainfully employed when the Democrats were in. He got work maybe a little more frequently than would otherwise be the case [laughs]. But he would go through periods of unemployment, when the Democrats were out of office. And when he was unemployed, he'd somehow or other arrange something until the Democrats got back in. But there'd be periods when we would have difficulty, but he came from a large family and our aunts—he had a lot of sisters—would somehow or other cooperate or make contributions. So our family survived during that period. You know, we got by. At the time you are going through it you don't think it is particularly bad, but in retrospect, it was a moderately unpleasant time right through 1939 or 1940. Then the war started to break out and Dad got involved working at one of the shipyards. And, during most of that time, right up till the time I got through high school, my mother was able to stay home. Then she went back to the shoe factory, and she was working in the shoe factory until I was maybe two years out of college.

I had done two stretches in the military. I got in at the very end of World War II. I graduated from high school in 1945. And I had good math scores, so I applied for one of these electronic groups in the Air Force. I got out quickly, got out as the war ended. And that actually provided most of the money for my tuition at Holy Cross. The GI Bill just provided everything but one semester. And in the year that I graduated, my father died that summer, at the age of fifty. And there was enough money somehow or other in the family to go to business school. But first, I did a quick stint, maybe a year and a half in Korea, as an aeronautical engineer. Then came back, finished one semester of business school, and went to work.

The reason I went into the actuarial business is that my degree was in mathematics. At least in those days, there were limited areas for applied mathematics. And the requirements to enter were extremely demanding, but there was almost a guarantee that the demand for actuaries would exceed the supply. I was security conscious. I felt I could meet the requirements and then I would be in control of them so unemployment wouldn't be a hazard. And it still isn't today. I would say I was security conscious because the Depression made me live with a certain insecurity. So it was a product of the Depression. Money was always in short supply. It was needed and it wasn't there so security became one of my early goals.

Finding Your Niche in the Market
"Nobody else knew how to do it."

As I said, actuaries were always in a situation where the demand exceeded the supply, so if you went down and asked for the job, at reasonable compensation, you usually got it. And I worked briefly in Chicago, then came back to Boston. And the nature of the actuarial science was you're taking a series of, at that time it was eight, examinations, and every year you get a raise. And so, I went to work in 1953, became an associate in the Society of Actuaries, that was '54, became a company actuary in 1956 or so. I got my fellowship in the Society of Actuaries in 1959, became vice-president in Actuary of Boston Liberty Life Insurance Company, in 1959. In 1964, I became executive vice-president of Federal Enterprises. That was my number two job. And in 1969 the president retired and, for one reason or another, they did not make me president but they made me vice chairman of the board. That was an awkward, awkward position. The company was dominated by Harvard people, with one exception, there was one Dartmouth guy there. So I was the only Holy Cross guy there. However, that had nothing to do with the fact that they didn't make me president.

But when they didn't make me president it was a situation that wasn't going to work out. So I went to Michigan. I had an opportunity to work in Michigan. I had three or four opportunities to go other places. And all that time I always made more money than I needed and was an investor.

My goal in the fifties, sixties, and early seventies was to rise as far as I could within the company, but at the same time, to accumulate assets that would produce an income independently of my own earnings. Why was that important? Because, in my own framework, assets independent of my own earnings let me determine how I would allocate my time and not let somebody else determine how I allocate my time. If I'm employed, some other authority, the one who is paying me for my time, determines how my time's employed. I've always had the feeling that I was a better judge of how I spent my time than somebody else. Now, that's the way I felt about it. I guess part of it is the nature of the profession. The nature of the actuarial profession is providing vehicles of financial security. I said to myself, if you're providing that you should at least think of your own security. So it was the nature of the thing: you became familiar with compound interest as a tool of the trade—a combination of compound interest and probability stats. If you'd do it early then you'd get the benefits of it all your life, so I became an investor early. So it was just an outgrowth of the profession, a by-product of the profession.

I was thirty years old, and I was vice president and financially, very comfortable. I was probably twenty-nine, thirty years old by the time I got married. I moved to Michigan as vice president of a company called Hawthorne Incorporated.

I went in as vice president and group actuary, and Hawthorne is about twice as big as Boston Liberty. So it was in some respects a step down and sideways. But while I was there, one of the people had this idea, and said to me, "We think it's a good idea. Why don't we form a company and you come with us? We don't have much money, but it's a good idea. We'll make you president, we'll give you a third of the company." And I looked at it, I thought about it for five or six, maybe five or six, minutes; then they finally said, "Come on." And I said, "Yeah, I'll take it." There was no question, it was substantially more money, it looked like a good opportunity. So I went to that company as president in 1972.

The company was called Summit, and the idea was right. And that company became extremely successful. It went from like three hundred thousand a year to maybe thirty-five, forty million dollars. It was insurance-related. And it involved risk management for state employees' unions on a national basis. We handled their insurance. We sold a specialty product that had never been offered in their union before. We were basically concentrating on the loan side, and if a state union member could not make his loan payment because of either death or disability we would make that payment to the union. We would assume that risk for the union, in return for a premium. And the state unions were frequently the last to get paid. They had high delinquency rates, so they were very amenable to taking us up.

And this became a country-wide success and moved into Canada. Hawthorne had been insuring the risk, but Summit was generally in the business of managing the risk. And it got too big for Hawthorne and we switched our contract with Hawthorne's full approval and above board, to a company in Tennessee. Things got too big for us too and we sold—lock, stock and barrel—our business to a company in Missouri in exchange for stock. And we made a lot of money. The stock appreciated significantly because the business was extremely profitable. And nobody else knew how to do it, although a lot of people attempted to. They were doing it unsuccessfully. We had just learned how and had command of the numbers, and so we could do it. Today, there are probably eight or ten other companies that can do it. But during the late '70s and early '80s, we were the only ones that could do it. So it was a financial success. Good for us, good for the company. Everyone was happy.

We completed that sale in 1975. We went from '72 generating this business, growing it, and then actually harvesting, getting the harvest in, in '75, '76. And I worked out my employment contract until early 1982, when it was acquired by an international company. It was just a natural evolution of what I was doing. Since then, I've been involved with tax shelters of various sorts, myself and my partner Scott.

Intellectual Capital
"I'm not sure there's anything more to my secret than attempting to find some worthwhile idea."

My success has come primarily not because the capital was important; it was the idea that was important. The idea that we had in Summit was important and it generated huge returns. Capital was a small factor. The idea was important, so the returns were inordinately high. In the book company the situation was similar. The capital played a role, but it was a small role. The idea was right and, so, ideas were the only valid resource, the most important resource. Capital was clearly subsidiary and just didn't enter into any of these transactions. I said, if ideas are important and I have a redundancy of assets, then I would like to deploy that redundancy in the area of searching out worthwhile ideas that are directed at growth on a broader scale, growth of society. Assets that have a redundant nature should be deployed to assist economic growth. Ideas are always going to be more important than throwing capital here, or giving capital to somebody in whom I have no confidence, or don't have any real conviction about what it is they're doing.

I'm not sure there's anything more to my secret than attempting to find some worthwhile idea. Now, let's say we interviewed a hundred and fifty or five hundred people, and ten people said, "Gee, I have an idea that makes sense. Nobody else could have possibly seen it because I have a view as I travel through my years in this world that is different from everybody else's view. I'm a peculiar combination of learning and data and that gives me a unique perspective on the world. I see something that would work. I've got some intellectual capital and I can use that intellectual capital in a productive way." All I'm saying is if five or ten people do that and implement it then I think they'll have a success. There's a great deal of intellectual capital present and I'd like to find a way to tap that capital.

If your thought processes are clear, if your ideas are reasonably lucid, then you will, more often than not, achieve what you want to achieve. Where you don't achieve that, quite often you have a failed, flawed idea, whether you're talking about philanthropy or business. You can't execute a poor idea, a poor concept with moderate efficiency and still achieve a great result. You can take a flawed idea and execute it perfectly and you've got a boondoggle. No amount of capital or labor will take a bad idea and turn it into a good result.

Time and the human mind are the ultimate resources, and money and material and labor are just subsidiary. And so if you haven't allocated the right intellectual resource to it, you've got a flawed idea and it will fail.

The Business of Christianity and the Christianity of Business
"There's no inherent conflict."

And somebody approached me with an idea that if possible, in this materialistic, secularized world, we could have a company that can operate consistently with Christian principles and still be successful. And I said, "Let me look at the idea." I looked at the idea and I said, "I think you've got a good idea." And so we started that business, Life Distributors. We started it in '78. This was not my idea but I recognized it.

Somebody who had been thinking about the market said, "I've got this idea. I think that there is a need in the United States for a distributor in the area of Christian literature. The stores need it, the publishers need it. There's a place there and I know how to run an inventory control system." And I said, "Yeah, let's structure it as a tax shelter because I'm gonna lose some money to begin with. I need a tax shelter." So I became one of the original ten investors in this company and became the director of it. I watched it. After the first year we got into some difficulty. We got by that. Then somewhere during the second year, some of the ten stockholders doubted the validity of the premise and so I became a sixty-five percent owner. From a fifteen percent owner up to a sixty-five percent owner. And that company I started—I functioned as chairman of the board from that point on, which was '81 or so—that company has become the largest distributor of Christian literature in the world.

There was a need in the Christian book-distributing field for an entity that distributes books. It's inefficient for each store to order directly from the publisher. It makes sense for each store to have a common source. And a national distributor with reliable credentials did not exist. So that market void could be filled. The idea was executed with success early on: the idea was sound, the void did in fact exist in nature, in the real world, so today seven thousand stores buy from this source every month. A similar idea was behind the original company I talked about when I first started out, Summit. There was a void in the state union market for a certain type of insurance, we exposed the marketplace to that need, and the marketplace responded and we had a lot of business.

Life Distributors was strictly an investment decision in a concept to which I could relate: the fact that you could run a business consistently with Christian principles and still be successful. I mean, it didn't necessarily have to be Christian. It could have been insurance, it could have been anything. You just need to apply Christian principles as your decision criteria. When it happens—and it doesn't often happen that they contradict each other—where you really have to make a decision, when the business decision says one thing and the Christian principle says another, then you opt for the Christian principle.

Here's an example: We were acquiring a company in Oregon and they had some financial difficulty, and we had to close the deal quickly. So we went through the whole contract in about two weeks, for timing reasons. This was during the Christmas season. And in the process they made a mistake. It was forty or fifty thousand dollars in our favor. And we were reasonably successful and they were having a bunch of financial difficulties. And usually in business, if I were part of a public company, I would have had to say, "We'll go to arbitration or we'll go to the court." And I'd come out all right. But we said, "Well, they need the money, we've got a long-term relationship with them. Their mistake was honest." If I were in a public company, I couldn't have done that. Let's manifest the Christian principle. It was an honest mistake on their part. And to hell with our gain.

There's a specific attempt here to have a Christian environment in the workplace. And nobody's going to come up and tell me that it's failing. I'm sure we have areas where it's a problem. But I had one individual come up and he said, "I just want to tell you that I can feel in this place the presence of God." He said, "I'm happy to work here, it's just a delightful place." Each Monday at work, the week always starts with some inspirational message that somebody from a selected department has put together. The whole company is invited, maybe forty percent of the afternoon shift will show up. One department will sponsor it for a month. So for four weeks, some individual will give a selected biblical passage as the message for the week. And they dedicate the week to doing the work of God. That style tends to permeate.

From time to time, few of our employees at Life Distributors would say that the company should be the most well-paying, benevolent organization, with zero or minimum profit. But if you attempted to do that then the business could not meet its obligation to the seven thousand stores that we have, many of whom say that their whole mission in life is the ministry that they have in the store. In order to assist them, which is our major goal, that's one of our purposes to create and have healthy Christian bookstores in the country, then we must be profitable. The reason we have to be profitable is that we have relatively huge inventories that are financed either by the bank or by the publisher. The criterion they use to evaluate us with for the extension of credit is, "Can you pay us back?" And if we're generating a profit then they're willing to extend us increasing credit for increasing growth.

The one thing that I do not buy is that there's an inherent conflict between running a business consistently and applying Christian principles to a business and conducting it very well. There's no inherent conflict. Now this particular business may be blessed in that it distributes books consistent with generally prescribed Christian principles and avoids other literature. But I do not think that in the other businesses which I've been engaged in, particularly the insurance business, there's a conflict between conducting your business as a Christian businessman and conducting it where optimization of profit or resources is the major goal. If somebody's willing to look at it short term and long term, I don't think there's any real conflict there. In fact I think there's a long-term disadvantage associated with conducting your business in a way inconsistent with Christian principles. Let's say you are running a mine, and you're not going to take care of the safety precautions and the coal dust because your competitors don't do it. I'm saying there may be a short-term benefit to not looking at the coal dust, but it's those short-term benefits that have some long-term disadvantages. And so, to the extent you're running a mine, it's just good business to have healthy employees for the long term. I think if you analyze it rigorously, there isn't a contradiction. It gets to be like solving a complex equation in which you're optimizing your overall prospects and not necessarily optimizing minor variables.

Broadened Horizons of Care
"That's the new problem: how do I put something back in?"

In the last three or four years, I found the money's coming in faster than I can really spend it. I never spend excessively. And I had no further financial need. My family had no further financial need. So, I was always continually aware that assets should work. Up until a certain point my assets were working for me. Whether I was a manager of a company working for somebody else or working for myself, I found that the goal was always that you grow. If you've got the company, as it grows, everyone associated with it has the opportunity to participate in its fruits. The only condition under which I could harmonize the personal goals of the employees with the goals of the corporation was when growth was present. So I always directed my activities to areas that were growing faster relative to the rest of the market. That's where opportunities were greater. Throughout my entire business experience, growth was the magic, the golden goose that provided all the gold to meet your need. So I was growth oriented and I had seen the benefits that growth had bestowed on customers as well as employees, in my own experience, on two or three different occasions. I had some conviction that economic growth can meet needs on a broader scale. So I'm pro-growth, pro-economic growth. I reached these conclusions empirically.

And I had stuff growing in a number of different ways. I thought all my personal needs were taken care of. My financial needs and my obligations, as far as my family was concerned, were fulfilled with a certain redundancy. In the last two or three years, it's been evolutionary. In terms of priority, my first priority is I'm going to take care of my basic needs, then I'm going to take care of my family's need. When I've got those taken care of then— I'm not by nature a consumption person; if the needs are taken care of, I don't have to invest. It's taken care of, it's completed. You know, I gotta go on to something that's a little different. There's no question, in the early years I'm doing it for the benefit of Brendan Dwyer. Well, I've taken care of Brendan Dwyer, I've even taken care of Brendan Dwyer's family. Maybe before I rack it up, there are some things that I can do. Not necessarily, you know, for Brendan Dwyer, but for others. Something that would enhance the opportunities for somebody else. And I'm saying growth does that, so I'm looking for something that would enhance economic growth this time.

It's like the guy who's had six ice cream cones, then the next one isn't worth anything. Or the guy that walks off the golf course, and he's been out there perspiring for four hours and he walks in and he wants a glass of beer the first time, but by the time he has his sixth glass of beer he doesn't want it anymore but he just keeps drinking.

Then I went through my last year's tax return and set my plans for the following year and I said, well, you're allocating forty percent of your resources to the government. That's fine, but maybe you should think about how you could be reallocating in a more consistent way. The businesses don't need your time to the same degree that they needed it before, so what can you do that's worthwhile? So it's been just evolutionary.

And I also felt an obligation to put something back in. I mean, put something back in and find a way to do it with some rationale and in a way that will do something worthwhile. That's the new problem: how do I put something back in? How can I return something to the system in a meaningful way? And I wanted to do it in a way in which it would make a difference. There are the obvious ways. You give a scholarship to some people. That, to me, wouldn't make any difference. I consider that a cop-out; there's something better. I think assets should be deployed more for long-term things.

I've gotten to the point where I'm investing for a two percent return as opposed to a ten percent, because the investment had decent social consequences. The way we used to measure things in the financial area is, in my way of thinking, a little obsolete. All I'm saying is I'm happy to deploy those assets or give them away, use them for a different type of return. I think our basic resource in this country isn't land and it isn't capital, it's labor and intellect. So something that enhances or develops the human potential—I'd be amenable to allocating assets in that way. When somebody comes in and asks me for a different purpose, I give him a thousand dollars but I don't have any convictions about it. I haven't yet selected the places where I want to allocate these resources. And I'm talking about doing something constructive over the next twenty years. I'm fifty-seven and if I have the opportunity for twenty years I'd like to do it in a way where it makes a little difference. If I do, I'll be happy. And if I don't I'm going to have a certain discomfort. I'm not going to lose sleep over it at night and I'm not going to throw over my business, but I'm going to be happy if I get some conviction that I'm allocating those resources in a way that's going to benefit this society. It's uncharted water. I don't have a plan yet. It's a larger issue and there are few people with whom I can discuss it.

In a professional foundation the director of the foundation is concerned with keeping his job and not making a mistake by allocating a resource to a bummer of a deal. But I'm not afraid to fail. I'm not afraid to allocate a resource that has a good, before-the-fact opportunity to achieve some success and that ultimately, for some reason or other, may not work out. I don't think the manager of a private foundation can tolerate that same degree of risk. I would think philanthropy, in the little I know about it, probably has a great many more failures than businesses, because few people want to make the effort to connect the resources that they want allocated to the result that they want to achieve. You need to have the guy who is allocating the resources be the guy who created them to begin with. When you delegate that mission to somebody else, then it loses something in the translation. Quite often, managers of philanthropic institutions tend to substitute their own goals for those of the guy who provided the resources. Quite often, those goals take a back seat to people's interest in keeping their jobs and avoiding a mistake.

I don't think you can subdivide your total life into compartments. When I get a conceptual framework, it should work in both business and philanthropy. It doesn't very often work in the philanthropic area. But I think there's a great potential for it to work in that area, if people thought about it more deeply. The same techniques which have produced significant results in the business area can be adopted to fulfill philanthropic goals. And if people with means take advantage of the opportunity to do this, I believe that they will end up being happier than if they don't.

The Moral Imperative
"There's a gap that exists between what we're actually doing and our potential. And narrowing the gap produces more happiness."

The time I give to philanthropy varies over the year. If I had to strike an average I would say forty to fifty hours a month. It might be nothing for three months, but it would average that amount. Now, I say that because I have the freedom to do that. My priorities are such that if business requires my presence, then it gets my presence for fifty or sixty hours a week. But if business is running smoothly, then I have more choices as to how I spend my time. And I allocate my time where I think it will make a difference. And my general perception is that twenty percent of the events accounts for eighty percent of the results. That's a standard estimate and I normally like to function in the critical twenty percent area, where they're going to influence results. And shy away from allocating time to the eighty percent that are only going to account for twenty percent of the results. So that's the way I allocate my time—which, I think, leaves me a certain amount of time for leisure.

I'm saying if I thought what I'd do would make a difference then fine, otherwise somebody else can come and take care of that. Whatever I get my satisfaction from comes from being able to make a difference. That's what makes me happy. That I've felt I've made a difference in a beneficial way. And I'm much more comfortable being involved in an idea that's my own, or one I can adopt as my own, as opposed to working for somebody else's idea. My involvement may be on a continuum anywhere from actively giving advice all the way over to simply saying, "I think it's a good idea; you should go ahead."

I would say my gifts tend to be two-tiered; I think of major gifts and then a number of minor ones. And anything else would be just in the nuisance area, a reflex action with no thought whatsoever. Like the United Way. I certainly respond, I have an obligation, but that's not enough to make any difference to them or me. But I do it because it's just an obligation, like a utility bill you have to pay.

I would say I've probably got five or six minor projects that I give to and I've got them lumped all together. But because they were relatively minor I could not sum enough conviction. One was a van for a Catholic missionary in Asia. These are all cash contributions to projects initiated by somebody else. A combination of cash and time to an entity known as "Lean on Me." And it's inner-city Detroit. It's a guy that I really believe in what he's doing, but I'm not sure I can help him very much. I'm comfortable about it but I'm saying if I do devote some time to him I'm not going to be able to make much of a difference. I conceive these projects like when sometimes you get stuck in the snow and by yourself you can't move fast but if somebody gives you a little push you might get over. Some of these things I look upon my role as being able to maybe give them a little push and get them some momentum. If I can, fine, if I can't, tough. But I'm not going to be the major giver because they got their role and they're doing fine. Another one is a group for world evangelization. I made a contribution to them. I can't sum enough conviction because I don't think they're going anyplace. But they are dedicated, sincere people. I got through doing them all at the end of the year and I knew that what I did was cop out on each of them. I would say, I don't want to say no, and I don't want to make a big enough gift, so I'll do something. So I give halfway between and feel more comfortable.

I guess I'm being mathematically oriented. I've always allocated assets on the basis of here's the asset and here's the return. Now in business that procedure is very formal and it is very rigorous and it's done with a certain precision. Well, that's the same process I go through with less rigor here. What's the good? What's the potential? And if I'm looking at Dillon Wilson's project in Boston and he's struggling but he's got a bunch of young kids there and two or three of them are going to make it, a small amount is going to make a big difference there. I'd not like to see him go under.

Most of today's 888 millionaires probably don't think beyond their own little business. They're devoting their seventy or eighty hours a week to that little business but they will, somewhere along the line, reach the point that says, "Well, this is a good business but, you know, what's the next step?" And I think that's terrific if they can summon enough conviction about community giving, the United Way, etc., but I can't. I'm saying I want to look for some things that have some higher potential. For example, Summit created maybe a hundred and fifty jobs relatively quickly. And it created meaningful jobs. It made a meaningful impact on people. Then we started Life Distributors. We're providing four hundred jobs in an atmosphere and in an environment that we attempt to say is Christian, and some people are having meaningful employment that might otherwise not have it. I'm saying that I had two ideas and as a result of implementing them I created four or five hundred jobs. There may be people who as a result of their experience have accumulated some intellectual capital and if they change their emphasis from self to a broader thing, they can deploy that intellectual capital for the benefit of some others. Then their capacity to generate worthwhile projects in a way will be superior to what some well-meaning but less well-equipped bureaucrat or politician might be able to generate. This guy's experience and motivation will be different from the experience and motivation that emanate from Washington. Now, many projects that emanate from Washington are pure, but the mix is different. I'm saying both can be good, but one can't generate what the other can generate.

We each have a potential and there's a gap that exists between what we're actually doing and our potential. Narrowing the gap produces more happiness and increases in that gap produce less happiness. I believe individuals try to be happy. So somebody who is functioning at less than their potential is not as happy. I'm not necessarily being critical of somebody else who is out there being a good American. I'm saying that they can be better. I could be a lot better. I'm not quarreling with that. That's why I'm trying to be better.

What criteria do I apply to ferret out what I get involved with? I guess I listen to people talk, I listen to them say what it is they're trying to do and how they're trying to do it. And then I bump it up against my own perception. That's the criterion on which I accept some and reject others. You almost have to go back and start with a whole set of values that some Sisters of Charity imbued me with and the Fathers at Holy Cross told me about. A lot of things have been programmed into me. You don't go through any great formal process, you simply listen to something and it comes out as either right or wrong. And I don't seem to have any great doubts in that area.

Maybe I'm coming at this circuitously. My thought process is always going to be micro, not macro. Many of the problems are micro in nature, as opposed to being macro. And a macro solution will not work to relieve something that is essentially heterogeneous and micro in nature. Individuals have a certain potential for achievement. And I'm looking for ways I can enhance the climate or the environment under which they can achieve their potential. Part of it's in economic terms, but part of it's in their whole being. In a company you try to breed an environment in which each individual can achieve his own personal and financial objectives. I guess in broad terms I think the United States, from a climate standpoint, should be able to do that. Now, I don't have enough influence to change the whole climate, but I might be able to influence a little arena or little spots in the same way that I've been able to influence some company. But I can only alter the scenery or the climate or the circumstances; people have to do the things that cause them to narrow the gap between what their potential for doing is and where they actually are. I think if they narrow that gap, they're becoming closer to what they can be, then they increase their own levels of happiness. And their unhappiness is measured by the gap that exists between what they are and what they can be.

Let me give you an example of my view of a flawed solution developed in a central bureaucracy. And that's the situation in which the government says that we should take care of dependent children. But that makes it financially attractive for single parents to remain single, particularly in black communities. The financial choice that produces the greatest benefit for them is to remain single and have babies. Welfare was an idea with a well-conceived social purpose, but somehow or other the idea was flawed and it hasn't worked.

Instead, I prefer backing individuals like Stan Bankridge. Stan's working with 750 young men on parole. He's attempting to take that one step further and not only help them, but also get the whole system remodeled conceptually from the standpoint of injecting caring and feeling into the system, and he's calling it love. That's where the judges got to care, and the probation officers care, and that's essentially a concept that he developed as a result of working within that system for some thirty years, analyzing statistics and data on who returns to jail and who doesn't return, and why they don't return. And making some policy suggestions and prescribing a remedy which, I think, will end up having a beneficial effect.

The Spirituality of Everyday Life
"To harmonize my activity with the roles that the Creator would like to have born."

I think that as you look at the world, there are parts of the world that are fine and there are certain imperfections that exist. Each of us has the capacity to improve that, just a little bit. That's your role. If you're doing that then you're going to be happier. A number of people have to work in order to get food, clothing, shelter. And they do not have time for anything else. But our society is advancing to the point where more and more people will have the opportunity to improve society a little bit. Let me use the analogy of the Bottle Law in Michigan. Each person returns their bottles and of necessity the whole state became cleaner. I'm no great advocate of the Bottle Law, but as a result of each individual altering their habit just slightly, the whole state became a lot cleaner.

Each individual has a different view of the world based on the seat that he's occupying. I share the Catholic view of the world, that's the one that I would like to advance. I think it's proper, I think that's the Creator's gift. That view tends to put me as some little person in some big structure, but I at least feel comfortable with the relationships, my relationship with the Creator and people all around.

I can look out there and see things that conform with my Catholic viewpoint and things that do not conform. And I have a capacity to maybe change something and bring them into line. If I can do that then I think I should. At certain times I can look up there and I can't do anything about it—well, that's that, so be it.

I don't consider myself an extremist when it comes to religion, but I think that people that are acting consistently with Christian principles are doing good. If it's consistent with the Almighty's plan and harmonized with the Almighty's plan then it's good. If it's divergent then. . . . Some of those Christian principles are cut and dried, like abortion and homosexuality. They're cut and dried. You've got to decide to live your life according to the way Christ told you to, or live it some other way. And one is right and one is wrong.

My role is to attempt, insofar as I can, to harmonize my activity with the roles that the Creator would like to have born. To the extent my activity harmonizes with the role He sees for me, then I'm going to have a peace and tranquillity in exercising that and in living, that you can't get in any other way. And when I'm in conflict with that, then I'm going to have a certain tension and disunity. So that's the way I see my role. Insofar as I can, I must determine what His role is for me, and try to live it. And whatever things or gifts He gives me, it's my obligation to use them in a way He would like them to be used.

2

Rebecca Jacobs: "Give Me Mexico, That's What I Want"

Jacobs tells a rags-to-riches story, complicated at the apex of her career by being a business woman in a man's world. At forty-seven years old, the owner of a chain of make-over salons that is spreading throughout North America, she still battles for respect and against insecurity.

"I'm helping people to help themselves, to like themselves better. . . . I sell self-respect. That's exactly what I sell." In the process, Rebecca Jacobs has herself gained self-respect. Originally intending only to improve her own physical appearance in order to get a job, Jacobs has ended up the largest franchise holder of a chain of make-over salons for women. Her contagious enthusiasm for the service and her charismatic personality proved to be the catalyst that turned her entrepreneurial aspirations and a business opportunity into good fortune. "I knew it was going to be successful. I just knew, because it had done so much for my life." Indeed, what it did for her life proved dramatic, for Jacobs is a premiere example of the coexistence of an inner domain of self-confident *individuality* and a worldly domain of *principality*.

Born just after the Depression, to a large extended family of European Jewish immigrants, Jacobs went to work at the tender age of eleven. Though she had to forgo college in order to help her family, she excelled in business by turning her jobs into learning opportunities. So, when it came to her first franchise, she was equal to the challenge. "I was training in my house, in my bathrobe, in between feeding my children, doing the books, laying out the ads, doing the public relations and getting a very quick MBA." As the business grew, Jacobs quickly learned what it takes to transform a small entrepreneurial firm to a large corporation. "I soon realized I couldn't be in everything. So I divorced myself from the bookkeeping, financial end of the business, and just ran the business." Despite her success, she remained modestly down to earth. "I realized real quick that I wasn't the smartest, I wasn't the

most important, I wasn't the best. And that the only way to get it was
to go out and hire it." Learning on the job, taking risks and hiring good
people, important as they were, proved less important than her great
expectations. "I'm a dreamer. I think that's one of the biggest assets that
I have. Imagination is the most wonderful thing, and I use it to make
those dreams come true. I just know I'm going to win."

Armed with such dreams and confidence, and unafraid to master
new skills, Jacobs reached a level of business success traditionally
reserved for men. Despite her success, she has repeatedly found herself
excluded, because of her gender, from the recognition commensurate
to her achievement. Although the professional men that she hired were
eager to work for her, her second husband openly discouraged her from
becoming an entrepreneur. Even having achieved such success, she
resents seemingly casual remarks about simply being lucky. "They
don't tell a man that he's lucky. A man is smart, I'm lucky!" Still, she
recognizes that she has been spared a good amount of prejudice because
of her position. "I'm sure it would have been different if I went to work
at the bottom of a big corporation." In the end, her biggest complaint
is that notwithstanding her extensive business empire and her publicly
expressed willingness to serve on executive boards of corporations and
philanthropic institutions, she has not been asked to do so. She says, "I
think it's because I'm a woman," and because her business serves
women.

As an entrepreneur and a mother of five, Jacobs missed the support
of an understanding husband. Torn by conflicting demands, she now
regrets some of her choices. "I think I missed a lot of their [my kids]
growing up." However, her primary concern is the impact of wealth on
their moral development. "Some of their values are wonderful, and
some of their values are not so wonderful. They're used to a lot of
things. They feel they deserve it; it's their birthright." She wonders if
the work ethic will have the same appeal to them as it did for her. "I
think the thing that's added to my success is, I was hungry. They are
never going to be hungry [and] I don't mean hungry for food." Despite
her reservations, she remains optimistic. All her children hold advanced degrees and two of them work in her company. "I'm kind of
grooming them, that's the whole joy of it, that's the fun. The fun is to
see my kids take over the business."

And what a business this has turned out to be. Her principality
extends throughout North America. "I have franchises in Massachusetts, Rhode Island, a lot of Ohio, Northern Canada, I go all the way to
Thunder Bay, the country of Mexico, oh, almost or all of Michigan.
Where else? A little bit of Kentucky, Indiana. It's now all one franchise.
I'm the lady you see on the television." When Jacobs entered the
cosmetic industry, her ability and inspiration led to the opening of one
salon after another. And, as the size of her company increased rapidly,
so did her reputation as a successful franchise operator. As a result,
franchise owners that wanted to sell would turn to her, thus adding to
her empire. Eventually, her expanding corporation became the biggest

competitor of the parent company. When the latter requests Jacobs' permission to produce and market make-over products, for which she holds the legal title, she, true to form, demands instead of money, the rights for further expansion—international this time. "You give me Mexico, that's what I want, and I'll give you the rights." Despite the phenomenal growth of her company she says, "I figure I'm in my infancy right now." However, the make-over market became stabilized, other owners are not as eager to sell, and competition is giving way to cooperation as all franchisees and the parent company are attempting to consolidate their gains by forming an association. So today, Jacobs is looking for new initiatives. In order to diversify beyond one market, she instructs one of her sons to scour the *Wall Street Journal* for businesses for sale, and Jacobs herself is entertaining the idea of joining a friend who is a venture capitalist.

Ultimately, Jacobs has a moral concern equal to her business empire. "This was a way of helping others and making some money off of it, which was unbelievable to me. In fact, I never even thought about the money, I just thought that I had to do this, to give this away." For her, money follows success and can make living easier. "It gives you the cream on top of the cake." However, the "cake" is the happiness that comes out of the "giving of one's self" and on that score money can be instrumental. "There is a God out there who watches all of us. And I think that in order to make a contribution and have a happy life, what we have to do is help others, and that will make you happier. Maybe that's selfish, but it does make me happier." Jacobs has provided her immediate and extended family with positions and market opportunities, helps some clients with reduced fees, is sensitive to her employees' needs, and looks after the broader community by contributing time and money to Jewish and other philanthropic organizations. Thus, despite guilt feelings for having so much money and an upbringing that emphasized the moral obligation of 'giving back,' Jacobs has discovered the most abiding philanthropic motivation; "those that aren't as charitable, don't get as much out of life." "That is why" she helps people, "whether they know about it or don't know about it."

BIOGRAPHICAL NARRATIVE

Modest Beginnings
"Things were very tough, but we were very happy."

I was born in Chicago, in fact Forest Park, where the rich people used to live. I lived on McIntyre and Purdy and really, that's inner-city Chicago now. My father had a gas station with another man, and my grandfather owned the corner drug store. I lived in the same house with seven aunts and uncles, two sisters, my grandmother and grandfather, my mother and father, and me. We had one basement, and it was all connected. I was born right after the Depression, and things were very tough, but we were very happy. It was a wonderful family life. When I was eleven, my little sister, who was nine, got polio. We had no Blue Cross, no insurance, so I had to go out and work. I've been working since I was eleven years old. We all did. And thank goodness for the March of Dimes. They supplemented my father's income so that my sister was able to avail herself with things like warm springs in Georgia, and modern technology for polio at that particular time. She probably wouldn't have had them if it had to be on my Dad's income. After I started my business, she lost weight and began walking with braces and crutches. By that time I gave her half of the business. She grew up to be a very nice young lady. Today, she is a wealthy, independent woman.

My sister and I are the franchise owners of Trim and True—the TT grouping. I have franchises in Massachusetts, Rhode Island, most of Ohio, Northern Canada—I go all the way up to Thunder Bay—the country of Mexico, almost all of Michigan, and a little bit of Kentucky and Indiana. I'm the lady you see on all the television ads. It is now all one franchise. But, it was different franchises before. What I've done is I've been in competition with the parent company, buying out franchises. The original franchise owner is RJR Nabisco. That's the parent company. But originally it was started by a woman and a man and the company went public. Then it was bought out, about eight to ten years ago, by Nabisco for seventy-two million dollars cash. It was a public company. But, they didn't try to buy me at that point.

At any rate, to get back to my family history. I was the oldest of three daughters. We were born around the Depression time and I remember feeling strapped for money all the time. I don't remember wearing original clothes. Even when I got married the first time at the age of sixteen, I borrowed underwear from one aunt, a wedding gown from somebody else, and shoes from somebody else. I don't remember too often wearing clothes that I went out and bought. We just didn't have the money. Now, I love clothes and I have a voracious appetite for pretty things, but I find it hard many times to spend a lot of money. It's against my grain to buy a dress over a hundred dollars. I think that's part of the old upbringing. Well, I'm getting much better in my older years.

There was one thing that was very important. Although were very poor, in every room of the house there was a little blue and white box for the Jewish National Fund. My grandmother used to say, "If something good happens then you put in money, even if it's just a penny. And if something bad happens you put in money, because it shouldn't happen again." So the principle of "pay back" is something I've been brought up with. I remember my grandmother, a little old lady crippled with osteoporosis, standing in the corner in front of the bakery every Sunday, collecting for whatever charity there was at the time. And that's played a very important role in my life. Just the fact that I was one of the lucky ones, smart but lucky, [teaches] you to give back in life and take care of those who don't have it. Especially if you're the most fortunate one, like I have been. So, this payback is in terms of time and money, that you can give to those that aren't as fortunate as you.

Though I went to work at age eleven, I continued going to school. I graduated from high school, and I had a little bit of college, not a lot. There wasn't any money for me to go to college, so I went to work all the time. In fact, I was doubly promoted once. In fact, I was very fat, and fat girls study a lot. Two summers in a row, I took summer school, so I was again doubly promoted. When I graduated in June, I was sixteen. I then got married in August and had a baby the following September. I got married very young and for all the wrong reasons. He was a dental student at the University of Wisconsin, so I went up and lived in Madison. He was a brother of one of my friends in high school and I stayed married to him for almost five years. He graduated as a dentist and we went to live in Arizona. At the time, he was a captain in the Army. But we were just so ill-suited for each other that it didn't work. So, I took my child and went home. I moved back to my mother's house.

After that, I went back to work again. I was a bookkeeper for a big building firm in Chicago. I actually ran the whole office. Then I met my next husband, who was twenty years older than I was. He was one of the contractors for this builder. We married about six, seven months later and went on to have four more children. We stayed married until about six or seven years ago. I stayed married to him for almost twenty years. It was also a wrong marriage. I was determined to make a go of it. I wasn't going to be a two-time loser. At first, he was a wealthy man. He was in the building business, but about fifteen or sixteen years ago, he lost all of his money. So I had to go out and feed my children. That's when I found Trim and True and started my first company.

All that time, I was fifty pounds overweight, so I went to Trim and True to lose weight in order to go out and get a job. I didn't feel that, looking the way I looked, and having the kind of low self-esteem that I had, I could really do anything. I heard about this thing called Trim and True. I had some money of my own saved up, and I gambled on it. I went there and it worked for me. Afterward, they asked me if I would open a salon in Chicago. Trim and True has been in business for about twenty-three years. For me, this was almost twenty-two years ago. So I said yes, I was going to open a salon here, and then go out and get a job in advertising or public relations. However, after a few months, I knew it was going to be successful so I devoted my full time to it. And that's how the business really got started.

The Confident Quest
"I'm the one that made the business grow."

When they asked me if I would open a salon in Chicago, it meant that I would buy a franchise. At the time, I didn't even know what the word meant, but I said yes anyway. So, I went to my husband's lawyer and got everything settled. We made a deal with them and I was going to start the salon in Chicago. In fact they offered me all of Illinois, but I said, "What would I want Illinois for? Just give me Chicago, that's where I live, that's all I want." And in those days, it was very inexpensive. In the past, I've paid as much as almost three million dollars to buy a franchise out, whereas the Chicago franchise only cost me two thousand dollars!

I knew it was going to be successful, because it had done so much for my life. This was a way of helping others, while making some money at the same time. It was unbelievable to me. In fact, I never even thought about the money, I just knew that I had to do this to help other people. Because the first salon was very busy, and the second even busier, and the third busier still, I began opening other salons. I have some principles of my own, and nobody works for me unless she or he is a former client and has come to my training. So, I was training in my house, in my bathrobe. In between feeding my children and running the salons myself, I was taking the money, doing the books, laying out the ads, doing the public relations; in short I was getting a very quick MBA.

Just before I married, when I was fifteen, and until my first baby was born, I worked for a man in Forest Park who had the largest shoe store in Illinois. This man was a very hard taskmaster, and I ran his office. He was almost to the point of bankruptcy, because it took a lot to fill up that big empty warehouse. His distributor wanted him to file Chapter 11, but this man wanted to make a go of the business. That's when I was brought in to help. I learned a lot from him. We laid out our own ads, and I directed the salesmen on the floor. I used to sit in a room above the floor to watch everything through a glass. And, boy, if a pencil fell on the floor, he'd say: "Did you see that? Why did you let that happen? You know these pencils are money. Time and money are important and we have to make payroll." He really taught me a lot about it, and I thank him a lot. He was a crazy, wonderful, mixed-up man, and he and his wife were very good to me. This was where I got some of the skills that I later applied to my own business.

I started my business and began training people in 1965. Took a small office that when I hired someone to work with me, there was hardly room for both of us. I always made my bills, and of course, that wasn't so easy, because my husband felt it was silly, and that it was never going to go. So, I never had a lot of encouragement. He wasn't much of a talker to begin with, so it was very difficult. He was very negative about the whole thing. When the business started to grow, I began opening salons in other areas, training people, and putting people in place. I then went from a small office to a bigger office. But I learned one thing real quick: I was always going to go first class, never second class. So, I went to the top lawyers, and accountants, who are still my accountants and lawyers and best friends today, and I have to tell you, these men treated me like I was their best female client, and that has never stopped. Never in my twenty-one years of business can I remember having a negative business reaction from a man because I was a woman.

I built a building, I put out a newspaper with a circulation of two hundred and fifty thousand copies, I'm building a second building right now, sixty thousand square feet. I've borrowed millions of dollars from the bank and I've done a lot of things in my career as a business woman. I hear women say these things can't be done, that we're being oppressed, but oppressed isn't the right word. Maybe we're being treated like second-class citizens. When I think about it logically, and I do all the time, I wonder. I'm sure it would have been different if I had started at the bottom of a big corporation like Ford Motor Company, Chrysler or GM. Then I probably would have run into a lot of prejudices, and maybe I would not have gotten to be the president. But I'm a winner, and I believe in winning in life. I set my own goals, and I'm a dreamer. I think that's one of the biggest assets that I have. Imagination is the most wonderful thing, and I use it to make those dreams come true. I just know I'm going to win.

I've been a winner and a dreamer since I've been a little girl. That's why I was dissatisfied with my self-image. I wasn't comfortable with the fact that I had lost fifty pounds nine times before. I'm also a very emotional person. For whatever reason, I can start eating again, and put the weight back on, so I really worked at keeping it off. That way of thinking goes back to my mother . . . she was an orphan, and she didn't have any living relatives. She came over on the boat from Europe with her mother and dad. They contracted TB or the flu or something on the boat and died. So she went into an orphanage. She met my father and got married when she was fifteen. He was twenty-seven or twenty-eight. All she had of her life were her three daughters, and she thought we were fabulous. She used to tell me, even when she was angry at me, "You're a wonderful, terrific person, you're very smart. I expect wonderful things from you, you are wonderful, and you are beautiful." I'd say, "How can you say I'm beautiful? Look at me, I'm so fat!" When I was eleven or twelve years old, I was short and I weighed a hundred and sixty-five pounds. I was the fattest kid in the class and she just thought I was her beautiful Rebecca! So when you hear those things all of your life, that's who you are programmed to be. You are what you think about, what you believe. This is an extremely important fact—especially in raising your children.

My business success was just gradual. I think the important thing that I realized real quick was that I wasn't the smartest, I wasn't the most important, I wasn't the best—despite what my mother said. And that the only way to get it was to go out and hire it, because there were other people that knew more about computers, more about marketing, and that goes back to going first class. Go out and find the very best. I'm a motivator, so I could always talk my way into hiring somebody who maybe I couldn't afford at that time. By the time I got through it with them, they were willing to take a chance with me, and come to work with me. So I've been very fortunate that way. I think another thing is that I soon realized I couldn't be everything. So, I divorced myself from the bookkeeping, financial end of the business. I'm the one that made the business grow. Though I made every deal, when I bought a new business, I would say, "I need two million dollars, get it for me." I'm involved in most decisions, but for example, buying the computers was never anything that I decided I was going to do. I hired people to do that. My sister is in the bookkeeping department. So, I just went about my business, building the business. I'm not one that really looks a lot at the financial end of things. So, regarding my gradual growth, I had one salon, then fifteen salons, twenty, fifty, a hundred, then two hundred salons and I couldn't believe it! Now, I'm running a thousand salons in the United States alone, and I haven't stopped. I figure I'm in my infancy right now.

Fashioning a Principality
"Give me Mexico, that's what I want."

I have a lot of dreams. I remember Chicago was doing real well, and then somebody came to me from Cleveland and said, "We want to retire, and we like the way you run your business. We'd like you to buy it." So I said, "That sounds like a very good idea." I never thought, "Well, gee, how can I run a business in Chicago *and* run one in Cleveland?" They came to me because they liked the way I ran my business. Having a Trim and True franchise is like starting a baby from birth. It's a very personal emotional thing. To give it up is not like having a furniture store. Maybe it is. I don't know. I think of it because it's such an emotional thing. Maybe it's because we're dealing with a service and it's people's lives, and I'm very involved with the people that work with me, very involved with my employees.

That's exciting. I mean, here I am, Rebecca Jacobs, housewife, mother of five. Whoever thought that I'd be doing all the things that I do! More salons to open up, more people to meet, another staff to win over, and television. It just sounds so exciting to me. My husband would say to me, "You're going to have a lot of money!" But it's never had anything to do with money, because I certainly had enough at that point. My kids were all going through college, they were all graduated. One is a doctor, another is a lawyer, and they all went to graduate school, not just undergraduate college. This is a very nice business. But it's the challenge of it, it's the excitement of this that I just love. I love what I'm doing.

After I purchased Cleveland, along came Mexico. I had something the parent company wanted contractually, and they needed it desperately. It was the rights to make-over products. No one could market these products in my area of Illinois, unless I approved it or unless I was the broker. It was just something that we had gotten in the contract and never even thought about at the time. I didn't imagine that I was going to become a product broker, and they really needed it because they were going national. So they offered me money, but I said, "No, I don't want it." They offered me a quarter of a million dollars for those rights, but I said, "Something is not right. I'll tell you what. You give me Mexico, that's what I want, and I'll give you the product rights you want." It wasn't very smart at the time. I'm sure that I could have put the money to use and made a lot more money on it, because Mexico is very tough.

I went and lived there for a year. I took my children and put them in an American school. I thought I was so smart and really knew what I was doing, and boy I had been so successful in Chicago, so I did everything there the way I did it here. I had it figured that I was going to spend a quarter of a million dollars. If I wasn't successful in one year—and that was my time limit, my plan, my strategy—if at that time I wasn't successful or lost the money, whichever came first, I was no longer going to continue in Mexico. In seven months and about two hundred thousand dollars later, I was saying to myself, What can I do? I can't seem to be successful. I'd advertise in the wrong places, the wrong ads, I would do everything I did in the United States, but it did not work in Mexico. So despite all of my expertise, I had to start all over again. And in the seventh month, everything finally started to click and I gave up on American-style salons. Everything was in Spanish and we turned things around. When I left, I had stayed there about a year, year and a half, it was going real nicely and I wound up getting an apartment in Acapulco and I'd go there every six weeks myself, and I loved it.

Then things began happening in Mexico in the last three, four years. Now, they're really hanging on by the skin of my teeth down there. I'm not spending any time down there now because my priorities have changed. I'm married to a wonderful man I adore. I don't enjoy being on the road as much as I used to. I do it in the United States, though, because it's easier for me. I can do one- or two-day trips, but to go down to Mexico, it's not as exciting and wonderful any more. So I don't want to put any funds in there until I know what's going to happen to the country. We used to have forty or fifty salons down there, now we're down under ten. We're kind of retrenching and I have some new management. We're just trying to hang on. I sold the apartment and I'm waiting to see what's going to happen.

After I purchased Mexico, a lady from Pittsburgh came to me and said, "Are you interested in buying us out?" For each franchise I paid much more of course. I think I paid a million for Cleveland or something like that. I don't really remember what it was, and Pittsburgh was over two. So I also went to Pittsburgh. I found that it was really easy for me to run my business in different cities. So I'm in Mexico now, and in Pittsburgh, Cleveland, and Chicago. And I had very dear friends up in Northern Michigan, which I loved. It's God's country up there and I knew they were going to retire one day, so I started wooing them, and telling them that I'd really like to buy their franchise. Last year, they decided they wanted to sell it, so I bought it from them. Now I spend a lot of time up there. Percentagewise, I paid more for that one than I did for any of the other franchises. It was a very small franchise, about eight salons, compared to Pittsburgh, which was thirty. I think I paid close to a million dollars for that. Really, it was very high; it's half the size of Cleveland.

Also, I could have had San Francisco. We were in strict negotiations for that one, but it had been sold to somebody else, to Trim and True International—which is privately owned. At that time, I had a lawyer who was a business advisor and a very dear friend. He said, "Don't be silly, the price is too high. It's astronomical. Absolutely, you shouldn't buy." And I listened to him. I've since learned that he's a terrific lawyer, but I have to go with my own gut. It's a lot better. What was meant to be, was meant to be, however, and I wasn't meant to have California. Nor was I meant to have Cincinnati, but I know I could have done a fantastic job in both of those places. What they sold California for was more than what he wanted me to pay for it at the time. The people who bought Cincinnati were capital venturers who paid close to two million. The woman that owned it was not doing anything with it. And she said: "Look, you're a fantastic operator. I know what you do here. You've always had the best in the United States. I want to sell it for this amount of money," and my lawyer said, "You can't pay her for what she thinks you're going to do with that business. You have to pay her for what the business is doing." And, you know, I suppose he was right, it was not meant to be for me to have Cincinnati or San Francisco. But when it came to Pittsburgh, he again said, "You can't do that, you can't pay that much money!" I said, "I'm paying it and that's it." I knew that was right for me and I bought it. I was never sorry. I paid that bank loan back in two years.

Although I always had Halifax and Norwich counties, Northern Michigan came with Northern Canada. Northern Michigan was always with Northern Canada. I would love to buy some more franchises. But they get harder and harder to buy, because the parent company now wants to buy them back, and people aren't so anxious to sell any more. There are sixty-one of us in the United States that own franchises, and then there are a few of them that own most of Europe. Nabisco is the parent company, but they have a subsidiary which is called Trim and True International. I am the largest franchise owner—second to the parent company. The next person who's close to me probably has about half the number of salons that I do. Nabisco has made some overtures to me. We have talked, but they haven't asked for direct collaboration because we have formed a Trim and True franchisee association, which is a very strong association. We have a lot of communities and we intermingle with International on a constant basis. In fact, last year I was on the planning committee. We did strategic planning for the next couple of years. And now, I'm on the public relations committee, their marketing. We have legal committees and we have program committees. We're very involved in the progress of our industry. When you have a franchise, ten percent off the top goes to Trim and True International. We're almost like a twenty five percent partner. That's very high. I pay all the expenses. For every dollar I take in they get ten cents. So, in some ways, whether they want to buy me out or not, the fact that I'm very successful benefits them. In terms of customers and reputation, I've always said that if any one franchise starts to fail, it's going to affect all of us. So we all have to stay successful. That's very important, that's why we have this association. We're very strong. We're not a large number, but we're very strong. We're very vocal people.

Discounting Success
"They don't tell a man that he's lucky. A man is smart; I'm lucky!"

Well, besides five children that went through college and grad school—that was a big venture—I have investments that my lawyers and my accountants have gotten in: shopping centers and real estate. I'm a participant, I'm not directing them, I'm not handling those businesses. But I'd love to do that. In fact, one of the things that I'd really like to do, and I think I've mentioned this in the newspaper and on the radios, would like to sit on some boards. I think I've got a lot to offer, but I'm never asked. I don't know why that is. Maybe, it's because I'm a woman. We don't have a lot of women on boards. In fact, I don't think Chrysler has any at all. I don't know about Ford or GM, but if they do, it's probably a Ph.D. economist. I understand that there are other areas that have been traditionally women's, like hospitals and social services. But, I would like to be on a board, I'd like to sit on Chrysler's board. I'd like to sit on a big company's board.

I have a lot to offer. Maybe I'm not a Ph.D., and I haven't finished college, but I think I'm involved. Everything I read today comes down to the way you treat your employees and your customers—that makes the difference. Have all the technology you can get, all the computer people you want, but the thing that's going to make the big difference is the way you treat your customers. Actually, the way you treat employees, and the way you treat customers. I think that I have a lot to offer in those fields. I don't know why I haven't been considered. I asked somebody once. And he said it's a very political thing. You have to work your way up, you have to know the right people. Well, I don't spend a lot of time doing that.

I used to say to myself, what do you mean lucky? I'm the one that's working from eight o'clock in the morning until ten, eleven o'clock at night. I dream about it at night, I set my goals, I'm out there, I'm learning to be a public speaker, I'm doing things and, by the way, that is something that I hate to do, and I don't like to do. It makes my heart beat real fast, my mouth dry, and I get very nervous from it. But, I'm working real hard, and I'm learning and I'm taking all the risks. I'm the one that's plunging ahead, and I'm the one that's taking the gamble on all these things, and they tell me I'm lucky! But they don't tell a man that he's lucky. A man is smart; I'm lucky! I think some of it is luck, in all of life there is luck, yes. I secretly think that everybody has a certain karma or aura. I have insisted and fought, and motivated and done everything that I could to make sure that all my kids have a college education. But despite my abilities and efforts, I feel less of a person, less of a smart person, because I don't have that college education, especially today.

I'm putting up a sixty-thousand-square-foot building for our offices—for Trim and True. We'll utilize a third of the building and the rest hopefully will be rental, and it will pay the mortgage payments. I've sold the building that we are in now. I am now a tenant. I am paying rent to a very nice man who's going to make it into a financial center. He's got lawyers upstairs, he's an insurance man, and he wants to get accountants. So, it will be like a financial center. This was my first building and I drove the architect crazy. I wanted a narrow, skinny building, and that's what I have, a narrow, skinny building. It's overbuilt for the area, and I didn't get what I put into it, but I've lived here ten, eleven years, and enjoyed every moment of it. It's a well-built, beautiful, gorgeous building, and I'm very proud of it. I thought it was the-end-all-be-all, and I'd never move. How could I ever use its twenty one thousand square feet? How could I ever use this much space? And of course, now we're just sitting on top of each other here! So, it's very exciting to be building a new building and the new building, of course, has audio-visual rooms, a new test kitchen and classrooms. It's just very exciting. We do all the printing work. We have a big department downstairs that does the printing for everything that we put out. However, our newspaper is too big so it's subcontracted.

I don't think the problem is that I don't come across as an executive. There have been articles on me in newspapers and in our business magazine. We have this magazine, Truths, which talks about my business success only. It's not that the business community doesn't know about my business acumen. I think it's because I'm a woman. I really and truly do. I used to think that maybe it's because I don't have the education skills, or I don't have the education. All I know is that I have not been asked. I serve on a lot of charities. I sit with the best men in the city, the biggest, most influential men in the city on the Boy Scouts. I'm one of the few women that sit on the board of the Boy Scouts and I'm hobnobbing, if you want to use that word, actually going to meetings on endowment plans and business things for the Boy Scouts, with heads of the biggest companies in the city. I also sit on the Symphony board, where I participate in the meetings.

Wealth and the Priorities of Life
"Money can't give you health, friends, love.
But it can give you peace of mind."

I think, all these years in business have changed me. I think I'm much more confident than I ever was. I am also much more selective and I prioritize differently. The things that are important to me have changed, my values are different. But I wonder if all that comes with age or it comes with success or money, maybe all three, I'm not sure. If somebody had asked me ten years ago who I was, I would have said I'm Rebecca Jacobs first. I always feel that I have to be true to my heart first. If I wasn't happy within me, I couldn't make other people happy. I know that's a little selfish, but I was always Rebecca Jacobs first. Then I was a mother. For many years of my life, unfortunately I was Rebecca Jacobs, mother, business lady. I'm sure I would much rather have been Rebecca Jacobs, wife, mother, business lady. That's the way it is right now. It moves a little but it's Rebecca Jacobs, wife, business lady, mother because my kids are older and they don't need me as much, and sometimes they need me a lot, so it's Rebecca Jacobs, wife, mother—and that's where my values are.

Twenty years ago, it was very important to wear the right thing, say the right thing, be at the right place and eat at the right restaurant. Today, putting on my blue jeans or my sweats, and going out to the cottage on Lake Michigan with just my family is probably the ultimate. We do it every chance we get. I'm married to a really nice adventurer. I never traveled in my whole life other than for business, until I met him. And since we've been married six years ago, I've been to Europe half a dozen times. We've done things like pick a location, with no reservations, and just drive the car for three weeks. We stop where we want to stop and it's been wonderful. I'm going to learn to ski. I used to run, but I don't run anymore. I understand it's not good for your body, so instead, I walk five miles every day in one hour—that's a very fast walk.

My values have changed. Money does not buy happiness. Health is extremely important. And being a nice person, loving kind of person is very important. I love the money, I love all the things it supports. I love my baseball season tickets, symphony tickets. I'm going to the Bolshoi ballet next week. I love the fact that a friend of mine called to say I got front row seats to see Pavarotti in Chicago at the opera house, and I can afford to get on a plane and go for the night and see Pavarotti and come back the next day. I love the theater, I love all the things that support me, I love them all. It's also made me realize how short life is. And how important family is.

It's those things that are important, so I put a lot of time and money into them. I take care of my mother and, as I said, I gave my sister half of the business. I have my other sister working for me now. She has six children. I've already put away money for her kids' college. That's really important to me. That's where my life is today.

Money can't give you health, friends, love. It can't give love. But it can give you peace of mind. It gives you security. You know you're going to eat and you know you're going to be able to do all those things. It gives you the cream on top of the cake. I never was unhappy when I was poor. There were ten, twelve or sixteen of us, in one house, but I have wonderful memories. I have memories of singing and going to the beach and going to the South Side to sleep because it was too hot in our house. The whole family was together, and these are wonderful memories. We had one car and everybody got in the car. I didn't like not having my own clothes, and I wish that I had had a few things that I didn't have—material things. Money can buy you material things and make life easier for you. For example, before my father died, I sent him to Israel because that was something that he really wanted to do. I made life easier for him. He got very sick, and I was able to fly him to Mayo Clinic and spend six weeks there, and I took him to the finest hospitals and doctors all over the world.

Every once in a while I consider myself wealthy and every once in a while I get very nervous. You see, I wasn't brought up to do this. I was taught to be a woman and a mother, and raise children, and bake cookies and make chicken soup and spaghetti, and have a man take care of me. I've never had a man support me yet. And I always think, oh God, what if my business dissolves in the air! What happens to me? And I say, well, hey, kid, you own a building and you have some outside investments and you've got net worth. You know you'll survive and so will your kids. But I don't think about that often, I don't think about the money end at all. I'm well off. I guess I don't think of myself as wealthy, I don't know why. But I don't think I'm financially secure enough. One of my imaginations and my dreams used to be that I'll be financially secure the day that I have one million dollars in liquid assets. That will be the day that I'm never going to have to worry again. They can take my business away, they can do whatever else and I will have enough money to live the rest of my life, myself and my children, on the dividends. But that was so many years ago, that million dollars has shrunk down to so little these days, I have not set a new figure. I feel more secure now that I'm married to an attorney, even though he's not a rich attorney. He's a middle-class, average, wonderful lawyer who doesn't make a lot of money. We certainly do not have to live at all like we lived, but I feel more secure because I think he'll take care of me the rest of my life, if something should happen and I need that. He has a career and an education and I guess that's something that I want.

I would feel more secure if I had an education. If something should happen now, and I'm out of a job, I could fall back on that. I have a friend that's going through this. He should have let his company go three or four years ago, he hung on much longer, and now he's liquidating. Thank God he doesn't have to go into Chapter 11. And he's worried, about what he's going to do. What do you do? I don't know how much money, I don't know what he does and doesn't have, but I figure with my job, who would want me? I'm mid-forties, don't have a college education, where would I get a job? They don't want me on the boards. Where would I go, who would hire me? Who would want me? Where would I go, about getting a job? If something happens to this business, what would I do, how would I support myself? Would I go back to being a bookkeeper? I could do that. You know, I don't know.

I've always wanted to share and have a wonderful special relationship and I'm very lucky that I have it now. I feel so much more secure, so much happier than I've ever been. My kids have been my only constant, all of my life. Now, they have lives of their own, and I really work very hard not to interfere. It's hard for me not to interfere. I get bubbly and excited and I say, "Let's do it this way, come on, let's go." I have to work real hard at not doing that. I've had to depend on them, even though I haven't done it financially. Maybe I have emotionally a little bit, but I have never depended on them financially. I don't ever want to. But I feel that for the first time in my life, I don't have to depend on them. I have someone that really wants me, wants to take care of me. Needs me, and that's something I need. It's a wonderful feeling.

There is something, cute or interesting, and I think about it often, but it doesn't help. Yes, I would love an honorary degree. I'm a tennis player, and I bought a boat, a houseboat. We have it out in Key West and my sister spends the winter down there because it's very difficult for her to move around here in her braces and crutches in the wintertime. She takes her housekeeper and goes down there. Every once in a while I go down there and it's wonderful, because it's on the water on the Canal Street Causeway. I fall out of bed and there's tennis, and I can exercise and it's a real nice place. For some reason, I love older people, and I love to listen to the stories they have to tell. I just have always had a comradeship with older people. There's a lot of older people there.

One day, next to me on the court was a black lady playing tennis, and I was watching her, and God she was fantastic. I mean unbelievable. We went to the steam room and it happened to be just her and I, and I started talking to her, you know, telling her how much I admired her tennis playing. I asked her what she did and she said she's a Ph.D. professor and teaches MBA at Harvard. I said, "O my God, I don't believe it, here you are an A tennis player, and you're a professor at Harvard." I said, "You're everything I want to be." I said, "When I grow up that's what I want to be." Then she said,

"What are you doing?" I was telling her. Then she asked, "What do you make?" and I started telling her, and she said, "Do you know what I make? Do you know what you make? Are you kidding, you want to be me?" I said, "I can't believe it, are you kidding?" That night I went back to my room and that's all I thought about the whole night. I'm in the business of giving life to people. I change people's lives. I'm helping people to help themselves, and it's wonderful.

Dealing with the Children
"They feel they deserve it (wealth); it's their birthright."

My oldest child is thirty. I had five children. I was married to a wealthy man, and my kids grew up in a wealthy household. Their father was a kind man, but not the most easy with money. I worried about their values about money all the time. They grew up with a housekeeper in the house, a swimming pool out back, and a mother driving a Cadillac. What kinds of values are they going to have? I think the one thing that's added to my success is that I was hungry. They're never going to be hungry. I don't mean hungry for food, but I was hungry. Then, on the other hand I'd say to myself, for God's sake, Rebecca, you've worked this hard, I mean I worked to have this housekeeper in the house, and to be able to have a swimming pool outside, and to be able to have the Cadillac if I wanted to drive it. Am I willing to give up all those things so my kids can be hungry? I'd say, well, I just have to give them more, I have to give them a lot of extra love. And I'm sure I could have done a better job. I don't think I did such a terrific job on all of them. I think that basically they are very kind, good-hearted, wonderful kids. Two of my children work here with me: one's a lawyer with an MBA and the other one has a degree in psychology and computer science; the doctor's wife works with me, and I have another daughter here. I've just gone into the Trim and True spa business. A daughter and her husband run that business.

I also have a daughter that's a nurse. She started working with me too, but it just didn't work out. She had a difficult problem with me all her life. She's my oldest child, her father was my first husband. When she was about two, we divorced and I have a lot of regrets about that. I wished that I had stayed married to one man and given the kids maybe a better support system with a good father and mother. There are a lot of things that I wish I could redo, but I know I can't. Everything that I've done, I've done with love, never with maliciousness. Never sat there and said, now who am I going to get today? So I've made mistakes, everybody makes mistakes. Being human is to make mistakes. But I never did them knowingly. I thought at the moment that I was doing the right thing.

Now, when I look back on it, I wish I could make some changes. For example, I would have tried to spend more time with my children when they were younger, even though I had the responsibility of feeding them and clothing them, being a mother and a father to them. I think I missed a lot of their growing up. By the time everything would get to me, I'd lose myself in a book, rather than go out and play with them or do something like that. I think if I had to do it over again, I would take plenty of time for books when I get older and can't do anything else; now's the time to go out and rough-house with them, be with them or do things together.

I go back to the question of what are their values. I think, it's interesting. Some of their values are wonderful, and some of their values are not so wonderful. One is very impressed with what money can buy and is very interested in buying a lot. But yet, he's a very kind, decent, wonderful guy. And I suppose he's used to a lot of, they're used to a lot of things. They feel they deserve it; it's their birthright. Because I didn't get to spend a lot of time with them, I had them all work. I made them all take typing as soon as they could, so all of them worked here as typists. And of course, when they got to college, they all thanked me for that. That's the best thing I could have ever done for them. At the beginning they hated me for it. I think I would have spent more time driving them to piano lessons and football and doing those kinds of things. Their father was never around, so it was on me. My family had no money, but I had piano lessons. We had no money, yet I had tap dancing lessons. My mother devoted her life to doing those things for me and my sisters, and I didn't. So my kids don't have the extras, they didn't play instruments. They didn't have dancing lessons. They didn't have all those extracurricular things after school which I think makes one well rounded. I hope they do that for themselves now that they're adults.

I haven't given shares of the company to my children, yet. Though, I set some of them in very good jobs, and nice salaries, but they've worked into them. I set up one of my sisters with half of the business, and the other sister is now working. The one sister, by the way, who is in a wheelchair, married a few years back. She's a blond, with rings on her fingers that run her wheelchair, and they're flashy. At times, when a guy saw money, I would get very nervous. It was a very big problem between us at the time. I just thought, if anything should happen to her I'd have him for my partner, so I persuaded her to sell me ten percent. So now, I'm a sixty percent owner and she's a forty percent owner, but we split the profits. For my other sister, I bought a franchise in Columbia, South Carolina. It was a small franchise offered to me but it would have done very nicely for her and her six children and her husband, who was a schoolteacher, and I got them all excited. And I sent them there, paid for all their expenses. My brother-in-law was going to run the business with my sister, but it just didn't work out. It was very unfortunate. They moved back to Chicago and it took a while before we got to be real close again—we were very close before—and she's now working for us. Her husband is teaching school again, and I'm doing everything I can to help her. I don't know if she's resentful. We've never talked about it.

I set up trusts for my kids. Everything is done, a revocable and irrevocable trust. If something should happen to me, they'd have the business. I wasn't married five years yet. My husband is an attorney and he has two children. I just did, I just changed my will and left him a big sum of money, but not the business. Right now, the trusts go just to the children. I didn't make a trust for the grandchildren. I do what my estate lawyers and estate planners tell me to do. I'm giving the children the business, because it's either selling it or giving it to them. Since they've been working here for years, and I'm kind of grooming them, that's the whole joy of it, that's the fun. The fun is to see my kids take over the business. And that's the one thing that prevents, or stops, me from selling—my kids like the business. They really like it.

We work as a team. We sit in here, and we don't leave this room until we all agree, the whole team, not just my children. My sister, and the kids that work for me, and my other sister, Sheila, sit on the team. My General Manager is a woman and Jody Boyle is a business, financial person. Jody is a CPA who doesn't want to do CPA work but loves the business end of it. So he's really the one that put the building together. He does the purchasing. Even though I have the final say, and I'm the chairman of the board, I try to run this business, ninety percent of the time, by the team. We present the problems, we do our strategic planning, we decide what we want to do, and we do it. We all have to agree on it. We also have my accountant and my lawyer. They came in the last couple years. We really haven't used their services as much. But I'm thinking about developing an outside board. Maybe that's a way of getting on a board myself. Asking some of these important men to sit on my board will help me because I think, the more educated opinions that we can get from intuitive people that are successful themselves, the more my business is going to grow. I want this business to keep on going.

We are also thinking about diversifying. If we ever decide we're going to go public, we're going to have to diversify. So we are taking a look. I have one son that reads the *Wall Street Journal* all the time. He brings me businesses for sale and we go take a look at them. So far, we haven't found one, but who knows what's next. We are looking in all kinds of areas. We're looking for businesses that are financially well, that are making money, unless we see a service business that I really would know myself. That way, we wouldn't have to depend on other people. It may relate to what we are doing now or it may not. We're in the wellness business, that's Trim and True, that's my workplace. But I'm looking for anything and everything. I have a friend right now who is a venture capitalist. I'm looking into getting in on his business. If he would want me, he'd want me not just for my money, but also for expertise when we go to buy other businesses. There would be three main partners, of which I would be one of the main ones, who would all share the responsibilities of looking and choosing and working it. It sounds extremely exciting to me.

Emissary of Kindness
"I help people to like themselves better.
I sell self-respect."

In terms of my public involvements, I've always felt that in life you conduct yourself. My mother always said, "Do unto others as you want others to do unto you." That's something that I've lived whether I've had wealth or I haven't had wealth. As a public person I think I have certain standards that I should live by, especially in the business that I'm in, or in the position I'm in. As a motivator, if I don't believe in what I say or do, like getting drunk every night and carrying on and dancing in the streets, and getting fat, then I'm never going to be good at it. Yeah, I think that's a responsibility. I think it's everybody's responsibility to be the best they can, to do unto others as they want others to do unto them.

I sacrifice. I do that. Everybody does, everyday. I bend backwards, bite my tongue. I think nobody wins in an argument. You can battle it out but you're still going to walk away, thinking the way you want to think. So I learned a long time ago that I have choices every day when I get up. One is to be happy, one is to be ugly, and those choices are mine and nobody else's. So there are certain things that you have to do to get the end result, which is to be happy, peaceful. Not, rah, rah, every moment of every day, but I have a philosophy that I guess includes sacrificing, or maybe just overlooking is a better word. If sixty percent of the time—in relationships with people, that is, marriages, children, business, mother, housekeeper, secretary—I feel pretty wonderful, and forty percent of the time I don't really like it, I'm really ahead of the game. If it's seventy and thirty I'm really getting up there, I'm really scoring. And if it's eighty, twenty, it's been a wonderful day. And I figure that when sixty percent of the time I'm quite unhappy and uncomfortable, and forty percent of the time this kid's pretty wonderful, then I take a real hard look and make some changes. I think that forty percent is that figure. If you are willing to put up with my forty percent, then the least I can do is put up with your forty percent, because we all got it. So, we just have to overlook, we have to smile, sacrifice, whatever you want to call it, and that's something you have to do to get that sixty percent.

I also feel guilty about having so much money. That's why I give a lot to charity. I guess it goes back to being lucky, really the guilt. I feel that I'm very lucky that I have so much. And sometimes I kind of feel bad when I think about our country, the way people live. When I go out to the baseball games in Chicago, and have to go in a bad section, I don't say, God I feel guilty that I have so much and they don't. I always just think that I'm quite lucky and I always ask myself, is there a little bit more that I could do to help others? But everybody's got to help themselves. I started with just being in a very poor neighborhood. If somebody really wants to upgrade themselves, then they can. And they just have to want to, and I think that our welfare system tries to free people that don't want to.

I think that we have to reeducate our people. I'd like to see parenting and peer relations being taught to them from grade one on, all the way through high school. I think a lot of them just were not equipped to become parents and live with other people. A family life kind of helps you with that, but making choices, realizing what's involved in marriage, why you get married, what to expect from people, and what to expect from yourself is hard to understand. I think that's really important, and if I could do anything in this world, I would change some of our educational systems; the way we teach our kids. I would teach parenting and peer relationships. I really would. I think that's really important to teach. Boys and girls should know how to take care of a child. I mean the physical end of taking care of a child. I don't think it's all instinctive. Certainly it can't be, not when I hear of mothers that leave their kids in garbage cans. I think there are physical things that you could actually teach people about the niceties of living with people. For example, how to get along, how to live with them. I think it would be good for family life, even when kids are growing up. Realizing that people are all different, that we're all different, and that everybody wants to be right. That doesn't mean I think we ought to throw out four words from our whole vocabulary: right, wrong, good, bad. But because I think differently than you think doesn't mean that I'm right and you're wrong, or that you're right and I'm wrong. It means that we both have different feelings this time. We can respect each other for those, rather than fight with each other.

I see in my salons, the Indian lady, the Catholic lady, the schoolteacher, the interior designer, the Ph.D. psychologist, the clerk, and the black and the white and the green and the yellow and they're all sitting, trying to look better. They're very compatible with each other because they have a common goal. I think that when you give people common goals, they all learn to respect each other, and they're working for something. I think you can contribute a little to peace this way. I try to do my share by helping people to help themselves, to like themselves better, to wear smiles, smiles as opposed to faces and lips. I sell self-respect. That's what I sell. That's what I got out of it. I came out looking halfway decent because of it. I think people, if they stay in the program, they learn that they can do anything they want to do, if they want to do it bad enough.

We also offer services for mentally retarded adults and children, we have reduced fees for people who can't afford to pay. Absolutely. That is not universal, that's what I do in my salons. I do that because I think it is a necessary thing. I think that if it helps a person to help himself, I'm going to really do it all the way. If somebody can't afford to pay me seven dollars, then they can pay me five or three or two, but I think it's important to pay something. Also we reevaluate the pay scales, and if they're not really trying then we don't renew the scholarship. But as long as the person is trying, believe me, I get paid back a hundred times. I could have made a lot more money. I could have raised the prices, stopped the pay scales, not given to my family. But I wouldn't have had as much fun. It would have been easy, but I wouldn't have had as much enjoyment.

The Spiritual Secret of Money
"I think those that aren't as charitable
don't get as much out of life."

I'm a very strong supporter of the March of Dimes. They helped my sister out. Now, they don't worry about a polio epidemic, it's birth defects. One out of every four or maybe seven children in this country today is born with some kind of a birth defect, and I think they deserve a normal life. So, I work very hard for the March of Dimes. I was just honored as Woman of the Year by the Horan Institute. It's in Canada, in Montreal. I was the Woman of the Year, two months ago in September, and five hundred friends came and honored me in Chicago and we raised about half a million dollars. It was the Chicago chapter that made me Woman of the Year, which was very exciting. I'm also a member of the Fashion Group, and I'm a member of the Boy Scouts. The Fashion Group is an international organization of women involved in fashion. It's really made up of the collectors, the shop owners, the designers and the specialists. We have scholarships and we raise money so that young kids can go to Merton School of Design; kids that can't afford it. We also have a room at the Chicago Historical Society where we keep anything that has to do with fashion, from books to old gowns from the nineteen hundreds, so that people can come in and see.

I'm also a very big worker and supporter of the Allied Jewish Campaign. Pilot Hospital is a nonsectarian hospital. You cannot pay to get in there, and it's a monstrous hospital, a research hospital. If you had all the money in the world you couldn't pay. You can give a donation, but you have to be recommended to go there, to take your case. And it's for anybody. They were the first ones to have something special, like the Ronald McDonald Houses, for leukemia children. They always had living quarters for parents, right on the hospital grounds, so that kids would not have to go to the hospital by themselves. I've been active on the Jewish Association for Retarded Adults, they just had a fair a couple of weeks ago. Holocaust Memorial Center, things within the Jewish Community I've been very involved in, and the non–Jewish Community, in the nonsectarian community. What else? I have a hard time saying no, I always have a hard time saying no. A lot of them I just give some money to. I don't like to do that though. I feel that if I'm going to do something, I'd rather put my time into it. But I can't do everything, so I try to divide my real time between March of Dimes, Boy Scouts, Symphony, and Allied Jewish Campaign.

My grandmother taught me to be involved in the community and I believe in God. There is a God that watches over all of us. Whatever religion you are. I think we all just practice different traditions, we put different names to different things, but I think there is a God out there who watches all of us. And I think that, in order to make a contribution and have a happy life, what we have to do is help others, and that will make you happier. Maybe that's selfish, but it does, it makes me happier. That is why I am able to help somebody. Directly, indirectly, whether they know about it or don't know about it. And, I think those that aren't as charitable, don't get as much out of life. I mean I just want to have it all. I don't want to miss anything. I guess that's the sad thing as you get older, and you start thinking of your own life, and being over. I think there's just so much to do and so many people to see, and so much loving to have out there, that I don't want it to end. It really is wonderful. And I don't think it can be that wonderful if you don't give of your self. I mean, that's just my opinion. I could be entirely wrong.

I have very dear friends, who are very uncharitable and they know it. In fact the other day we were talking. They just bought four boats. They haven't got a yacht yet, but they will. They were talking and someone said, "What's the name of the boat?" One of them said, "Well, I think we should name it Selfish, because that's what we are." They both started to laugh and thought that was really cute because that's what they are. But, obviously, they're happy, that's the way they want to be. Everybody can't be the same. There can't be all givers and all takers, some of us have to be givers and some of us have to be takers. So I'm one of those that was kind of brought up to be a giver and it gives me a lot of pleasure.

I'm in the Allied Jewish Campaign because I'm Jewish and I'm very proud of Israel. I've been there several times to see how they live. I have an Israeli son-in-law, and in-laws that live in Israel, and I see how they live, with the threat of war, and the things that happen down there. They are trying to work for peace and all the rest, and I just think that I'm the lucky one, that I'm living here, and if they're going to do all the hard work, that's something I should do. Most of the money I give goes to that. I mean it's a big chunk of my money, and it's from me, not the company. I give for my sister too. I give for both of us. I tell her, this is what we're going to give to the Allied Jewish Campaign and this is what we're going to give there, and she says, "You're right, let's do it." Probably, we give over a hundred thousand dollars.

There's so much to give to that I haven't thought about starting my own fund. I believe in our city and I think one of the ways to make our city greater is to teach the young kids. The inner-city kids, or even suburbia, I say you work Girl Scouts, I do Boy Scouts, and we see a lot of resurgence of Boy

Scouts right now, especially in the city. Families, fathers and mothers are getting involved as scoutmasters, and I think that those young people will have a better chance of fulfilling their dreams than those that are just out there, you know.

I have really stayed away from politics and just this last couple of years I have been giving more money to politics. In fact, tonight I'm going to a fund-raiser for a woman judge that I've been asked to help. I did some stuff with the Democrats, I gave some money to Jimmy Carter, I find I really like to get involved, I've been asked to do more than I am doing, and contribute more and then get involved. But I just think there's too much; I can't do everything. I have enough with my husband, my children, my family, my business and the charities I do. Politics has never been one that I really had much of an interest in, not until lately. If I could change something, I would have changed the welfare system. I would like to go through the neighborhoods and make the houses better and I just think education is real important. People, poor white and black, are stuck. And I think that's terrible, because they're not educated and they don't understand that they can go out, get another job, get another house.

3

Benjamin Ellman: The Recipe for Entrepreneurial Success

His is a tale of learning, from one's travels, benefactors, and mistakes. Ellman, fifty-six, began as a traveling salesman and is now a successful manufacturer of light fixtures. Ellman narrates a drama in which learning leads to success. The older and more successful you get "the more you discover what you don't know," what you need to learn, and how to learn it.

For Benjamin Ellman, the virtuous use of wealth is a function of learning. Even after years of learning, "it's important to know," says Ellman, "that the older you get, the more you find out what you don't know." He repeatedly enjoins the *gnosis* imagery of experience, questioning, and insight to describe the dynamics of search and knowledge that mark his financial journey. Building and maintaining a business is an endeavor made both possible and moral by pursuing knowledge. The 56-year-old native of Chicago grew up very comfortably, his father owning a chain of dime stores. The bulk of his wealth, however, was made, and remade, on his own.

Ellman undergoes several liminal quests, each initiated by a period of not knowing and culminating in a series of (on one occasion, literal) enlightenments. The good fortune of insight is as much *achieved*, according to Ellman, as it is bestowed. Persevering in the quest for knowledge, he finds guides in business and philanthropy that direct him on his way.

Kemons Wilson, the Holiday Inn magnate who personally guided him to prosperity, Ellman found while combing Middle America for sales prospects in the early sixties. He recalls seeing on those trips "more and more what was going to be happening" in the food service industry, "what we take for granted today." His account of his first embracing of opportunity is a dramatic *tour de force*. Like Jay Gatsby, he spies the green light of fertile expectation, "all lit up and gorgeous." His expectation, unlike Gatsby's, is fulfilled: Ellman's light was a genuine sign, advertising Holiday Inns, the franchise that contracted for his light fixtures and made his fortune.

In the end, Ellman's *principality* and *individuality* are built on knowledge. This is particularly evident in his account of gaining back what he lost after turning the reigns of his company over to another manager. "Kellogg Business School put out a program on emerging companies and I fell in love with that program. It said that the successful emerging companies are the ones where the individual who starts the company, the entrepreneur, the owner, can get around his ego and bring in somebody from the outside who can make the company grow in a more third-party way. . . . The company lost seven and a half million dollars. The answer was: I made a very serious error in judgment by bringing the people in." In remarking that "to most people, I am my company," he delineates two complementary manifestations of his *principality*: his business, and the ideal he seeks to approximate of being the autonomous individual—i.e., one who respects community rights and whose personal rights are respected, one who takes charge of his own affairs and is neither pushed around by nor pushes around others.

Guides to knowledge are as instrumental in philanthropy as they are to business. Other Jewish philanthropists provide the major spur for Ellman's charitable involvement. Early in his rise, they take him under their wing and recruit him to become engaged in Jewish causes. "They would ask me to participate. And I went through a young leadership group that they were putting together in those days. . . . And I became rather interested in things like welfare."

Through his leadership positions in the Jewish Community Center Association, he administers and implements a number of community and social welfare programs. He gives to "the whole pot pourri" of community charities (e.g., United Way, Jewish Federation, schools, hospitals). And at his plant, Ellman pursues a humanistic strategy, tending to the needs of his workers as he tends to those of the community at large.

Ellman comments extensively on the personal satisfaction he gets from his giving, and how in general those who give get more out of their philanthropy than their beneficiaries do. Philanthropy supplements his business and makes him "a more well-rounded person." Consistent with his belief in the level of personal autonomy we have identified as *hyperagency*, he prefers private giving to government transfers via taxes, since the first form, by allowing the individual the choice of where to give, provides more giver satisfaction.

Ellman shows no reserve about calling himself a wealthy man, though he is not eager to discuss wealth (such talk he finds "distasteful"). With respect to his own lifestyle, Ellman does not skimp on anything, but engages in "conservative"—i.e., tasteful as opposed to conspicuous—consumption, which conforms to the familiar self-presentation of the wealthy as productively virtuous.

BIOGRAPHICAL NARRATIVE

The Question
"I was looking around for something to do."

I was born in Chicago, from a Jewish family. I'm Jewish. My father was born in Chicago and his father was born in Chicago. My father owned a five-and-dime store in the ladies' ready-to-wear and haberdashery business. My mother came from Oxford, Ohio, where her father, my grandfather, was a rabbi, servicing the needs of Jewish people of the Ohio Valley. He rode. He was circuit riding, basically, because there was only one rabbi in all of the Valley. And, my family, my mother's family, kind of ended up in and around Chicago where they had small stores in small towns. My grandfather had a store back in the 1890s and my father had a store. And I was raised very comfortably in Chicago. My sister and myself were raised from a very middle-class family background. During the second world war, my father bought a couple of small stores in some small towns so we started to make some more money and we moved to a nicer home than the flat we had lived in. But we had a very nice life. I mean, we went to a public high school in Chicago, which at that time was one of the finest school systems in our state. It was made up of many, many Jewish families living in that area. Chicago has a relatively small Jewish population, compared to other cities. But it's an old population. And in those days they tended to live in the same area. That's not true today but they did then. Anyway, when I graduated high school, I went off to college at the Ohio State University.

My father could afford to send me to college. I graduated high school in 1950. Even though this was a very fine school district, still probably only about 40 percent of the graduates of the high school went to college, mainly because people couldn't afford it in those days.

I graduated college in 1954. When I graduated college, with a degree in business administration, the Korean War was on. So we still had the draft around. Practically all of us joined ROTC, when we first went to college. We wanted to complete our college degree before going into the service. I joined the Naval ROTC, and at the end of my junior year, between your junior and senior years in college, they'd send you to summer camp. I went to a summer camp at the Naval Air Station in Pensacola, Florida. And they took me for a ride in a jet trainer and I fell in love with flying. So when I came back to college for my senior year, I changed. I went to the Air Force ROTC, I said I wanted to go to pilot training when I finish college. They explained to me that I would have to sign on for four and a half years of active duty rather than the two years' requirement I had. Since I did not want to go into my father's business—I didn't like it—it seemed a good opportunity. And I really didn't know what I wanted to do. So I signed on for four and a half years' active duty. When I graduated college, I got my commission as a second lieutenant in the Air Force. I went immediately to pilot training. I spent nine months in pilot training. I became a pilot in the Air Force and was on my way to be sent to Korea when the war ended. I was then sent to Belgium where I served two and a half years as a fighter pilot in the 72d fighter interceptor squadron. After coming back to the States, I got out of the Air Force in 1959.

I married when I was about 28–29 years old. My wife was eight years younger than me. And we had three children. Unfortunately, after 17 years of marriage, my wife, who was very healthy and was a dancer and many things, had an unexplained stroke, and died, very unexpectedly, when she was 35 years old and left me with three small children. And it was quite sudden. I remained single for about three years and then remarried another lady and picked up four more children in the process. So that's how I happen to have seven children, ranging in age from 28 down to 17.

After I got out of the Air Force I was looking around for something to do. I had a cousin of mine, an older fella, who was a manufacturers' representative of a group of companies in the hardware industry. He represented one company that manufactured light fixtures. And he got mad at them and quit and he came to me, knowing I was looking for something to do and said, "Why don't we start a light fixture company?" Well, I didn't know what he had in mind. After he explained it I said, "All right, fine." So we each put up $500. We named the company Eagle Incorporated because that is the name of my old squadron from the Air Force, Eagle Squadron. But we didn't get along very well and six months into this partnership I bought him out for the original $500.

Pursuing the Vision
"It had this great big gold sign, all lit up and gorgeous."

I started to travel the United States myself because I've always been pretty good at selling—I'm a good salesman. I wasn't manufacturing anything. What I did was I'd buy the fixtures from a shop in Springfield and then I had somebody in Chicago shellac them, and so forth. And I'd go out and sell them and then I'd come back and pack them and ship them and that's how the company started. As I traveled around the United States in those days in the early '60s, I began to see more and more what was going to be happening in the food service industry. That it was made up of many small companies and that there would be an opportunity for someone to build a larger company and that this was a field where restaurants were going to grow. That people were going to eat their meals outside the home. All of the things that we take for granted today were starting to happen in the early '60s. So my company became a very large manufacturing company rather than just a sales company. Because I couldn't find people to make things for me, little by little I started manufacturing things that I couldn't buy from somebody else. And today the company's a publicly owned company and we do about $37 million in sales.

And we have factories in Indiana, Nebraska, Chicago and Edmonton, Alberta. And we're very much of a vertically integrated manufacturing company. And that's basically the background of my company. And that's how I got started.

There are many decisions that you make in life. I've always felt, the difference between successful people and very successful people is that the most successful people I know have one thing in common. They have a unique ability to take advantage of opportunities. Everybody gets opportunities but most people don't recognize them as opportunities. I can think of a number of those opportunities that came along and probably pushed me into certain paths. One of them I remember, specifically. I was traveling across Iowa. This is in 1961—sometime in '61, I believe. And I was headed across Iowa towards Des Moines. It's a long drive. It's a long drive out there, late at night. And in those days, they didn't have any motels or nice hotels. You either had the old hotel in the downtown area or a bunch of crummy little rooms, around the outskirts. And I couldn't afford the hotel, so I used to stay in these crummy rooms all over the country. As anybody in the traveling world can tell ya—I pull into Des Moines and I saw a Holiday Inn. I had never seen one before. It was beautiful. It had this great big gold sign. It was all lit up and it was gorgeous. I couldn't believe this place. It had carpets on the floor. It was air conditioned. Had a nice restaurant. I had never seen anything like this. And I went and introduced myself to the manager and the room was very reasonably priced and I asked him what kind of place this was. Well the manager happened to be the franchisee and he talked to me. We sat up half the night talking about Holiday Inns and about this fella Kamens Wilson who started Holiday Inn and what he was and everything else. And I got so excited that the next morning instead of continuing on out West to Omaha, I turned around and drove to Memphis, Tennessee. It's a long drive. And I went up to Holiday Inn's and introduced myself to Kamens Wilson who was the chairman of the board of Holiday Inn. And by then Holiday Inn was a fairly substantial organization. Not what it is today, of course. But it was pretty big.

Kamens Wilson was the type of person who liked to talk to young people like me. And we spent about three hours where he talked to me about the future. 'Cuz in those days, according to the statistics, probably 98 percent of the people in this country had never traveled more than 25 miles from where they were born. And he said this was all going to change. And all of the things that we take for granted today he told me about in 1961. He then turned me over to their director of purchasing and they specified for use at Holiday Inn restaurants and coffee shops my fixture, an Eagle light fixture. That happened in the early 1960s. I never forgot that conversation. And of course I used that to go ahead and build my business as to what was going to happen in this industry. But in addition, that light fixture of mine was specified in—Holiday Inn put out a very thick book of specs about how you're supposed to build these things. And in one corner of one page, the specifications for the light fixtures happen to be my company's light fixtures. And I learned my second good lesson from that also: Sometimes it's not what you are that counts, it's what people think you are that counts. And people all over the world didn't think of Eagle as a company just starting and a little garage-type operation which it actually was. 'Cuz if they were specified by Holiday Inn to fill, you know, one of their requirements, they must be a very substantial company. So I started to gain national and eventually international recognition for my product because of this. So that, I think, is a benchmark in getting me to where I'm now—it's one of the most prominent examples I know of taking advantage of opportunity.

I've got a very large net worth. A net worth in excess of over eight million dollars. Which is significant. However, it's not a terribly liquid net worth. Because I've been a risk-taker practically all my life and I've always built and kept building. It's only recently that I've decided that possibly I should become somewhat more conservative in my philosophies and attempt to consolidate my gains. So up until now I've been accumulating net worth as a by-product of all the things that I do. It hasn't always worked out. And it's important to know that the older you get, the older one gets, the more you find out what you don't know.

Reversals of Fortune
"You have to learn things all the time."

I've had some significant reversals in my fortunes in recent years in that—about four years ago, I felt the company was as big and as strong as I could make it. The company had been doing exceedingly well for all these years. I thought I needed to bring someone in from the outside who would add organizational strengths that I did not have. So I brought this fella in to be the president, the chief operating officer because he had operated a $900 million division for a Fortune 500 multi-billion-dollar company. I made the assumption that he would bring to the company the kinds of maturity and organizational and management skills that I didn't have, because I really had built this company from scratch and was very much an entrepreneur. That's a classical syndrome. In fact, Kellogg Business School put out a program on emerging companies and I fell in love with that program. It said that the successful emerging companies—emerging company's a company that successfully goes from $10 million to $100 million—are the ones where the individual who starts the company, the entrepreneur, the owner, can get around his ego and bring in somebody from the outside who can make the company grow in a more third-party way, someone who has not been as personally involved as the entrepreneur is. Well, I believed that and without going into a lot of detail, I brought the gentleman in, and this company had never lost money in its 23-year existence, and in two years, from 1981–82, the company lost $7½ million. The answer was: I made a very serious error in judgment by bringing the people in. They didn't have the experience. They had never been involved in a smaller company. They were only involved in multi-billion-dollar companies where they had many committees that made many decisions.

What they were doing wrong is a series of many things. They were trying to take a $30 million company and operate it like a multi-billion-dollar company. They were incurring enormous expenses without looking into the bottom lines. Because they had been used to getting budgets from corporate headquarters and dealing with those budgets. They moved a factory from Cleveland to Chicago without really doing a study of what would happen when they attempted to do that. Did they have the proper wiring? Did they have the proper engineering skills? Did they get enough people that were going to move with the factory? and so forth and so on. Well, when they had done that in the large corporations they had many people handling all those details. They forgot that they don't have people handling those details in situations like this. They have to be handled by themselves. And when everything fell apart for that move, they didn't know what to do. They just, they had nobody to go to. They didn't have anyone to go to and had nobody to fall back on. They had never been involved in money.

Basically they couldn't make decisions. Couldn't make decisions. And the company fell apart under his management. I had to come back into the company in 1983, in 1984 rather. Take it over again and get the company back to profitability which I did in 1984 and 1985. So what I learned from this experience was (a) I was probably a better manager than I thought I was, (b) that necessarily coming from large well managed companies does not mean that someone can succeed in a different kind of atmosphere. So the major thing I've learned in this business is that you're just not always right. I had been very successful in my major decisions over all these years and I was terribly unsuccessful in this one. You just got to learn, you have to learn things all the time. I'm much more conservative now. The company lost that much money that I have to be conservative. Also, I would, in the earlier years, I would make large leaps because I'd been successful in whatever we did—the company had been successful. Now, I have to take a series of smaller steps because we're not as successful and we don't have the wherewithal behind us to do some of these things that we did at one time. I feel that I made a serious error in judgment on the people I brought in and then I compounded the error by not watching it very carefully and then I compounded the compounding of the compounding by procrastinating for a period of time because I didn't want to question my own decisions.

This company was built around me. Everybody in the United States thinks about this company as me personally. I felt that was wrong. I felt that there's no way you can be successful in business if things revolve around one individual and you want to grow larger. But, that's not necessarily true. Look what's happening today with Lee Iacocca and many other people. Individuals who are heading up businesses are becoming more connected with their businesses. I made the mistake of thinking it was wrong. I read too many books put out by various business schools that really had no practice in being in business. And I made a serious error of judgment. So what I've learned from all of this, really, is to go more with my gut feeling about what's happening than what someone else tells me to do. And I enjoy being back in the driver's seat. I wish that it hadn't happened because it makes a lot of things we do more difficult to do right now. But I enjoy what I'm doing.

One of these days I will write a case study on what I've learned about running a business in the last two and a half years—it's a lot different from what I learned previously. I think I'm a much better operator today than I was two and half years ago. And I don't blame the people because I'm the one who put the people in place. I blame literally myself on this situation because the net result was, for example, in one year, on $30 million in sales we lost $3.8 million. Now the next year, on the exact same $30 million in sales, we made $300,000. So we have a $4.1 million turn-around on the exact same dollar sales. So you say, what in the world was happening? What was happening is that the people running the business that lost all the money weren't really operating the business on a day-to-day basis. They were operating it by writing things down on paper, and the things weren't working and they wouldn't recognize that these things wouldn't work. They were manufacturing a product that was bad and were throwing it out the door. And, it's just that, when you operate in a large business environment, you have so many safety nets of people who have been working different areas for so many years, and so many systems that it's difficult to make a mistake. But when you have to make these decisions all the time, right down to how many people you need or do you have enough electrical power in a facility and you've never done that before, or maybe you did that way back in your history when you were starting out, but now, you forgot about it, or you lost that skill, then you are courting disaster.

I think the future is great now that we've got everything on track. The company's prospects are excellent. I have more confidence in myself as an operator. I lost confidence in myself, I thought I was a good salesman, but not a good operator. Now I recognize also my weaknesses in that I am not enough of a detailed person and I get bored very easily and my attention span is not as great as it should be so I have to develop people under me that are going to pay attention to those details. So what I changed is I am much more patient with people. I am now trying to develop people that have worked for me that I can bring up in my manner of management which I don't think is bad now, rather than try to buy it from the outside, so I've changed. I've become more conservative on what we should do and how we should go about doing it. I anticipate five years from today, the company will be doing $100 million in volume. We'll be making seven or eight percent after taxes—which is what it used to make. I will operate as the chairman of the board and the chief executive officer and I will have developed in five years an individual who will at time be the executive vice president of the company or the president and chief operating officer of the company running the day-to-day operations.

Wealth and Virtue
"Money has never ever been a big factor to me."

Financial security means to me that I have no debt and that my income, regardless of what would happen to me, would continue to be at what it is today. And that depends to a great extent on the stability of this business. 'Cuz a good part of my income comes from this business. So that's why I do not consider myself financially secure. In 1981 I did not feel this way. 'Cuz we had the net worth in the background. We don't now. It's gonna take me several years to feel that way again. I can have whatever I want today, but I don't know for how long. Financial security is really a by-product of what it is we do. I don't think it's all that important. Although it's becoming more important to me the older I get. It wasn't that much, I never thought about it that much when I was getting financially secure. And when I turned around one day and all of a sudden noticed I had this very large net worth, it kind of surprised me. But I never thought about it until we lost all that money and now I think about it more than I did. And when I make this recovery, I think that I probably will convert a lot of things that I have into cash and different types of more secure investments.

We're a very conservative community, Chicago. We have old families in Chicago, but not really as much as they do up East. So, ostentatious display is not something that we would like, so we don't do it. But we don't consciously not do it. It's just that it's not part of our lifestyle. So we don't really think about it one way or the other. I've never owned a yacht, but you know, if I wanted a yacht, I'd get a yacht, I guess. I just don't necessarily want it. I went through a series of owning some speedboats for a while because I liked them. It cost me a lot of money before I got out of them. But I didn't do it for a lifestyle thing. I just did it 'cuz it sounded kind of nice and interesting. It was fun. It didn't work out, financially, so I got rid of them. Most people like myself, who have an income in excess of four or five hundred thousand dollars a year, they can do whatever they want to do. I mean, there's nothing that they can't afford to buy, if they want to do it. I've always lived up to what I made, you know.

Money has never ever been a big factor to me. Ever. Ever. It's never been something that really affected me one way or the other. It's been a by-product of what it is I do. I spend my money on the things people normally do. Clothes, trips, whatever I want, you know. Children. You know, that sort of thing. I set up trust funds for my children some years ago. Irrevocable trust funds. And when they reach certain ages, they get money and income and if they blow it, that's their responsibility, you know. There's nothing else I can think of to do.

I don't like talking about money. I grew up in a family that talked about money and I hate that. They talked about so and so's got this. Or so and so's got that or you know, we've got so much so we can afford to do this. It wasn't in a bad way, but I've never felt that it was worth talking about that much.

I've never thought of doing things because it's the particular right thing to do, except if it was the right thing for *me* to do. I've always been a doer. All my life I've always been a leader. I've always been able to do a lot of things. I'm a good salesman. I've got pretty good ideas—I'm fairly intelligent. So whenever I got involved in something, I've gotten to a leadership role because I immediately placed there. And I like to do it. I mean, I don't like people telling me what to do. I think that I've probably taken on too many things because I just wanted to do it. And it was wrong and I probably spread myself way too thin in a lot of ways. I'm talking about business and philanthropic things.

Philanthropic Initiation
"You pick up the right things from the right people."

My first roles in philanthropy or in civic activities really came about through the Jewish community. Chicago is a very small community. It's a fairly large town but for us that have been born here, it's a rather small town. Everybody knows everybody in this town. If you are fairly successful in your business, everybody knows it. It's a conservative community but it's a very nice community. And, people are expected in Chicago to take their place in community activities, if you do well. I became involved initially with things like the Jewish Community Centers' Association, with approximately 17,000 members of which 8 or 9 thousand are Jewish and the balance are non-Jewish. It's on a large campus. We have many, many facilities. It's one of the premiere agencies in our community and in the United States when it comes to Jewish Community Centers. It's been in the forefront of many things, of doing pilot programs with the mentally retarded, with all kinds of social welfare, with the aged. Sort of the premiere United Fund or United Way agency in Chicago.

I began to get involved, I'd say 1966, '67, when I was still starting to become fairly successful in life. And I was engaged in doing things in the community. I felt that my parents, although they were traditional in a religious sense, were never big participants in the Jewish community. I don't know why I felt this.

I guess if I can put my finger on it, I was exposed by elder people in this community who I had a lot of respect for. People who had built businesses. Who were nice people. Who had helped me out. And they brought me in to some of these activities and exposed me to the needs. And I felt it was important that you give. As you do better, that you give something back.

They were business connections. But, they took upon another role too. My parents died quite young. My parents died in 1965. My father was 67, my mother was 57. They died quite young. So I had a marvelous life until then. When I was starting to become more successful and affluent, instead of, you know, talking about things, maybe with your father and mother, that you would normally, I would be talking about those kinds of things with other people. So some of these other people whom I admired a lot were very interested in Jewish community activities and they got me involved. And I saw the needs in it. It just seemed important that somebody had helped my antecedents when they came to this country many years ago and that I should probably do the same thing. So that's how I first got involved in giving some moneys, let's say, to Jewish activities. And then, they would ask me to participate. And I went through a young leadership group that they were putting together in those days—the Jewish Federation here in Chicago. And I became rather interested in things like welfare. You know, care of the mentally retarded, care of older people, problems of broken homes. I got the knowledge of that, which I had never known about. And it interested me. And I then became very much involved. Then, because of that and because I am a leadership-type person, I became presidents of things. I became on boards of directors and I became presidents. And from then, I went from that into the general community to where I'm involved today in other things that aren't necessarily Jewish.

You pick up the right things from the right people and you turn it toward doing the right things for you. As I said, Chicago is much more conservative than many communities. When we ask people for money in this town, it's done in a different way. It's not done like it is in many communities where it's put upon you as this is what you must do. It's not done that way in Chicago. In fact, Chicago is a very poor community for giving, compared to other Jewish communities. I mean they publish books on what people give; we don't do that in Chicago. I think that if we did that, people would give more but at the same time, I don't think it would be the right way. That's another way I'm just a product of my environment, I guess; that's how I grew up.

The Rewards of Philanthropy
"I just really think that giving is a part of getting."

I'm a very traditional person. In fact, I think being Jewish has done a lot of things for me. It gave me the education, the background. The reason I am what I am today is partly because of my environment which is a Jewish environment. That's helped me a lot. I am not a profoundly religious person by any stretch of the imagination. But I do believe in roots. And I think it's important to have those roots. And I think one of the roots I happen to have is by religion. Which among Jewish people, if you're involved with many of them, it's hard for them to express why they are involved but it's important to them that they are.

I feel personally, and it's only my own philosophy, that we're always better off helping people rather than asking some nebulous third party to do it, such as the government or something like that. I think it's more efficient. I think it's proper. I think it's proper that when you do well, a part of what you do should go back into helping other people who don't do as well. Whether it's in money or in time. And either one, by the way, can be very important. It's nice when you can do both.

I think basically, when people give, they give for themselves. But I think that they get more out of it down the line than what they think they'll get out of it. I'm not talking about the normal gifts you have to make in the form of business where you give to this because this guy gets you to give to it. That kind of stuff where you're suppliers and that sort of thing. I'm talking about major gifts. I just think that people who give major gifts get a feeling of contributing in one way or another. I don't know how everybody feels. But most people. I feel very good about it. Sometimes it's a stretch to do some of the things that I've done in the past. And sometimes I've done it when economically it was difficult for me to finally get it done. For example, I had made some major gifts and when I had my economic difficulty I had to put a hold on paying off those pledges. And it never bothered me. I knew I'd get them eventually paid off, which I have done. It didn't bother me that because of my particular circumstances right then I couldn't live up to my obligations. Some people might talk. That doesn't bother me one way or the other. You do things for yourself. You don't do things for everybody else. Again, it has nothing to do with status because I really don't think you get status from giving. I think you get self-satisfaction. I think that's very good. I just really think that giving is a part of getting. I think you get back a lot, too.

First of all obviously you feel satisfied. Because you've done something. Secondly, in many instances where you've done things, you can actually see concrete results of people that have huge things happen to them in their lives. I remember I was president, for two years, of the Jewish Community Centers Association. And it was unbelievable what I learned about the numbers of people in this community whose life literally depended on that agency. I mean, if they didn't get the subvention so their kids could go to camps or to day-care centers or some of their older people were taken care of in the elderly homes and got meals and I mean, their whole life depended on this institution. And you see instances where children have gone on from very humble beginnings and gone on to become major contributors to, not only themselves, but back to the community. You know, that's just great. I think that those are things you get a lot of self-satisfaction, you feel real good about that. And I think that's important.

And I do it too because it's interesting. I think that you get involved with things that are different from things that you do in a business way of life and that's good because it makes you a more well-rounded person. When I get involved in the university or community center, or a hospital or something like that, that's giving me something back, not just in a philanthropic or a social welfare way, but it's almost like an interest other than what I do on a daily business basis, which is important. It makes me more well-rounded. I mean, you know. My business, outside of talking to anybody in the industry, is kind of dull to discuss with anyone. I don't like to discuss it. Not because I'm afraid to discuss it, it's just that I would think it would bore most people to death. They're not interested in it. It's just a different type of thing. I don't necessarily like listening to anybody else's stuff, either. So when I get involved in other areas, it just widens my scopes of interest and expands my mind. And I enjoy it. So I think that's a lot of the reasons I do those things today.

I think the minute someone starts to help, they make a difference. I guess that's what I'm trying to tell you. They make a difference in their own lives, you see. You know, there are people who give money in much different circumstances than mine. When I give money, what the hell have I given? I haven't given anything that's gonna bother me or take something away from anybody. I haven't ever had a situation where one of my children couldn't go to college or couldn't have an automobile. There wasn't one single thing that I ever denied myself from the moneys I gave. Ever. But I think that there are people that I've seen that have denied themselves the moneys they give. Now the amounts might be different and the size. But God almighty, I mean. Those people are doing a lot more. So to them it's more meaningful. Sometimes I wonder, what I give, if it made a difference. I don't know.

And I'm very intimately involved with the Boy Scouts. I'm on the executive council of the Boy Scouts and I'm involved with inner-city kids, but I'm trying to keep my involvement to a minimum until I get things back on track with this company. Yet, I still do a few things that I'm good at for these institutions. I don't spend a lot of time in a lot of these areas. In fact, I've pulled back from spending the time. I've told the various people in these various activities that I'm available to do some of the things that they think I can do better for them. However, until I get things more worked out here, I'm not going to spend as much time in these areas. I've done that in practically every area right now, if things get worked out I'll get back to it. Because I enjoy it. I enjoy doing it. There's also the hospital, Jewish Hospital. It's part of Loyola University. I'm on their board of trustees. We had a fundraising. I'm giving them $40,000 over a period of four or five years. The Jewish Community Center. We had a major building—Kiersten Ellman Day Care Center. That was my late wife—it was named after her. So I made a major $150,000 commitment to that.

What attracts me obviously is a whole pot pourri of things. There's a lot of things that attract you. Helping people, you know. Here's a typical example of things I don't like. I've always been a big supporter of Israel through the United Jewish Appeal. But I've been very aggravated about this whole assault in Lebanon, what's been going on in the West Bank and their lack of ability to negotiate. I won't stop giving, I'll still support that but I won't give them as much. It bothers me, aggravates me. I don't like doing that. It's just bothersome. I feel that I've got the right to display my interest or lack of interest or dislike by what I give. I don't have the right to tell them what to do. I don't have the right to walk in and say, hey, you do this or I won't do this 'cuz I think that's for the birds. But I do think I have the right to express myself. And I can change anything. I don't have any lifetime commitments.

I don't like giving basically to political action committees. It's not that I don't give politically, I do and I am involved in giving politically. The reason I don't like to give through PACs is because they don't necessarily represent me. So I don't like to give to PACs. I'm not saying they're wrong. I'm sure they're right. But they represent special interests as a group. But I'm a special interest as an individual, not as a group. I can't compromise on that score. So I don't give to PACs for that reason. I certainly don't give to groups that I don't like. For example, I don't like radical groups, either left or right. I think that people tend to radicalize things, either left or right—I won't give to either one of those kinds of groups on either side. I wouldn't give to the John Birch Society, nor would I give to the Civil Liberties Union. I just think both of them are too radical. I've thought about starting a private foundation. But I never really had the liquid wherewithal to do it yet. One of these days I may do it.

Fundraising Counsel
"You don't really know everything."

I've been involved in a lot of fundraising over the years. I've stopped trying to judge people. I don't judge people as much as maybe I did when I was younger, because you don't really know everything. And you can only really judge yourself. When I'm out raising money, I'm making some major calls, some major people in the community, soliciting their help. Like we're in the midst of a major capital fund drive for the University of Chicago where I'm on the Board of Trustees. So I sit down and discuss with them why the University of Chicago deserves to be supported. I don't talk about them, that they should have to give money, or they shouldn't have to give money to charities and stuff like that. That's not my business. What I'm there to talk with them about is why U of C is a good investment for them to make. And then attempt to have them do it. But I would never tell them that it's their duty to give money. And if they say no, I don't think less of them. If they don't, if they say yes, I don't think more of them.

The one thing that I've always had to talk to people that get involved in fundraising is to get them away from thinking that you only concentrate on where you can get the bigger gifts. I know that it sounds better to do that, but you lose, you lose the reason for the existence of the operation, if you do that. I mean, if you solicit only the big people, so to speak, the board members, the movers and shakers of the institution only. They only go out and solicit, let's say, the major givers. I realize that that's the right thing to do, from a business standpoint, from a waste-of-time perspective. But then they lose the sense of propriety. Because if they're not talking to the people who are giving, in many ways more generously, because of their where-withal, and they're not getting involved with them, then they've lost the aspects of why we're raising the money in the first place.

When you're talking about the practicality of raising money. Obviously, it's the old 80/20 rule, okay—80 percent of your money comes from 20 percent of your people. And you have to concentrate your efforts on those people from a very practical standpoint. But, if the fundraising people lose the sense of why they're doing it and just get caught up with meeting the goals, then you've failed. I never like to get involved with something like that. I think that's dead wrong.

There is a group of very powerful people in the community. I am certainly not one of them. We have in the community a very, very upper-tier power structure that is made up of, is called River City, which is made up of about 12 or 14 businesses that are the largest businesses in this community. And the chief executive officers of each of these companies make up what is called Chicago Pioneers. And they certainly make a power elite in the community. And I'm certainly not a member of that. But, those people are not necessarily inherited wealth people. Many of them are, came up through the ranks of these companies, some of them. And when you go to have a major fund drive in this town the first thing you do is go after the Chicago Pioneers—you go to the Chicago Pioneers to make your presentation. They sit down and talk about it as a group. They don't give as a group, by the way. They give individually. But, they've done an awful lot for the city.

Personal Credo
"I believe . . . I think . . ."

I believe that people are individuals. I believe in the free enterprise system and I do not believe that everybody is equal. I think that the world is diverse and different, that's important because I don't like people telling me what I should believe. My social philosophy is very simple. I think about the individual a lot. I really think the individual is terribly important and the rights of the individual are important but the rights of the masses are important too and how do you balance it. So my social philosophy is one of equality for everybody. I really believe that, but I don't believe all people are equal. I think if you took a bunch of people and you gave them all the same help, certain ones would rise in different areas regardless of race, creed, color or anything like that. So I think you should give everybody a shot at doing it, but you should reward the ones that do it and don't reward the ones that don't do it. I don't believe in social welfare that much. I believe in not letting people starve, obviously.

But I do believe in the individual giving to help other people. I think that philanthropy for the individual is much more important than from the government. If I were to look at it from a business sense I think it makes more sense to give it individually than to be taxed and give it through that way. 'Cuz at least you're giving to the things that you as an individual want to give to, which is more important.

I think people tend to think people who have done well financially are lucky. I think that's the basic stereotype. And the reason—and I can understand why they do that, because in a sense they say, there's that guy doing it. I'm just as good as him. I don't think everybody does, but a lot people. That's natural, it's human nature. Also people tend to think you're a lot wiser than you are, just because you've been successful at business. That's not true, either. You might be wiser in certain areas. I mean, over the years, you know, people have come to me with these ideas and plans because they really want to hear me expound on them and that doesn't make a lot of sense because I may know nothing about these things but just because I've been successful, they think that you're successful at everything, and that's not true. So you get stereotyped as wiser, smarter, more intelligent, more lucky. Quite possibly, more ruthless.

I've always believed that the quality of the environment where a person works is really important. You get much more success that way. So I've worked very hard at making that quality of the workplace a good place to be, in making sure the place is well lighted, cheerful. That supervisors are not hard-nosed. And that everybody gets the right to speak up and talk. People in my company, I don't ask them to call me Mr. anything. They call me by my first name. And I like that to go throughout the company. I like the supervisory personnel not to wear coats and ties but to be very loose. We have a very loose dress code. And a very good benefit package. I've always insisted on having a good medical program. A good pension program for people. We've got an excellent one by the way. It's never a question of whether I can squeeze more out from my workers. I mean, you have to look at things from a business point of view. I think that you have to. The bottom line, see? But you also have to look at it from the morality of the whole situation.

4

Gretchen Dowell: The Uneasy Intersection of Wealth, Family, and Identity

Dowell recounts a rocky adolescence and youthful estrangement, followed by a return to the fold to help in her stepfather's political career. At forty-one, she has launched her own career in state politics, arts endowment, and progressive philanthropy.

"A lot of my background was shaped by the fact that my parents were divorced when I was young." Thus Gretchen Dowell opens her narrative by setting up the first act of her life's drama. What follows is a story of *initiation*. She repeatedly attempts to deal with troubles of identity and estrangement from her wealth by searching for love and a sense of belonging that a family can offer. When describing a fight sparked by her first marriage, she would say to her mother and stepfather, "All I want from you is your love and you don't know that. And all I want to give you guys is my love and that's all. I want a relationship. . . ." Family is the source of her problems with wealth and identity; and eventually it is family that provides the solution.

While Gretchen was growing up, her mother was unable to develop a caring relationship with her, and her father, though more successful in relating to her, was living 3,000 miles away in the West Coast. "When she [my mother] was in the house, she was upstairs in her room, because we always had nurses or cooks or somebody who was taking care of us. So my interactions with her were buffered." My brother "is more like her and I'm more like my father. . . . And she was more comfortable with him, not as comfortable with me as a girl." Frustrated by this quandary, she reached for a family wherever she could find one. When left alone at her family's apartment, she would visit the superintendent's family in the basement, because "they would take care of me." In this family, "there wasn't the tension. You could just sort of sit and sort of be, you know. You could watch TV together. Together, I mean that's the big thing. This was a real family."

Gretchen Dowell knew that her family was wealthy, but in her eyes, the wealth was entangled with painful personal struggles. On the one hand, armed with her father's values of discipline and self-sufficiency, she did not fully embrace an identity of wealth. "I never asked my family for money. I would go through my brother." Money bred bitter feelings, fostered dependence, and caused self-doubt. "[I had] a real dislike of money from very, very early. And, in my family I never saw money bring happiness. And that includes all the cast of characters I named." On the other hand, she did not abandon wealth, either: "you know, I didn't like the way they used it, and yet I was not ready to just throw myself out in the street." Like many inherited women of her generation, her negative experiences did not deter her from seeing that money was a valuable asset. "I've always felt the great potential that money has."

Unable to find love and understanding with her mother and new stepfather and convinced that her "dream of dreams" of living with her father's family could not become reality, Gretchen resigned herself to going to an out-of-state boarding school. There, further separated from every supportive relationship, she reached the nadir of her pain and confusion. Mired in the anguish of *liminality*, she described her school years as in a "fog." At graduation, she felt "burned out" and went on to college only because she "didn't know what else to do." An early marriage to an ethnic screenwriter, family's rejection of him and eventual divorce proved another false start in finding a family. But as she struggled to assert herself and acquire the independence a profession can offer, she put everything on the line. Finally, "one day . . . [I] packed a bag and left. I went to a hotel for women on the South Side. . . . I really needed to be by myself. I knew pretty well that this is what I wanted to do. I did not go through this divorce just to go back in the same role with my family, I mean that was very much on my mind."

Up to this point, Dowell's relationship with her stepfather was shaped by mixed emotions. His wealth and famous family name intensified her conflicts of identity while his large circle of relatives was a source of like-minded people, who shared similar experiences. But now her stepfather's request that she take charge of his philanthropy was the watershed of Gretchen's transformation. The reunion with her family was at once the reconstitution of family relationships on a more equal footing and the beginning of a new, effacacious relation to inherited wealth. Thus, with the entrepreneurial virtues of hard work and achievement, over the next few years, the stage was set for the climactic act of her moral drama. "So when it came to my time, . . . I decided it was time for me to stop being critical and to do something on my own. . . . to risk, to put it out there, to see if I can do some [philanthropy and public service.]"

When her stepfather passed away, he passed on to Gretchen wealth, a philanthropic identity, and an exposure to state politics that empowered her to pursue her vision of the good society. Anxious to separate her own abilities from her received identity, she was eager to give all her time and energy to causes she believed in. But she was adamant about not using her wealth. "So I got involved in politics, really thinking through stuff and doing it myself. That was my big motive, to do it myself but to succeed and not spend much money." Later she will distinguish herself as the first female to head a government agency in her adopted state. Finally, she had arrived to a visible position with important responsibilities and challenges, a position based on merit rather than privilege. "At that time, I was proving myself, you know, I was on the line. It was public. . . . It was a great deal of satisfaction for me."

Today, she still employs professionals to handle her money and remains unclear about the details of her finances. But now she feels more at ease in giving big sums away. Her philanthropy is shaped by her emphasis on active involvement and the establishment of relationships with the recipient organizations. The "tricky" part is to find the right organization and create a relationship. "It's not just giving money, saying, 'Here, here's a proposal,' and 'Yes, I agree with your objectives.' " Her progressive work on peace and helping other inherited wealthy to come to grips with their money is born from her experience. "I think the goal of peace is so long-term that to me, it's more of an organization process and leadership question rather than a [specific issue]." Thus, her highest, most sublime goal is union with others through nourishing relationships. What "keeps alive . . . spirituality" is allowing "myself to be touched and nourished by other people and nourishing other people." With a new marriage and three stepchildren, a professional identity and a philanthropic career, Gretchen Dowell has arrived home.

BIOGRAPHICAL NARRATIVE

An Ordeal of Separations
"I was this poor, little, rich girl."

A lot of my background was shaped by the fact that my parents were divorced when I was very young. In fact, I don't remember them living together. We were in San Diego, Mother's home town. But when I was four, my brother and I, he's about a year and a half older than I am, moved to Philadelphia because my mother had remarried. Then every summer we would spend three months with my father in San Diego, and so we went back and forth. So that sort of just shaped my childhood. In Philadelphia, I went to the Presbyterian Church School in the very beginning, and then to Larchemont—a private girls' school. It was on the West Side and within walking distance. My mother subsequently got divorced, and then in the '50s she met my stepfather, Creighton Stevens. They got married in about '55, and we moved to South Carolina in the middle of the Columbia River Valley on a mountain. It was a cattle ranch. And I was not very happy about moving to South Carolina. In Philadelphia there were more kids like, you know, from the same background. Also, I was very pleased with school. It had taken me a while to get into—a couple of years. I really liked it a lot and I was getting good grades and I was sort of waking up to this. I was achieving, I was getting attention or whatever you want to call it, but I was also enjoying the ideas.

In Philadelphia you can't help but see the way other people live who don't have money and you get an idea that you've got it. We were different because we were wealthy—I forget now how old I was, but we had horseback riding lessons in Heathe Park and I went to dancing school. When we first moved to Philly, we lived in an apartment building where the superintendent of the building, I think he was Swedish, and his family would take care of me. I don't know if my brother was around, but they'd take care of me. I remember going down to their apartment in the basement to watch TV and stay with them, you know, like when my mom was on a trip or something, or the maid was out and nobody was home. This was before my mother's third husband and she were divorced. So she's been married four times. Creighton was the last. But there was a very short marriage before my father. There was my father. Then there was the marriage which was the reason we moved to Philadelphia. Then there was the divorce. And then she met Cray in Philadelphia and so we moved from the West Coast to Pennsylvania. Now I visited these people in the basement and got a sense that they were different and I liked it, you see. That's the thing. I mean, they had this dog, there was the father, the mother in the kitchen. They would cook. And they had an older daughter. They had a daughter who was like, I don't know, 18 or 19 and going to college, a community college or something. She'd come in and out. I mean, she's older and everything. But it was a real, a feeling of I don't know. There wasn't the tension. You could just sort of sit and sort of be, you know. You could watch TV together. Together, I mean that's the big thing. This was a real family.

I was 12, but Cray had been in our lives for about four or five years. We were in Philly and in fact that was a very happy time. His family has an estate right outside of Philadelphia, about 45 minutes away, so Mother and Cray and my brother and I would go out—Cray had a small house on the family estate. And we had some very nice times there. But once we got into South Carolina, there was this big cattle ranch; and you know, Mother was all of a sudden Jean Stevens, and both Cray and Mother had a very strong sense of wanting to do things for the city so were very busy. Cray was very much involved in something called the South Carolina Industrial Development Commission and Mother was very involved in helping bonds get passed for education. So they were out making a lot of speeches and doing a lot of things like that. So after a year, I registered my unhappiness with the arrangement because the nearest school was about an hour away—there was a bunch of us kids who were driven down to school and then back in the afternoon and so I was pretty isolated.

I was lobbying to live with my father in San Diego. Had it all planned out, where I'd go to the high school where my mother went to and all that kind of stuff. She still had family in San Diego. So I really wanted to get back there and live with my father and stepmother who had a much saner kind of life. And to me it was very normal. The life of my mother, to me, was very abnormal. So, I was attempting to engineer my great escape and go back and live with my father which was the dream of my dreams. And that did not happen. And I, of course, blame my mother a lot for that. But, I also would sort of say now, Why did my father not fight for me more? And I think in some ways my mother was responsible for that. My mother is emotionally a very strong person. She's very strong and it was like, "If she's not happy with me, I'm not gonna let her be with you [my father]." You know, there was that kind of conflict within her. She's very capable and I think she did end up saying, "Well, you know, we're going to send her off to boarding school and we're going to do this and we're going to do that and we've got the money and you don't have the money to spend on her." Unfortunately, I guess, I didn't react openly to what was happening. I have a tendency to hold grudges and resentment within and to just not talk. Just get real silent, withdrawn, and basically in some ways take it out more on myself.

In fact, even before we went to South Carolina, I really argued strenu-ously for me to stay in Philadelphia. My stepfather was very conciliatory, saying, "Well, come down to South Carolina, we want to live together as a family unit." I'll never forget, he used the words "family unit," family unit! But, I felt real betrayed. My experience was really classic, where I was the one who came home in the afternoon and evening, there was no mother, no Cray, my brother wasn't around. And literally, you know, I was this poor, little, rich girl who's having dinner in this huge dining room with the butler. This was the family unit! I was so angry that year because there was no commitment on their part and I was just furious with them. And I said, "Look, this is it. I'm not getting an education. You guys aren't around. You know, I love the cook and I think the butler's neat but this is not—" and it was cold. We were up on this mountaintop and it was cold and windy.

So I ended up in a boarding school in Memphis, Tennessee. I stayed for five years, and oh, it was awful. But it wasn't my decision. It was decided that I wasn't going to go to San Diego. And that was a real blow to me. And I fought it as much as I could, but I felt my father wasn't willing to fight for it. So that really was a blow to me. So I went down to Memphis but I was so homesick. There was emotionally, at that time, a real schism between my father and me, because I emotionally felt abandoned by him, that it didn't work out that I'd go to San Diego. I look back on it and just go, "whaa, whaa, whaa." And I felt like the emotional anchor was gone. And then for whatever tattered comfort my family gave me I wasn't with them. I wasn't even in South Carolina, which was a hopeless mess but I didn't even have the cook and the butler, you know. I didn't even have those mainstays. I really felt, emotionally, I was a basket case. So, I remember I would be in class, and sometimes I'd just break into tears, and I wasn't happy, and I wanted to leave and I didn't know where I wanted to go or, all that kind of stuff. But, I stayed on.

After the first year, the eighth grade had elected me as its president of the ninth grade class. And I made some friends and one thing led to another. So, I went ahead and stayed there. And the rest of the time was sort of up and down. It's a real sort of fog in my mind about the period. I think it was in the eleventh grade, I was in a depression. I slept most of the year and it's like a real break in time. I also gained weight. The families send cookies. So you have all of that. I knew I wasn't really working that hard. There was a group of girls that I got very close to. There were about five of us. And at that time it was the French New Wave. And I went to see all of those French New-Wave movies which were existentialist, a fact that would confirm all the bleak feelings I was feeling inside anyway.

All my friends were intellectually precocious. We all were. And my girlfriends were all involved in broken families. They were all very bright; probably we were brighter than the grades we were getting and stuff like that. And we were sort of in the same situation the three closest friends were in—two of them, their parents were divorced, or one was. I think her mother had just died or was in the process of dying. In fact, two of their mothers were dying. That's right, and the tensions within those families where father and mother were not getting along before they were ill, and the illness lingered on for a couple of years. This was an exclusive school. One of my best friends, her family was the Davis family of Godwin Davis so there was, that. And we hung out at her house a lot, although both of her parents were—I mean it was a zoo, an emotional zoo. So there was like, us three or four of us sort of girlfriends, who are very close and then everybody else in the, not everybody, but a lot of the other folks in the girls' school to us were mindless, you know. We did not have a debutante and there was never any pressure. I mean, we just stayed out of that stuff a lot and there wasn't any pressure in my family. My mother really didn't approve of that.

And my niche or image was very important. I had long, long hair, was sort of a rebel. We're into the 1960s now. And I was sort of influenced by existentialism. Not really knowing what it is. Sort of a pseudo-intellectual. More intellectual than the others but not really. Bright enough to be able to pick stuff up but not having the inner quiet to sit and really dig into things, and not needing to. While I was at school I got an allowance and it got sent—let's see, to the school bank or something. I can't quite remember. And, that was another thing. I never asked my family for money. If I needed any money, I would go through my brother [laughter]. But I refused to ask them directly for money. Because everybody around them was asking them for money and I refused to be like everybody else around them. I was not going to be just one more handout. I would not ask my mother for money from the time I was like eight or nine.

The Predicament of Wealth
"In my family I never saw money bring happiness."

My mother came from money. Her mother had money. Her family was an old, relatively old, family in the Southwest. They moved out to the Southwest in the 1880s, or so. They got into tin mining and then with World War I, they got into trolley-building. They had Perkins Trolleys and all of that kind of stuff. So the Perkins family was where her money came from. My father did not have money. And so that was, to me, a real choice of values from the very beginning and I chose my father's over my mother's. I just didn't like her use of money. When I look back on it, in addition to whatever kinds of mother-daughter conflicts naturally arose, there was also to me a very strong set of morals that I disapproved of—hers and my grandfather's, who had control of the money. My mother's father I didn't like. I found him to be very abrasive and very brash about trying to buy people. Using money to buy affection as a substitute for affection within the family. And being very, to me, very insensitive, not only to me, but also to my mother and that kind of stuff. So, there were just natural tensions and for me, as I say, very moral, very deep moral feelings, very early on, around money. Very early.

When I was four or five years old, I remember just creating a moral structure around the way that my father lived, his view of work in the world. How he physically was involved with the world. He worked with his hands a lot. He was a detective and he was born in Utah in a small place called Halnon and his father ran a clinic and was a doctor—the only doctor in that area. And evidently his father was supposedly very brilliant but a very difficult person. Sort of cold and distant. But my father was very, very bright and worked his way through college. He did a lot of hands-on kind of stuff. He liked to fish, to hunt. His secretary said he had an incredible ability to look at the scene about the accident and to know immediately what had happened. He had a sort of three-dimensional sense. I just admired him a lot. I never remember him, as we were growing up, going to the police station. He worked out of the house. And so, he was very much around a lot of the time. So anyway, you know, that dynamic was very early in my life. He died about 13 years ago.

You know, I never remember them together. And Mother never said anything against my father. I mean, she was really good about that. I don't remember her bad mouthing him or anything like that. And the same about my father. I mean, obviously there was a lot of pain in the divorce. There was a lot of hurt. I remember one time my father saying that when they got divorced he didn't take anything from the marriage. In fact, he just left the household and lived on a boat. In San Diego they have marinas and so forth and he lived on a boat in the marina. He didn't want anything from the marriage, materially. And yet I think there was some bitterness because there was no doubt that my mother had plenty of money and I think Dad just sort of walked away from an unpleasant situation rather than maybe even getting what he brought to the marriage, whatever that was. Whether it was a sofa or chair or something. He took a material bath in a way. It's sort of, "I'm not going to argue with that. I'm just going to walk away." There's so much of, I think, style too.

The fact that my father was not afraid to do that and my mother was always, and still is, you know, feeling she needs money. And that's a big drive in her life. She needs the money to live. She couldn't live without it. And I mean, a lot of money, disposable income. And the relationship between her and her father, who controlled some of her trust funds and stuff like that, was the same, you know, "Dad, I need money. Give me my money." So that relationship was very colored around that and they both allowed it to happen. And I, very early, I just didn't like that. And emotionally, the battles between Mother and me have only subsided in the last couple of years. So, you know, I'm 41 so that's 39 years of a very strong morality that I've held and judged her, too, you know, very disapprovingly in my moral structure, around money.

These circumstances contributed to my strong sense of morality. The way I've lived, to me there was, from the very beginning, a strong value for doing things yourself, for being able to be independent. Not needing people around you. And even in the relationship like between Mother and me and Derek, my brother, she has a—and I don't know if this is related to money or just her personality, but even now, and I laugh about it now. But, I mean it's like, she'd be sitting here and she wants to get a cup of coffee or something, she'd say, "Oh, Gretchen, will you do this for me?" you know. It's getting other people to do things for her. And she's almost mechanically phobic, I mean to ridiculous extents. Watching her helplessness used to just drive me crazy. But now, like I say, I just sort of look at her and say, well, you know, she's 67 and so she's mellowed some. She doesn't react like she used to. And the same thing with my stepfather to a large extent. He had obviously grown up with a lot of servants around him, and he was used to that, you know.

To me, that's a real moral thing that you do it for yourself. You know how to do it for yourself. You can be independent. You don't need to have people around. You can be self-reliant. A real self-reliant kind of individualistic goal. I wanted to prove that you can do it. I had a real dislike of money from very, very early. And, in my family I never saw money bring happiness. It never has. And that includes all the cast of characters I named. But, I didn't feel that the money was made the wrong way. I know that is part of morality for some people, but with the Stevenses and then, you know, the Perkinses, I'm sure they were robber-barons, the monopolies, exploitation of labor and people and all of that kind of stuff. You know, the Stevenses have been very good through the years with philanthropy and sort of switching that around to a certain extent.

For me in fact, if anything, money somehow or other, was bad, I just had no respect for it. Really, I just didn't like it, I didn't like what I'd seen it had done. And I saw that as being so much a part of our life. And of course, once Mother married Cray, I mean, the name Stevens is synonymous with money. So, I saw so many people around Cray who I thought were demeaning themselves; he unfortunately had a trait of picking some of the least principled people to work with. So a lot of his great visions that both he and Mother had, a lot of them didn't get implemented because he was a very poor judge of people. And the characters that he brought around, a lot of them were just there for the money. And the kinds of money that got siphoned off of good projects in large salaries, expense accounts, I mean—Drinking, I mean, I have a big thing against liquor. I mean I did for years. I mean, I didn't myself drink until my 20s because Cray overindulged the people around him. This fed this whole sense of, you know, there was no morality there. I didn't get a sense that there's a spark to life, that they can enjoy other people and they enjoy themselves or if they can't that they can figure out how to get there. And there was none of that with my mother and stepfather. They were like bogged down in their own emotional misery. And unfortunately got more and more bogged down as they got older. And the money helped them dig their emotional pitfalls. Didn't help at all.

That was just the whole vibe around them, particularly around my stepfather. I mean, you'd have these people around for dinner and stuff like that, just being around him. First of all, if you were a guest at this farm it was like a feudal manor. It had a swimming pool and horses and this and that. If you were a guest, I mean, everything that you wanted was right there: all the booze you can drink, all the food you can eat, all these things that people in America dream of—oh my God, you'd walk into this little guest house and everything was filled, the refrigerator was filled. You walk in, you open up the medicine cabinet and there was Elizabeth Arden everything. And people are just like, my God, they're not used to that. They're not used to walking into something that spoke so much of "Here it is, take it." And that kind of feeling went very much into his work, and everything that he did. So there was something inside of me that said, I don't want to be like everybody else around them. I mean, I don't want to be treated like just another, you know, psychopath. I was observing all of this, reacting to it, trying to be different, but feeling being trapped by it. Absolutely trapped by it.

And my brother, from very, very early when we went to Philadelphia and my parents were divorced, my mother treated my brother very much like a young man. From age eight and so forth, we would go out to dinner and Mother would give him the money to pay for the meal. He was the young gentleman. And he was given, you know, he always had plenty of cash. I mean, he had no problems asking for money. No problems. And I got him to buy me the comic books and stuff like that but I would—when I was a kid, I'd rather do without than ask. I didn't miss it, you know. He'd come home with the comic books and he'd always buy me a couple I liked; so he sort of looked after me in that way. But he was fitting into that morality play along with my stepfather and my mother. I felt like he was sort of like a court jester to a certain extent. And we, I'm not real good about hiding what I'm feeling. If I don't like the way someone's behaving I'm not a pleasant person. I'm not unpleasant. I can sort of sit there and be like a black hole, you know. I won't necessarily fight with people but that was my way of sort of protesting. And my brother and I did not get along for quite a while because I saw him drinking too much. I saw him not taking hold of himself. And just sort of following in Cray's footsteps. It was so easy.

And it's interesting. When we first moved down to South Carolina and my mother first married Cray, I remember Cray saying something about adopting me. And I remember he and I were talking and I don't remember talking about that with Mother or Derek present. So it was just him and me. Cray and me talking about his adopting me. And I remember being very much aware of two things. I felt, one, a great loyalty to my father and that somehow or other I couldn't do that. And two was, you know, for all the magic that a Stevens name would have, that Cray still basically—I don't know how to say this—was never sure if anybody loved him for himself. There was just too much money around. And so I felt very strongly also that I would lose moral leverage, as well as some personal respect for myself if I chose to be adopted by Cray and get the Stevens name. That somehow or other I would never be able to morally stand up to him and say, I love you, but not because of anything I can get from you.

Nevertheless a Legacy of Care
"All of my immediate family . . . in some ways were visionaries."

I don't know if I'd call my father an intellectual but he loved ideas, he loved history. I remember sitting around the table and him getting excited talking about forces in history, the Communist revolution and what happened in the Soviet Union and Germany and, you know, really getting excited about things that had depth and more meaning to it. Before I was aware of, you know, we were talking along those lines. He was involved in politics and you know, this attempting to have, you know, better vision, bring a better vision into the world. That kind of thing. And so was my mother. All of my immediate family, my stepfather, my mother, my father, in some ways were visionaries. They wanted to see the world be a better place for people. That was very strong in all three of them. The way they chose to do it is very different. And sort of to get back to what I was saying, there just seemed to be a very principledness about my father and a kind of trustworthiness and the kind of thing that when he decided to do something that he would do it. It was a kind of a commitment. I respected, and I loved him. So that this added more on to it.

And the things that I remember from my mother very early on, she loves to read. So my images of her have been very sedentary. And when she was in the house, she was upstairs in her room, because we always had nurses or cooks or somebody who was taking care of us. So my interactions with her were buffered. And of course, with a brother who's a year and a half older and there's a lot of those kinds of divisions—he's more like her and I'm more like my father. And she was more comfortable with him, not as comfortable with me as a girl. Her mother died when she was three or four, in childbirth with her sister, my aunt. I can understand that she had a lot of resentments. She never had a mother. And so that was played out in our relationship a lot. And she didn't learn anywhere either. She sure didn't. And I think in some ways she felt unprepared, and I think she felt inade-quate, and I think she felt that if she were a good mother she might even be jealous in some ways. Here I have one, and she didn't. She never had a mother. And I think that really always was at a deep part of her, and I've seen just pieces of it.

We have battled through the years but I remember in my 20s, realizing, in one of our huge battles that we had, that she really wanted just someone to take care of her. And I remember looking at her and thinking, I'm just going to have to get off of my resenting that she was never my mother because she never will be. Now, when I visit her, we're both older, the battles are gone. Like some other lifetime. If we ever talked about morals or morality, of what people ought to do or how we ought to live, we would probably abstractly agree but disagree on how we've lived those.

My mother's a very strange person in many ways. I mean, there's a side of her, for all this, where she doesn't like pretense. She may indulge in her own pretenses but they're not social pretenses in a way. They're like whatever she needs, you know, whatever all of us need to get around in the world. I mean, there's an earthiness and a generosity about her. When we were in Philadelphia, she volunteered through the Junior League to work in a drug abuse program with teenagers who were in, I think, South Philadelphia, in the reformatory there. And for five years, she worked in that program really as a volunteer social worker, working with the teenag-ers and with their families. She was influenced strongly by a sense of caring for others. In fact I just heard her recently talking about it. She had a real vision about how she wanted the world to be. And that was one way that she evidenced that.

But this caring didn't carry over into her lifestyle, from my eyes. She spent a lot of money on clothes, a lot of money on furniture and things like fresh cut flowers every day. To me they were totally unnecessary. I think I had a sense of the waste and the unnecessity of it. I don't think I really was aware that there were mechanisms to help other people. But it used to pain me to see people that I knew were either emotionally or somehow or other not able to help themselves and it made me feel guilty. I mean there was a sense of guilt. There was a sense of pain. And not knowing what the mechanism was to give to them, to help them.

The interesting thing is that I think emotionally I was able to have these feelings because my mother felt that way. I mean, my mother had those feelings for other people. She did, or she wouldn't be working with the teenage drug abuse people. But somehow or other there was a big gap between those feelings and what she spent in her own daily life. I mean in terms of money, she had, you know, concerns for general welfare. She was very much involved in civil rights kinds of things, always very involved and very conscious of any kind of discrimination against blacks. And her working in the drug abuse program was tied to those concerns. And yet, I'm not aware of her saying to herself, okay, instead of spending a thousand dollars on flowers, I'm gonna take that thousand dollars and give it to this group that helps blacks or that helps drug abusers. That's what I mean by the mechanism being absent.

Searching for Direction
"I really needed to be by myself."

When I graduated, I was really burned out with school; I had lost the purpose of, you know, why am I doing this. I really didn't want to go on, but I didn't know what else to do. I went to Theodora Brooks. It's in Wilkes-Barre, Pennsylvania. It's northwest of Philadelphia. And I was really not happy. Why was I in college? And, at Theodora Brooks I had a couple of roommates that were okay. I was so far off in my own little stuff that it was really—the world was not reaching through.

My first Thanksgiving in college, I went into Philly. We still had the apartment. And some friends of my family's were there and met this young man, Claudio, and he was so abrasive and so obnoxious, I thought he was great [laughter]. And so we started dating. And my family came to Philadelphia for Christmas and they met him and he was not impressed with them at all, so that was even better. I thought that was really super. And so I continued to date him. He was Portuguese, from down in Delaware. No money. His grandparents were immigrants from Oporto and they still spoke Portuguese. Claudio was a screenwriter. I remember one time my mother said, "Well, he's very nice but of course, you know that nothing's going to happen. You know, it's very nice to have him around and to date him for awhile, but that's it."

Just what happened was that the relationship became a real battleground where at 18, I announced to my family that I was going to get married to Claudio. What happened was about two or three months of intense fighting for everything I was feeling. It's such a classic, textbook sort of thing. I felt like I had to take a stand. I had to get away. I loved the guy. And it was a real question of love versus money. I'd had it and that was my message to them. I mean, we had screaming, shouting fights and my main message was you guys are so full with this money business and your this and your that, you've lost love. All of this kind of tension I was feeling. And so, we just fought around and around in circles but my main message, like I say is, I love *you*, not your money. I don't care about the money, take it. All I want from you is your love and you don't know that. And all I want to give you guys is my love and that's all. I want a relationship and not all the other junk. And so they disinherited me, they stole my jewelry, you know.

It was traumatic. I had gone to Wilmington, during some of this I had gone down to visit with Claudio's parents. And I called my family and said where I was because they didn't know. I had slipped out at night. I had taken some money from them. And you know, I was not, I'm not going to say I was an honest, up-front person on some of this stuff. And so, I called them and I said, "I just want to let you know where I am. I lied to you. I said I was going to do such and such but I'm down here in Wilmington with Claudio's parents." And they said, "Well, we have your jewelry case and we're going to keep it." And I said, "That's fine, you go ahead and keep it. I don't care." So I mean, their tactic to get me to do what they want was the very message I was trying to get through to them which is that I don't care about the money. And so, they said, "Well, okay, we'll disinherit you," and I said, "Fine. Go ahead and do that." "We'll take your jewelry." "Okay. That means something to you. It doesn't mean that much to me. You take it." And they did. And then there was one more scene where my brother, whom I saw as just an emissary of them, was sent out. He was sent up to Philadelphia to try to buy off Claudio for $25,000 if he would just leave me. You know, not talk to me anymore. This is textbook. That conversation took place walking through Heathe Park, and Claudio said no. You're ridiculous and this is crazy and all that. My brother, Claudio, and myself walking through Heathe Park with this strange conversation. My brother's trying to buy off Claudio. And so we'd go through this for, I don't know, several months, like I say. In many ways, it was just a real moral battlefield. So we did get married and then we went back to Philadelphia.

My parents didn't come to the wedding. We were married in a county courthouse. Afterward his family had a little family gathering and stuff like that. And then we went back to Philadelphia and lived in his apartment which was on the South Side. I was 18 and he's 6 years older so he was 24.

He was a screenwriter. So, you don't work a lot when you're a screenwriter. And I was feeling like, well, you know, I've made my stand and I've said what I have to say and I was feeling a little bit lonely, all that kind of stuff. What happened next was that my family started calling up. It would either be Mother or sometimes my brother. It wasn't Creighton or his son—he had one son from a previous marriage, who was younger. So we had some kind of a reconciliation. And then they got—I don't know whether it was maybe through an introduction or something but anyway, Claudio got a small job for a movie or something so we went out to the West Coast, to Los Angeles. And we lived out there and he was working on a scenario, and we went down to Tijuana, you know, on the set and all this kind of stuff.

After that he wanted to come back, so we came back that fall. He didn't like anything else that was coming out of Los Angeles so we went back to Philadelphia. We drove through South Carolina where they, somehow or other it came out, "Why don't you come up through South Carolina when you go from Los Angeles to Philadelphia?" And at that time I was pregnant and so I thought, well, you know, okay, let's see what this is like. So we went to the farm and everyone was being very nice to each other. And about the second night, my mother made some kind of a remark or something that just drove me wild and I was furious and so it started off all the old fights again and we left about midnight and drove straight up through Wilmington to his parents. And I had a miscarriage the day after I got back up to Wilmington. And I didn't really blame them because I knew that I really wasn't ready for the child and I really didn't want it and I was having trouble eating and stuff like that so I think that my whole body was just emotionally upset. So I didn't really blame them for it.

We went back to Philadelphia and I realized that I wanted to go back to college and so there was an arrangement with my family—they paid for my college. So I went back. Went to a small college in Philly called Sparrow College. It used to be on—it's closed up now—Bettez and Byrne streets. It's a college that Mother went to for about a year or two. There was a handful of good teachers and so I finished there and in the meantime they were giving me a small allowance and Claudio decided to go back to college. So he went back to Curtis. We worked out an allowance. I mean, it was enough to pay the rent and get food and they took care of my college bills. They got sent to them directly. And so we did that. And the thing is frankly, I had, throughout all of this, questions of whether I could earn my own living. You know, I didn't like the way they used money, and yet was not ready to just throw myself out in the streets. I didn't like the fact that I just didn't go out and see what would happen. I was afraid. But, I finished college with honors.

I majored in English language and literature. I'd always wanted to be a teacher, so I went to Penn Teachers College and did start teaching in high school in Philadelphia. And then we'd been married about four years, and things weren't working out too good. I was older and he was older. He had started getting very conservative and very racist. And I was teaching in a school with blacks and hispanics and that was just a lot of real bad problems. And so we started going to a marriage counselor. We went for about a year and then I really wanted to separate. It was real painful for several months and finally one day Claudio went to work and I—he was working in a real estate company—instead of going off to my job I called in sick and then packed a bag and left. I went up to a hotel for women on the South Side. And I didn't tell my family where I was going. And I didn't tell Claudio where I was going. I really needed to be by myself. I knew pretty well that this is what I wanted to do. This was about '69, '68. And there was one teacher that I worked with that I told—that was a friend. This was something that I was not being manipulated by my family. It was something that I was going to do for myself. I did not go through this divorce just to go back in the same role with my family. I mean, that was very much on my mind. We began divorce proceedings which at first were amiable and then my husband got a lawyer and I ended up getting a lawyer and it took about a year. It was sad for me because I ended up having to—I had a small trust fund, a very small trust fund, and I ended up giving Claudio half of it—about $50,000. And just buying him out is what it came down to. So that was not pleasant.

Reconciliation
"I did go to work for (my stepfather) which was different from being such a rebel for so many years."

I worked until the summer of '69, and then the summer of '70, Cray decided that he was going to run for reelection as mayor of Columbia and he wanted me to come to South Carolina, you know, and help the campaign and so on. And so I did. I went down to South Carolina, I guess it was August or September of 1970, and helped the campaign. He lost, and it was a very bitter defeat for him, very, very hard. He did not take in reality too well. I had tried to tell him his opponent was very good. And, you know, tried to cushion him about the obvious fact that he was going to lose, and the night of the election when he heard the news he was very bitter, and afterwards he was very bitter. He felt like the people of Columbia had slapped him in the face. And he felt that they owed him to be re-elected. You know, that he should be re-elected just because of what he had done. And so he had a real, as one would say, attitude problem. And so, I mean, it was just crazy. It was too bad.

Despite all these battles and everything, I loved my family very much and I think one of the hardest things was to see the pain that they were in and the kinds of things they caused themselves and that they wouldn't allow me or anybody else who truly loved them to help them in any way.

And they really kept any real love out. I mean, that's my experience of my stepfather and Mother until recently, until the last couple of years. And that was really sad. I'd had my battles with them and now he was asking me to come back to South Carolina and I did. I was in Columbia and I enjoyed Columbia, and I got to know some young people who were in government. And so I ended up staying in Columbia. I worked at a black junior college teaching English for about a year and a half and then Cray was sort of recovering from the defeat and he started, not very subtly, saying that he wanted me to work with him. He had this new project that he was doing and so forth and so on. In some ways, it was like he was trying to turn a new page, you know. It was like, okay, the defeat was over. It took him several months to get over that. And he was trying to put his affairs in order.

He had been in politics for about eight years and he wanted me to come work for him around his whole philanthropic giving. And the issue that was posed to me was that he was getting on in years, in his late '50s and that politics had made sort of a shambles of his giving. He had given to a lot of little charities and boy scout stuff and that he wanted to get clear about what his true concerns were and to try to get his money to be as focused to accomplish what his real concerns were. And so, I went to work for him in his office. He did not go to the office [laughter]. He was up at the farm most of the time. He had an office up at the farm and he had an office down in Columbia. And I did go to work for him which was different from being such a rebel for so many years.

So I worked for him for about a year and it had its ups and downs and all kinds of things and then he got ill. In September 1972, he looked like he had cancer. He went to Sloan Kettering and they did an operation and sure enough, very bad pancreatic cancer and they just couldn't do anything. He came back and he was quite scared and pretty much everything stopped. And then he went out to Fort Lauderdale. There was, you know, a couple of months where he was okay, you know. I'd go up to the farm on the weekends and stuff like that, and then he just went downhill pretty fast and I flew out to Fort Lauderdale, where he had a house, in January. He died in February '73. And about a year before, a year and a half or so, Mom and Cray were divorced. So they were divorced during that time. That's when I got—when he died is when I got my basic inheritance. It was the first time that I had any kind of money that was my own. To some extent he treated me as a daughter. The thing of course with the Stevens family is that the grandfather sets up trust funds that, you know, would go through generations—for blood relatives. And I wasn't that. And that's very strong in the Stevens family—who's blood and who isn't. What he essentially did was take a trust fund that he had control over and equally divide it among my brother and me and his son Cray. So we each got an equal third of the trust fund. Young Cray, of course, benefited from the other trust funds too, but it has been quite adequate for my brother and me.

Also, Mother, in their divorce, got quite a big settlement. And she has benefited throughout her life from the trust fund that was set up by her mother, I guess. And thank God it's a trust fund that she could never invade because she would have spent every penny of it. She gets the interest off of that and then she got quite a good settlement when she divorced from Cray which she quickly spent and it was millions or something and she spent so much of it. Don't give her any cash. It's gone. But now she's settled down. She's in San Diego and she did buy a house and she has redone it quite a bit. But she's living fairly well within her means, more or less. And my brother is attempting to ride herd on her although she's a great one for calling him up and saying, "Well, find me $25,000. I just made a commitment for such-and-such."

Arrival at Responsibility
"When it came to my time . . . I decided to stop being critical and to do something on my own."

I don't consider myself a Stevens. I don't use the name and I wasn't adopted. About a year and a half ago the University of South Carolina opened up Cray's archives and I went down for a weekend. And Creighton Jr., Cray's son, referred to Derek and me as his brother and sister. And yet, you know, I think there's been some jealousy because Cray spent more time with Derek and me than he did with Cray Jr. And I think that Cray was the kind of person who could never express affection. And I remember when Cray died, I just decided to acknowledge that we loved each other very much and I knew that. And that was that. And I think that Cray Jr. doesn't really know or believe that his father really loved him, which he did. But Cray, big Cray, played such games with you and he could be cool in a way to the people he loved—have servants or secretaries call you. In other words, he'd never deal with you directly and in a way he—I mean there was so much pain inside of him that he wasn't easy to be with.

After Crieghton died, his brother called a guy by the name of Roland Maxwell who, in the very beginning when Cray was mayor, used to run Cray's business in blind trust. And so Cray's brother called Roland and said, "We're concerned about Gretchen and the money and so forth. Would you be her financial advisor? Would you help her invest it?" and so forth. And I knew Roland. And I didn't particularly like him. He was pretty abrasive. He reminded me a lot of my grandfather—very money oriented, very conservative, and all that kind of stuff. And he saw me as a social do-gooder and not having much money sense. And so, he came to me and he said, "Why don't we share an office in Columbia, and I'll invest your money." And he's got—his wife has money. And he's got his own money and everything and he's made a bunch. So, there was no sense of his leeching off me. It was more of a mutual kind of thing. I knew I didn't know anything about investing. In fact, if anything, I handed it over to him. And it was like, I don't want to hear about it. I kept that inheritance at an arm's length for a long, long, time, and I started working in the community.

At that time I was really seriously thinking about leaving Columbia. Cray was dead. My brother was still in South Carolina, in Columbia, but we weren't real close. And, he had fallen in Cray's footsteps. He was an alcoholic, my brother. I just felt like he was over there somewhere. We didn't have much in common. There was a foundation that had just been set up in San Bernardino called Sentinel Foundation which was set up by rich kids, inherited wealth folks, and I was thinking about joining them. Actually, I had, about a year and a half or two years before that, become sort of a member of a loose group of rich kids, who would meet in Philadelphia every several months to talk about what it was like growing up with money.

I knew what was happening out in San Bernardino. And I knew that I wanted to put my roots down somewhere. Cray's death liberated me in many ways, because I'd become very much a caretaker of him. I felt very much needing to take care of him. And Mother was out of my life and I felt that very much for her too, for all the battles and all of this and all of that, I felt very much tied into them—their neediness, you know, in many ways. I say that in a sense that any parent or child feels. That you try to make your parents happy. For me it was a very natural kind of thing. So, when Cray died, it was in some ways a relief because it was a burden psychologically, emotionally. He wasn't somebody that you could sit down and say, "Well, what do you want? How can I help you?" There was none of that kind of discussion.

In the past, both Mother and Cray were out making speeches and doing good you know. Really turning themselves over for the city's good, trying to help. So when it came to my time, that had been '74, I decided it was time for me to stop being critical and to do something on my own. I remember really thinking, I've been critical for a lot of years. And now it's time to really see what I can build instead of being critical of what is. What does it take to really do something? What's the constructive path? What is it that I want to do? And it's time for me to risk, to put it out there, to see if I can do some of this.

The next stage that occurred for me was basically, I had lunch with somebody on the Columbia City Council, a friend, somebody who used to work for Cray, a black man. And he had an appointment to make. He could nominate two people to the Columbia Small Business Commission and he wanted to appoint me and somebody else or nominate me. And I said, "Yes, go ahead." And it was very interesting because I remember thinking, "Well, if I get this appointment to the Small Business Commission, then this is my commitment to the Columbia community. This is the vehicle that my interests will take. I was looking for something. And if it doesn't come through, then I'll probably go to San Bernardino and Sentinel.

And I was interested in philanthropy. And having worked with Cray, I've always felt the great potential that money has. That money, when you get outside of all the emotional stuff and everything, is a tool and that it can bring great opportunity in the hands of bright people, good leadership, and a good organization. And those things need to be lined up. Money, in and of itself, I have seen to be destructive to organizations or to individuals, leaders, who couldn't handle it. But I think that there is a real obligation from the philanthropist's point of view as well, to go in and be able to sense out where is the growth of that organization. How much can they handle. How much is good from one source. I think too much money can be worse in some ways than not very much. But at the same time I was very much wanting to be involved on my own, to really be in a community and to do things that I believed in.

Achievement Spawned by Effort
"I was proving myself. I was on the line. It was public."

The rezoning thing came through, and I ended up being on the Small Business Commission for six years and I was on a subdivision committee for four to five years. And I was very conscientious. And, really did a lot of things and pushed for a lot of things that needed to happen at that time. In other words, I just jumped into Columbia, South Carolina. And so through that I got involved in, behind the scenes to a certain extent, doing a citywide coalition about the city ordinance and got it passed. So by doing all those logistics and handling and thinking that through, I was just getting more and more involved in politics and government.

I mean, all of a sudden, it was like it's time for me to dig in and do it myself and see what I can do. And, so I got involved in city politics and stuff and, you know, really thinking through stuff and doing it myself. That was my big motive, to do it myself but to succeed and not spend much money. I'm still not spending much money. I had money in the bank but my whole ethic was not to spend much. Although probably compared to some of the other kids that I know, I mean I didn't wear tennis shoes, I didn't drive a Volkswagen, but, anyway. So a lot of my money, I really didn't touch it. I didn't give any away either. I really, really didn't need it. I just let Roland reinvest it. I wanted to know what government was all about, city government and neighborhood stuff and then I got involved in some legislation at the South Carolina General Assembly. And I started lobbying for it.

I knew Cray had a horrible time with the general assembly—his being a Republican and they were Democratic. You know, I heard what a huge fight he had with them. I was really curious about how to be a reformer in circumstances that are not favorable to you and how can you get it done.

How can you move the state ahead in some ways? And what are the skills that I need to learn? And so, I better jump in and learn them. And the enabling legislation got passed for this new department and Governor Richards called me up; he was the governor then. And he said, "I'm having some problems with the guy who's acting director and will you step in as acting director and there will be a special assembly in about six months. If the funding doesn't pass, you're out of a job. If the funding passes you'll be director of this department." And he sort of apologetically said, "Well, and after a year you could step down." You know, that kind of thing or something like that. And I said, "Well, let me think about it." And I called some of my friends that I had made in the legislature and I said, "Would you help me?" And they said yes. So I went back and I said okay. And that was that—so I was acting director of the Department of South Carolina Cultural Heritage.

So, one day I was in this office in state government. When I was in the office with Roland, the most I had ever managed was a half-time secretary and I didn't even manage there because Roland did. And the next day I walked into this department of 100 employees and about seven or eight state agencies, some were state and federal with several millions of dollars' budget. We had a real fight to get it, but the funding passed and so I became the first director of that state department, the first woman in the South Carolina cabinet at that time.

So I believed in the legislation and I felt that it was time for me to know how state legislature worked because it was so pervasive in the state.There was no home rule for cities. So in my work at City Hall I just knew that so much was dependent on the state legislature. I knew that I was free to do that. I had enough money at that time in the bank. I mean, I don't ever remember ever saying to Roland I need the money that I have. I had worked as a high school teacher. And the one thing that really drained me about teaching, particularly in the South, was that I felt that I was getting symptoms of problems, if you will. I mean, I was getting kids who couldn't read and they were in junior high school, even in junior college. So I kept thinking, well, I want to get more to the root problems, you know. I felt a little bit ineffective in a classroom. I mean I enjoyed teaching to some extent but I wanted to do more, have more of an impact. And the legislature, the general assembly was part of that.

I had to learn a lot, real, real fast. I mean it was fascinating and I just really worked myself to death for about three years. I was really working real hard. It was like a campaign. It was a new department and we had to go back before the legislature in a year and so there was just a lot of stuff going on. But at that time, I was proving myself, you know. I was on the line. It was public. It was not a popular thing and I had to make it popular in a very short time. It was a great deal of satisfaction for me. Because it worked out well and I learned a lot. I spoke from a position of some power and some prestige. You know I had a title and all this kind of stuff and I was getting paid by the state. I was part of the governor's cabinet and my position helped a lot in cutting through the bureaucracy because since I was the director of the department, that means I talked to the director of finance and administration or his assistant and cut through a lot of crap, and people in the bureaucracy treated me better than if I were just a department or agency head or something. So I used that as much as I could.

The Department of South Carolina Cultural Heritage brought together the South Carolina Arts Council and the historic preservation program, a couple of museums, state museums, and several other agencies in that vein. Since South Carolina was so poor, everything that the legislature thought was not necessary and a frill and didn't have anything to do with government, they did not want to spend money on. So that was a real challenge. I feel that government is so strong in our society and that if something is not recognized in government then it doesn't have a kind of cultural, social, place for recognition. Because American society is so influenced by government, by what happens to it, state and local, our government leaders are people who listen to and reflect of where we are in society in many ways. I think the government is a mechanism, if you will. It's not the-end-all-and-be-all, but it's a very powerful mechanism where people can have legitimate platforms.

Lingering Fears of Dependence
"Emotionally, there's still that sort of little kid inside
who says who's going to take care of me?"

And I became paid which was nice. I had gotten paid when I was a high school teacher but it was minimum. But this was a real salary. It was important to get paid. It really was. It was a hard job, it was public service and so I got paid good, fairly good. And yeah, I liked that a lot. I was also sickened at how much was taken out with FICA, the federal taxes and stuff like that, and what my gross was and what the net was. And many times I thought, Jesus Christ, you know. I was getting paid before when I was a high school teacher. Yet several times I had left my check at the office because I didn't even think about it. I didn't even, you know, the check was so little. I mean, one time my supervising teacher said, sort of embarrassed or something, he said, "Your paycheck has been in the office for a week or ten days. You never picked it up." And, I sort of laughed at myself because, you know, it was so little, you know, that I didn't need it to live on. I didn't even think about it to live off. And it's like, God, how do other people manage?!

The good news and bad news is that I, for whatever reason, psychologically, I needed this. I know in the abstract that I could buy anything I want. Every once in a while I suddenly just say that to myself. But what I wonder is why do I need to say that to myself. Why is it that I need to be able to go into a place and know that I have the money? And I wonder because I think, well, I feel many times a real classification around how much money you have by shops of clothes, by restaurants, by all of that kind of stuff, particularly living in Philadelphia. And I got real sensitive to that. And I either bristle to it or else I'll go the reverse and take it like sort of a put-down.

I'm just so aware of many times where I get in situations that I need to have that money to be able to do things that I want to do. That I'd like to do. And I wonder well, what about people who don't have it? Now, that feeling hasn't made any difference in how I set priorities in my own life. But I must say that that's an underlying, I guess, anxiety or tension or something. There's always the possibility of the Depression or something. That somehow or other I would lose my money. Or earlier, when I was very young and I had come to a logical conclusion that I didn't agree with my family's values. It was like well, how am I going to survive in this world? That kind of thing. And yet there's another side of me that I was also proving, while I was taking the job in the department and working, that I could make it. That I could get a job that I believed in, that was challenging and exciting, and that I could earn, you know. As I sat down with the reality of it, I could deal with it. And I know that on another side of me, there's a sort of a fear, fantasy fear.

There's two things. I know I could earn it and I know that I could scale my lifestyle to be happy within what I'm earning. That's one thing I know I could do. The other thing is the fear that somehow or other it won't be enough or that I'd have to—it'd be painful to go through this transition. And it's sort of like I don't want to go through that pain of transition. And that I wouldn't be able to travel as much as I do, whatever I get in my head that I really want to do. But I know I can. So, it's really in some ways, an unbounded fear. It's just there. It's a tension. And I intellectually, I know that I can deal with it, but emotionally, there's still that sort of little kid inside who says who's going to take care of me? Somehow the money allows me to feel that, okay, I'll be taken care of. At least I have the money so that I'm okay.

I don't feel that if I lose everything I can ever get it back. I have never chosen to make money with my money. I don't think in those ways. I wouldn't want to spend my energy that way. I mean, even now I don't spend my money on things or objects. What I choose to spend my money on, overall, are my travel, usually for a conference, for what I consider my work to be, which is all non-profit. There's also a certain kind of creature comfort, if you will. I have a nice house that I own. A car that I like. It's a Honda, but not luxurious, you know, it runs well. But not a BMW or anything like that. I spend money on food. I like good food, you know. Going to a nice restaurant occasionally. An excellent restaurant occasionally and usually a good local place. But that adds up. And it's something my husband and I do. I have three credit cards and I'm paying those bills by month. I look at them and I think, God, you know, this seems like more than

I ought to spend. Whether it was a book or a restaurant or a wedding present, it all adds up, you know, every little item. That's okay, that's okay and then I add it all up, and it's disconcerting. About four times a year I'll spend more money than usual on clothes.

When I was working in the department, about three, or four times a year I'd go to New York, to Bloomingdale's. But I don't buy Ralph Lauren, you know, a jacket for $400. I love sales. I'm a sucker for sales. And I buy things. And it's like going for value in a way. It's like I refuse to pay what I consider too much money for clothes and yet when I get something I'll wear it. If I like it, I'll wear it. And if not, after a year or two I'll give it away. Give it away to either—in the last couple of years there's a cleaning lady who worked for us. And she'd take them to her church. In Philly, before I came down here, I took three bags of clothes that I just hadn't worn in a couple of years to Kindness House around the corner and they distributed them through their thrift shop to homeless and people like that. But I still have clothes that I've had for years.

I don't spend money like my brother, [laughter] who just bought a boat. I don't spend money on objects. He bought it. But then he had to outfit the whole damn thing, you know, which my mother loved. It's out in San Diego. She called and she said, "Oh, it's so exciting, Derek has got all this, you know," so she thought it was great. Then you have to take care of it which is a big expense. You're only going to be on it for so much out of the year. And there are all these kinds of things. A friend of mine just told me of a donor of a foundation in Georgia who has a boat in Portland. A large boat, like a yacht or something. He's been very interested in the Canadian coast. And he leases it to non-profits to invite potential donors and past donors for a trip around the waters of British Columbia and then he goes along and fishes [laughter]. So he has the boat, but he also has it for nonprofit purposes and he uses it for himself so that's a neat combination. But for somebody like me that's too wild, that's too expensive, that's too costly. Of course, this is an evaluation relative to priorities. If you're going to spend x-thousands of dollars on that, which is purely personal for pleasure and all this, what about other places where that money ought to go? It's a real ought to. It's a real ought to and should.

Persistent Skirmishes with Money
"They never tell me how much is in there."

I don't have a sense about how much of my annual income is spent in terms of consumption, or in terms of social purposes. A couple of times I've sat down and attempted to go through a budget; nevertheless, I have some kind of an idea of how much I spend, let's say, each month. Actually, the way it works is that I have an office in South Carolina and now it's been moved to Arizona where this financial advisor lives. We have two accounts, a liquid asset account where a lot of the income, you know, when municipal bonds mature go into there and so forth. And then I have a small, little checking account. But most of the money is in my liquid asset account and he believes, and I think rightfully, that you ought always to be liquid up to a certain amount so that there's quite a bit in there. But they never tell me how much is in there. They may say, there's so much in your account, your checking account. It's always the smaller amount. And that's when I get my, sort of, I'll call up the secretary and say, "Wire so much money to my checking account." And in a way, it's not good because I just feel the least spent on me, the better. That's where I come from. The least spent, the better.

My morality is a real hard thing for me to justify. I feel like I have to earn money being spent, in some way. For example, if I'm in New York for a meeting, then I might go buy my clothes. Let's say if I've realized that I've got some meetings, you know, like if in the wintertime there are meetings and I need new dresses for these kinds of meetings or something like that. I'll go into the junior department sometimes and buy things cheaper that will fit me. So I can buy more things for less. But like, for me, I might buy $500 to $600, rarely more than that at a time. And that's enough.

So my budget never worked out very well. Because it always broke down around how much I could spend for myself. And there's a kind of thing of not wanting to hem myself in and yet really not wanting to face how much I do spend and not wanting to cut back. I think that's really the heart of it. I spend more money on myself than I could earn. And when I say *on myself*, I mean my husband and myself, the household and that includes utilities and groceries, you know, just running a household. Doing property taxes, insurance I mean, the whole bit. Just running a family of two and a dog. And sometimes my husband's children. He's got three daughters. Running that, plus whatever I spend on myself separately. So feeling that I spend too much and knowing that I could never earn as much as I do spend, and yet not wanting to consciously cut back. Let's say I spend, just off the top of my head, around $60,000 a year with what I'm talking about. And I know I could never earn that. And this is not after taxes. Oh, let's not talk about taxes! How much of my money goes into taxes, huge! And so, there's that. I think part of it is I just don't face it, in a way. I mean, I do and I don't. The thing I hate to do is call up the office and ask my secretary, who's the sweetest, dear, motherly woman, to send me, wire me money. This is my own money! And she never gives me a hassle. Whatever I want is fine, you know. And I set it up that way. I set it up that way because I don't want to make it easy for myself. I don't trust myself in some ways with it.

My financial advisor is politically the antithesis of where I am. He's just very conservative and yet, he doesn't ever give me a hassle. He'll give me his opinion and he's very good. He says, "You know, whatever you want to do is what we'll do." He says, "This is your money, so here's my advice. If you want to follow it fine. And if you want me to do something else, I'll do it." You know, I've sent him perspectuses on business ventures and stuff and he's a straight shooter. He says. "You know, this is what I think." Most things he doesn't like. And he's very good. He'll say, "If you want to do this, it's fine." No guilt trip. He's really good about it. But there's a real conservative part of me, financially conservative, I think I should not touch it. That I shouldn't give it away. I shouldn't do any of this stuff. I mean there's another part of me, it's only been recently, I'd say like last year. Let's see, '84 I gave the most away. And then this year I'll be giving even more away and last year was because of the elections. I gave more away, hard money to political candidates around the election issues, than ever before. In 1984, it was, total, it was around 150. That's hard non-deductible, political contributions and soft deductible contributions. And this year it's—I'd say $100,000 a little over 100 is soft. And probably closer to 35, hard money.

Everything that I've done has been sort of in the non-profit area or teaching high school, junior college. When I was working in the department it was all non-profit stuff. And it's—learning. I felt like I was really learning about the government and was learning how to work in a disciplined way—our office was open at 8 o'clock in the morning. So I had to be there organizing, managing, plus all the communications, speeches and stuff. So I was really pushing myself in many new ways to learn skills that I felt were important and to implement some of my visions of what I wanted to see happen. So, I worked real hard and I didn't give myself much peace. I mean my whole formula is to work until I'm exhausted. Not to take vacations. I mean, it's a real formula for in fact, in '83–'84, I got sick, very sick for a year.

The Demands of Conscientious Philanthropy
"You have goals and a vision, but how do you best realize those with your money?"

Back in '81, I got involved in nuclear issues. I was at a Family Fund board meeting and Helen Caldicott came and talked, gave her sort of talk, and that really affected me a lot. And we went ahead and gave her, I think the first general support grant for her project. And that really hit me. For about two weeks, I'd find myself talking with someone and then all of a sudden just like verbatim quoting, you know, just almost paraphrasing what she had said. And so it really touched me on a very deep level. And I started working with Citizens for Social Justice, which originated out of South Carolina by Glenda Andrewes, wife of Rupert Andrewes, the congressman.

And then in Philly, as I was saying, there was this group of funders and foundations who came together to do several things. One was, they were very progressive funders who wanted to get other foundations into funding the nuclear area. They wanted to provide good information because it's a very thorny, complicated topic and a lot of people want to keep it at arm's length. They wanted to get more funders and more money and better giving and just sort of demystify the complexity of the issue. And so there were about 10 or 12 funders who would meet every six weeks or so and we did a series of conferences, like seven conferences over about two years only for other funders and foundation people, around various aspects of the topic. Executive Directors, that was the level. We wanted the professionals. The foundation executive directors. And I had known some of them through the years, but through this mechanism, this funding steering committee for peace, nuclear arms control, I became a working component of it. I did it for several reasons. One is that I thought the whole idea of getting more foundations in the area was good, to broaden giving because there wasn't enough money. It just needed more groups. Again, the focus of the group was more informed giving. The whole reason why I started working for Cray around his philanthropy was you have goals and a vision, but how do you best realize those with your money? That whole question of here's your money, here's what you want to see the world be, how do you focus that money so that you realize those goals as best as possible? A very complicated thing to do well.

I'm starting to formalize my giving more. As I'm giving more away, I realize that there needs to be more work with the organizations or the individual, that—how do I say this—in order to realize that vision that the individual or foundation has of what they want to create with their money, that needs to be articulated or understood by whoever's giving the money. So that, number one, you need to find organizations or individuals who can begin to carry, to do work that will go forward to that vision. And finding those organizations and individuals is tricky to a certain extent. And then working with them, creating that relationship. It's not just giving money, saying, "Here, here's a proposal, and yes, I agree with your objectives. Your objectives fit my objectives, and da, da, da." What you're looking at, you're looking at as colleagues or allies so that you're both trying to fulfill the same vision. And I think that's the best role in my view that a funder can take without meddling. The balance is a fine one, a fine tightrope.

I was feeling the need to sit down and sharpen my own vision, exactly where is it that I want to go. What is it that I want to create, what's the conceptual framework for this. So this summer, I proposed to a friend of mine who runs an organization, a peace organization, whom I respect a lot, that I knew wanted to get into foundation work, that he work part-time for me as a consultant around funding and he's doing that. And he's excellent because he knows a lot of the organizations. He knows the people. And he can sit down and have these kinds of conversations that frankly I don't want to spend the time on. But I feel like in order to spend my money well, those need to take place. So that's a real big step for me because before I got Bill, I really, I had this thing that I had to do it myself. And now I'm realizing that I didn't want to spend the time to do those and yet I felt that I needed to, so there was a real conflict within me. So I understood why I was giving to organizations, but there wasn't the kind of communication and the kind of relationship-building that in my view is what really works, the difference between just being a funder and being a good funder.

There aren't many funders that I know who really get into the psyche of the organization. They don't meddle. But they know what's going on in the organization. They know the strengths and the weaknesses and they're there to help the organization. They go to the regional meetings. They go to dinners or they talk to people in the field and stuff like that. And they're really there to sort of feel out what's going on. And that doesn't mean they're going to fund them forever, but to me that's the responsible funder. So I'm moving into that area and at the same time having this person is enabling me to sharpen my vision and conceptual framework so that I'm not only sharper but it's a deeper understanding of why I'm funding this group and not that group.

Utopian Vision and Pragmatic Action
"The goal of peace is so long-term that to me, it's more of an organization and process and leadership question."

In January I started a working relationship without pay with an author, Herman Peiser, who's a sociologist and philosopher and has written several books. And he and I have been talking for about a year or so on the larger questions of how to sustain large-scale political and social change with many people involved. I don't like to use the word "movement" because I think it's too unified, and what we're talking about is something very diverse and something that's sustained. This is one of the things that has interested me obviously through the years. It's a continuing thread. So I started working with him on my own part. He's not only been reading books on political and social change and various aspects of it, but also doing in-depth interviews with people who've been activists. People, either from what I call sort of a hard political point of view or religious one, who have gotten active because of religious convictions or because of visionary convictions, moral convictions or new age psychological. The whole area— how and why they didn't come back or have they been able to sustain their commitment throughout the years; what happens in bleak times and so forth and so on.

This has provided a lot of self-discipline and structure for me, pursuing the questions that I have all my life in various ways either as an activist or as a funder or as someone who's sitting in the living room sort of reading the paper and saying, What can I do to help the world in the way that I want to see it come about? And so that really in the last year, since January, has propelled me very far and really was, to me, the midstep in getting, hiring this consultant.

The consultant was one of the people that I interviewed. And after listening to him—even though I knew him very well—I talked to him and interviewed him for about four or five hours. I thought, this is the type of person with sensitivity and intellectual framework but also humanity, morality about him that—and we were friends—that I trust. I trust him to represent me around money issues. And also, that's very important for me to be able to say to him, "I'm confused abut this." Which is very hard for me to say or "I don't know." I have problems talking about money to other people, presenting my own ability to contribute. Frankly, I said to him, "I need you and I want you to buffer me because I am not good with organizations and sitting and asking hard questions when I'm the donor. It's a role that is difficult for me to play." So I am sort of maturing beyond my feeling I have to do it myself and realizing that for various emotional reasons I wasn't doing it the way I wanted it to be done. Getting him in has freed me up to deal with some of these other issues that go on, like what kind of framework am I looking at.

It's a larger framework of many parts and I find a great interest in social, political change organizations that have links to grass roots and have some kind of a national focus and coordination. The issue still is very much peace, anti-nuclear and within that realizing that it's at a stalemate right now for many, many reasons. Trying to find out which are the groups that I feel need to be around, institutionalized in the good sense of the word. How can we help them through this transition time? Like the "Freeze" is having a hell of a time for obvious reasons. Can they make the transition? I think that it's important in many ways that they do. From just the "Freeze" legislation to a whole grassroots network which is large, larger than what they know. Some kind of a national linkup.

My approach in many ways is not so much the nuclear era as what's the movement and the issue around that. The goal for the "Freeze group" really is to continue as an organization. But I think also that they have to broaden out because the peace activity is not around that legislation anymore. The "Freeze" legislation as an issue is pretty well dead in my view. The activity and the peace out around the country is pretty much around Central America now. I think the goal of peace is so long-term that to me, it's more of an organization and process and leadership question rather than the substance. An issue like a comprehensive test ban, it's good. Of course it's good, but the issues in this are so much out of our hands in so many ways. It's more of a grassroots kind of national linkup.

It's a very long-term goal. It entails the kind of education in a very broad active sense that I don't think we're used to. Personally, I'm granting funding to a whole range of organizations now. The largest gift that I gave last year I guess was close to $10,000. It would be to a group in New Jersey, a non-profit group that was doing voter education, encouraging registration, getting out the vote for a specific congressman in this congressional area—someone who got through, who nicely got re-elected, Derek Morrison.

Patterns of Giving
"I have in the past not given money to organizations if I'm actively involved."

In the last couple of years there are several groups of funders who are coming around, wanting information in terms of being able to target the money. And I help set up a group called the Future Fund which is a group of funders who are interested in politics. They have hired a man who lives in Lincoln to go around the country to states that are important electorally and to find out what's going on: what's happening in the senate race there, what's happening in the congressional race, what are the non-profit organizations that are doing good non-profit work that is supporting the electoral stuff, who are the candidates who are hardworking, what are their chances, what's the Democratic party look like in that state, can it deliver? If it's not delivering, is there another mechanism that will deliver, do they need money, is it hard, is it soft? We have a monthly meeting and he reports to us. He writes a report about what's happening in these states. That's all hard money and we've got a mailing list and so forth and it's like you need to give $1,000 to be on the mailing list and receive these reports and so on and so forth and budget's around $80,000 a year to maintain this. So that's one piece. It's just information for funders who are interested in the political developments, but want to target their money on the local level. I give a little under $4,000.

As a contributor, I see myself doing that for a while. It's a good information network. So there's this new mechanism. The mechanism through which I gave the $10,000 last year is another one. It's called the May Coalition. Again, this was formed out of the funders' initiative to a large extent, getting all of the new deal coalition folks together—environment, blacks, hispanics, nuclear peace groups. Labor—they've got their own gang, you know, they may sit in and out. Anybody who's non-profit, and many of them have PAC arms. League of Women Voters sat in and out. So people wearing different hats but coming together as a sort of under the non-profit umbrella. And through this mechanism saying to the funders, "Okay, we as a group have got grassroots people out there who'll come up with ten congressional candidates throughout the nation that agree on what we think are good fit with all of our issues. These are people that fit our purposes which wasn't easy, okay. Here are the ten guys, men, women, whoever, who we feel are good." It's not easy, because you have somebody who's good on environment but not good on abortion let's say or this, that, and the other thing so they have to slug it out.

I have in the past not given money to organizations if I'm actively involved—because I feel that, from my experience, giving money alters the relationship. So to be an active member in the day-to-day operations and a donor at the same time bothers me. The largest gift that I give mainly is $10,000 at this time. Although this year I have committed to a $25,000—it's a throw-back, it's a very emotional thing. It's to the South Carolina Arts Center which my family started in many ways. And it was for a room in a marvelous antebellum house. I don't know exactly the date it was built, but I used to be on the board of the center representing Cray, I know them very well, it's excellently run, so I have confidence in them. They were also doing an excellent renovation job on this house. And so anyway the room I bought for my mother is to commemorate, well, not to commemorate—it's just a plaque with her name on it from her loving family. I tried to get my brother to go in on it with me but he wouldn't. And she spent ten years as chairman of that organization and it was doing two things. One it was to honor her—she's still alive—and to express love and admiration for her. And the other was to help the arts center raise the money. It was to help them meet a challenge grant. If they could raise $500,000, they would get $500,000. And they were doing a good job.

People—other young inherited—will send me proposals that I have to respond to. And usually those are fairly spiritual. I'll give them a check for a couple of hundred dollars or something. I think it's a pretty good group. I like them personally, but that's more relationship stuff that doesn't really fit into my vision of what I'm trying to do. For example, Marion Huntman sent me a proposal. She does something in Puget Sound called the Yiddish Theater. I like Marion a lot and I just have confidence that she's good and they wanted to take a trip to Europe for a couple of months in the summer to do some work so she sent me a proposal. And we had a really good talk in June at the last meeting I attended. So, by relationship stuff, I mean helping people that I like or that touch me in some way even though I think they may be goofy. And even though I might not believe in what they're doing or think they're out to lunch in some ways or whatever, I just have to realize that in some ways, there's a personal relationship basis so that I have a hard time saying no. And with other friends of mine who have come to me for a donation I'll say that. I'll just be up front and say, "I'm having trouble with this." I feel awkward, uncomfortable. Yet I try to talk as openly about it—the mixing of friendship and contributing.

A number of funders and executive directors of foundations are actually out there looking for groups to fund. And sometimes it's good and sometimes it isn't. The part that, as in any kind of a network or trade association—you can call it that—like if Martin Burroughs calls, it's very hard to say no to Martin. There's a kind of a hierarchy. Martin's been around. People respect him. I respect him, from when I first met him. Also, you're flattered he calls you; it's like getting a call from the President. It's very hard in the end. Oh my God, he's asking me to do this and it's very hard to sit and say okay, what do I really believe and what are my interests in this thing and what do I need to say—what's the hard stuff I need to say. The other side of it too is that Martin may help you someday. You find a lot of that and I think that's the bad side of the funder network. But you know, they don't expect you to give big amounts.

The Spiritual Path
"I'd say the world can be better than it is. I can be better than I am. The people around me and relationships can be better."

I think the American society has real ambivalence towards people of wealth. I think there's an envy. I think people think: "I want to be there. If I work real hard I can be there." And I think someone has told me that in the last year or so there have been more people of wealth created, that is, over a million dollars, there's been a rise in the number of people with that kind of wealth. So I think in our society that there is a lot of desire for that wealth and money.

Do wealthy people set an agenda? Well in my experience, what it means is that you can participate, do so-called "upper-class things." We all know that there are all those, you know, differentiations once you get in there—whether you're a newcomer, old family, all those kinds of stuff—so it's sort of a myth in some ways. At the same time in a public way, particularly in South Carolina, in many, many ways, the only few people who really spoke out were of upper class, old family and money. I know in some places like New York, obviously you have people who've earned money, having power and all that. And they have a place. They've earned their place. So they set agendas. They can do things and so forth. But I didn't find that so much in the South. So it varies.

My perspective about the world and about my use of the money is a combination of spirituality and a morality. They're very close. Just a deep moral sense about the relationships between people, between people and institutions including government, and between nations. A moral basis for those relationships. How I think it ought to be and the difference between what it is and what it ought to be. Closing the gap is what drives me a lot. I don't have an organized religious house if you will. I don't have a kind of a spiritual practice. And I think that for me it was secular, spiritual, moral, humanist, if you will. Replenishing that and nourishing that is a problem. I can't deny it. And I don't have that outside faith context. I feel that those who do have it, do have more strength. So as I say for those of us who are secular, spiritual humanists, I think it is tougher. It's tougher to have the reserves.

I guess for those who don't have the faith perspective that others have, who don't have an outside practice, other people, the whole relationship, personal relationships of being, allowing themselves to be touched and nourished by other people and nourishing other people keeps alive the spirituality, the drive, the moral imperative, whatever you call it. Just friendship, very deep, good friendship, honest friendship, trusting friendship and friends that you can kid around with, be honest about with, friends that you can call up when you're lonely and who, through thick and thin, are there.

Through my illness, I've learned many lessons related to perspective. To be sort of able to step back and say to yourself, okay, don't get so involved in this one thing. Just step back. Step back a little. Get some perspective. So those kinds of things that allow little things in life to feed the spiritual. Like when I work real hard and I just feel drained, like my whole body is like a brick wall—yuck. Just to be able to go outside here and take the dog and just sit on the grass, see the trees and the sky and nature—very big replenishing, spiritual, moral source, it's very deep. And allowing those kinds of quote-unquote "little" things to feed me and they do, they really do, and to do those kinds of things that allow those opportunities to happen, I think that's the biggest lesson that I re-learn and re-learn and re-learn.

What keeps me going? That's the question I ask [laughter]. What keeps me going is a belief that things could be better. It is not interesting taking care of number one only. It doesn't feed me, doesn't excite me. What do I get excited about? I get excited about good ideas. I get excited about organization stuff. I get excited about good leaders and friends who can have a conceptual as well as a human perspective of things and who can talk about the deeper kinds of drives about why we need peace and how this will be, and about organizations that look good. I get so excited about—somebody just told me about it—a new organization called Another Solution. That's sort of exciting. It's a visibly different slant from the old social change stuff. Can it work, how do people react to it? Is this feeding the larger, these deeper questions that I'm working for myself? Is this an organizational way to do that, to sort of move people, educate them in the larger sense of the word, which is the issue of who they are and the moral potential of who they are. I mean, I'd say the world can be better than it is. I can be better than I am. The people around me and relationships can be better.

I'm probably more of a progressive in some ways. I find the conservatives don't get excited about these things. In general, they are satisfied with the world the way it is. I'm wanting to change the world, and a lot of my focus is on change, and people who are doing a good job at that in organizations who have got the organizational and the intellectual skills and the heart and the morality and the spiritual and putting it all together. I could sit and get really excited about reading books about such issues. The people who think and talk the way I do, happen to be all progressives, for the most part. Now in some ways I don't believe that all this stuff is automatically good. You'd probably call me more of a neo-liberal in a way; I think it's time to re-think some things in terms of just what good have certain policies really brought. I get very unhappy when the progressive side gets caught up with this symbolism, like let's say busing, not being able to qualify it for maybe it's good in this situation but maybe it's not good in this situation. To really deal with the reality of it. We get caught up in our own history, in our own symbolism about history, we have no room for real critique. I get real unhappy with that, especially since there is no room for that. People have emotional stakes, but this is the 1980s, not 1965 for example. So I am sort of trying to get beyond left and right, but still have moral principles. What's real? It's very complicated, and it's not easy. Since January, I've been trying to step back, doing more reading, talking and writing. Putting some pieces together. Saying, yes, okay; yes, it is complex; yes, it is confusing but how can I do a little bit about it, and still enjoy the people that I'm working with? And that keeps me going.

5

Norman Stryker: Expunging the Guilt of Unmerited Wealth

The fifty-nine-year-old author, political analyst, and philanthropist recounts a lifelong struggle to overcome the guilt he received along with his inheritance. By writing books and starting organizations that combat a political-economic system which perpetuates undue privilege, Stryker comes to feel meritorious in his own right.

For Norman Stryker the tribulations of being born rich are a daily burden. The grandson of a renowned entrepreneur, he was brought up in a family of great wealth and progressive philanthropy. However, early on he realized that he was a victim of his fortune, vulnerable to the jealousy of others and his own low self-esteem. Troubled by his unearned riches, he became oppressed by a pervasive sense of guilt. How Stryker expunges his sin of unmerited wealth by dedicating his money and talents on behalf of "the underpowered segments of society" is his story of *purgation*.

As a child of wealth Stryker felt painfully different from his schoolmates. "When a chauffeur would drive us to school, I would insist that he drop us several blocks away from school." Entering the adult world of employment and philanthropy only reinforced his youthful embarrassment. "Being different in money is no different from having a harelip or clubfoot or green hair, except that this difference makes people envious of you, instead of sympathetic." Besides the social stigma of having more money than others, Stryker lacked the confidence of the self-made rich. "The worse thing that money has done to me was to make me have less self respect than I ought to. [It made] me atone. For what sin? I don't know. But, there needn't be anything very much more than having money I didn't earn."

Feeling isolated from others and undeserving of his wealth filled Stryker's life with "anguish," "conflict," and "agony." His attempts to relate to others in social and philanthropic circles became undermined by a self-admitted paranoia. Did they want to be his friends for himself or his money? he wondered. Was he free to refuse a request for charity or did the solicitors know the extent of his wealth and would judge him harshly? Anxious and confused he yearned for an emotional anchor. Yet, the responsibilities of a regular job that organize most people's life were rendered superfluous by his wealth. "Nobody tells me to report to work at nine. Nobody says the assignment for the day. . . . A person in my position has to carve out every goddamn day of his life."

Not surprisingly, much of Stryker's adult life was a long, unhappy quest for productive work. Following the advice of a family mentor, he went to Washington in search of a government career. After two unsuccessful positions in the executive branch, two jobs in Congress, a position in an electoral campaign, a stint as a journalist, and an effort to start a newspaper, Stryker did not feel any closer to his goal. Even his family life suffered a downward spiral. A string of three marriages ended in divorce, each having failed to provide the happiness that he sought.

However, despite these apparent failures, Stryker was on to something. His interests in social justice and progressive politics sparked by the example of his famous grandfather and the ideals of his beloved mentor had become his guiding lights. Stryker started writing about the influence of money in politics and became an idealistic, radical journalist. To his amazement, he finally had found his niche. "I was just very happy being an activist. I even got over the hatred of raising money, and found it a challenge." Still, in a fashion typical of the *hyperagency* of the wealthy, Stryker established a series of four organizations, where he could work instead of working for someone else.

Notwithstanding his mixed feelings about his parents, Stryker is grateful to them for his early apprenticeship on the board of his family's foundation, where he learned the lessons about "the responsibility of wealth and the obligation to give it away." Later, this knowledge proves instrumental by helping Stryker to combine his philanthropy and activism. Speaking about the current organization, Americans Against Lobbying, which he personally funds, Stryker insists, "What I do is philanthropy; I put money into it without the expectation of any return. I put my own energy into it without compensation, except psychic, and it's in a public cause that I happen to consider very important."

For Stryker, the privileged access of the wealthy to the political system perpetuates social inequality. Whether he is exposing lobbying interests or fostering independent journalism, the goal of his books and other organizational efforts was to "get people to understand how they get screwed." Demystifying the political process and making politicians accountable became his way of providing the "leverage" to balance the scales of power. In government, as in philanthropy, the ultimate guarantee of fairness is "to have a multiplicity of decision makers."

After years of struggle, Stryker is able to recognize himself as virtuous. "The things I'm most proud of are first, the books I've written—because I know that the merit of those has zero to do with the amount of money I have—and second, the social inventions—the organizations that I've helped bring into being." His productive "investment" of wealth and his personal accomplishments on behalf of the politically weak have released him from the grip of guilt. Now, he says, "I'm getting more relaxed about spending [my inheritance] on myself and giving it to others." But more than that, Stryker can admit that at last the sin has been washed away; "I'm really not such a bad guy. I'm really quite a good guy."

BIOGRAPHICAL NARRATIVE

Philanthropic Initiation
"So I grew up in a tradition of class people."

I was born in New York but raised in Houston. Houston is my hometown. Father was a trust officer. My mother was the third daughter of Augustus Nussbaum, who is the man most singly responsible for starting Randolph Company. Actually, Randolph was the name of one of the two partners. Randolph was the salesman and Nussbaum was the organizer and developer. And I intend before I die to write a biography of Nussbaum because he was an extraordinarily farsighted and courageous philanthropist. The public interest in the book would be about how he started Randolph Petroleum but my main interest in it would be the way he engaged in philanthropy. He gave away, I believe, $61 million which would be equivalent, he died in '32, would be the equivalent of half a billion today, I guess. I won't give you the bulk, the full screen on him, but he became interested in the South and the cause of blacks. In the only biography which has been done of him, which is a poor job, there is a speech he gave in 1911 before a black YMCA and if you excerpted that and put it on a wall poster, you'd think it was Martin Luther King talking. He was imaginative in his philanthropy. One of the things he did when there was not merely "separate but equal," but zero black schools in the rural South, he put up challenge grants to local governments to build black schools. They were called Nussbaum and they had two pictures, I'm told: Abraham Lincoln's and Augustus Nussbaum's.

My grandfather also got in touch with a Southern liberal activist, who had started out to be a preacher, Alfred Hannibal. He was one of several people that Nussbaum had asked to provide a short memo on what can be done about improving things in the South. And Alfred Hannibal said, "Give freewheeling discretionary fellowships, no strings attached." The recipients could do anything they wanted for a year. Actually, this idea was the predecessor of the Graham grants. And Alfred Hannibal handed the memo to Clifford Cavanagh and thought no more about it. Nussbaum called him from Detroit and Hannibal went to Detroit and Nussbaum showed him around the processing plant and Hannibal didn't make any connection with the memo, and after lunch Nussbaum said, "Dr. Hannibal, you have a splendid idea about these fellowships," pulled out a checkbook, and said, "How much would it cost to start?" And many eminent people came out of those Nussbaum fellowships. So I grew up in a tradition of class people.

Dad served on the board of the Nussbaum Fund along with Mother. And my parents were not so hot parents in many ways, but an exception to that observation is in bringing their kids into philanthropy. They had previously been doing their philanthropy on a personal basis, making decisions all themselves without a staff. But, shortly after the war—we were all grown by that time—they set up the Horace C. Stryker Family Fund and put their three children on the board. And that's what now, 38 years later, is the Stryker Fund and it's gonna spend itself out of existence next May or June and that too is in keeping with Nussbaum's philosophy that each generation should finance its own philanthropy and he stipulated in his will, or in the charter of the Nussbaum Fund that it should be spent out within 25 years of his death. But my parents also gave to each one of their three children, I think it was half a million dollars, back in the early '50s, to start up our own foundations, so we could get a taste of what it was like to make our own decisions.

I would like in principle to involve my kids in my giving—I have five of them and they are very, very different people. And I have tried to encourage them. I wanted very, very badly to get them involved with the Stryker Fund and that's the trouble with it. In those days I was even more unwise than I am now and I pushed and pushed and pushed and the kids' reaction was to pull back and think, "My God, what's Dad trying to do to us?" But, I'm proud to say that three of my kids now sit on the Stryker Fund board and have taken an active part in it. And they're all imbued to one degree or another with the responsibility of wealth and the obligation to give it away.

So I grew up in Houston, and went to a private school there. A school that my mother was the key person in starting because she didn't see a school she considered good enough for her children in Houston—that's the best side of my mother. Then I went on to Yale. I majored in history but my Yale years were during the war and Yale was all screwed up. I spent half my college education in the Navy, then I went to Washington to see Alfred Hannibal, who turned out to be my real father. He wanted me very much to have a career in government. He ended up as a foreign attaché to the State Department and was very friendly with Mrs. Roosevelt and to a certain extent President Roosevelt. So I came down to Washington after college to try to find a job in 1947 and there were no jobs around but I happened to hear of a government internship program that the Goodman Foundation was then running, aiming to give immediate college graduates two or three rotating assignments in the government in hopes of attracting them to a career in government and to compress this—I came to Washington in '48, and started.

Daily Labor
"I get a big kick out of . . . making something happen that wouldn't have happened."

In the year I had to wait for that internship I worked for a newspaper in Houston, then I came here and interned for the Department of the Interior and then up on the hill for Stan Powel. Later, went on to the Senate side with Jim Duncan. After that came the Stevenson campaign of '52, and directorship of research for a democratic organization, '52–'56. Next, I founded a newspaper in Alexandria, Virginia with three other people. Four years of that—expensive and unhappy. And then Kennedy was elected and everybody was going into the New Frontier. I went too, in the State Department, but I was a bad fit and I was eased out of the government. I started writing and have written five books, starting in '62 and ending, the fourth one was finished in '73. My first family broke up, first marriage broke up. But anyway, six months on the *Baltimore Sun Times*. A year in public policy school as a freshman at the age of 49. Disillusioned by that. Married again and went to Boston for five years. Second marriage broke up. Third marriage disaster and after that I wrote a book, fifth book about lawyers and came back down to New York and became an activist. Started a political action committee having to do with the environment and I found out I was just very happy being an activist. I even got over the hatred of raising money, and found it a challenge. After that ended, I found myself wishing for that again and I've since formed three organizations having to do with a favorite subject of mine—money and politics.

My first organization was called Citizens for Honest Voting, which was an attempt to get a public service media effort to get people to check off the box in the tax return for presidential funding. Second, I plagiarized myself. In the late sixties, I invented and started the Fund for Investigative Journalism. It granted stipends to freelance reporters to supplement the income that they got from the low paying magazines that were the only ones that would print serious investigative stuff. And Jack Burns, who was the first executive director of that, had the far-sightedness to give a little known reporter named Herbert Lundberg his first $250 to check out the lead on a massacre in Laos and when that paid off, the Fund gave Lundberg a grant for $3,000 and that produced the massacre story. And I always cite that as the biggest bang for a buck I know of in philanthropy anywhere. In '83, I started the Project for Investigative Reporting on Money and Politics which works in the same way that the Fund for Investigative Journalism does, only on this specific subject. Burns is back in harness now with me. And the third, those two are C-3 tax deductible entities, and the project that I'm spending most of my time on is a non–C-3 organization called Americans Against Lobbying which mainly publishes irreverent ads in local papers around the country spotlighting the campaign finance inequities of the local congressmen. And that's stirred up a good deal of hell. And I'm also occasionally doing radio commentaries, although not as many of them as I in principle would like to do. So that's my life story.

I pride myself with—this is gonna sound immodest but if I don't blow my horn, who will?—I think I'm a pretty or a very good social inventor. I get a big kick out of creating something or making something possible, making something happen that wouldn't have happened. I'm, I think I'm good at inventing new institutions, such as the Fund for Investigative Journalism.

I'm also helping out to create a media data base by congressional district, to enable public interest organizations after they've made an analysis, to put pressure on congressmen. National studies that the League of Women Voters does and other issues here in Washington do not affect congressmen and senators. They couldn't care less what appears in the *Washington Post* and the *New York Times* 'cause their constituents don't see it. And that's the philosophy behind the local ads and the localized press releases. We sent out three hundred individually tailored press releases in the '84 campaign spotlighting the PAC history of that many congressmen, and sent it to the local media. The response has been terrific, terrific. We got 124, by count, 124 calls from reporters around the country, a harvest of clippings.

The Stryker Fund
"The decision was to spend it out."

Issues of social justice were also worked through in the family fund. My sister is dead and my brother got out of the Stryker Fund because he didn't share the goals of the board, he didn't share the social action, the social reform goals of the board. The Stryker Fund went through several incarnations and modes of operation. One of the nicest stories I tell about my mother is that when my brother said he didn't want to go to any more meetings, he started to vote by mail. And there was a project on corporate responsibility and he felt that it would embarrass him in the board room of Randolph where he's been a hardworking, conscientious and excellent board member for years. And he said, he wrote on his ballot, "If this grant goes through, I'll resign." And so there we were, he and his wife voting against, I and my wife voting for and that left it up to Mother. And one of the important considerations to her in institutionalizing the family philanthropy was to make sure we got together once in a while and so if she voted for it, there was the strong possibility of undermining her personal goal. And she said, "It's a good project," voted for it; my brother resigned. Then my nieces and nephews and later my own children began to people the board. First you had to be 21 to get on it, later 18.

We've given away three quarters of a million to a million. And when some trusts, 20–year charitable trusts, began to fall in, my parents gave to already-taken-care-of grandchildren instead of to the Stryker Fund. So that cut back on the amount of money they had to give away. And so there was the decision to either cut back the giving and perpetuate the Stryker Fund or keep on giving the same amount and spend it out, spend the capital out and the decision was to spend it out. That was the way my parents set it up. That was unchangeable at that point.

I have mixed views about the demise of the Stryker Fund. On the one hand, the negative feelings are, I think it's fair to say, that this has been at the cutting edge of progressive philanthropy—progressive in the political sense. And Carney Nicholson, who's been the executive director now for 22 years, had a genius for traveling around the country and ferreting out diamonds in the rough. And we're the only foundation that I know that has applicants appear before the full board and that has been enormously exciting. It makes for hard work. Our meetings are all-day Saturday. We give an hour to each applicant, six on Saturday and three on Sunday morning and then we vote on Sunday afternoon. And that has been just very exciting.

I would recommend that to anybody, any foundation that wanted to have more interesting meetings, 'cause (a) you're looking at flesh and blood and you can ask questions of a person that you can't ask of a piece of paper and (b) particularly for those projects that hinge on the quality of one person, on the leadership of the organization, you get a chance to make an assessment. I was the president for twelve years before we began to rotate it among my nephews and nieces and children. And I wish now I had spent more time with them. Instead, I was always busy, involved in either writing a book or something else. But in any case, I did not serve on the board because, first of all, I think they would have had real reluctance in having more than one member of a given family on the board, but (a) I wasn't interested in it and (b) I would not have had anything to contribute. In fact, I would have been likely a thorn in their side.

The Sin
"The worst thing inherited wealth has done for me is to make me atone."

When I was growing up, it was not a secret that we were wealthy, I mean, versus all the other people in my class. I mean, one only had to look at our house and garden. Wealth created a huge guilt. In that respect, I shared the experience of an enormous number of inherited-wealth people. When a chauffeur would drive us to school, I would insist that he drop us several blocks away from school, and I had that story repeated to me any number of times. I like to say that being different in money is no different from having a harelip or clubfoot or green hair, except that, that difference makes people envious of you, instead of sympathetic.

I don't want to overdo the poor little rich boy; but a person in my position has to carve out every goddamn day of his life unless he chooses, as I sometimes wish I had chosen, to just apply a profession, e.g., newspapering. Newspaper reporter was what I started out being, and I wanted to become a professional at that. And many of my cousins have not chosen a profession—I'm judging them by my standards, not by theirs—and have led lives of what I would call emptiness.

I envy the apparent lack of guilt or conflict of people who made their own fortune. And, actually, I'm thinking of one person, one of my really close friends, who's a lawyer, but he's really a real estate investor and makes deals, puts together deals. He grew up in a very modest background here in Washington, and I think his net worth equals or exceeds mine. I think, he probably has access to more money in principal, and he makes big gifts to his kids' schools. For example, he gave a running track. He is very generous and makes gifts that I would not dream of making; someday I might. But he made it all on his own, he carved out his own money; and I didn't make a goddamn cent of it.

I don't own a yacht but I used to have an airplane—I used it for flying myself and my family up to Newport. I wouldn't dream of having a corporate jet. My brother owns a jet plane, but I wouldn't dream of spending that amount of money on anything that he does. But it's interesting. He had a certain size jet, and he was going to move up the ladder, and it was going to cost him a million, a million and a half more to buy a bigger one. He said to this person: "But I deserve it. I made it and I deserve to treat myself to this. I inherited. I am richer now than I was, you know. I built my fortune. I started with x and now it's 2x and I did it through hard work." And he's right, he has worked hard. Unlike me, he has more self-respect and pride about his money and he has had through his life, I think, less anguish, conflict, guilt.

The feelings of guilt put me through much agony. For a long, long, long time, it gave me low self-esteem: who am I to deserve all this good fortune? And it made me paranoid, well, paranoid in two respects: One, when I came to Washington, I felt with considerable justification that people liked me to some extent, greater or lesser extent, because of my money. Everybody that looked at me, secretly had a dollar sign. I no longer feel that, I think I'm more realistic about that. I know that people to some extent treat me much more favorably than if I didn't have and give away money. And to some extent I enjoy that. I take advantage of it. On the other hand, when I came to Washington, when anybody asked me to give, say, to the Heart Ball, or any of the more conventional charities, if anybody asked me to give to a charity, I behaved as if they had an X-ray vision into my bank account and knew exactly what I had, exactly what I spent on myself, exactly what I had to give away. No amount I gave was right; it was either too low, or too high. I've gotten over that. I give to the things I want to.

The worst thing that money has done to me was to make me have less self-respect than I ought to. 'Cause I'm really not such a bad guy. I'm really quite a good guy. I think the worst thing it has done for me is to make me atone—for what sin? I don't know. But, there needn't be anything very much more than having money I didn't earn. And being more fortunate than others, for reasons I didn't have the least to do with. And so, it has always made me frantic about making use of every golden moment to save the world and atone. And until recently it's given me a less-than-usual capacity to just enjoy myself. The last couple of days, I've begun to run out of gas on this project that I've been working a couple of years on. I have to decide for myself: should I continue this or shouldn't I? Those decisions are not available to most people. You report for work or you don't get paid. Nobody tells me to report to work at nine. Nobody says the assignment for the day.

As a result of the guilt and constantly having to evaluate and decide what to do, I wasn't able to take real vacations where I'd let go of everything and recreate. I regret the times when I was underwhelming as a parent and cheated myself as well as my kids of just relaxing. We used to have a place up on Newport and Dad would have to spend half of every day writing his book. That's the worst thing money did for me. The best thing? I didn't have to do anything that I didn't want to, and I don't underestimate the joy and advantage of that. Some people have to collect garbage whether they hate it or not. Others, a lot of idealistic people that worked for the government, were on the public policy side of, for example, HUD and have since gone out and let rich people in, using the same issues they were trying to resolve in the first place and I haven't had to do that.

I think most people think well of me and have regard for the fact that I'm always involved in one cause or another. However, other people look at me with dollar signs in their eyes. I mean this comes through most clearly when somebody, whom I haven't seen in seven, eight years says: "I'm coming to town and just love to see ya. And won't you take a ticket to the benefit?" and you know that goddamn well, the only reason they haven't seen you for seven years is that you're not very close friends. And that pisses me off. It's funny [laughter] but part of the reason I enjoy raising money is that I can pull all the same tactics that have been pulled on me!

Though, it's gonna sound self-serving and pompous, I think, I'm different from most rich people, because I think I devote myself more to causes than most rich people do. However, I do so at a great, great personal benefit. Of course, leaving aside the underendowed capacity to enjoy myself but I'm getting over that. I just spent a week down in Florida, and I goddamn hated to come back. Anyway, the last 5 to 10 years, I'm trying to reach the 50-percent maximum in my giving, I mean, I think most often, most of the time, I do it and if that was raised to 60 percent, I would still do it. One of my neuroses is fear of running out of things. I fear running out of money. I've just discovered how irrational that is. And so, I'm going on 60 now and, I mean what the hell am I gonna do with all that money?

New Bearings
"I guess I'm more relaxed both about spending it and giving it away."

If there were an Olympic event in inattentiveness to money management, my own personal management, I would win at least a silver, if not a gold. So, I haven't concentrated on money management; in fact, just the opposite. I've been neglectful, inattentive and as a result, I'm sure I've missed out on a lot of opportunities. I have recently shifted financial managers and the new ones asked the outrageous question: what do you want, what are you goals? What do you want to do with the money? Why do you want to make it? And one trait I used to have, I have it much less now, that I hated about myself, was that I was generous, giving thousands of dollars to people distant from me or not closely related to me, but I was shamefully niggardly when it came to people close to me. And I think I always wondered, I know that was true about my mother and I suspect she got it from my grandfather. But, I have that.

The change of investment management set me to thinking about what the hell I did want money for. I'm just as eager to have them make a maximum return on it, but I guess I'm more relaxed both about spending it and giving it away. I don't give money away in large hunks; the $10,000 grant is on the high side for me. I'm taking to making a lot of challenge grants to help organizations reach out and get new people. These are various permutations of the challenge grant. You either give it for increases that people give this year over last year or for new givers or for gifts. For example, the Coalition for Creative Energy, that's probably the wrong name. I gave several thousand dollars on the condition that they could get individual attorneys to give a thousand dollars each. And that has been extraordinarily successful in getting organizations a greater base of support. I look for the oddball organizations, relatively friendless organizations to do that. A lady friend, for example, is involved with a small fund whose main activity is to bring a writer in residence to The American University and I gave a challenge grant for increments and new givers. One person gave $80 that only gave $10 the year before, and another person who hadn't given for five years, also gave. That's a turnover.

Despite the fact that I disapprove of people who avoid paying taxes—having railed against them—I am damned if I want to give a dollar that I don't have to, to build B-1 bombers and MX missiles. I prefer to give to charity the maximum amount that I can deduct from taxes. Last year that was close to $400,000. I gave it to the Norman P. Stryker Family Fund which is in a way a parking place. I don't have to think of causes to give to all at one time. And my children do the same thing. They give their year-end gifts to the Norman P. Stryker Family Fund and then draw out of that—like my second son, who is the celeb of the family—he plays lead guitar for McCoy Tyner. But he insists on anonymity four times over, he doesn't share my intention for giving to social action, social reform. He wants to feed people. And so, I'm pulling out my wallet now to make a note to get in touch with an organization that feeds people in New York to ask them in what way a challenge grant could help them. I'll take that out of his balance.

I have a hard time getting myself to look over all the proposals and I've just hired an assistant, mainly to help me with the Americans Against Lobbying work. I cannot go over these proposals with him in the office, because I'm too easily distracted by phones and other things. I think, he's just newly on and I think he is horrified by the snap way I make decisions, but I will not respond to an application that has the appearance of a fishing expedition sent broadside to a number of foundations, and I am the expert in detecting those.

The money I use is basically my own wealth and four trusts. One of those trusts I have the use, I can invade the principal of and the other two I cannot. I can only get the income and the rest in the principal goes on to my children. My parents, using primarily my mother's money, that's the source of the big wealth, my parents set up these trusts years and years ago. And so I have control over half the money, no control over the principal of the other half. I don't know whether it's half and half or not. My net worth is somewhere around eight million now, and a fairly big part of it goes out to alimony to my first wife. But I don't live high. I live very comfortably, as I said, I'm getting more relaxed about spending it on myself and giving it to others.

The Politics of Money
"I'm trying to get people to understand how they get screwed."

One of my tenets of philanthropy is I'm not interested in giving by and large to organizations that have broad bases of support. For example, I would never give to Red Cross, not because there's anything wrong with the Red Cross but it has a huge base of support. On the other hand, there are public interest organizations that either don't know how to write a letter to a foundation or are doing something that does not attract broad support that I'm delighted to and take great pride in helping out. And, another of my tenets is that I have no interest in becoming a permanent supporter of an organization. I think I am ready to give a lot of money to an organization to build a bridge from where it is now to cross a pond to dry land, but I will not give a dime to that same organization, worthy although its efforts are, that's gonna merely build a dock out in the middle of the pond and when my money runs out, they're only in the middle of the pond and they're just as bad off as they were before. I'm happy to make, build a path for an organization towards something permanent and self-sufficient.

I am not paid. What I do is philanthropy; I put money into it without the expectation of any return. I put my own energy into it without compensation except psychic, and it's in a public cause that I happen to consider very important. What I do, follows in the line of books on public policy that I wrote and I think I have something of a role in making that subject less arcane and mysterious to the public and more particularly to office holders. Now I feel I'm going at the root cause of the policy problems—the lobbyists for groups that have the money to contribute to senators' and congressmen's campaigns get the first entree. Access is the most precious thing a congressman or senator has to offer. There are only 24 hours in a day and clearly, the lobbyists are lined up eight deep and the one who gets in to see the man can always present him with a persuasive memorandum. That's no trick. If the congressman is inclined to do something, the lobbyists are skilled at making that action clothed with public interest and national interest. That's what I like doing. I guess I'm trying to do in the field of money and politics what I did in the field of public policy. Trying to get people to understand how they get screwed.

The law requires a donor to a private foundation to pass the money through to public foundations, public charities. And there have been many years in which I've had a substantial overflow and that I've had to park it so to speak in Habitat or some other public charity which has a donor-advised fund. I also give time to what I want. I abhor sitting on boards; I will not in most cases. If a good friend asks me to serve on a board and really leans on me, I occasionally will, but I almost always find out that it's a goddamn waste of time. I associate myself with "the usual suspects," the so-called liberal funders. I am less a peacenik, although I am no less ideologically. But my juices don't flow about Central America. One of the things that I dislike about my recent work is that I've become a specialist about money and politics. I don't get enough variety.

On a broader level, I think poverty has persisted because "them who has gets." You know. It's as simple as that. And there are institutional, political barriers that have kept the distribution of income almost exactly the same. I've read a study of income quintiles that goes back to 1910; it shows that income distribution hasn't changed. Or more tellingly, I think it was 1945–1975 or 1980, a period when the size of the pie was just expanding enormously. However, though the shares changed, it was as if you had a rigid structure bolted in place. The share of the tenth quintile went from 42 to 43. And the share of the lower quintile—don't hold me to the figures—went from 5 to 5.8 percent. So, I think that, those who have money are able to put it to use to make more.

Gore Vidal is right in saying that there aren't two political parties in this country. There's only one party—the property party—and it has two wings. I am a Democrat but I'm more and more a disaffected Democrat when I see the Democratic party raising its money in thousand dollar dinners. Who the hell can come to thousand dollar dinners other than fat cats and lobbyists? When I see Ted Jameson in the House raising PAC money like hell for all his colleagues, going around bending, twisting their arms, you know. So, the wealthy are wealthy, because "them that has gets." And you know, it's not as ironclad. When you come to individual cases, you have people like my friend the lawyer, real estate developer. But in the macro picture, there's very little movement.

Though in terms of taxes, I advocated, for want of anything better or profound, just wiping the slate clean and doing what the 13th Amendment, or 16th Amendment provided—tax incomes from whatever source derived—wipe out all the preferences. But the one I had philosophical trouble with was wiping out the charitable deduction. Because I think it's a plus to have a multiplicity of decision makers rather than government. I especially, I came to Washington as a rabid New Dealer and at that time, the government was the solution to all deals. I've now become more and more Republican in my view of government programs. I have a fear of big government, particularly with regard to individuals, but I think, it's good to, it's a plus to encourage philanthropy. Philanthropy is just that—a multiplicity of decision makers as to how to benefit the public wheel.

Atonement
"I give leverage to the underpowered
segments of society."

The things I'm most proud of are first, the books I've written—because I know that the merit of those has zero to do with the amount of money I have—and second, the social inventions—the organizations that I've helped bring into being. I have been able to have some research assistants but still the quality of those books was purely mine and when people say, "Oh are you the Stryker?" I take enormous pride in that. Because I did that as a profession and a couple of the books, two books on public policy have been on the bestseller list. Not at the top, but, they've been successful, especially critically. Also, I have taken pride in that the organizations I have started I could have bankrolled myself, but I didn't. I have not been a major donor in any of those money and politics organizations. But if I decide next year to resign, which I'm probably gonna do, to back away from being full-time involved in Americans Against Lobbying, well, I may pay the salary of a person to keep that going. And that would be for me a lot of money, compared to the size of my usual gifts.

I am fortunate in having a number of opportunities where $5 or $10,000 from me can make a big difference in the life of the organization. I write to my rich friends about the merit of my particular projects. In a million dollar campaign or project, a thousand dollars is the pea under 189 mattresses. But if it's $75,000, a thousand dollars is something. It makes a dent. And, for example, a person from the NAACP Washington D.C. chapter called me up and wanted to have lunch. I started to say to myself, well you know, the NAACP has a broad base of support . . . But then I went and instead of saying, "Nah, I won't play." I said, "Well, let me see how I can be creative in offering a matching grant." And they went away. I offered a matching grant of $5,000 and said, if this works, come back to me. And that's the way I like to work. Well they haven't come back to me yet. But every matching grant, every challenge grant that I have given in the last couple of years has been matched.

Overall, I think there are two or three contributions that I made. The thing that I take the greatest pride in is the institutions and ideas I've brought into being as something of a social inventor. Second, I've tried to give to things that give leverage to the underpowered segments of society and to make public interest organizations, that are fighting the fights I believe in, more effective. I mean, I would have died to give computers to any one of a number of little organizations. They magnify so much their ability. And I have looked for opportunities where small amounts of money from me can make a big difference. I advanced money to people that had cash flows. I've lent money to organizations, given the challenge. You know, I just have tried to use my money in a way that it produced leverage, had leverage.

One of the organizations that I had a hand in starting was New York Unaffiliated Reporters which started in 1975. One of my tenets is that nothing ever changes without a focal point of full-time energy. The saying that a camel is a horse produced by a committee. Committees don't produce anything in the way of change. And the thing I mainly did was to put up the money to hire a marvelous woman to bring this thing together, to bring the unaffiliated reporters together and form an organization. And I had edited out of my mind the extent to which I personally involved myself, but they are now naming an award after me. That's very pleasing and I take great pride in the fact that I had a role or that people think I had a role in bringing that into being. It was then a hundred, a hundred and fifty members and now I got more than two thousand. I made it possible for a silkgrafist who was wasting his time in sign shops to get into a career as an artist. I'm very proud of that.

My father used to say and this is not original with him. Although not a religious man, nor am I in the conventional sense, he believed that each human being has a hereafter and it is not amorphous or in heaven. It is tangible, palpable, measurable. And it consists of all the people who live on, who you've touched in your life for better or for worse, and live on after you. And that is as good a precept for daily living as I can think of. I get into trouble when people start investing qualities of mercy or justice in a deity because I see so many exceptions to that. So I guess I believe in a separate creator of the physical universe and I marvel. Your new child is just a marvel of systems, automatic, incredible. But when you stop dealing with X as a creator and start investing morals or goals or qualities to it, I fall off the wagon.

I guess I got my inspiration from Alfred Hannibal. But I guess the bigger answer is I got it from Augustus Nussbaum. Partly through my parents, partly through Alfred Hannibal. But Alfred Hannibal was the inspiration. When my own father died, I cried when I learned of his death. I cried once in the day surrounding his funeral. But when Alfred Hannibal died, you could tell. I was an honorary pallbearer and I was just a mess. And if I'll write that book about my grandfather I know just who I'm gonna dedicate it to. Even though I hadn't thought about it before.

6

Laura Madison: "The Call"

The Biblical imperative given the physician, "Heal thyself," is neatly applicable to Madison. The sixty-three-year-old Chicago heiress survives a catastrophic marriage and personal illness, as she gradually develops a philanthropic career to enhance "the health of humanity" and her own.

Growing up on the fashionable North Shore of Chicago, Laura Madison was something of a debutante without a cause. "I was brought up in a very, very narrow-minded atmosphere and I did everything I was told to. . . . Yet I was always a rebel." Now sixty-three and living in New York, Laura Madison, ex-debutante, is still a rebel, but with a keenly articulated cause: the health of humanity. Yet in coming to her philosophy of healing love, Madison had first to heal herself. Her story features motifs of *healing* and *awakening*. Madison suffers through intense periods of liminality for which her resistance to Chicago social customs is but a modest blueprint for what she must endure. These lifelong struggles revolve around the emotional and physical turmoil of sickness and death. Encounters with such affliction become personal crises of identity and vocation.

Madison undergoes two particularly trying *liminal* periods. There are first, the debutante days alluded to above, in which she must weather her brother's death, her father's acute depression (brought on by the Depression), his subsequent physical illness, and the chronic unreliability of her mother ("she's about eight years old and always has been a very spoiled child"). Although she had long questioned her blue-blood conventions, her first avenue of escape was to marry a blue blood. Yet their years together actually bring her to the brink of suicide.

The turning point comes when, after twenty years, she hears a voice tell her that "no one [else] will rescue you," and that she must "let go" of her ego in order to save herself. Slowly, Madison heeds "the call." She recants her old values, meditates, goes back to school, travels, but most importantly, *practices* an ethos of caring: "From then on, I have let in anybody who wants to come in. I listen and I go where I think I'm needed."

This resolution of *liminality* brings Madison a new moral identity associated with a new relation to money as a "tool" for making a difference in the world. Being "totally loving" explicitly entails a more instrumental orientation toward wealth. Her identity is solidified as she gets involved in various projects—whether charitable or profit-making—directed toward awakening the *human potential* in others (i.e., toward awakening the potential for individuals to become "as human as they possibly can"). Ignorance of this human potential is, to her, the ultimate evil. Thus, Madison attempts to replicate in others the culmination of her liminal quest. Her own healing and her return home to a new understanding of her wealth form the content of this replication. She directs outward into the lives of others the cure discovered through her own healing drama. She assumes the role of a steward to whom resources have been lent to be marshaled for the world's restoration. Permeating her giving-orientation is a desire to really *make a difference with her contribution.* Unlike many inherited wealthy, she is willing to delve into the principal of her inherited capital "without a second thought" if doing so would prove useful.

The ethos of stewardship carries over into her frugal lifestyle and disinclination to consume. Wealth is subordinate to health, but not essential to it. Thus, financial security—which to her "means I don't have to think about money particularly"—does not facilitate one's ability to "let go." This attitude relates to her implicit belief that America is a meritocracy where anyone, who really wants to, can make a fortune; and also to her *micro-orientation to social reform*—her notion that the key to social change is individual spirituality (the attainment of "integrity," and not structural reform).

Madison's philosophy and practice are identified in her stewardship, the roots of which are traceable to the noblesse oblige orientation of her North Shore antecedents. But this orientation has evolved—mutated, as it were, through sickness into health, and from ignorance to knowledge—into a holistic, "New Age" emphasis on the health of the earth and of humanity.

BIOGRAPHICAL NARRATIVE

Family Background
"My father came from a rough diamond who made a hell of a lot of money."

I was born in Chicago in the most conservative, upper, upper-class situation you could ask for, where what you wore, what you ate, how you held a spoon and who you spoke to was more important than anything else in the world. And then on top of that, I was a Catholic and that's why I say, how I got out of it all, I will never, never know.

My family name is O'Hara. It means nothing to anybody. My father came from a long line of timber barons who had bought huge holdings of land all over the U.S. His grandfather made and lost everything he had. Made a million dollars two or three times and lost every cent of it—a kind of person you could be in those days. And then, my father came into money as third generation. And so, he wanted to spend his life studying birds—he was a scientist; an ornithologist. He didn't have any income from that because he had all the money he needed anyhow. And, he worked harder than many people I know who are working for money. Very interesting person. And he was very, very broad in his thinking except for things having to do with women. Women weren't goods and chattels, but they were there to be protected and taken care of by men. They were not meant to have any ideas and thoughts of their own. And, this is where he really let me down, 'cause I had the same kind of mind he had. So, because I was a girl, what I thought was ignored. And, I was the jam in the sandwich; that is, two boys with me in the middle. He used to call me Sugar or Sugarplum.

Well, my mother came down from the Larrauchette family, old town American, just plain American, because you know, the Larrauchettes had been in this country for three generations by then. Her father was a Kirby. Her mother was a Larrauchette. And her grandfather had come over from—her great grandfather had come over from France. Her grandfather was Jacques Larrauchette the composer. He was an American composer and church organist.

My great grandfather was the head of the family. He had eight children and every single one of them was able to make a living in the arts—that's how talented they all were. So, he was the head of the whole thing. Anyhow, his father came over and was in Louisiana for quite a while, I think with the Huguenots or something. I don't know this history very well. He was an importer of fine furniture, and brought over a great deal of the furniture that's in the White House. When Jackie Kennedy was decorating it, she was dealing with a lot of the stuff that he brought over and sold to the White House, way back then.

My father came from a rough diamond who made a hell of a lot of money. His father had bought land all over the United States. I mean huge, thousands of acres of land, among other pieces of land, along the Mississippi Delta. That's a lot of land and there was a town in Mississippi where the land was. And he bought the whole town and all the land around it and put all the Indians to work. He practically bought the Indians with the town. I mean, you know, the things they did in those days were fantastic. I remember my father telling me about how anybody who had a lot of money practically owned the trains immediately. Even then my father was very concerned about people. Because I remember him telling me that these people had just tons of money and rode the trains wherever they were going, and he talked about the people working on the tracks making in one year what those guys spent in a day. I remember him being aware and concerned about this and talking about the way the pendulum goes back and forth. It was about the time that unions were coming along and he would say the same thing's going to happen with the unions, that happened with the rich people before there were unions: they're going to take advantage of the other people. Unions will get so strong that the poor will suffer from the unions. He was very astute about a lot of stuff.

The Estrangement
"I was told not to ask her into the house again."

I went to a private school and we had servants in the house. Just like everybody else I was with. I didn't know what wealthy meant. I didn't know that anybody was any different, I was so protected. But, you couldn't have made me arrogant if you killed yourself doing it. I just couldn't be arrogant. I don't know what arrogant means. Actually, it was just the opposite. I had a very, very poor idea of who I was or what anything was all about. I just tried to be a good girl. It was awful. My, ideas were not looked for, in any way. I spent my whole time listening to what I was told I should do and shouldn't do and I never even thought for myself what life was about or anything. It was a kind of vacuum that I was brought up in. I never read the papers. I would listen to my father saying what a terrible person he thought Roosevelt was—that sort of thing.

When I was taking those religion courses at Barnard almost all the students were either Catholics or Jews. And to me that was very interesting because the people who cared about what's happening to humanity and where we're going and what it's all about—are the people who had fundamental training and thinking that way.

Probably I have a very similar background in a funny sort of way, even though I was taught to look for what a Jew looked like and you didn't speak to them. I was brought up in a very, very narrow minded atmosphere and I did everything I was told to do. I went to confession every Saturday and I tried to be a good girl. That's about it. And when I got married, the same thing. I was not thinking for myself; I was going by the book. Yet, I was always a rebel. I was always a maverick in a sense—a total contradiction. Underneath it all I was always thinking, why did I have to wear gloves to go to town? Why does my father talk about people as top drawer and second drawer and stuff like that, as if those people are worth knowing and other people aren't? And from the very first, the first person that I had a crush on was the plumber's son. I mean, I just never accepted that any people were really different from any other people. But it was obvious that those were people who weren't worth talking to—you just didn't get involved with them. They worked for you. You can be very polite and nice to them but they're not people that you could possibly have any kind of interaction of minds or thoughts or any other. You're superior to them.

I brought a little girl in off the street one time. My mother was away and she came in. And this child was just—I can still remember her carried away. She had never seen a house like ours. The thing that impressed her the most was that the toilet seats were white. Painted toilet seats to her were the height of wonders [laughter]. So my mother came home and—they were trained to be very polite—the child was told it was time to go home and I was told not to ask her into the house again. And I never understood why. I was never told anything about anybody else being less or anything else but the whole attitude and behavior of everybody was "You just don't trust those people." And really, by the time I was grown and married, I was pretty much of a snob in a way. And yet I didn't believe it. Anyhow, what actually happened . . .

My mother's ninety-two; however, I figure she's about eight years old. Always has been and has never gone beyond that. She is like a very spoiled child. Never was she able to relate to me in any way, shape, or manner. The only kind of attention I ever got from her that made me feel as if there was any relationship between us at all, was when I was sick. And then she'd fuss over that and worry about it and come in and give me medicine and tell me what I had to do and stuff like that. But otherwise, there was no communication; I could not tell her about anything that mattered to me and have her respond. She didn't know how. She was terribly, terribly jealous because I thought the way my father thought. She couldn't talk to him about anything that was important to him other than, whatever there was between them. Nevertheless, he loved her very much.

Still, she was terribly jealous of me because I related to my father on levels that she couldn't get near to, talking about science and about what was going on in the world and all sorts of things. And he talked to me in a way as if I were an equal. When he talked with me he'd get excited about things. For instance, he was crazy about *Life* magazine. And *Life* magazine really was very mind-broadening in those days 'cause we didn't have TV or anything else. And he would get all excited about the things shown in *Life* magazine, and he would talk about all sorts of things, which she could never get onto that level at all to save herself. There is only one thing that she wanted to talk to me about: how I dressed, what parties I was going to and what everybody had on. But, I could never remember what anybody had on because I didn't give a damn. Of course, it was just impossible to tell her that as a kid.

The Formative Years
"Lack of caring is a very hard thing to deal with."

I was a debutante. I did the whole thing. And the thing that's so hysterical about it was that I could see that that was not what I wanted in my life. And so I said: "Look, if you want me to come out, I'll come out. And I'll dress up and go to all the parties. I like parties but don't think I'm doing it—don't think you're doing it for me. If I do it, it will be because of you. I know why you want me to do it, and that is to make me a puppet on strings, and put me out there for all your friends to see."

That was the picture I saw. So, I came out, and I had a very intense year and a half or two years in the coming-out process—going to parties every night and staying up till four in the morning, sleeping all day and, I loved it. I had an absolute ball. I met a lot of wonderful people. I loved to dance, I love music. I loved all the excitement; but, I didn't care about alcohol, thank God. That was again something funny. My parents told me that the only thing I could drink was sherry. Well, you can get drunker on sherry than anything in the world. So, I had a glass of sherry every once in a while; but, I never really liked alcohol at all.

It's just so unaware, my parents' relation to me was just totally unaware. When I was ten years old, I got double mastoid, and I was sent out to a Santa Fe boarding school because I was so sick that they didn't think I was going to survive. I had an older brother who was two years older than I was. He and I were all there was for each other because our parents were always going out and doing things and really were not relating to us at all. So, we related to each other, and we were very, very close. And while I was at boarding school in Santa Fe, my brother died. He was at boarding school too. He went to Archbishop Carol School, and he got mastoid. At the time, there were no antibiotics for it, and it turned into spinal meningitis. And they couldn't do anything. So, he died while I was at boarding school in New Mexico. My parents knew somebody in the town, and asked them to come up and take me out for lunch and tell me my brother died, which they did. And I couldn't believe it. When I got home, my mother had changed his room into a girl's room, and put a fancy decoration. I was never into that kind of stuff; I was kind of a tomboy. I wasn't really interested in pretty clothes and pretty stuff. She'd done this dressing table all up in pretty colors and glass thing, and about half his things were still in the room, and she turned the room into my room! When I tried to talk about my brother, she told me how terrible it was for her, which is the way it's always been. If I'm sick, she says, "I've been sicker." If I say, "I'm tired," she says, "You're not, you're too young to be tired." I mean, this is the way that it's always been with my mother.

She didn't know how to take care of us. She was a child. I mean, I know that now; and I really feel sorry for her because she doesn't know how to relate to anybody, poor soul. But, it was god-awful while that lasted. However, it forced me out in a way. It forced me to take care of myself. But I think, lack of love is a very hard thing to deal with, and if you can become a loving person in spite of that, you've come quite a ways. Anyhow, caring is what it is. The only thing she cared about was my physical being and that

I think is the reason I was sick so much. I mean, literally, that's the way we worked. Psychologically, we don't know we're doing it; but, if you find that the only way you can make somebody care about you is to get sick, you're going to get sick. And my father did something equally amazing. He had been used to working all his life for nothing, because he had a really good income—his father was dead by then. Well, when the Depression came, his next door neighbor committed suicide—I'll never forget that. And he was really in a slump because of this terrific social desire to be socially prominent, he was very concerned about how he appeared, what he did and all this sort of thing. And the only thing he could see to make money on was to pump gas, and that to him was the very lowest thing anybody could possibly do. I can remember him sitting very depressively and saying to me, "You know, the only thing that I'm good for is to pump gas."

Within about a year or two, he developed rheumatoid arthritis to such a degree that he couldn't take care of himself or my mother or us, which was the only way to get out of an absolutely intolerable situation and try to make money in some other way. But, he didn't know how to. The only thing he knew was ornithology. And the thing that's so pitiful about the whole thing is that he wrote everything that the ornithologists of today use as their bible. When I went to the Natural History Museum a couple of years ago, I asked someone in the ornithology department if they'd ever heard of my father, they said "Yeah, he's everything we need. We look up from him." Well, he never got paid a cent for that; but, today he'd have been perfectly well off, if he had done it—hadn't he volunteered to do it.

He lost a lot of his wealth. He didn't lose all of it. My aunt had a great deal of money and she took care of us during his sickness. On top of that, I never felt it at all. We continued to have servants, we continued to live just the same way. But, I never had my own private money. I just lived in a rich way all my life, growing up. And then, I married a very rich man. His name was Darwin Madison. And he was from Chicago. And his father was a partner of Sears. So, there was a lot of money there. He's deceased. My husband, I think when I married him, I married my mother. And I understand that's what we all do. We all marry our mothers—that's a very interesting point of view.

Hitting Bottom
"Really on the verge of suicide."

So what happened was, when I married, I was trying to get out of this awful situation of being at home with my mother, who was just impossible, and my father, who was terribly ill. And my mother, whenever she didn't like something I did, she'd threaten to tell my father and upset him and I knew he was too sick to be bothered with that kind of thing. So, I had that on top of everything else. Just unbelievable! So, I tried. I married this man because I thought I was Florence Nightingale. He was crippled. And he was crippled emotionally as well as physically which was really a humdinger. He was about, emotionally, he was my mother's age. Intellectually, he was my father's. He was very intelligent, very bright and very, very helpless. And so I married him to take care of him and that's just what I got. And I ended up having four kids and taking care of him on top of all of that. And my kids had no idea—I became kind of a shrew because I was so overloaded and I wasn't getting any help whatsoever from him. It wasn't that he didn't want to. Again, he was just like my mother. He was a little boy who was used to being taken care of all his life; and he didn't know how to help me in any shape, way or manner.

And so, I had four kids and at the end of—I don't know, twenty years of marriage or something like that, I knew I was going into the loony bin if I didn't get out. So, I picked up with my youngest child and moved to New York. And I spent two years here, kind of really on the verge of suicide; every day just thinking how am I going to end it. But, the excuse I had was my son: there were good schools here and I could put him in a good school. My son saved my life. He really did. If I hadn't had that child, I don't know what would have happened. 'Cause he gave me an excuse to get away from an impossible life, and not be absolutely thrown out by the community because I was married to a cripple and to walk out on a cripple was the utter end. But I was able to say that my child was very, very bright and needed a better education and that I was bringing him to New York for this reason, and my husband went along with it. By that time we were living in Georgia. We moved down there because of his father's—that's something else hysterical. His father bought a lot of timberlands in Georgia [laughter]—so I moved back into timber on my husband's side as well as on my father's.

My husband was never able to disagree to anything. He was just a kind of a sweet, sweet person who would agree to anything and never understood anything. The worst thing he ever called me was a radical activist. And that was the worst thing he could think of to call me. We were never married in the true sense of being married; we just lived together and had children. So, I stayed up here and he stayed down there. But he came up quite often because he had doctors up here and he would stay with me when he came up for holidays with the kids. We'd get together, and I'd go up to West Egg, and the kids were there. And I'd live in my part of the house, and he'd live in his own part of the house—really crazy, the whole thing. But anyhow, for two years I went through this total despair.

The Call to Healing
"Nobody is going to rescue you."

One morning I woke up and I heard words, just as clearly as if somebody walked in the room and spoke to me. The words were something I never would have thought of: "Nobody is going to rescue you." And it was the most extraordinary thing that ever happened to me. You'd have thought I'd just get a gun and finish it off. But instead of that, it suddenly dawned on me that I'd been sitting there and I'd been paralyzed for years and years and years, thinking that my husband or my mother or some knight on a white charger or somebody would make it work. And the minute I realized that—that it just was never going to happen, it was like putting a rocket under me and I started to move. I didn't do anything very exciting. But little by little I began to think over my values and throw out all the things that didn't make sense which was most of the values that I'd been trained in.

Four years later my son went off to boarding school and I bought this house. And I walked in the alley one day and again, I heard a voice and the wind almost blew me down as I came into the alley. And the voice said, "If you really believe what you think you believe, you've gotta let go." So I came into the house, the telephone rang and this—not the most responsible person in my mind—person who had people with inventions come to him and he'd make stock offerings for them, he was on the line. And a friend of mine had made a cigarette that was not cancer producing and I'd been interested in putting some money in that. So, I wanted to buy stock in it, and I met this man, and he had thought I was very interesting and intelligent. So, he was on the phone and he was buttering me up about how intelligent I was and how he had something he thought I'd be interested in. I also had decided about three or four days before that I was going to become a mineralogist at Barnard.

What I meant when I said to let go of your ego is that, life is all about letting go of your children, letting go of your ego, letting go of your money, letting go of everything that you think is contributing to you; and rather finding out who you are, and where you're coming from, what is inside of you, which is everything you need. And anyhow, the message was: "You've got to let go." And I walked into the house, and I realized that all that time I'd been kind of trying, trying to hold the ranks to everything, trying to control everything, trying to keep everything together. Because it just seems like too much to have a husband who wasn't able to make anything work, that it was all up to me. And of course the children really resented me because he was the good, sweet one and smiled and was lovely all the time. And I was the one who said, "You've got to brush your teeth and you've got to get up and do what you're meant to do. . . . " Just kept at them all the time. So that's been a long, hard struggle with them, even after he died. It's pretty good now; but, it's been tough because they could not understand why I would walk out on that beautiful man.

The call. I've just come in from hearing these words: "You got to let go." And the telephone rings and this guy says, "I'll pay your way to Colorado and back and put you up for three or four days if you'll come out to something I know you'll be interested in" and I say, "What is it?" And he says, "I'm not going to tell you." And this is something I would never, never in the world agree to. So, I said, "Well, I'll call you back." It was too big a blow. And I got my calendar out and looked it up and of course there wasn't a single thing on the calendar. So, I thought, you got to let go. If that's true, what have I got to lose? This is a good way to find out what letting go is like. So the tickets came the next day. I went to Colorado and a woman met me, who is somebody I could go to tomorrow if I lost everything I had and she'd put me up for the rest of my life. I haven't a doubt in the world about it. The meeting was all about geothermal strain and they didn't know anything about me signing up for a mineralogy course. They wanted me to put money in this thing. I put it in and it quadrupled, quite a large amount of money quadrupled in about four or five months. I got two independent studies out in the mountains of Colorado for my mineralogy classes with a mineralogist. And I just had one great thing happen after another, just from that one time of letting go.

The New Path
"I listen and I go where I think I'm needed."

From then on, I have let anybody who wants to come in, in. I listen, and I go where I think I'm needed. I do what seems to be working toward helping humanity, which as I say is my prime goal. It's the only thing I'm interested in in the world—the health of humanity. To really relate to other human beings all over the world—whoever they are, wherever they are. I mean, human beings having an opportunity to be truly human which very few people are. People don't even know what it is to be human. To be human is to be a spiritual person as well as a physical, mental, emotional person. In making a oneness that's healing the earth, healing the rifts between people, all that sort of thing: that's what I'm really interested in. And wherever I see any chance to get involved or see that I'm supposed to be doing something about it, that's what I'm interested in.

Before anything else comes the welfare of humanity. Whether it's charity or something financially lucrative—it doesn't make any difference. Maybe financially lucrative can end up doing more for humanity than charity can. So I feel the whole business scene needs to be turned around so that the poor don't get poorer while the rich get richer. The banks are very self-serving, and even though I've had bankers argue with me who really don't think that's true, I believe it is. Those are just a few little basic ideas that I wanted to get across.

At one point, my husband was going through all sorts of things because I wasn't living with him any more. And he was saying to me, "What are you going to do with my money?" And I was saying: "Well, it's all right. You don't have to leave it to me. You can do anything you'd like with it." But, I was saying to God, "If I am left that money, I will do my utmost to see that it really goes in places where it will do something worthwhile for people." And so, that's been my direction, and I've really bitten off a huge bite. Boy, I would be very happy to have just enough to do the things I like to do. I live very simply, very inexpensively because I'm very economical. Some of my friends who are dependent on other people for their money, quite often spend a lot more in a year than I do. I guess the Depression did that to me. I remember my family, my father gave me an allowance of $100 a month to really take care of myself. And I was so proud that I would come back with maybe $25. I would buy a record, one record at a time, of a symphony. You see, at that time the records were 48s and a symphony would sometimes be five records. So, I'm very saving and very careful, I've only learned in the last ten years how to be giving of my money. It was hard for me to use it on myself, or for that matter, to use it on anybody. And I'm learning to have an entirely different relationship to money. So many people think of money as love. I think of money as a tool that can be used in any way. It can be used for harm, good or whatever.

Though, I felt like just wanting to get rid of money at times, I feel a real responsibility to see that it goes in the right places. For instance, I own a lot of timberland in Georgia. I'd like to sell it. But if I sell it, those trees are going to be felled and the land is either going to be turned into what I call asparagus farms or real estate that is just destroying the land. So, I feel a responsibility to keep it and shepherd it. I don't want to. I mean, it isn't what I really want to do. I know exactly what I want to do. So right at this moment, I'm trying very hard to get it so it's almost computerized and it's going out and it's doing what I want it to do. And yet I feel I have to be a steward of it all. I cannot just give it all away and have it frittered or put into things that are not helping humanity. So, it's that responsibility. And the worst part is the paperwork. I get piles every single solitary day. And, I go through them, as I said, because I don't want to miss something that's important that I can contribute to that'll make a difference. I'm getting better and better at throwing it out though.

I actually get, I don't do an awful lot myself. I find the people who are doing worthwhile things. I don't know why I think of New Synergy Academy as an example. That is a group that I've been working with and which has been going on for about ten or eleven years. They are going into all the alternative energy problems of the world trying to work out ways of growing things without using a lot of fossil fuels. And instead of using a lot of poisons to kill the insects, they bring in other insects to balance things out. So, I give them money and I go and see what they're doing and I get involved in what they're doing and they know me and I know them. I really don't contribute much to things that I don't really get into and get to know the people.

One of the things that I've been interested in is George Winston's music. I've been working with him quite a lot and he is making people aware of the earth and how important it is to love the earth. I've been in touch with Tim Lefkowitz. In fact, I went to El Salvador with Tim and a bunch of people who wanted to do a satellite thing between the El Salvadorans and some of the universities in this country. That never took place because they have a crazy idea about where and how they were going to get their money. And I couldn't help finance the whole thing so it didn't take place. But, I keep in touch with Tim and he turns up here quite often and we talk about what's happening in El Salvador. And I give money to Oxfam because I think they're doing very worthwhile work. I try to find things that are really making a difference and that are not just squandering money in funny sorts of ways. There are several people who are making movies. I think that communications is probably one of the places that's gonna make the biggest difference. And the more people that good ideas can go out to, the more chance there is that things will change, and people will see things differently.

I have no rule of thumb for deciding how much to give away each year. This year [laughter], well, let me think of what my income is. It isn't such an awful lot. I give away practically all my income. But I never know. I just give what I think I can give whenever something comes up that looks as if it needs it, without going into the principal too much. That's the way I'd like to do it. If I had it really well organized, I'd know exactly how much I put out and how much I have. Actually, what I've been working on very, very hard is to get a clear picture of just how much money I really have to use. And that is very difficult because the income from these trusts is—I have not yet been able to get these people to sit down and tell me exactly how much. I have an accountant in Georgia that I'm hoping—I've asked him about a month ago to put on a sheet of paper just how much money went into what, what was expended in the last year. And that's what he's supposed to be doing. And I wait, and I wait, and I wait and they're very sloppy about coming back with what I ask for. Tomorrow I should call him and pin him down again. I'm trying very hard to really have a clear picture of exactly what I can use, what I can't. However, I plow my way through all of it. I can't have people advise me because the people who advise me are the people who are handling my money. They are conservative and so absolutely appalled at the things that I'm interested in. But, they go along with me; but, they . . . [laughter] their minds are being blown all the time, so it's kind of funny. But, I would go into my principal without a second thought if there was something that I felt I could really make a difference in and I didn't have enough.

Investing with the Heart
"I also stand a chance of losing."

Right now, I'm kind of poor. I'm in debt in fact, because I put a great deal of money into a group who call themselves Responsible Venturists. And these people are trying to invest money in things that are socially responsible. These people are just taking it and trying to make money with it and I may get something back. They are doing things like buying land, and trying to see that the land is properly developed. They were supposed to pay off the loan that I took out in order to give them the money. However, the money hasn't come back, and I'm left with a loan that I have to get rid of. I've never owed anybody anything, and I don't want to start now. I don't feel stuck on this one, not yet, but I may be. And if I am it's all right, because the people I gave it to are people whose hearts are in the right place. They will not have wasted it. It will have gone to things that were worthwhile, even if I don't get it back. So, I just may not have as much money which will be fine.

I don't have millions and millions of dollars to spend. I do have some millions of dollars, but they are in trusts. So fortunately, I don't have to get involved with that. My own personal money is a couple of million dollars. It's not a lot of money, but, it's enough to make a difference. And that is what I'm talking about. I guess maybe it's about three million, I don't know what it is. And I put $500,000 of it into that project. Now, there's another group who are doing something very, very interesting with the fishing industry. I have written out a letter of credit for them for a million dollars. And I stand a chance to make a lot of money, but, I also stand a chance of losing all of that. If I lose that, I'll just be left with the income from the trust, which will keep me alive and kicking and eating and all of that and that will be all right too. So, I'm in a very funny position right at this moment. I may not have any money at all one of these days to speak of. I mean, I won't have any money that will make me a rich woman. But I will have enough money to eat and to pay the taxes and do that and that will be it.

Strangely enough, most of my friends are poor at this point. I mean, they really are. They're very creative people who have very little money. Just enough to get by, wondering whether they're going to have enough to eat the next week. Really creative people who want to do something wonderful with movies or on the stage or with art or something like that. They're the people that I see the most of and that I really love. And I find them so much more . . . , well, it's interesting, because for years I knew nothing but people who really were terribly wealthy, though they were very caring people. But, I really think they were non-thinking in a lot of ways. It was that same thing about going by the book. It's a whole kind of a doctrine of how to behave and what you do, and it's all done without very much thinking behind it.

Part of it is noblesse oblige and a lot of it is penny wise and pound foolish. They'll spend $5,000 and not be able to spend $25 on something. You know that funny kind of psychology that makes one think, oh, my God, $25 is a lot to spend for that! And yet something else will come up and they'll spend $5,000 for that without even thinking about it. That's part of it. It's kind of no understanding of what money really is to them. It's just, "I've got a hell of a lot of money, and I use it the way my friends use it." It's a whole lot of non-thinking stuff and it really doesn't affect the fact that they're caring, loving people to the people that they're involved with and totally unaware of the rest of the world. They protect each other by reinforcing each other in what they say and do. It seems to me that there are more people with a lot of money who think and act that way than otherwise. It's a kind of an unconsciousness of anything other than a kind of a protected, safe life. Living on yachts, wearing the right thing and going to the right country club and doing all sorts of things together and only doing it with people in the same kind of financial situation. So that nobody's ever embarrassed because they can't do what somebody else is doing because everybody has a lot of money, and they just don't know that anything else exists because they keep it out of their minds.

At this point, I feel financially secure, and for me, it means I don't have to think about money particularly, I guess. Though, I remember buying skim milk instead of regular milk during the Depression, so that I'd save two cents. But, I've never been concerned. I've often thought about what it'd be like not to have any money. I used to think of running away and then I would think I wouldn't know how to take care of myself. But I always thought I could do something, I could work. Even now I think, if suddenly I didn't have a cent, there are a lot of things I could do.

I have friends who really do have to think about whether they're gonna stay in their own apartment or be thrown out and not have anywhere to go. And I talk with them and listen to them. But, I don't give them money. Because, well, I give them money if they ask for it. But there is something about giving money to somebody that you have a real relationship with that can hurt the relationship. And they don't want it hurt and I don't want it hurt. In that they might feel that they owed me something, or that they had to get it back in some way and they wouldn't be sure that they could do it. I often say to them, "Look, if somehow or other I can make things work for you, let me know 'cause I don't want you to . . . if I can help, I want to help." But, I don't say, "Look, here's $500 that will get you over the hump, take it." Because there's all this pride. The thing about money that I found more than anything else is that a lot of people think money is love, for instance. That's one of the big things. Or they think that money can get you whatever you want or can help you to change somebody else's mind. Instead of seeing it as a tool to create some kind of a balance in the world.

Responsibility and the Ethics of Wealth
"I have an opportunity to really make a difference if I see something that a large amount of money could do."

The conditions of wealth and poverty in our society have come about for a million reasons. There isn't any one answer to that. And it didn't happen overnight either. And yet, I kind of believe that with enough ingenuity and hard work, even today, somebody who really wants money, feels that money is that important to them, can make a lot of money. I just wouldn't want it, that's the trouble. Money means very little to me other than it keeps me warm. Yet, one of the things that's been so crazy to me is that I've always been very careful with what I have, even when I didn't have very much. And my friends who have very little aren't careful with it at all. And every once in a while I say to myself, you darn fool, why are you being so frugal?

If I lived the way most wealthy people do, I would guess there was an advantage in being wealthy. I don't see any advantage for me to be wealthy. I really have no desire. For instance, if I wanted to, I could have a chauffeur, dressed to the teeth, and give parties and live the old kind of life. I think of being wealthy as being dolled up and just spending money like water. So, I don't think of myself as wealthy, I guess, which is pretty funny. I don't want any of it. The only advantage I can see to having money at this point, and I suppose that's being wealthy, is that I have an opportunity to really make a difference if I see something that a large amount of money could do more for than a small amount of money could, because I have a large amount to put in it. For me, being wealthy has no advantage. Having enough money to eat and to be warm and to be dressed decently and sleep in a comfortable bed and have something over my head is all I want. So I'm really a very poor example for you to be talking to.

Every once in a while I say to myself, well, you know, I really could do something that was just a lot of fun and has no particular value at all. It's nice to know I can do it, and I might do it. I've finally learned to be nice to myself, to be good to myself. For years I was really being kind of a rich pauper. And some of my children have done that a little bit too. I had to learn that there's no reason in the world why you can't enjoy things, as long as you're not depriving anybody else. I can't go up to Balducci's without feeling kind of guilty. It is probably the most lavish food store I've ever been in. It's got every kind of food you could ask for, terribly high prices and people just spend tremendous amounts of money there.

So, I walk in there. I marched in that June 6th march you know, the 12th, whatever it was, with Thich Nhat Hanh, who came from Vietnam and came over with a boat of people and saw all the suffering that went on. And he was saying something about, he can't go into an American supermarket without feeling sick when he thinks of the people that he had left who aren't getting enough to eat. And I go into those places having heard him say that, I don't know how aware I was before I heard him say it, but I go into a place like that where there's just cornucopias of everything, and I feel guilty. I feel uncomfortable, but I don't see any way to turn it around. And yet I'm ready to if something comes along that will make something better for somebody else by turning it around. In the meantime, I can't kind of see what can be done.

If the people in the government get the idea of serving the people, that will do it. But, that isn't what's in their minds, at the moment, that I know of. Serving the people, I guess it means what dear Mr. Jefferson and the people who wrote the Declaration of Independence meant, what they really wanted to do. And I just think, the government today has lost all track of what that was about. What's needed is that the people are taken care of. The old are not junked. The young are listened to, and the people in between are given a chance to lead the fullest life they're capable of leading.

I do support somewhat, political candidates. Usually things to get more Democrats into the Senate, that sort of thing. Not that I'm for Democrats or Republicans either. But I think the Democrats are more humanistic than the Republicans, that's all. And I, strangely enough, I think Mr. Reagan has done some pretty good things. And by mistake, not because it was the way he wanted to do it. But he has not been handing out money, quite the way the government did before, to people who took it for granted that it was coming all the time and got very lazy and very sloppy about how they used it. People have really been forced to make their money go as far as they could make it go and use it wisely and that has been a boon for dear Mr. Reagan. But it's just been by accident. It hasn't been because he really cares about people, as far as I can make out. Personally, I would be interested to do something in the way of an international . . . global communications project. I find myself a little fuzzy sometimes about what I really do stand for and not stand for. I think I have some kind of really a hard-core basic something in the back of it all, but it doesn't always come out very well when I try to express it.

The Mission
"What it means, really, basically is being totally loving."

My spiritual path is Buddhist. Buddhism, Islam, Christianity, Judaism—what else is there? [laughter] It's the words. Whatever. But no Americanism. Americanism won't do. That's out.

And I'm very grateful for my Catholic background. I graduated from Barnard in 1979. When it was the right time to go to college, my father's point of view was that any woman who went to college lost her femininity. So, you can see what I came from. How I got where I am, I'll never know. But, anyhow. I took three courses every semester. I'd take science. I was allowed to do this because the geology department that I had signed up for folded. And I found out about the School of Developmental Studies and said, "I'm half scientist and half artist anyhow so how about letting me do this?" So I'd take a science course and an art course, hands-on art course, every semester and then I'd take philosophy or religion in between just to pull everything together. And probably the best teacher at Barnard was a religion teacher. He was fantastic. And so I was just using the philosophy and religion and things like that to bring art and science together, to make it kind of a whole. And it worked like a dream. My horizons just expanded endlessly. It was a wonderful experience. It was terribly difficult at times because I never had any science in school at all. But I knew I was a scientist. I had a beautiful time doing it.

Money does not allow you to speak your mind more freely. I think that somewhere in your life you've got to get to a point where you say, what do I stand for, what matters to me? Is integrity more important than anything else, or isn't it? If integrity's more important than anything else, even if I'm out on the street, and have nothing, I'd rather be there than live a life that I can't live. And the people I know are far deeper than most of the people that have money that I know. I think you have the opportunity to speak your mind, no matter what. It's up to you. I'm thinking of two people right now that I know who are really on the edge of not having anything. Not even having enough to eat. And they are deeper and clearer thinkers than almost anybody I've known in a long time. They have had money and they have lost it and they've gotten it back. They've gone up and down all their lives, and have never been really totally secure. And actually, I don't think anybody's financially secure. I don't think I am. I said "yes," before but, I don't think I really am. Tomorrow the whole world could blow up. I think that the situation in our economy today is so crazy that I could be out on the street with everybody else tomorrow and I've thought about that and thought well, everybody else will be out there so that's fine. I'd hate to be sticking out as a sore thumb while everybody else was suffering and I wasn't. I'd give them what I had but that wouldn't do much good. I'd just join them by doing that.

I don't think "the poor are always with us" is the right answer anyhow, and I don't think it's true that for a rich person to be saved is as hard as the camel getting through the eye of the needle. I think the two have nothing to do with what being a human being's all about. Because being a human being isn't dependent on being poor or rich to my mind. It's dependent on being aware and caring and conscious and responding to whatever you can respond to when the need arises. For instance, on the streets here there are people begging all the time. Some of them are having emotional, mental trouble so much that it's kind of hard to speak to them because they can be almost violent and it's kind of frightening. But whenever I can, if somebody asks me for money and I feel that I can speak to them, I ask them what's happening in their lives. And if they are unable to find any place that can shelter them, and if they're young, I try to send them up to a place in the Bowery district, where they are doing wonderful things for young people— taking them in, teaching, educating them, giving them jobs.

I've done a lot of work for hospitals and things like that. What I'm trying to do desperately is write. I'm trying to make space for writing. Writing about how I see life and what's important in being human. How to be a human being. I heard somebody doing a sermon the other day about how we think that other people are less human than we are and that this is what all wars are based on. And that's what's behind all the things. We think the poor are less human than we are. We think the rich are less human than we are. And the prejudice against the rich is in a way as awful as the prejudice against the poor.

Wherever possible, I want to open the way, even just in a conversation, for all other human beings to have the opportunity to become the human that they are, that they don't even know they are. Because we haven't touched what being human is yet. I don't know if there are any people on earth today who are really there. There are a few that are on the verge, or on the edge of getting in there. There are a few that know, but it's very hard to hold onto this knowledge day in and day out. What it means, really, basically is being totally loving. That's a big one. I think my goal is to become the most truly human person that I am capable of being and in doing that I'll do all the rest of it. That's what really is my mission.

I think the obligation is to be true to yourself. I just think that's the obligation for everything. Shakespeare had it right. "To thine own self to be true then it follows as the . . ." I don't know how it goes, but everything else goes right. In the term philanthropy, I think there's a certain sense that I'm more giving than you are. But, I don't think I own it. I guess that's it. I really don't think I own my money, any more than I own my children. I think I'm renting it. It's given to me to use properly. And I have to do the best I can and maybe that's why I think I have to be true to myself first. I am different. I am different from a lot of people.

My grandfather, my great grandfather might have exploited people. It doesn't bother me in the slightest because all these things keep turning over. There's a great cyclical stuff going on and I don't know. Even if he did exploit people, the money kept right on moving to somebody and maybe it did a lot of good at the same time. I don't know how you really pin that one down. I'm not coming from guilt at all. That's the funny thing. I've never understood that. I haven't felt very much guilt in my life. Maybe because I really haven't had any mean thoughts to speak of. I've never wanted to do somebody else in or win at their expense. I've never really wanted that kind of thing. And I've never wanted to be more, to have more what I wanted to be is a more loving person and I'm learning that.

The main problem is narrow mindedness. It's, I guess it's ignorance and I think ignorance is probably the greatest problem. Because when people know, usually they're pretty good. It's when they don't know and they think that things are different from the way they really are that is when the trouble begins. They hurt themselves and others a lot. I guess ignorance is the problem, not groups or categories of people. The minute you categorize anybody or anything, forget it.

It's ignorance of how wonderful the world could be if everybody could be truly human. It's ignorance of how giving gets, instead of just waiting to get gifts. It's really ignorance of how much beauty there is in the world or even if you get down to how absolutely extraordinary being alive is. It's ignorance of what matters. And what matters more than anything else is your own integrity, nothing else.

7

Ross and Beverly Geiger: God's Regents

The Geigers, a couple in their mid-sixties, became evangelical Christians twenty years ago. They had by then already accumulated a fortune which they attribute to a work ethic imbued in them by immigrant parents. The consequent doubling of their fortune, through smart investment, they attribute to God, and seek with their wealth to do His bidding.

"Millionaires and the extremely wealthy," sighs Beverly Geiger, "I'll tell you, they are so confident in their wealth, that leads them away from Christ, and that's a pity. That is a pity because they can't take it with them and often they think they can send American Express on ahead with them. They can't and that's the unfortunate part." Beverly and her husband Ross feel they can bear witness to this account from both sides now. Once focused entirely on this world and making money in it, the born-again Geigers have readjusted their *principality* to coincide with their newfound spirituality. What they feel they discover in the process is that the Lord increases their revenues threefold.

Prior to their conversion, the Geigers (Ross especially) defined themselves by what they conceived as their self-made ascendance from poverty to wealth. "In New Rochelle you either wound up at the foundry or at Cabot Cranes." Ross did indeed work at the former, as his father and uncles worked at Cabot. But he was determined not to "wind up" there. "I had one goal, and that was to make money. And I wanted to find out, as I progressed in life, if I could make more money. I found by trying different things that indeed I could." Geiger rises from bank teller to owner of his own bank—in this, fortune contributes as well as the virtue of hard work. (Geiger's career catapults, for instance, when he catches his first employer embezzling.) "Then I decided, 'Well, if I'm making billionaires out of millionaires, I might as well become a billionaire.' So then I became a billionaire and built thousands of houses." As a realtor, indeed in any money-making venture, Geiger has the Midas touch and an accompanying regal attitude. "I've always had the ability to, without an education in economics, I had the ability to pretty much determine when the economic situation would change." Beverly Geiger likewise has a sixth, monetary sense. Formerly Beverly Gianelli, the daughter of Italian immigrants enjoyed an even steeper rise from rags to riches than her husband, becoming his legal partner and commercial peer. "I never looked at my wife as anything but my partner," Geiger confides. Says Beverly: "It was unusual in those days for women to be as prominent and head of a large company and so forth. . . . Of course I had all the money I needed then, that's why I urged him to try and retire in '78 but I realized myself that it was useless."

The Geigers became ends unto themselves, too self-sufficient, they admit. "As confident as I was and successful as I was, I didn't really feel I needed anybody," Ross confesses. They felt religious enough, and as for others, Beverly says: "I couldn't give two hoots about you, or the next guy, or the other guy. I couldn't care about my fellow man. No, I cared in a minor degree but I'm burdened today, that's the difference. . . . It's a burden today, we didn't put it on ourselves, believe me."

The change was drastic, sudden, dramatic; enforced by a conversion to an evangelical faith, and accomplished with Biblical precedent: *A little child shall lead them*. "One of these days I will write a book about it," explains Ross. "I was led to become a Christian and accept Jesus Christ as my savior by my seven-year-old grandson." Steven begged his grandfather to accept the Lord, and Ross became a believer. Beverly had become converted a few months before.

"We're no longer selfish. We used to play golf and bridge and just do the things we wanted to do. Now our priorities [have shifted], everything the Lord wants is number one. Now it's the Lord that controls our lives, and that's the primary directive." Prayer meetings displaced board meetings. All the zeal the Geigers had put into accumulating land, they now devote to saving souls. Their time and money are given over to mission work and to administering two family trusts turned religious charities. "Oh I tell you, what we haven't gone through spiritually. You see, I know the battle that's there. So now my burden and Ross's is for the lost people so they can get through it all. And that's why we are thinking entirely differently."

As the Lord's stewards, however, the Geigers find themselves wealthier than ever. "That shows the Lord has a sense of humor," Ross chuckles. "Even though I have given this money away in the last few years, the Lord has blessed my investments to the point where I am almost taking back more, a lot more, than I'm giving away. So if He keeps on doing that, I'll have to give a lot more to keep up."

"It's phenomenal," Beverly continues. "The scripture says you cannot out-give the Lord. Yeah, that's right. God blesses us and we keep making more."

Their spiritual conversion not only coincides with monetary gains, but confirms their lifestyle and missionary agenda as well. The Lord, for instance, dictated to Beverly that she and Ross should buy their dream house. While in prayer on the balcony of her apartment, she says, "the Lord gave it to me loud and clear." It is the Lord who orders their crusade against the "abomination" of homosexuality, the Lord who helps them reap success. "I led a boy to Christ who was a homosexual, a drug addict, and an alcoholic. You should see that boy today! He is a fine young man in this town, excellent!" Thus, belief in God invests the Geigers with remarkable certitude and clarity about their mission. Though cautioning against the "confidence" that "leads you away from Christ," they nonetheless tend to see much harmony between their plans and the Divine Will.

BIOGRAPHICAL NARRATIVE

Crossing to the Better Side of the Tracks
"I wanted to find out, as I progressed in life, if I could make more money."

BEVERLY: I was born in 1919, and I grew up in New York City. I lived on the outskirts of a small section of Queens, and went through college at Our Lady of Mercy in New York. I graduated from college about '39, '40, something like that. I worked for three years. In fact I was going on to study medicine but my dilemma was whether to continue in the field of medicine. My school had given me a scholarship, in fact to Manhattan College, and my dilemma was whether to get married or pursue a career. I did not feel I could put them both together. We were dating and he wanted to marry me and I was going to marry him. I knew in my heart that to be married and have children and all that, I could not pursue my career with the kind of time it would need, so, I gave that part up and married. We got married in '41, and we had two children, two daughters. One came in '44 and one in '47.

ROSS: Well, I was born in 1918 and raised in New Rochelle, New York, which wasn't too far from New York City and in New Rochelle we had two factories. We had the local foundry and Cabot Cranes which was a crane manufacturer. So in New Rochelle, you either wound up at the foundry or at Cabot Cranes where most of my relatives and my father worked. So that was the outcome. So as a young man, when I got out of high school, I wound up at the foundry even though I had taken a business course at a business school. While I was at the foundry, the opportunity came up to get a job in a bank. In those days, things were very difficult, so, when that type of opportunity came up, there were many applicants. About 700 applicants for this particular job. At the time, it boiled down to someone else and myself and I thought the other fellow would get the job because he came from a proper family on the right side of the tracks and I came from a working-class family and did not come from the right side of the tracks. But fortunately, we both went to the same business school, Public Business School of New Rochelle, so when the chairman and president of the bank checked the other fellow out with me, there was no contest because I was ranked very high in the business school. So I got the job, and then I went to the foundry, and told them I was leaving because I got a job in a bank. Then they offered to put me in the office, but I said, "No, I don't want to work for the factory." So, I wound up as a teller at a bank. Then I took a banking—they had a training school with a five year course at the bank, and I took the course in two years. I competed with people who had master's degrees and business experience in banks and many other degrees, and I wound up with the highest mark they ever had in the banking school.

Then in the bank, I caught the president of the bank stealing from the bank. The president wound up going to jail and I wound up going to work for the government as one of the youngest bank examiners in the country. I am not a college graduate. I took specialized courses. I studied accounting to the point where I was able to have an accounting practice with another fellow who happened to be a CPA and I knew as much about accounting as he did. After being a bank examiner, I was in charge of a mortgage department in the bank, and I started to do real estate in my spare time, and decided that I could go out on my own. I also studied real estate law because I thought that was important, so I knew real estate law and accounting. So I have no graduate degrees, I just studied, because I could use that knowledge in my business, both in accounting and law. In other words, if I had gone on to school to become a lawyer I could have gone on or been an accountant. Instead I was using both those fields in my business and going into the real estate business.

Right after the war, with the financial background that I had, I found that I was far superior to those in the business. It didn't take long before I was doing exceptionally well and selling thousands and thousands and making billionaires out of millionaires. So then I decided, "Well, if I'm making billionaires out of millionaires, I might as well become a billionaire." So then I became a billionaire and built thousands of houses. When I was about thirty-eight years old I had already earned sufficient monies so I retired, and I came to Florida and bought the house. This is down in Miami Beach. There is a country club down there. I bought a house across the street from the country club. I had the boat in the backyard and the swimming pool and the golf course were across the street and after a few months I said to my wife, "I'll be like the rest of these fellows. I'll be drinking all of the time, that's all I'll do. I better go back to work," and that's when I set up a mortgage company with the bank. I was the chairman. It was the late fifties.

I've always had the ability to, without an education in economics, I had the ability to pretty much determine when the economic situation would to change. Even when I had my mortgage company, ninety days before the bottom fell out of the real estate business, I liquidated the company. I will never forget that, because in January we had subdivisions in Florida that had been built, financed, and were fully completed. By April of that year, some of those same subdivisions had like forty or fifty percent foreclosures. Then again I would be building and the same thing would happen there. I would go along and build and all of a sudden I'd get the feeling that things would change. I'd sell out all of my enterprises and coast for a while and then go back in again. We've kind of picked up so that's why I felt I was always blessed. Whether it was my own knowledge that accomplished this thing or not, I used to say that the Lord had the say and not me.

I always feel very comfortable that if I lose every dime I have now, that I could go back and do it all over again; it wouldn't bother me in the slightest. I just feel I could, I mean you build up a confidence. I think the most important thing that young people overlook is the fact that if you get the knowledge and you have the ability regardless of the situation or time and so forth you can always be successful.

That's why I think, I'm very sure that if you took all the wealth in the country and everybody put it in a pile and dispersed it to all the people, it wouldn't take long for the same people to go and get the money all back again.

BEVERLY: I was in business with him.

ROSS: My wife joined me and she got to the point where she was able to become sales manager and advise forty or fifty salesmen while giving me more time to go out and build more homes throughout Connecticut. When we were working together we also were raising a family.

BEVERLY: Usually I would try to work my hours around the children, so, much of my work I did at night—I was in the office during the time they were in school and I would keep that, try to get back in sometime around four so they wouldn't be alone. We had a housekeeper but I didn't want the housekeeper raising my children. It was unusual in those days for women to be as prominent as I was and head of a large company and so forth. Today it's not, but then it was.

My parents were immigrants. They came from Italy. My father was just a common laborer. My mother was a very brilliant woman with no education, very brilliant. As a kid, I was very, very poor. We were extremely poor, we lived in a poor section, raised in a horrible neighborhood and my mother had six children and every one of them she sent to college, every one of them. Her three daughters all became nurses; my mother insisted that was a good profession for us. Fortunately it happened that I liked it so it was okay, but one is a college professor at the University of Delaware. She was insistent upon an education. On the other hand, Ross was an only child. He was extremely motivated.

Ross: And I would compete with all of the college people.

Beverly: He was always self-motivated; despite the fact that his father had about a sixth grade education, he was a machinist and his mother a housewife. My father was a laborer and Mother was a housewife and a seamstress on the side, she worked as a seamstress. Also, my father had maybe the equivalent of a sixth grade education, my mother no schooling at all. Show you how important school is, my mother was smarter than my father. Without my mother none of us would have made it.

Ross: I had a drive that I got from one of my uncles because I had no brothers and sisters. Once I married, I had one goal, and that was to make money. I wanted to find out, as I progressed in life, if I could make more money. I found by trying different things that indeed I could. I was very successful in insurance and selling life insurance but I couldn't make money fast enough doing that. But when I got into real estate, I found I could do that and I could get paid very well for what I was doing and building made it easier to accumulate money. Also my background in accounting helped tremendously because in order to accumulate money, you also have to know the tax laws.

Beverly: Well, making money was a high priority for him, but not me.

Ross: It sure was for me. That's why she wanted me to quit and I tried quitting when I was thirty-eight, because we felt we had enough at that time and I could afford it. But I wasn't satisfied, then I had an opportunity to buy a controlling interest in a bank of Connecticut so now this was another challenge, another field instead of buildings now. So I took over and bought this bank. That was in '64. I decided I better run the bank so I became the president of the bank and met with the directors and decided that I would take less salary than the previous president running the bank but on the condition that if I developed the bank I would get a percentage of the increase of the earnings of the bank. In short order I turned the bank around and it became one of the most successful banks in the state of Connecticut to the point where, because of this little formula on the percentage of the profits, I was making more money than most of the bankers in the state. I made my first million there in my thirties. I was about thirty-five.

Beverly: After that, it was easy. Still would be easy if I let him work but I won't.

Ross: I finally quit from the bank because I built the bank up to the point where I joined some other bankers involved in a holding company. I sold my controlling interest in my bank at a tremendous profit. I was ready to retire. I also pledged that I wouldn't go back to work. As my wife said, if I had kept it up, I probably would just keep on going making money. I felt that I should just take it easy and there is no point to it after a while. I've got two daughters, no sons to take over anything. So what was the point to keep on going?

BEVERLY: We had plenty.

ROSS: We had more than we could ever spend.

BEVERLY: We didn't know what we were going to do with it at this point. We had no idea, we figured the children, the grandchildren and so forth that's what— We had no particular goal at that point beyond that and just to live well, play golf, and so forth ourselves.

ROSS: Later we changed completely and decided that we would eventually, as requested during our lifetime, give away most of the funds.

The Confidence of the Self-Made
"As successful as I was, I didn't really feel I needed anybody."

BEVERLY: Ross was very self righteous. He thought, "I made my money honest, I did this, I did that," and I kept saying that "that had nothing to do with it because you were honest or because of this." It was a very difficult thing for him to see what we were trying to do. So then myself and my daughter's family prayed for him, for God to give him the wisdom to see it because he could not see this, he said, "Well, I made my money honest." I said, "What are you talking about?"

ROSS: I felt I was a pretty terrific guy.

BEVERLY: However, if you ask me, that confidence leads you away from Christ, not to Christ.

ROSS: Mostly.

BEVERLY: I have a very difficult time with the people here who are very wealthy.

ROSS: Most people have that problem. I mean most of our neighbors have that problem.

BEVERLY: Millionaires and the extremely wealthy. I'll tell you, they are so confident in their wealth that their confidence leads them away from Christ, and that's a pity. That is a pity because they can't take it with them, though often they seem to think they can send American Express on ahead with them. They can't and that's the unfortunate part.

ROSS: I had a problem joining and becoming a Christian because of the fact that being as confident as I was and as successful as I was, I didn't really feel that I needed anybody.

BEVERLY: He didn't feel he needed Christ to help him.

ROSS: So if I'd felt the Lord had helped me all my life, what more could I do? What was the purpose of the whole thing? I'd go to a breakfast or luncheon and hear a story about a man who was a drunk or somebody else was on drugs or they ran around with women and now they need to become a Christian to get over these things, well, I never did any of those things.

BEVERLY: That was a crutch, he said. He said they have a crutch.

Ross: And I had made all my money honestly so I had no—
Beverly: Nothing to repent for.

Before Conversion
"We met the usual appeal things."

Ross: God changes your life, which in my case— As a successful businessman I feel you can get quickly successful but you have to be a pretty good gambler. It just so happened that as a young boy, when I was twelve, thirteen years old my father taught me how to gamble, so I was a tremendous gambler. I could play cards with the best and usually the majority of the time, ninety percent of the times, I'd win. I could shoot crap, I used to go to caddy, my father told me how to gamble so I didn't have to caddy. Instead, I'd go up there late and wait for the other fellows to come in and play crap with them or cards earlier and would win the money so I didn't have to go out and carry a bag, I could win money from them because he had taught me how to do it.

I got to the point where I could go into a gambling casino and win several thousands of dollars and go away a winner. I did that almost ninety-eight percent of the time so I was a very successful gambler. I'd go to the horse races. I don't feel anybody can beat the horses but you can win a race so long as you bet one or two or three races that you figure you have the odds in your favor, you can make money. You can't beat the horses anymore than you can break the casino, but you can be satisfied to go away a winner and not try to break the casino, you can come out very well.

When I became a Christian I went back to Atlantic City. I happened to go up to New Jersey. Atlantic City had just opened up gambling casinos and I went back and I told the Lord I was going in to see what it was all about, but if I won any money I would give it away to a mission down here in Florida with the migrant workers. I went into one casino, I wasn't there for more than fifteen minutes when I won three or four thousand dollars. But now as I was winning the money and looking around the casino I had a different attitude. I started to look at the people who are throwing away their money; most of them don't know how to gamble and most of them are losers. I went to another casino and the same thing happened again, I won several thousand again in a short period of time. I came back to Florida, gave all the money that I won to the mission and never went back to casinos again. I had no interest in going back.

Beverly: Now the thing is the desire was removed, now he couldn't do it himself.

Ross: I don't even play cards in my own club because I know that if I play cards with members of the club, I have a tremendous edge over them because I'm too good at it. I wouldn't play with them.

BEVERLY: But you see his desire to gamble was completely removed, God showed him first the people, see the people were people who couldn't afford it. He told me "I saw people through different eyes" and now he just doesn't have the slightest inclination to go to the horse races or the gambling casino, nothing, absolutely nothing. That is something that God himself removes from you. I mean it's, you can't do it for yourself. That happened in '77.

ROSS: By that time I wasn't working, I was retired.

BEVERLY: We were going to have fun, just play golf, play bridge—we had been doing that. I enjoyed it very much. He was fifty-five at the time. I started a little bit earlier than that. Playing a lot of bridge and golf and I'm the club champion.

ROSS: Oh, we had plenty of things to do.

BEVERLY: Golf took a lot of my time and I loved it. And bridge took a lot of time. It's a thinking women's game, and I enjoyed it.

ROSS: We were also, we were very active as ballroom dancers, as a matter of fact we were very good at it. We did a lot of things together. I was different than most husbands. In fact when they talk about liberation, I always thought of my wife as my partner and she was liberated the first day she married me because I never looked at my wife as anything but my partner. We shared everything, never worried about money, never had a discussion over money in all the years we are married. She had anything I had, which was a lot. I had accountants and lawyers tell me, "Oh you got to be careful. After all, if your wife leaves you, you got to make sure you got the money, you got the control." I never had that attitude. Many times she had, she would make money in her own name so we never worried about it. Money was never a problem between us.

BEVERLY: But you see Christ has been the icing on the cake for us. That's been the fantastic part. We were spending it on ourselves and on the children, and giving away—

ROSS: —maybe a few thousand dollars.

BEVERLY: That was very little considering what we had. We met the usual appeal things like that.

ROSS: Red Cross, or things that came around like the hospital.

BEVERLY: To me, it was a bother, they bothered me. Oh, before that when I was a member of the Catholic church with children growing up, we were much more generous then to the Catholic church. We gave to the nuns, we did a lot of things when the children were young and then all this hypocrisy started, I don't even want to go into it. I just thought the whole thing was a fraud. Catholicism insofar as what they say and what they did were two different things. You see, I looked up at people then, which I don't today.

ROSS: Yeah, that's the difference, that's the big difference as a Christian, you don't put anybody on any pedestals, unfortunately as a Catholic—

BEVERLY: Priests were on a pedestal, nuns were on pedestals, I did that which was wrong but that is something that—

ROSS: Now as we go forward and are giving away certain amounts of money, it takes time and effort to give it away because you better be prudent about what you're doing.

BEVERLY: We didn't change our use of money right away, not right away.

ROSS: Now we've started to get a different attitude.

BEVERLY: As we've studied scripture.

Conversion to Care
"I cared in a minor degree but I'm burdened today, that's the difference."

ROSS: What was so incredible was the way I became a Christian. One of these days I will write a book about it. I was led to become a Christian and accept Jesus Christ as my savior by my seven-year-old grandson. Nobody believes me. But my seven-year-old grandson—.

BEVERLY: My daughter's son. One of three grandsons, yeah, my daughter Dawn, she is in Virginia right now. She was my spiritual mother. It was her grandson, her child. It sounds crazy but it's true.

ROSS: And it was a very interesting situation. I was leaving to go to Europe and part of my trip was going to take me into the old land, Israel. My wife wanted to follow the travels of the Apostle Paul. I had my young grandson over at the house the night before I was going to leave and I noticed, passing the room where he was staying, he was kneeling alongside his bed, and he was praying for my salvation.

BEVERLY: And crying, crying. But he has been praying for a long time.

ROSS: When I saw that, that affected me and the next morning I'm beginning to leave on my trip, my grandson came up to me and said, "Are you going to accept the Lord before you leave on your trip?" and I said, "I don't know now, Steven, I think I am going be traveling the Holy Land and so forth, maybe when I come back after I've had a chance to travel the Holy Land and so forth maybe I will have a different perspective." And he turned to look at me and said, "Pop," he called me Pop, he said, "If you were to accept the Lord before you leave I would feel that I would see you again in Heaven, after all you are going to be traveling on boats and ships and planes and something could happen to you and I would feel a lot better if you would accept Him before you leave."

BEVERLY: He said, "I'll never see you again if something happens. If you don't do it before—"

ROSS: So I got on my knees with him and came over and I made a commitment to the Lord.

BEVERLY: Yeah, the difficulty I had, as well as he had, was I couldn't understand where they were coming from. My daughter, I felt, I found her offensive, the same as Ross did and I'm telling the truth. I did. I said, "Dawn, what are you talking about?" "Don't you know who Jesus Christ is, don't you know?" I said, "You mean you went to Catholic school and you went even as a child and you don't know who He was? Of course He's God and man and He went to the cross to die." She said, "Mom you don't understand." Well, everything was Mom you don't understand. Finally the Holy Spirit really got a hold of me that one day after three months of intensive study, nobody could explain it to me. I think that's why I'm so burdened for people, to explain it to them. Then after I came to understand and received Him as my lord and savior, I couldn't wait to tell Ross about the Bible. We lived on the ocean then and we'd take a five mile walk on the ocean, I'd tell him all the stories in the Bible and he'd go, "yes and yes and yes" and I was crushed because he felt no need. He said, "I've made all these decisions all my life. I don't have to go to Christ for every little thing I do in my life." I said, "He wants your whole life, He wants the little things as well as the big things, He wants to give you eternal life, if you are going to give Him control of your life, you have got to go for everything." He said, "Everything I did I made my own decision" and that was the hardest thing, and he was successful.

He knows he has eternal life now, there is no question about that, he knows that, how it's going to help him. He knows once he gets the spirit of God in him, the direction he is going to go in. You see you have a different direction of motivation, there is no question about it. God Himself gives you a completely different perspective and that's where you change the most, in your perspective on life. It's just so different. God Himself takes you as He takes a child, and you just start to grow. Before, I think we were very selfish, by and large we lived unto ourselves really and I couldn't give two hoots about you, or the next guy, or the other guy. I couldn't care about my fellow man. No. I cared in a minor degree but I'm burdened today, that's the difference. See my husband too was someone who cares, but there's a difference, it's a burden today, we didn't put it on ourselves, believe me.

And I've led people to Christ. So many are saved, I see the change in their lives, they all change, they just have to accept Christ. It's fantastic, you should have seen what this girl was into, this young lady. She got married at fifteen, had two children by two different men, she's got a third husband, she said she had a demon coming to her room and when I got all of this on how Satan has struggled for her soul, oh the battle we went through, to get her to church, it took me five months to get this young lady to go to church. Oh I tell you, what we haven't gone through spiritually. You see, I know the battle that's there. So now my burden and Ross's is for the lost people so they can get through it all. And that's why we are thinking entirely differently. We're no longer selfish—we used to play golf and bridge and just do the things we wanted to do. Now our priorities, everything the Lord wants is number one. Now it's the Lord that controls our lives, and see that's the primary directive, it's everything *He* wants and He guides and directs and shows us what He wants—including, for example, this house.

The Unity of Spiritual and Material Wants
"The Lord wants you to have that house."

BEVERLY: I lived on the ocean. I was perfectly satisfied. We always had a big home but I was perfectly satisfied with a three bedroom apartment on the ocean, beautiful place on the ocean. Ross was used to houses in different places and so forth and he kept asking and I just didn't want a house and the help and the whole problem. Then one day in praying I said "Lord," I had arthritis by the way and I had come down here, the doctor told me to stay in Florida and that's the reason we came here permanently. And one day in prayer on the ocean, I had been praying for a place to live. Well, it turns out the man next door wants to get married and all you have to do is see that he gets married, I can have that place and I'll have it all settled. In my mind I had it settled as mine. In the meantime, it took him three years to get married and I'm waiting for him to get married, in fact he still hasn't gotten married. He said he would sell it to me when he got married and he was living in the apartment right adjacent. In the meantime, Ross starts to look around at the houses here, and I said "Lord because my husband is in business," and we discussed this, I said "If the slightest little thing goes wrong with any of these houses, then we don't go along with it because he could make any deal work and I don't want that, I don't want of the flesh, I want it really coming from You. Lord, any little thing that goes wrong, I'll sell the house."

ROSS: We get ready to go see another house, get control of contract and the owner calls up and says, "Well we've decided not to let the washer and dryer go with the deal."

BEVERLY: And I asked the Lord to make it stupid. Make it something stupid so I would know it was from Him. OK now, washer and dryer, seven hundred thousand dollar house, how much more stupid do you want? so the Lord did it.

ROSS: So this is where we told him to forget the deal.

BEVERLY: That's right and the broker said to me—

ROSS: She said, "I'll buy you ten washers and dryers."

BEVERLY: I said, "You don't understand, the Lord does not want me to buy this house."

ROSS: Her commission would have been over forty thousand dollars so—

BEVERLY: So she's going to buy me—I said, "No you don't understand, the Lord does not want me to have this house," so this went on, like this, stupid, I said "Lord let it be stupid, let something really dumb go wrong so I can't make a mistake." Now Ross had, this has happened not once, it happened about four times, stupid, stupid things went wrong each time so it looked like it was going to be a habit, stupid things were going to go wrong, so now Harvey, the man in this house, died three weeks before, Ross went to the club, met the man by accident—

Ross: No, met the sons.

Beverly: The sons, not the man, they sat and had lunch and the son said to come see the house, they haven't had it on the market yet, they haven't had it appraised yet, nothing, and Ross saw it and was impressed, we saw nothing like it, it had carpets, nothing like it is today, but you saw the floor plan having been in real estate, he saw the floor plan and he said to me, "Would you please take a look at this house" and I said, "Oh please, not another house, I think the Lord is trying to give us a message, no houses," and he said, "No, please just look at this one," and I said "OK." I came and looked at it from one end to the other and I said, "Ross, if there is a house I could work with and fix it over," I said, "if the floor plan was right and I think I could do something with the house, but make sure you really want that house." I still didn't want a house and I kept trying—

And in prayer on the balcony, in my apartment, the Lord gave it to me very loud and clear: "You are trusting Me for everything but your health" because I came here because of my health and He said to me, "You are not trusting Me," and I said, "But Lord I can't go in a house, I have to be on the ocean and my doctor said this," and I gave the Lord all the reasons and He said, "You trust Me for everything but your health," well I said, "all right, I'll go with whatever You say," and then when it came to this house and I saw it, I saw it once, I said, "It's possible," so he took me back and we saw it twice and I'm standing there in the living room and Ross said to me, "What should we offer for this house?" and he and I both wrote it on a slip of paper—

Ross: I said, "Well, before you just tell me, write it down and I'll write it down and then see how close we are in what we think we should pay for the house."

Beverly: We had the exact price, the exact price, we both came up with the same thing and we thought that was incredible. I mean we had been in the business, we came close before but never this exact, so then my husband offered it to the son and said this is the price—

Ross: Well we took the same attitude, that if something crazy happens, forget it.

Beverly: Not one penny Lord, not one penny different, not one penny. We won't pay more or less. Nothing, it had to be that or else so the man said, "I don't know, we don't even have it appraised yet, let me speak to my brother and let's see what he says." He called Ross the next day and said, "You bought it." All the brokers in the meantime, because it was the most desirable lot in the area, were bombarding in to see the house, and he showed it only to us. Nobody. Now you start to see the Lord working. Now my son-in-law had said in the past, "Remember little things, make sure it's nothing coming from you." I said, "I'm trying very hard for you guys." I said, "You know how I am." He said, "Go to the elders of your church," at that time we had been going to a church in Miami, and I said, "OK I'm willing to go." And I told him about the house and he said, "Make sure you have it appraised," and we went through the whole thing and he said to me, "Take it, it's a lesson from the Lord." He said, "There is no question in my mind that the Lord wants you to have that house." I said, "OK, I like it," the money and so forth and I kept telling the Lord about it. He/She wants it this way, now it came to one little item. We found the pool had a rusted—

ROSS: The heater was leaking.

BEVERLY: Oh that's it Lord, I told Ross . . .

ROSS: So we start the closing. I said, "We have one problem and that's the pool heater, so I think you ought to be able to help me do something about the water heater." I says, "I think a new one is worth about nine hundred dollars," the man said "No, that's an oversize pool heater, you need a bigger one than that, suppose I give you fifteen hundred dollars."

BEVERLY: Now that's the difference. Then there wasn't one thing that ever went wrong with the entire deal from beginning to end and at the end the man said, "I want you to have this Hammond organ." He did not know how we felt about the house. That's how good everything went. I'm positive, there is no question, God made it very clear to me.

ROSS: The relationship on the deal has been the very best.

BEVERLY: And the people were wonderful. A lot of people, even the workmen that came here, I needed something for the marble, I shared the gospel with them, though they were Christian I didn't know these people from Adam. I never knew them. I'd call a man and say "Demolish my whole kitchen," and the man who came here said to me, "Oh, Mrs., do you realize that this is black walnut?" He said, "Oh, I can't fix it but I'll send a man that could." What does he send me but another Christian from another church. I couldn't believe it, he did a magnificent job with the whole kitchen. So this is how the whole house went for a year. I didn't know these people and God sent them. God meant that people should hear the gospel, people I hired. I don't know. That's one of the things, there were so many things like that.

ROSS: Well it's not our house, it's His house because—

BEVERLY: It is, it's His house.

ROSS: He will eventually get the house.

BEVERLY: Yes, it's His house, there's no question about that. We have a personal relationship with Jesus Christ, and that's where it is all at.

ROSS: When I went to Israel, I met a group from the church that we were attending and the minister baptized me in the Jordan River, I had my first holy communion—

BEVERLY: We both were baptized in the Jordan River.

Ross: And then I went to the tomb where Jesus was supposed to be buried and there is where I had my first holy communion as a Christian, so I really did it. Though I was a Catholic, I felt I was looking for a change, I felt, we had some problems with the Catholic church at mass and we were sort of . . .

Beverly: We had seen hypocrisy. I became a Christian one year before him, only one year. Well, after I became a Christian, I went to where the children were learning the Bible, you see I didn't go to a church because it was a Presbyterian—that had nothing to do with it. I wanted to go where there was teaching the Bible. This was in 1976. And in '76 I went there because my son-in-law and my daughter were going there and they were teaching Genesis. That's the reason I started in the book of Genesis at that point and I went there just to study scripture but whether I went to church or not I was hearing the same gospel message, excellent gospel message, and I heard it over and over again and I asked many people what's different from what I believed to be Catholic and what you're trying to tell me. This was three months before I really understood the message. Dawn had told me something similar to what I told you but I didn't quite understand it yet and then as I started studying Genesis and the scripture, I saw the redemption plan, and in the book of Revelations I started to see the whole promise of redemption through the entire scripture. Then three months later, in January, I was positive I knew and I asked the Lord for reassurance and He promised to give it to me, and He did. God changed my life as I learned and studied, He did it so gently and quietly—

Ross: Another thing that people should realize is that— and this shows the Lord has a sense of humor. Even though I have given this money away in the last few years, the Lord has blessed my investments to the point where I am almost taking back more, a lot more, than I'm giving away. So if He keeps on doing that, I'll have to give a lot more to keep up.

Beverly: It's phenomenal. And the scripture says you cannot out-give the Lord. Yeah, that's right. God blesses us and we keep making more.

Ross: I put a substantial amount of money in the stock market about a year and a half, less then a year and a half ago, and I'm making, I've increased that money over sixty percent.

Beverly: It's incredible.

Ross: I bought some other investments in bonds and other things that I did, that have gone up tremendously in value, so as these—

Beverly: In Zachariah, you cannot out-give God, and that's exactly what we were finding, the more we keep giving the more He keeps piling it in, and I can't believe it.

Ross: It's really, when you stop and think about it, it's comical.

Missionaries of the Word
"For the people who never had a chance
to understand the gospel."

Ross: When my son-in-law went on to Bible College, I was very happy that he did and of course helped support him to go through Wilkes as he had three children and he needed some assistance. And then as I started to think more about it and as we got more active in the mission circles, then I started to make certain moves about getting ready to do something. I thought it would be a good idea instead of holding back until we die, to start to do something now.

Beverly: Well, the thing is, the children were coming into a tremendous sum of money at this point, both of my daughters and my grandchildren. That is how we had the will set up at that point. They became trained in a tremendous amount of wealth and the grandchildren, of course everybody was involved, fancy houses and my daughter had a big fancy house, she had the three children, she gave all that up and took all the profits from that house that Ross had helped them to accumulate to this point, they gave it all up and spent their money to go to Wilkes Bible College. They went and he had to have support through the years. . . .

Ross: Well, we helped.

Beverly: A little bit, but we didn't give them much. The bulk of the money came from their own commitment to the Lord. They took the money, God really provided the money, and they gave up the swimming pool, and all of it. God is so gracious. They have a house now, a very small modest house, but right outside their door the community swimming pool, tennis courts and God saying, you're doing this for Me, I'm going to give it right back. Gave it right back to them but they don't own it, but they have the use of it and the children are not in any way deprived, it's amazing how that house was there waiting for them and that's how it was. They only had three weeks to get a house and they asked for guidance and direction and someone had picked that house out for them and told them, they just walked into it, it was amazing. At that point their values, my daughter said her values started to change because having gone to Johns Hopkins, having lived in the high social strata and so forth, money was very important to her, very important, far more so to her than it was to me because she lived it. She said she just had to get a totally different attitude around money. She was changed by that. With us as we would talk, we were very gradually discussing what to do with the money. At the time, my daughter had said, "You know, we don't really need that much anymore" and then there would be a need amongst the Christians, the missionaries, this one or that one, that's how it started, very slowly. Well, she would bring this to our attention or someone else did. We would give her, the missionary there or someone there, and "Oh this one wants to go to Wilkes Bible College." It started very gradually, before we knew it, in '83.

Ross: So I set up a couple charitable trusts in 1983 and because of my ability in investments, the amazing thing was that the two trusts I set up in '83 may have increased tremendously in value.

Beverly: You should see what God is doing, it's incredible. It's not his effort, Ross knows it.

Ross: I bought some discounted government securities and in a short period of time they increased in value tremendously, so that's—I set up a foundation too.

Beverly: On no effort on his part at all, none. I think it's really incredible. And the foundation is charitable. Two charitable trusts and a foundation all to go for the propagation of the gospel.

Ross: We work several different ways, we work with some organizations, we work with individuals who we feel could be helped, somebody who wants to go to Bible college and needs assistance, we help him. My wife and I administer these trusts. What we are doing now is we are bringing in also my son-in-law and my daughter and we—

Beverly: We also have someone else on the board—

Ross: They have some suggestions where they want to help somebody—

Beverly: We set the guidelines down and the guidelines are predominantly the gospel. That is, the foundation is set up only for the people who never had a chance to understand the gospel.

Ross: We've built a second story on our house; upstairs we have a guest apartment. Many times ministers will come in the area to preach or to speak and so forth; we'll invite them to use the facilities.

Beverly: Or missionaries. And the Lord, I ask Him to bring people too. And the charitable trusts, have a similar statement of purpose. Both of them.

Ross: We chose to have these different vehicles because at the time, they were discouraging me from setting up a foundation because of the fact that in lieu of certain laws and so forth, in the event of my death, so therefore I set up this charitable trust. After I did that, then I decided after studying estate laws, it would be wiser to have a foundation particularly while I'm alive so that I can teach my children who in turn can be part of that and be able to operate it intelligently when I'm gone. The foundation works out better with your estate. In other words, now it makes it simpler in your estate, you say in your estate your monies will go to the foundation which is already set up and operating.

Beverly: Well actually what happened originally was when Ross tried to set something up, it was extremely difficult to get a lawyer or somebody familiar in what we wanted to do because most people who are in this field are completely unsafe.

Ross: Mostly secular lawyers, it is very difficult to find people who do—

Beverly: And they are secular and they don't understand what you are trying to do. They think you've gone low, they think you've gone bats. So this is the difficulty and we tried to set up a regular program for giving and it was very difficult, we found people were not too honest.

Ross: No, as a matter of fact they were the worst— I have found since becoming a Christian and also from giving my funds away, because of the fact of my background, I usually, when I get involved in an organization, say I was to get involved in a Christian community foundation, I would want financial statements—I would look, I would ask for financial statements and so forth so I could check to see how, if they were legitimate. I want to know what are they doing because to be honest with you I have found people who have set up things like that, who are not really carrying out, doing what they say that they are.

Beverly: They called themselves Christians but—

Ross: But like all charitable organizations there are good ones and some that aren't so great. In my view, the ones that aren't so great are the ones who are spending the biggest portion of their assets, of their contributions on raising funds, rather than giving it away—

Beverly: And on salaries. Then there is a difference between Christian folks; people call themselves Christian but unless they are truly "born again" they are not Christian.

Ross: They have to follow the Bible. . . .

Beverly: No, if they're not born again, they're not Christian. I can call myself one but anyone can call themself anything. That creates a criterion where . . . Christ the Lord and Savior . . . not that we don't sin, of course, you'd be a stupid fool if you say we don't, but the thing is, there is a difference.

Ross: Let's face it, there are many organizations around, even on TV where they really raise tremendous amounts of money but that doesn't say that they are doing what they should be doing with that money. I mean that's, if they're using it for the wrong things, doing things that they shouldn't be doing, then you don't want to be bothered. The focus of our two trusts and the foundation is international. Actually, it could be domestic or international.

Beverly: Right now we are helping people in China and Russia. Wherever God shows us He needs—

Ross: And then we try to travel and as we've traveled we find things, for instance we traveled to China and we've gotten, we were very impressed with what's happening there. The amazing thing is that so many people have become Christians in China without any missionaries, without any churches, without any Bibles, yet these people become Christians, it's absolutely amazing. It's mind boggling so I find things like that, where we met some people there that would help. We went to Hong Kong and finally, helped establish a Bible college in Hong Kong, some people did a nice job. So as you go along in life you find different areas that make sense. There is another man that we know who's doing a wonderful job and he's saving people from third world countries and he's training them in the Christian scriptures and evangelism so they can go back to their countries and develop churches and make Christians out of people there.

We have another friend, another man God brought to us this winter and he's a doctor, he's from Pakistan and his wife is an obstetrician and he is an internist, no, he's a surgeon, and he trained in this country and he was in the Connecticut area. He gave over $300,000 a year. He gave up an income of over $300,000 to go back to Pakistan to be a missionary. To help the people, so if a man is willing to do that you ought to help him.

BEVERLY: But he is truly of the Lord.

Now we spend most of our time giving and teaching the scripture here, teaching people. I have a Jewish boy now in my class, and he was trying to understand the Hebrew scriptures, and he understood the covenant, the blood covenant, most people don't understand the covenant. They don't understand how seriously God took the blood covenant, and you have to take it from the Hebrew perspective in order for you to really understand what did it mean in the Hebrew culture and it was an extremely solemn binding. And now, that young man is in the class, and he's a stockbroker and he's very prominent, so of course, we spend a lot of time now with individuals who truly want to understand. Now he is not a Christian yet, but I will tell you I see God working in this young man, and until he truly understands, but until God, God's spirit illuminates him, he's going to be frustrated. He is seeking, I mean he is trying to understand.

We didn't mention it, but we also give for children to get a Christian education, to study the Bible. But they have to go to the schools, where the Bible is being taught. I'm not going to send them to any school, no, I want them to have Christian values, what the Bible says. Every year, this is a perpetual . . .

ROSS: Well, we invest the funds and we've built up, if this particular school we support runs out of funds we give them additional funds.

BEVERLY: The amount we disperse is not fixed, it depends upon the number of youngsters that they get. See we don't know, it's how many youngsters are applying.

ROSS: If they need ten thousand because they've only got so many but if they need fifteen and they only made twelve, we give them the difference.

BEVERLY: We have one black little girl whose father was sexually abusing this child, the aunt took her away from him and she is raising that child. She only has a job and there is no way she could support this child so in order for her to have a Christian education we put her in the school.

ROSS: There is a Chinese girl that we put through the school. She became the valedictorian of the school.

BEVERLY: It is easier to reach people when they are young. Older and especially older wealthy people are more difficult.

Ross: If you don't reach them, if you wait too long to reach these people, if they are older, if they start to get up into sixty-five or seventy, then they have gotten to the point where their money is almost like their god; they've got to hoard it. They don't want to spend it, they hoard it, they won't spend it.

Beverly: Actually statistics are such that only one percent of the people over sixty come to Christ and that had been my experience here. It's much easier to witness, and to even have a life-changing experience, I found people over sixty, the most difficult age for witnessing to. And I have my people to pray for at the club, they are so secure in what they want, like their structure at the club and the parties and they have gotten to know each other and every week it's another different kind of a party, it's a social thing. They stay so together like that you can't pull them apart from what they're doing to let them know that there is another way, unless something happens in their life, a great tragedy or a sickness.

Ross: I got in there under the wire. I became a Christian at fifty-nine. Fifty-eight and nine months.

Beverly: I mean some of these people are retired executives, tremendous executives, and these people have been witnessed to and say, "It's OK for you but me, I'm going to do what I've always known." See they are more comfortable in what they have always known and they don't realize that they are perishing, they truly don't see that there is a heaven and a hell, they don't see that difference.

Ross: Church, for them, is maybe Easter Sunday or Christmas; they don't think about such a place to go to.

Beverly: Right, Easter Sunday, when they go to a church—

Ross: They just go play golf most Sundays.

Beverly: Right. When they go to a church it's a very liberal church that the pastor tickles areas with pretty little sermonettes and that's it. They go to church and so they think they are people who go to church and say God is going to give me credit for going to church, and they don't honestly understand a thing about what the Lord did. They don't know a thing, nor are they even willing to be receptive to it. There are a few exceptions but they are such minor ones, one man came to Christ at 83, my own mother is 83.

Ross: Well, we went out for Mother's Day with a couple probably around eighty and it's very difficult to reach them when they are at that kind of an age.

Beverly: I shared the gospel with them on Mother's Day, we took them out for brunch and yet, it is like you are talking to nobody, there is a blank wall. Their little world is playing golf, playing bridge and going to dinner. Of course, wealth in general is the issue, because wealthy people are self-sufficient unto themselves. "I'm me, I made it and I don't need anything." Ross said it.

Ross: I had that problem myself.

Beverly: He was so self-righteous, we couldn't get through but God says the self-righteous would be very difficult. He says so in the scripture.

Ross: As an only child, I never needed any assistance. Nobody helped me from the beginning of my life until I was successful so I never felt I needed any help.

The Work of Philanthropy
"I'm spending more time now than I used to spend when I was . . . making a living."

Beverly: Now all these are people that we find out about and then help through our trust or the foundation.

Ross: In financial terms, we'll be averaging, at the rate we're going now, we gradually have been building it up, close to a total of $200,000 per year.

Beverly: As the need comes, we can increase it as we see, as God gives us a picture of what He wants us to do.

Ross: As I take principal for myself and continue to build the foundation, with investments and so forth, I have to disperse from the foundation at a certain percentage. Same thing with the trust. Plus the fact that what I do now is I give most of my income away in addition to the trust and the foundation. I give away to religious organizations as much as I can for tax purposes, though I'm limited to some extent by taxes. It could be much higher than two-hundred thousand.

Beverly: More like three, three-fifty for the year, counting everything, at this point, but the foundation is just starting, it's in its infancy and it isn't fully funded yet. We want to give everything away. Absolutely, it's all going to the foundation or the two trusts.

Ross: Yeah, as a matter of fact by setting up the trust you take current money away from your principal. Now, you set up a trust, so that value reduces your estate and you've done that.

Beverly: We can't take that money back from the trust. As I said before, you can't out-give God and that's the truth, I'll tell you. We'll have to set up a board which we are in the process of doing, and the children will take it over and besides we see that they are responsible and so far it looks that way. Everything is for the Lord, except for the amount which we will leave for the children and the grandchildren's education.

Ross: They will be well educated.

Beverly: Education, whatever they need. But outright money is not, not too early in their life, believe me. They will get it later because I do believe money can be a curse. Now Dawn shares this sensitivity about money.

Ross: Yes, no question.

Beverly: My other daughter became a Christian too.

Ross: The same. She has no problem about it.

BEVERLY: She became a Christian the same year he did and she was also baptized in the Jordan. She came to Israel last time with us.

ROSS: Well, I usually check out, if I feel I'm interested in an organization then I really study them because I want to make sure that they are running their organization properly and they are doing what they say they are doing. I have found that that's necessary, that's why I think, actually to give money away and spend, it takes time. I find that I'm spending more time now than I used to spend when I was working and making a living.

BEVERLY: I can't even play golf, I play once or twice a year now. I'm so busy.

ROSS: I bring in a secretary and she's on vacation, she's away right now, and I have an office at the other end of the house here. Before I set my own foundation up, I had a foundation which was part of another umbrella organization. So the largest gift, this year, was through the umbrella foundation.

BEVERLY: We're anticipating this to be much larger by the end of the year. At least, minimum of two hundred and fifty thousand.

ROSS: Minimum two-fifty, it will probably be over that.

BEVERLY: Between two-fifty, three-fifty, minimum. Cash, everything is in cash.

ROSS: Not everything, we give them some properties . . .

BEVERLY: Yeah, but we've given most of those away.

ROSS: And this is to establish the foundation and then this foundation is just starting now.

BEVERLY: We're just getting started.

ROSS: Well in '85, the largest [gift] was again, over fifty thousand. As a matter of fact, well even this year was a hundred thousand dollars and last year was over fifty thousand. Well I gave to my foundations. Not the trusts, they get an income of close to a hundred and fifty thousand a year which is dispersed to charities. These are the Geiger Charitable Trust, and the Fundamentalist Fellowship Trust.

BEVERLY: Yeah, trust one and two, we give them by number, number one and two.

ROSS: But we do not try to reach a certain percentage of our income going to charity each year. Because if something comes up and looks good, we might do a lot more. Last year we were interested in Billy Graham because he came to our area and had a big crusade, so we gave to that.

ROSS: We made a donation to that.

BEVERLY: This year we have already sent out a lot because he had a big conference in Amsterdam with all the third world countries.

ROSS: We usually have prayer, we ask the Lord to show us where He wants it to go. If we are making over five hundred, we're giving away an awful lot of that.

BEVERLY: We usually ask the Lord, He shows us where to give. Basically, for God's people, missions, Bible College, graduate school, pastors and ministers from third world countries. A lot of those come over for additional training. We try to set up a program where they would teach evangelism in the Bible colleges there. We set up a program and supported it. We not only give money but we give ourselves to each of these projects.

Ross: I mean even with the migrant workers here, not only did I give them funds, but I worked with them. I even set up their books.

Beverly: He balanced their books but he doesn't balance our own checkbook!

Ross: Set up their books and everything else for them and try to help them in their own organization.

Beverly: Right, so we give ourselves and I taught them, I had classes up there. We give at least forty hours a week of our time.

Ross: We're both busier now than we were before.

Beverly: We have a full-time secretary.

Ross: Oftentimes I go in like a financial consultant to organizations, like there is a Christian law school in Arizona that I've acted as their financial consultant to, not only of funds but also to guide them as best as I could. My situation is that even though I didn't have the college degree, with the studies I had, I feel like I went through college.

Hearts, Not Systems
"I would start not with changing society, but with changing individuals."

Ross: The reason I mentioned international charity is I feel strongly that although many Americans are missionaries and are doing good work, we feel as time is passing that the new situations in the world will require missionaries from third world countries. The country of Korea is doing a fantastic job; Africa is doing a fantastic job. We find Christians in other parts of the world, it's absolutely phenomenal. You have a huge church in Korea. There are churches where they have a hundred and fifty thousand, or two hundred and fifty thousand members. You don't find that in the United States, but you can find that in third world countries like Korea. It's amazing.

Beverly: And we are very concerned with our United States, the way we are going; because our nation was set up on Christian precepts even though it was never fully a Christian nation, but it was on the precepts, even the Constitution and the way it was set up, but we have people now who think nothing of divorce, of abortion; and homosexuality is becoming an alternate lifestyle. God calls it an abomination. I led a boy to Christ who was a homosexual, a drug addict, and an alcoholic. You should see that boy today! He is a fine young man in this town, excellent! God's changed his whole life, but he didn't understand before. He too had been a Catholic, and I told him his life was going down the tubes, there was no place he was going, but God took that life and raised him up. Now you see, that young man inherited money and it did nothing but ruin him. He said anything, whatever depravity—

Ross: He was looking for everything.

Beverly: Any depravity, the bigger the better, which was the next depravity? People would tip him, he used to be, he was a decorator, they would tip him with Quaaludes. His sister shared with me that he was a homosexual, she's a Christian, she said, "Will you pray with me about my brother?" She had a certain will. We started to pray together. Somebody gave him Quaaludes that were contaminated and he overdosed. He was unconscious and he was taken to the hospital as dead. And I said, "God will take him, I'm positive He will." I said, "Let's pray that God will turn that brother of yours around." I said, "God will honor us in prayer." He is a beautiful Christian today, beautiful.

Ross: But there are things that we won't contribute to. I don't feel as led to, I won't contribute to organizations that call themselves Christian and do not follow the scriptures of the Bible.

Beverly: Or liberal organizations.

Ross: I might make a mistake, but if I catch up to them, then I'll drop them as contributees.

Beverly: Any liberal who reads the Bible as, "You can take it the way you feel like it," no way, I don't believe that. That's definitely too broad. God's always been very consistent. I know television says that, our news says that, our culture says that. But I am diametrically opposed to that.

Ross: We're fighting situations today where everything is self, self, self. People don't think about God, they only think about themselves.

Beverly: It is selfishness, predominantly. If it feels good, do it, that's the thinking today. If it feels good, do it. It's humanism in the schools that youngsters need to reject and you have to be very careful. Unless you raise them in a godly home, truly worshipping the Lord first, foremost and always, the children are going to live with serious problems later because of what they are teaching them in school. They are giving them birth control pills, and abortions are rampant. How long is God going to take this kind of thing? How long before He does something to this nation? We haven't known a war, we haven't known anything here, we have only had to lay the plenty, but think why. We have had more missionaries going out, God has used this nation. We have housed the Jew. The nation of Israel is very important to the Lord. Well, whether we agree with many of the Jewish things or not, that's nothing, that's God's problem. I don't agree with them always, but we still don't condemn them. I mean we don't make it difficult for them, we don't crucify them. With what they did to Jesus, that's between God and them. Many of them are coming to Christ today, more Jews are coming to Christ in the United States than have since Christ came, can you believe that? Those are the statistics. It's incredible. Still, everything we do in this nation, we are turning our backs on God. They took prayer out of the school, "In God we trust," they tried to take it off the coin. I mean how much more are they going to take away? How long is God going to let us do it? I fear for my own nation, I really do.

ROSS: Now, of course, you have the liberals who are in charge of this nation and doing this stuff.

BEVERLY: You have your media very much and then you have the liberals who are into all kinds of sin for themselves, making excuses for their sin and saying it's OK.

ROSS: Television is a very bad influence—

BEVERLY: Television, it's anything to make money, from a television stand-point—

ROSS: The media people are mostly agnostic and don't give you a point of view about God.

BEVERLY: But it's not that, I don't believe that, you see a businessman is smart enough to change his ways if the people didn't want this. So as long as he is making money at it, yes, he'll give you the clothes you want. He follows the desires of the people. And that's why I would start, not with changing society but with changing individuals. There is no other answer, to me, the only answer to society is Christ. Then, if I am a Christian, I have this guideline—that Christ is most important in my life, guiding how I'm going to conduct my life.

ROSS: People will know where you are coming from. For instance, if I play golf with some of my club members, many men, when they play golf or cards or something else, they will use the Lord's name in vain. They know where I am coming from, how I feel about it, so, they apologize to me. Let's face it, if you missed a golf ball, did Jesus make you miss that golf ball or did you do it yourself? So why do you pick on Him, why do you turn around and use His name in vain?

BEVERLY: If they swear, and say, "Gee, I'm sorry, Ross or Bev." Don't apologize to me, apologize to the one whose name you took. I say, "He happens to be my friend," and I will stop them in their tracks. So, and usually they come here, in fact we just had a group here the other night, we try to reach out with the gospel. It's very hard to reach out to rich people, very hard because they are settled in their ways, they have it made so they think—

ROSS: But we are reaching quite a few of them.

BEVERLY: And then when they get sick they know where to go, when they are really, when they're down, they have—the money can't buy it.

ROSS: The amazing thing about the wealthy person is when he becomes, when he has a major problem or becomes ill, then he looks for Christ.

BEVERLY: "Pray for me." I have a doctor, all through the years I was praying for a doctor friend of ours from the Yale-New Haven clinic. He was a Yale man, tremendous doctor, bone marrow surgeon. I would pray for his salvation, for ten years and he'd say, "I'm not ready, I'm not ready." He liked gambling too much. We used to go to the races, and we went to gambling casinos together, then when we became Christians, he didn't understand what happened to us. He thought well it's another phase, they are into something, some other phase. Well the phase never finished and it was getting stronger and stronger and stronger. He thought it was just some other tangent that we're on, that's what he thought, it was another something that we just—

So this doctor now had rejected Christ right along and he said to me, "Oh, well," he said, "Bev, you and Ross, it's OK for you, but I liked Ross better as a gambler than I do as a Bible teacher." If I started at the beginning he would cut me off somewhere along the line. He would say, "It's for you and Ross but it's not for me." So he went on and guess what happened to him? He got cancer in his own specialty, leukemia, and then he said to me, "Oh Bev, would you pray for me?" At first I didn't say anything, later on I said to him, "If you don't believe in prayer, why should we pray?" And later on when I had a chance to talk to him compassionately, he said, "Oh, every little bit helps." "All right, Rob, we'll pray for you," and he started to get better, but this was not part of Jesus at all. He started to get better, what happens, he got better for a little while and he got sick again, very sick. On April 15—I shall never forget the day, because of income tax day—he had called us up the day before, he was ready to accept Christ and this man was dying and he said, "You are the only one who will believe me." And I went over there and I led him to Christ and I said to him "How should we pray?" And he said, "I want peace, I have no peace, I want peace." I said, "Alright," so we prayed. I said, "Lord, manifest yourself to him now and show you care, that you are really real and what I'm telling him is the truth." Within several days I went back again, he said, "Tony, for sixty-six years Satan has had me, the only intelligent decision I ever made in my life was to receive Christ, I have the most beautiful peace." He said, "It's fantastic," so I said, "All right, now what else would you like me to pray for?" he said, "More peace." So I said "All right, I'll pray for more peace." He had the most magnificent death, which should have been a horrible death with the kind of cancer he had, the doctors told his wife and everyone, he's going to be really bad. No way, he just slipped off. And he did die in June.

Ross: He died June first.

Beverly: June first, and he was a Christian for six weeks, too bad, he said, that he didn't have his life to turn over to Christ. "Too bad," he said, "I resisted so long." He said that, from his own mouth. He said, "Because what you are telling me is true." See only the spirit of God—

Ross: So the wealthy man can't take it with him and so what is he going to do with his wealth?

Beverly: And he was wealthy too. He couldn't take it with him, but he was hard, very hard and I was just thinking of him in prayer.

Ross: Now, possibly it can happen that some people make their wealth on the backs of other people. Possibly, yeah—

Beverly: I would think so, I would think so.

Ross: —depending on what kind of business they were in.

Beverly: But I don't think the average, I think when they say the backs of other people, I think you could say like the abortionists, who really are misusing the people and they call it pro-choice but they are not telling the people the true alternatives. They only want it their way so they are not giving the people the alternatives, I think that kind of people, yes.

Ross: I guess another possibility would be people who hire migrant workers. Well, they could take advantage of them.

Beverly: That's another thing, the ministry we were working with—

Ross: We have seen it in Florida because we've helped a minister down here in Florida who has been dealing with the migrants and because they certainly have been taken advantage of.

Beverly: I too went in the migrant camps and I taught them evangelism at the black church, I did there, and I went into the migrant camps with Ross.

Ross: The minister, we're talking about, was black and he's been helping me. Then, of course, there are a lot of Haitians who are migrants and working on the farms and so forth and they are taken advantage of tremendously.

Beverly: Yes, I think they were abused and misused, yes, but remember those orange growers are not the real wealthy men.

Ross: I don't think you have to do those types of things to make money. I feel when I made money, when I was in the building business I had many people working for me and I had such a relationship with the contractors who worked for me that many times I made them into bigger organizations by their working for me. We had a fabulous relationship with them. I guess, sometimes it may be necessary to talk to people in our ministry, if we know that they are exploiting somebody else.

Beverly: If they're, oh, I would definitely tell them, I would definitely speak up.

Ross: As a matter of fact we've gotten, we've had some problems—

Beverly: I've done it with the migrants. In fact we would try to work through the mission to help relocate them if they were under this dominion of a man who's abusing them and misusing them. We get them relocated. We get them out of there. So and if the man, many of them would not want to listen, there is no question, they don't care, but these are the Shylock type of people, these are not the true wealthy people. With the wealthy people, like we have here at the country club, like the Grand Union heiress, the Avon heiress, the really wealthy are not like that. There are the Shylock types, but I don't think they are the real wealthy people, I don't.

Ross: Top notch executives that retire from General Motors or Ford and so, we have a lot of them around here.

BEVERLY: All these people are rather upstanding people. I find them upstanding people, that's why it's hard to reach them with the gospel, that's the reason. Same reason it was hard for my husband. Many of these people are upstanding. It's hard to reach them. They have been self-sufficient into themselves.

8

Dale Jayson: "Just Strive for Perfection"

The ex-All Pro halfback has parlayed education and fame into a standout second career as the owner of an appliance distributorship. Growing up in Arkansas in the sixties, Jayson had to be "twice as good" as white players to make his college team; but once given the ball, he insists on one's personal responsibility to run with it. Having secured his own future, he devotes substantial time helping other black athletes build a future after sports.

"You could feel like we were in a struggle. A struggle for equality," says Dale Jayson, referring to his lifelong effort to blaze a trail for himself and other blacks to follow. Jayson is a self-proclaimed "pioneer," from his schoolboy days in Texarkana, Arkansas to pro football stardom and, later, business success, in St. Louis. Inspired by his father, who insisted Dale do better than drive a truck in Texarkana, Jayson sets his goals on becoming a pro football player: "It was something that was tangible to me that gave me more of a mission."

Virtue and vision fuel Jayson's trail-blazing path. The good fortune of being "blessed with athletic talents" is tempered by the hardship of prejudice (e.g., having to play twice "or maybe three times" as well as college teammates in order to start), but in turn is overcome through the virtue of hard work. He stars, first at Rutgers University, where he followed in the footsteps of his idol Paul Robeson, then with the St. Louis Cardinals. Yet relatively early in his first career, bitter disappointments (injuries, contract disputes) teach Jayson that professional football is "not a game, but a business"; and that even in one of the few realms where a black man could claim membership in an elite, his options were limited. Once again, though, virtue would triumph over misfortune for Dale Jayson—but this time, in another realm of competition.

The time had come to strike a new path. Jayson learns the appliance distributorship trade during off-seasons. And at the same time he fulfills a promise he gave to his father to complete his college degree. At the ripe old age of 29 he retires from football, and with "every penny" he and Marla Jayson saved, he purchases a distributorship.

Jayson is even more a pioneer in the market than he was on the gridiron. He is the first black man in the region (perhaps in the country) to own a GE appliance distributorship. Though the odds are against him, the opportunities are promising. One need not stop doing business due to age or injury. In the distributorship game, one can advance from player (employee), to coach (manager), to *owner*. "Instead of the show, I'm involved. I'm involved in the high level, man." Jayson works night and day, outhustling the competition. His one outlet soon expands to three, and he becomes the most successful distributor in the regional market.

Along this path to a success exceeding his celebrated football career, Jayson picks up "concepts," sometimes in the form of pithy sayings, which he codifies into a formula for success. "If your ship does not know to what port it is due, there's no wind favorable to you" means: "You have to have some clear-cut goals and strive for perfection." This in turn means working very hard, perfecting even the most tedious tasks: "On the road to success, it's empty. Most of the people are at the rest stop. . . . Being successful is boring. The secret to success is developing the habits of doing things that non-successful people don't like to do." And to truly succeed, one must not just think positively, but *affirmatively*: "I've eliminated three words from my vocabulary: 'If' and 'I wish.' Most people who use those words are losers."

The primary concept Jayson identifies as "self-actualization," the striving to maximize all one's God-given talents. This informs his social relations, his family life, and philanthropy as well as his business pursuits. Because people are social creatures, "to reach the highest degree of self-actualization, you have to work for the good of others." Jayson therefore takes other athletes under his wing to show them the right way to have a *principality* of ownership to go with their *individuality* of fame. By the same token, one cannot work so much for others as to limit their chances of self-actualizing. Thus, Jayson speaks of curbing welfare benefits, of even making benefits contingent on ethical behavior and diligence, in order to encourage others to "develop their God-given talents." His attitude in this respect has been identified (in the likes of his friends Andrew Young and Maynard Jackson) as the New Black Conservatism.

Because self-actualization is for the greater glory of God, spirituality sanctions wealth and fame. "It's easier for a rich man to get to heaven," Jayson remarks, because a poor man might need to sin to keep his belly full. Further, to be "Christlike" means, for Jayson, literally to take on the attributes of a god. The aim is reflected in *how* he speaks as much as in what he says. One will notice in the interview that Jayson tends to proclaim, "I say, what's wrong with this country? I think we've got to look at freedom"; even on occasion, to refer to himself in the third person or the first person plural. The tone is never boastful, rather it is proud.

Jayson strives to be a model for others to emulate. "I want to set an image so that others can say, 'hey, I want to be like him.' " Along with the other black businessmen, and the athletes turned businessmen especially, whom he guides, there are his sons, Dale Jr., and Jay Jayson (the names are very telling) whom he especially molds to follow in his footsteps. Both attend Rutgers where they play football, and from where Jayson hopes and expects them to graduate into the NFL. They have also been schooled in the family business, and Dale looks forward bringing them into his company. As Jayson vowed not to suffer as his father had, so now he looks forward to setting up his children so they will not have to endure all he has. But they must endure *some* if they are to be like their father since their father has overcome so much—and since overcoming is the means of self-actualizing. That Jayson can to some extent orchestrate where his sons must struggle and where they need not is an impressive indicator of his extraordinary *principality* and *individuality*.

BIOGRAPHICAL NARRATIVE

Up from Texarkana
"I really wanted to be a professional football player because that gave me recognition."

I was born and raised in a small town in southwest Arkansas, Texarkana, Arkansas in 1944. Neither of my parents had any kind of theoretical schooling whatsoever—algebra and so forth. We were not poor, we were not well off. But we were about average for a black family from that area. I spent eighteen years there, through high school. I was fortunate enough to be blessed with some athletic talents. I was able to get a scholarship after high school to go to Rutgers University. So I played football at Rutgers and went there for four years.

Then I became a number one draft choice with the St. Louis Cardinals, which was a long-term goal of mine. Ever since I was twelve years old, I dreamed of being a professional football player; it was something that was tangible to me. You saw so many blacks in Texarkana, Arkansas who were unemployed. I figured there were pro football contracts worth fifty, sixty thousand dollars a year. And I said, wow, you know, that's what I want to be in life. You couldn't be anything but a teacher or some hard laborer, a truck driver like my dad was and I thought I wanted to be more than that. My mother was a domestic worker and I'd watch television and see all the people out in the world and I really wanted to be a professional football player because that gave me recognition. Because you couldn't really get it down here on account of the prejudice of people in Arkansas. The fact that you had to go to separate dining areas, separate restrooms, separate water fountains, and you had to ride in the back of the bus—that had an effect on me as a kid down in Arkansas. That's not what I wanted.

You could feel like we were in a struggle, a struggle for equality. I say, the only thing I could hope to be down in Texarkana, Arkansas was a schoolteacher or a bus or truck driver, like my father was, or work out of one of the refineries and low-end jobs back then. But we didn't have to work in the summer. My father did not want us to take low-end jobs. He says, "Son, *I'm* working like this. I don't want *you* guys to work like this." My father did not let us work. He would not let us stoop to do the only kind of jobs we'd be able to get back then. I stayed home and we played ball, and we didn't do anything in the summer. My father worked very hard. He had a good job for a black man in Arkansas. He drove a truck for a cement company and they made pretty decent money back in those days. He had a very good job for a black laborer who had no education.

I never missed a meal. I never had no shoes to wear. We always had shoes. We always was neat, clean. My mother used to work two jobs as a domestic worker. I had my access to a car when I was sixteen years old. No, we were not poor. We had two parents that were very hard workers and that had good common sense. And I say we always owned our own house, and we settled with what we had.

We were a very close family, very religious family. I think my teachers cared about me, about helping us to get an education. The school was completely segregated. All of my teachers were black. The first white person I really knew was the guy who came from Rutgers and said he was trying to recruit me. My first friendship with a white was on a trip to visit colleges. I think sports and my involvement in sports, et cetera, gave me exposure that I wouldn't have ordinarily gotten if I were just an average black boy who was not an athlete.The fact that I was able to go with my brother when he went to school, and stay with him in the summer. All of these things shaped me, because in order to be what you want . . . So I got an exposure down there that made me broaden my experience, which broadened my scope on life.

I had an older brother who was a good athlete. He got a football scholarship to go to the Prairie View College in Missouri and I spent a couple summers with him and got a little broader exposure. I can remember as a kid, my father and brother and I went out for a drive to California and I was thirteen, fourteen years old and my Dad took me to a football game and a baseball game. That's when the Dodgers used to play in the Coliseum and I told my Dad, I said, "Dad, I want to be on that team." So, all of those kinds of things, I think, led me or gave me the desires to develop those God-given talents. I was already a pretty good athlete. I was one of the best around for my age in junior high school. I was really good. I had size, I had speed, and I had the will.

The Pioneer
"I grew up in an era when we were trying to make changes in the country."

One of the reasons I chose Rutgers as the school to go to was because of its history—the fact that Paul Robeson, one of the first blacks to play professional football, went to Rutgers. I looked at the offers that I had coming out of high school— I had a lot of offers, I had seven scholarships out of high school to play college football and that was when things were very difficult for blacks down South. All the schools were contacting me—Big Ten schools, Pac 8, Big 8 schools, et cetera. No black athletes at this time were playing in the Southeast Conference, in the Deep South, in 1963.

And Rutgers had just had an enormous season. At that time they had a senior tailback, Roy Lee, and I wanted to go there. Not only to play halfback but because I thought Rutgers would do more than produce athletes, I thought they could produce pioneers. I thought that there's where I wanted to go to school and that's why I made my choice.

Why would I use the word "pioneer" with "athlete"? Well, I guess what I was trying to do is sightsee it out before. The state of the climate at that point had a definite effect on me because of the fact that changes were trying to be made in the movement with Martin Luther King. So it made me very conscious back then of the fact that I could be a prime leader, because I had options. They talked to me about those kinds of opportunities. "Now, you can be, if you develop your talents, you could possibly be the first black to play down in the Southeast Conference," et cetera. We were the first pioneers. I first started to want to be a pioneer when I heard of Jackie Robinson being the first black to play baseball. I was looking up to people like Rafer Johnson, the first black decathlete, who I'd met at a track meet in Houston, and Phil Gibson, and Arthur Ashe.

They talked about Dale Jayson being the first black to play in the Southeast Conference. I thought about it back when I was playing in high school—you had your Martin Luther King giving blacks those first opportunities so I grew up in an era when we were trying to make changes in the country, as far as opportunities for blacks, et cetera. I can remember then trying to get my older brother to transfer from Prairie View to play down at Arkansas State, which was a local college in the Texarkana area. They said that he could be the first black to play ball in the Deep South. And I heard of Abner Haynes who was a football player who played in North Texas State. He was the first black that really played and made a name for himself in Texas. None of the Southeast or Southwest Conference teams were playing blacks. The smaller teams started playing blacks before any of the Southeast Conference started using blacks in the athletic program. My first cousin who graduated two years after me in high school became the first black to play down in the Southeast Conference. His name was Jerome Lattimore.

And I can never forget when I went off to college, my father said something to me, he said, "Son, if you get an education, with the kind of common sense you're going to inherit from your mother and your father, you'll be a hard person to beat around." I promised my dad I would get that education.

It was a real big adjustment to make from a very small town to come to Rutgers where blacks weren't around the school. A great adjustment. My father and mother moved to New Jersey shortly after I went to Rutgers. My father got a job at Rutgers. I moved them, practically, to New Jersey 'cause I didn't want my mother and father to be down in Arkansas at that time. All of us went to New Jersey because you had a certain freedom there, you could mix with the races, etc. I didn't want my parents to stay down in Arkansas where it was so racist.

Having What It Takes
"Son, you got to be twice as good."

I was behind when I came. When I went out to Rutgers I was behind because of what I was exposed to in an all-segregated black high school— coming to Rutgers I was competing with those kids out there. I was behind; I had to work hard, work my butt off just to keep up. I got two C's and two D's my first semester. They put me on probation. It scared the hell out of me. So, not only did I start off behind, I also was playing ball, which was very demanding. But I was determined to get the education. I was determined to be the very best football player I could be.

I remember when I was sixteen years old, I broke my leg right below my knee playing football, a compound fracture. They told me I would never be able to play football again. I would be lucky to walk again. But because of the determination that I had back then I told the doctor, "Who are you to determine that I can't play football again?" I felt so strongly that I was an individual, I was able to overcome that. Who was he to tell me that I would not be a professional football player? At sixteen years old I said I want to be a professional football player. So I broke my leg, it was a real bad break. I did that my sophomore year in high school but I came back the next year and I made All-State in four sports. I would not let that stop me. So, I always have been a very determined person. And I think a person has to have something in them to overcome that kind of adversity. So, the kinds of problems that I had in the classroom, I just worked a little harder to get over.

I became very disillusioned by my sophomore year in college. I thought that I was better, but they were playing the white kids in front of me. And I came home and I talked to my dad about it because I was very disgusted, and he said, "Son, you got to be twice as good, or maybe three times as good." I said, "Dad, that's not fair." He said, "Well, that's life." Here is a guy with no formal education. So I said, if that's what it takes, then I am going to be twice as good. If that's what it takes for me then I will have to work twice as hard. Despite that, I found that God is a fair God and I believe that. So if that's the case then if you want it, you have to work harder. So I developed a philosophy back in my sophomore year of high school that I would have to work twice as hard just to get the opportunity. So, that became my philosophy: whatever it takes, you do it.

I became an All-American. And I was a good student. I became a good student, majored in political science. I didn't graduate on time. I didn't graduate from Rutgers. I graduated from Saint Louis University. I came here in 1967 and moved my family here in 1968. I got married while I was in college. I married my junior year in college. I had a kid my senior year in college, and then I had a kid right after I graduated from college. So I had two boys when I was twenty-two years old. Lovely wife whom I am still married to. I've got two sons now, little Junior who's twenty and Jay who's nineteen. And both are starting football players for Rutgers today. I felt so proud last week. It was exactly twenty years ago, 1966, I played in the Sugar Bowl. In 1986, my two sons played in the Sugar Bowl for Rutgers.

A Rude Awakening
"Please, Lord, don't let me be a . . . has-been."

I came here to St. Louis and played football and I was an instant success. I was on the All-Star team. And I improved my first year. Hey, this was a dream come true. You know, I worked all my life for this. I thought about being that professional athlete and all of a sudden I'm a professional athlete now. Making more money than I ever imagined that I would make. It was 1967, I had a bonus of $75,000. And I was making $32,000 a year. And I thought I had all the money in the world. It was a lot of money then. It was a good start. I don't know anybody twenty-two that was making that kind of money back then. I thought that I had a hell of a year. So, I thought that was it. I became an instant success.

But I became very disillusioned my rookie year because I was looking for some endorsements. I was looking for commercials, et cetera. So I came back out my second year with a contract that paid me $32,000. I said I deserved more than that: I was the franchise; I was the team; I was three-fourths of the offense last year and I deserve to be compensated accordingly. This game of football, it's a business. . . . Not like college, where it's rah rah rah for Rutgers. Win a game for Rutgers. This damn thing is a business. I went down there and I played my behind off . . . three-fourths of the offense, and hey, these people say "Here, this is a contract. You've got to abide by it. You're not going to break it. This is a business." So okay, I'm going to treat it as if it is a business.

So, I got hurt in my second year and I was leading the NFL in rushing, scoring. I got hurt and I was in the hospital. What can I do for the rest of my life if I can't play football? I've got a family to support. I've got two kids. What am I going to do? I thought, as soon as I get out of this hospital I'm going to get a real job. So I went out to the General Electric and got a job in the off-season in 1968. I worked seven off-seasons. Because of my influence on the football field, I could sit down with the vice president of the GE and I said, "I need a job, I want to work in the off-season. Is there anything that you can do?"

He said, "Well, we don't have any jobs for part-time workers. But we do have an opening for an agent where you can do a job, making, oh, fifteen thousand dollars for PR." I said, "Is there anything else you've got?" "Well," he said, "I probably can create a position for you to learn the business on a six-month basis working in distributor development. You could learn the wholesale end of the business and the retail end of the business but I can only pay you two hundred dollars per week." So I said, "I tell you what, give me the two hundred dollar a week job and I'll work in the off-season." And that's what I did. I worked in off-seasons for around seven years. I learned the retail end of it and the wholesale end of it. I went to school at night to finish my degree at Saint Louis University. I took thirty-six hours, then twelve hours after I played with the St. Louis Cardinals. I worked everyday from nine to five to get my degree and education. My dad always said, "Son, a promise is a promise." So, I went and I got my education.

Like I said, I became disillusioned by certain things. I met certain pro athletes because my brother was playing in New York for the New York Jets and I was playing for Rutgers and I used to go up on Sundays and watch them play after our game on Saturdays. . . . I'll never forget when I first came to play with the Cardinals, they called me in to talk to me after they had drafted me and so forth, and I met Roland George who was my hero. I saw him, met him, sat with him and I saw what he was doing. I met with some athletes who were working as PR agents at that time. And the idea of me doing something like that didn't sit right with me at all. And I got down on my knees and I said, "Please, Lord, don't let me be all poor and turn out like someone like he just turned out to be after he left the game." We were not making money after we left the game . . . So that's another reason why I went out and got myself a job in the off-season, so that I wouldn't turn out like the people that can't play this game any more. I saw that and I did not want to be a has-been.

Strategies for Success
"Doing the things that non-successful people don't like to do."

I've eliminated three words from my vocabulary: "If" and "I wish." Most people who use those words are losers. I've seen people who say "If" and "I wish" and they're losers. "If I would have done this," "I wish I would have done that." I promised myself I'd prepare myself so that I won't be sorry about what I did in the past. That's why I went and got my degree: not to say those words, and to take the kind of path I've taken to become who I am today.

I train a lot of guys who, like me, used to be athletes, and I take pride in that. I work on their attitudes. I used to want them to grasp the business. Now I work on them having and developing the right mental frame and attitude to be successful. You see, on the road to success, it's empty. Most of the people are at the rest stop, saying "If I would have," and "I wish I had." Having the right mental attitude helps you get disciplined. The discipline to come in every day and do the same thing and try to perfect what you did yesterday. Being successful is boring. The secret to success is developing the habits of doing the things that non-successful people don't like to do. Now, how do you develop the habit? Well, say I've got a family to support. I need to put a roof over their head. I need to send my kids to college, et cetera. That's not a strong enough motive to make you develop the habits that the non-successful people don't like to do. Purpose is the only thing that will make you do it.

Once I got the job at GE, I decided I won't do another business. I got really involved. GE hired their first black distributor in 1968. I was with them in Detroit. I got involved in it. A couple of off-seasons, I worked my butt off for them to justify to the GE directors and the General Electric Corporation that if they were sincere about increasing the number of blacks in the company, they had to have a black distributor trainer. I was very instrumental at GE. First I had this black distributor training program. I implemented the training program and I hired the first ten blacks that were going to do the job. This is when I was twenty-three or twenty-four years old. So I got very deeply involved in my off-season employment. I got deeply involved in pioneering, helping others to see that there is a change. That we can have access to the things that the majority has. So I got very deeply involved in it. To a degree that when I turned twenty-nine years old I said, I'm through with football. I don't want to play any more football. I want to be a businessman. So I retired at twenty-nine. And, just when I turned thirty I bought my first distributorship. I saved every penny to do that. My wife and I, we saved. Because when I was twenty-three I knew I wanted my own distributorship. And when I was going to Saint Louis University I'd run across a two-line sentence that said, "If your ship does not know to what port it is due, there's no wind favorable to you." You've got to have some clear-cut goals and objectives. And you have to work toward them.

And along with that concept, I ran across a concept called the concept of self-actualization. And that concept says that each individual human being should be given an opportunity to develop their God-given talents. It says man is a social creature, and can only grow through group activity. To reach the highest degree of self-actualization, you have to work for the good of others. Happiness. They say, what is happiness? Is happiness eating and drinking and being very merry and everything is going my way with the absence of conflict or tension, or is happiness achieving a basic purpose in life? I think it's the latter because I can remember when I was twelve years old, and I said, "I'm going to be a professional football player." The closer I came to becoming a professional football player, the happier I was. When I got a scholarship to Rutgers, it got me close to it. Then I became an All-American, the happier I became. Then I signed that contract, I was the happiest man in the world. I set a goal, and then I achieved that goal. That was happiness. There was no person any happier than Dale Jayson in 1967 when I signed my contract with the St. Louis Cardinals. I worked from twelve years old until twenty-one to obtain that. And I obtained it. So that concept came more and more to me. When I was twenty-three I thought I wanted to own a distributorship. When I signed that sales agreement in the middle of 1975, about eleven years ago, I became very happy.

That first store I had trouble getting. Why? Because it is a big store. "Too big for one man and plus that store has been bankrupt twice and we think you cannot make it alone in that store." I say, "Well, give me a shot at it." "No, we don't want you to just throw your money out. We don't think you're capable of running that particular store." I said, "Give me a chance. I can run it." "Hey, nobody has been able to make it at this particular store. We need somebody with some experience." I said, "Well, what about if I go out and get myself a partner?" They said, "That may work." So I went out and got myself a partner by the name of Douglas. It was Douglas-Jayson Distributors for three years.

Douglas was a white man. There were no black men with that kind of experience. So, I got Douglas who was an ex-automobile dealer. He became my partner, I was partners with him for three years. And the reason Douglas and I severed our relationship was because Douglas underestimated the will of Dale Jayson. Douglas underestimated the strong desire I had to succeed and we didn't see eye-to-eye on running the distributorship operations. And the store was doing very poorly, the store was bankrupt again in '78, but I bought him out of the bankrupt corporation. The store went bankrupt three times. But I made it a winner.

In New Jersey, when I lived there, there was a guy by the name of Rod Hammet and another guy, Paul Dean Honeycut. They advertised consistently on TV, all the time. So I said, hey, I need somebody to get me a gimmick. And I started mine. We were "The Superstar outlet." I have a cape, animation, would be flying through the air, and I do all my commercials with my cape on. So, right now, I am a lot more popular as an appliance distributor than I was as a football player, because I buy my own time on TV. And I started a totally different kind of merchandising.

I realize that the nature of appliance business is repeat business. My job is to keep our customers happy. If I keep my customers happy, they will continue to come back to me. But in order to do that, I have to do that through people. So I take a personal interest in the people who work for me, to develop them, so that they understand that if we keep the customers happy, we all are going to have a job. I take pride in making sure that my customers are treated fairly. We don't have any control over a lot of things, but there are things that we *do* have control over to make sure that we deal with the customers the way they want.

I purchased this second distributorship three months ago. It was a loser. Nobody wanted this store. They were going to close this store down. I bought the guy out at this store 'cause I thought I could make it a winner. And when I put in my bid for this store, all the local distributors protested my buying of the store because I'd have a comparative advantage over them. But I won. How? Consistency. Courage. You know that little saying that says, "Courage marks a man." That's true. Especially the kind of courage that man draws on when struggling to make progress. He takes two steps forward, and falls back one. Especially the kind of courage that keeps you doing what you have to do again and again.

Two weeks from now I'll purchase my third distributorship in Miami, Florida. This one lost seven hundred and seventy thousand dollars last year; in fact, fifty thousand dollars to date. But with God's help, and good discipline, I ought to be able to turn it around. You turn things around with people. I bring in people that I've trained. Just strive for perfection. The closer you come to perfect, the more secure you are. Good enough is never your best. You must take pride in performance.

Take pride in performance, personal pride. Put your personal pride in and zip it up. You can say whatever you want to about pride. But there's got to be a high amount of it—whatever is necessary to get. If it takes working sixteen, seventeen hours, get the job done. That must be the price paid for success. Success is something that's not just laid on the desk. Success is something that you have to go out and earn. You got to pay the price. Nobody asks a person the price he had to pay to be successful. They say you are a winner or you are a loser. More than training them, let them know that they are raising their expectations of themselves. And be fair— fair, but demanding. We became the first one hundred percent owned and operated distributors of GE in the country. Be two years this coming May.

Political Views and Future Plans
"That's what I want to do, work for freedom."

I've got other plans. I'm going to buy me a football team. There's people, certain people that have certain ideas about black athletes: that we can compete down on the football field, but we can't coach and we're not bright enough to be businessmen. We just can't coach. Oh, we can play it, but we can't coach it. We can't general manage it. The only thing I can do is own one. That's my goal.

I learned that when I was playing professional football. They asked me about coaching. People were always asking, "Hey, Dale, why don't you go after coaching?" I said, "Be real. Do you see anything that I could be coaching?" I don't want to be no assistant coach. I want to be the head coach. I don't see any head coaches that are black since I've been out of the game, and I don't see no head coaches on the horizon. And there's only one or two out of all these major colleges in this country. That's a shame. That's a shame.

I'll always be able to keep folks' respect and I'll always demand their respect. And I told the owners of the Cardinals that I'm a human being first and a football player second. And I say, I want them to treat me that way. Because it's a business. It's a system. There's one thing I learned, it's a system that has no conscience, nor does it have a memory.

Let's think about when we send eighteen-year-old kids to Vietnam. We taught them how to fight. A lot of them got killed there. A lot of them come back drug addicts, shell-shocked. And what do we do for them? We spit on them when they came back, but *we* told them to go over there! It's a system, and a system has no morals.

We draw lines in a system. Dale Jayson Distributors is a system. Is it bad that a system has no conscience or memory? Is it bad or is it life? That's life as we know it here on this earth. So that means that I have to look out for Dale Jayson first of all. So that means that I'm selfish, as we all are. For a democracy says do what you have to do to get over, even if you do a selfish thing. When I'm working here, I'm very selfish. I average eighteen hours a day, very selfishly, in 1979 and '80 and '81. People benefited through that, they got jobs, very good jobs. So I did that selfishly, but others benefited too. Well, Reagan ran for president because he wanted to be president of the United States, very selfish. Along with his selfishness he needs to help others. Lee Iacocca went to Chrysler Corporation, he said, "Hey, I'm going to make this thing work. I'm going to take a million for a salary and I'm going to do this and this and this." He did it all selfishly and look at all the jobs he saved in the country. A lot of people benefited from him.

Have a strong commitment to the purpose, whatever it is. See, as I mentioned earlier, a ship does not go to her port on her own. You've got to have some clear-cut goals and objectives. That's the purpose. Now, the other side of it is, hey, everybody I know of is in search of happiness. Is happiness eating and drinking and being merry and everything going my way, the absence of conflict or tension? Or is happiness the closer and closer you are to achieving a basic purpose in life, the happier you are? You cannot have happiness unless you have goals, whatever the goals may be. I mean you set those goals, but, hey, you may set goals like a wino. He has a goal and objective in life—to get a bottle of wine. And that gives him a purpose. Man's basic purpose on earth is to set goals and objectives and to obtain those goals and objectives. That's existing. That's existing on earth.

Freedom for the black man is one common denominator. You've got the right to ride on the front of the bus, go to the same restrooms, go to the same hotels, vote. But we do not have the access to capital. We don't own the hotels, we don't own the companies, so who is going to appoint the black Americans? Who is going to develop more black businessmen? The more black businessmen running this country, the closer we come to obtaining our freedom. That's what I want to do, work for freedom. Freedom in this kind of a country is economic. You can be red, white, and blue, and yet very poor, in bondage, because of economics.

So I donate a lot of money to my favorite charity organizations and freedom causes. I am a close friend of Andrew Young, who I've become closer to within the last six or seven years. One of the things I've been able to accomplish through my efforts at GE and my relationship with Mayor Young was to make a black executives organization. My efforts and time now lean more to working with the association. Working within the economic stream to make this accessible to other blacks. No question about it, what I have accomplished has inspired others to do likewise. So I tell those who want a lot of my time to go speak here and go speak there, "I can't." I do have a family that I have to raise. I do have some goals and objectives in life and I do want to set an image so that others can say, "Hey, I want to be like him. I want to be a football player, and also a successful businessman." I do talk to a lot of individuals. I'm talking to Darren Wirth of the San Antonio Spurs at 12:30 today. Darren wants to plan for his days after professional basketball. He wants to learn about the GE appliance-distributor training program. Mark Carpenter who was the split end for Kansas City, he was talking to me about life after football. How I planned my career, and why I chose to go the certain way that I've chosen. And I want to show how I'm involved. I'm involved in the high level, man.

There is no question in my mind that we can lick this drug problem in this country, right now, right now, if you leave the politics out of it. If you're caught dealing, then the punishment that they give you should be awful. And you're not going to get no high priced attorney who's going to get you out. We should have a method of holding the attorneys accountable for their actions. And we should limit the number of attorneys that we put into the market each year. Because they are the ones that change the judicial system. Hold them accountable for their decisions. Let's make sure that when we're fighting, the truth wins all the time. Let's protect the innocent. And let's punish the guilty.

Let's help our people get off welfare 'cause welfare does not lead to long-term progress. Let's hold our people on welfare accountable. If they're going to get the welfare checks, let's just not sit around and watch them.

Let's take the welfare checks and give them to our principals in our schools. And the welfare checks would depend upon, did the school kids come to school today? Did they behave in school today, and did they learn? Did your kids study at home, at night? Did you have your kid in at a reasonable time? Let's make them accountable. Man is a creature of habit, period. Now, if you develop a habit of going out to the mailbox once a month for a check, it is very difficult to make that person understand that he has to get up in the morning at eight o'clock and work till five o'clock, and have a job that he's productive in to get the check. Welfare is not answer. It's only a short-term solution to a disastrous time.

I'm not trying to set up a little world. I am trying to have a voice. I'm working to have a voice. Nobody wants to deal with or respect anyone unless they have been successful. But I have been successful. I think that people will now listen to what I have to say.

I'm going to leave something for my children, that's why I'm working. This is my basic philosophy. I feel that I should provide for them the opportunity. And I'm going to do for them as much as I can, so that Dale Jayson and the Dale Jayson family never has to worry about where a dollar's coming in. I try to teach my kids that if you've got money, the other problems that you may have can be very insignificant. You'll be able to enjoy all the things in life on this earth. All the things that God put on this earth. They haven't done that yet. We are taking a trip this year to go to Europe. We were going to go to Europe last year, but the kind of problems they had over there, we decided not to go so we went down to the Bahamas. I like to travel.

And I want my kids to go into business with me. We've talked about that from day one. They grew up with me in business. They did not know me that well as an athlete. They were still young. But they know me as a business-man. I've always taken them to my office and told them, "You have to earn the right to sit in this chair." If they didn't get good grades in school, I'd say, "Fine, I'll just drop one of the S's off Dale Jayson and Sons." I've always been that kind of kidder. They've kind of taken the same path I have. They'd like to be professional football players. They're not only good athletes, but they went to the same university I went to, Rutgers. Right now their goal is to be professional football players. And after they become professional football players, they'd like to work with their dad in business. So, I try to be a kind of a role model. "I don't want to be like John Doe down the street, I want to be like my dad." I've always wanted my boys to grow up with respect for their fellow man. I think that my boys ought to really go out and be a real contributing factor, to help others develop their God-given talents. I think you can only reach the highest degree of self-development as you help others. I think first of all you have to develop to the fullest. Now, once I feel that I am at the point where I have developed myself to a certain degree, then I must spend all my time helping others develop their God-given talents, whatever they be. Jackie Robinson gave all of us the opportunity to play baseball. If everyone had the right to go out and develop their life, think what this country would be like today!

When we think about this country, about this world, we think about the great men that went out and were pioneers in search of their purpose in life and how what they have done has made life so much more rewarding, so much easier for those who follow. Before we start to deny a person that opportunity, we should look back and think about if these individuals or great human beings that we read about today were denied their opportunities. Where would this world be today? That's how I keep things in perspective. Just look back. If the whole world would have done that, where would I be today? So, I think if there is anything that I believe in truly it's talent. Who am I, an earthly man, to deny someone the right to give back to God? Who am I, who are you, who is this guy, how can we do that? It's not fair.

The Gospel of Freedom and Responsibility
"You just can't be on this earth and do
what you want to do."

I'm a religious guy. I was born that way. My family's very religious. I probably look at it a little differently now than my parents do, but I still go to church. I think that there is a Supreme Being that is more powerful than I. You see, one of my secrets to business is increasing productivity. And I can show you how religion relates back to business. I believe that the best way to increase productivity is through accountability. I look at what welfare checks do to people. They don't have to be accountable. They're not punching the clock, they don't have to be accountable. If there's no accountability, there's no work, no productivity. I hold my people accountable, and I hold myself accountable. Now, just think about what the world would be like if we knew what it'd be like after we die. Somewhere down the line, I heard that the things that you do on this earth, you're going to be held accountable for after you die. And that fear of what's going to happen after I die is the thing that keeps me on the straight and narrow path here on earth. That's why I'm not a murderer, that's why I'm not a dope dealer, et cetera. There is someone who created us all. He is the Supreme Being. I believe in that Supreme Being. Hey, you just can't be on this earth and do what you want to do. So, that fear, that accountability keeps me going to church. It keeps things in perspective. It helps me with my discipline. I pray to the Lord to help me be a disciplined person, a Christian, Christ-like. So, yes, I am a very religious person and I will continue to go to church, will continue to worship the Lord. The troubles that we have over the course of the day, over the course of the week, the way you keep your sanity is you go home and say to some Supreme Being, "I need help with my discipline so that I can get through these problems, so I can get through the day."

I think it's easier for a rich man to get to heaven than it is for a poor man. It says in the Bible, "Thou shalt not steal." You have to steal to keep your belly full, so you can exist. It's very difficult to stay married and poor. I mean, you look at the ghetto and how poor it is, that's where you have most of your divorces. That's where you have all your illegitimate kids et cetera. Because there is nothing there to hold them together. I mean, if I get a divorce from my wife, I got a lot at risk. But if you got nothing and you get a divorce then what happens? It's easier for me to love everybody because I'm rich. The Bible says love everybody. Jesus said love yourself as thy neighbor, love thy neighbor as thyself. It's hard to love your neighbor et cetera when you ain't got nothing. It's easier to hate when you're poor.

I don't think it's a sin to be materialistic as long as you put God first. I mean, you can have materialist kinds of things as long as you put God in front of them. You don't want to worship your personal wealth more than your God.

What's wrong with the people in this country? This country is a beautiful country. I would say it has its problems, but this is the best country by far for me as a black person. I still say it goes back to one thing. We all should understand we are all human beings, we are all God's children. That as a country, we should all be responsive to all the demands of all the people. I think what has made this country as prosperous as it is, is that it has worked towards that end. You see, in order to grow, man has to have the ability. But freedom is the essential condition. I say, what's wrong with this country? I think that we've got to look at freedom. Freedom is due to everybody. Every human being should have an opportunity to develop his God-given talents. You see the greatest gift that God gives man is talent. The greatest gift that we can give back to God is the utilization of that talent. When a person denies you the right to give back to God the greatest gift He gives man, it kills your spirit. And the Bible says that the only thing that will live forever is your spirit. So I think, what we've done in this country, we've got a lot of people out here that are dead spiritually, because of racial discrimination blocking their ability to give back to God the greatest gift that He gives man. When that happens it kills your spirit.

Courage is God given. Courage marks the man. There is a special kind of courage a man must have, when he is struggling to make his mark. When he takes two steps forward and falls back one and walks alone in the dark. That is a special kind of courage that divides the men from the boys—to do what you have to do again and again and again. There's an old saying that says, "If you tell me something that's worth living for, you also got to show me something that's worth dying for." I'll die physically before I'll let you kill me spiritually. So I am looking to make sure my spirit is not killed, and you can kill the spirit by racial discrimination. And you say, what's wrong with the black community? Well, in the black community there are a lot of dead spirits. How you awaken the spirit is by giving every individual an opportunity to develop those God-given talents.

As we become responsive, and demanding of all the people in our society, the more healthy our society becomes. When we start taking a personal interest in all the people in our society, you know, and helping them to develop those God-given talents, the more progress we will have within our society. You know, there has to be consistency in what we do. Once we become inconsistent at what we do, then that's going to have an effect on the entire population. Consistency, I think, is the key to fairness and progress. I think accountability and consistency are things that we need to work on in this country. Hold people accountable for their actions. Make sure we're consistent in our punishment regardless of who that person may be. We don't do things because it makes political sense to do it, we make decisions because it's the right thing to do. It's the best thing to do.

9

June Radkey: Launching a
Business and Reconstituting
Her Life

June Radkey, sixty, housewife-turned-entrepreneur, finds the recipe for fortune late in life, and with it renews her self-respect. A homemaker on the verge of a breakdown when her children leave home, Radkey pursues her dream of owning a calzone shop that features her special recipe. The shop turns into a lucrative franchise.

In the past, June Radkey deferred most decisions to her husband and focused on her home. But with her children grown, she faced a major psychological breakdown. She averted this by becoming an entrepreneur. For her it was a matter of necessity: "I didn't do it for women's liberation or for financial reasons. We were financially fine. I didn't want to show up my husband. I just felt, like the doctor told me, 'you have to, to save your sanity.' " Radkey thus dramatically transforms her identity from conflicted homemaker to confident entrepreneur, starting up an exceptionally successful calzone restaurant chain. But the *principality* she works so hard to construct, it turns out, is not just her business, but her revitalized life. "This is a shot in the arm every time I go into one of the June's. . . . It's a wonderful feeling. It's absolutely a wonderful feeling. For three people that started this. . . . [Now,] the company has over three thousand employees."

June Radkey's story is mainly one of *initiation*, but also reflects elements of *healing, gnosis, awakening*, and *Odyssey* (for, much like the Homeric hero, she meets every difficulty with an inventive solution). As she builds her calzone company, Radkey undergoes a radical separation from her customary family relations, takes up a new persona as a vibrant entrepreneur, and reconstitutes her family and her place within it. Radkey narrates her story in terms of perilous journeys and adventures. "Only God above knows what I went through. And me." She would risk all to save her sanity, and gain self-knowledge and rehabilitation. But her gamble pays off magnificently, for she wins back all she puts at stake. She accepts a friendly buy-out offer arranged by a long-term customer, and thus with her newfound sense of accomplishment and identity, returns to a more self-governed domestic setting. "Now, I just want my family to be healthy and be good citizens. There's nothing else really that I want." Remaining active in the company in a limited role (via promotions and public relations), and at the center of the newly reconstituted family, Radkey enjoys the best of both worlds.

With her quest for sanity and entrepreneurial efforts consuming a great deal of her attention, Radkey has yet to give much attention to a broad philanthropic agenda. Her philanthropy relates to organizations of which she is a member. The bulk of her giving goes to her church and church-related social clubs, as well as the lady's club to which she belongs. She also donates money to the soup kitchen in which her son is involved. Her community service includes speaking engagements where she tells other women they can succeed just as she has.

But in fact, giving to her children becomes her highest priority. "I feel, if I can help my children while we're still alive, I'd rather do it now, not when I'm six feet under. Whatever I've got coming, I give a share to my kids." She provides them a financial start by employing them in the business, sets up a trust from which children and grandchildren benefit during her lifetime; and in other ways, liberates her sons from their father's demands that they be engineers like himself. Her emphasis on her children reiterates the major reason for starting her business venture in the first place: her kids, once her whole life, were now moving away from her. But, her business offers June a way to gather her children around her, once more.

Thus, Radkey has come full circle. But for one who has gone around the world, home, though it be familiar, is never the same as when last seen. Radkey has quested after "sanity," financial success, and most important, family. Because she has experienced so much on her journeys, June's homecoming is yet another new adventure (partly because she has orchestrated it): an initiation into something rich and strange.

BIOGRAPHICAL NARRATIVE

The Crisis
"If you want to save yourself, you've got to go out and do something for yourself."

I was losing my brother. He had cancer. And I was having some problems in my life—as almost every family does. And, I went to the doctor because I wasn't feeling well. And this is where it all started. So the doctor said to me, "Mrs. Radkey, I'm not giving you any medication." After he examined me and everything, he says, "There is really nothing wrong with you," and at that time I was going through my change of life also. He says, "I feel that you just have to get out of the house and start doing something for yourself." My children are grown now, and my husband happens to be a mechanical engineer so he had his own business, so he had his thing going, and the doctor just felt that I was just a very lonely person and that I had to get out and do something, and get to work. So, he says "Why don't you go out and get yourself a job, right now?" He says, "From just talking to you and examining you," he says, "you are on the verge of a nervous break- down. But, I don't feel that the medication is going to help you." He says, "I think you should just go out and get yourself a job." I say, "Well, I'm just a high school graduate, I don't know, you know, I'm a housewife. I've never worked for anybody."

As I was talking to him I thought of my idea again. My idea came back to me. And this doctor is from Sardinia so, I said, "You know, I do have an idea for starting up a little calzone shop, Dr. Savona." He says, "A calzone shop?" and I said, "Well, you know I'm Italian, I already developed the recipe of the bread, and I can make a variety of them with meat and vegetables." His comments were like this: "That sounds terrific." He says, "You know I'm Sardinian. We used to eat calzones all the time." "Well, do you like the idea?" He says, "I think it's fantastic." He says, "What are you waiting for?" I told him that my husband didn't agree. He says, "Well, he is doing his thing; if you want to save yourself, you have got to go out and do something for yourself, Mrs. Radkey"—at that time no one called me by my first name. So he adds, "I want you to go home. I want you to do some serious thinking; I'm not going to put you on any medication but I am all for this idea of yours. Just go and start small." I say, "But he won't even back me up; I have to have my own money and all that." He says, "You just go home and do some thinking, and come back to me in two weeks. Let me know what you're going to do."

Well, we used to live in Grove City. So I left and I'm driving and all of a sudden, looked up and I'm in Grove City. I stopped the car and I thought, My God, how did I get to Grove City from Bexley where his office was? From the time I left his office, believe it or not, I didn't remember anything. How I got to Grove City, I just don't know, I mean, I was in a state of I don't know what. And I just sat there, and I started crying and I thought, oh, my God, I could have killed somebody! So I just sat in the car and I was emotionally upset, and I said, I'm going to do something. This is it. I said, I don't care who I'm going to hurt, but I'm going to do it.

Becoming an Entrepreneur
"I was positive that I was going to make it."

I went back home, I changed my clothes—I did my usual shopping on Friday in the Eastland Market. On Fridays, I used to always get my fish from Peter. And, so I walked in and Peter says, "Good afternoon Mrs. Radkey. How are you?" and I say, "Fine, thank you." When I said fine thank you he looks up from the counter and he says, "Are you okay?" I said, "Yes" and he said, "Okay, what can I get for you?" I told him the fish I wanted. So he got it for me and comes back and he says, "Mrs. Radkey, are you sure you are all right? You're not your same you know bubbly personality." And I said, "I'm okay, Peter," I thanked him and I took the fish, paid him and I started to walk out of the market. At that time, the market had a very bad reputation because it was during the hippie time. With the long hair and the marijuana just starting to come into the Columbus area. So this market—my kids, my two sons, used to always tell me, "Just go to Peter's, don't go through the market because there is a hangout there, where the kids just all hang out and sit on the floor with the long hair and blah, blah."

I'll never forget that day as long as I live. I didn't even think of Tommy and my son Kenny, my two boys, instead of walking out of the market, like I always did, for the first time, I walked through that market, believe it or not. It was meant to be. I'll never forget it. I start walking and I see a little cheese shop, a gift shop and all of a sudden, there was a little shop there and this girl, this blond girl is selling wooden shoes. The wooden Dutch shoes that the kids used to wear at that time. And I'm just standing there and I'm just looking and it was just eleven by ten and she says, "May I help you?" and I say, "No, honey, I'm just looking." So I was just kind of staring, you know, to pass time, so she says, "Are you sure I can't help you? I have everything at cost today." She adds, "Tomorrow is my last day here." And she says, "I'll give you a good price if you buy two pairs." And I says, "I'm sorry honey, I'm not interested in your shoes." And I started to walk away and she says, "Are you all right, ma'am?" And I said, "Yes, why?" She says, "Well, I just thought to ask if you're all right." I says to myself, that's funny what's the matter with me? That's two people already asking me if I'm all right.

So I started to walk away and then I thought . . . and I went back and I said, "How much rent do you pay here?" And the girl looked at me and she told me. And she says, "Why?" I says, "I want to rent this space." She says, "Oh, that's fine," she says, "and I'll give you a good price on my shoes." I said, "I don't want your shoes. I wanted to know the rent because I want this space." She said, "It's $150, ma'am. If you don't want my shoes, what are you going to put in here? This space is so small, you can put hardly anything in here." And I said, "For what I'm going to do, this spot is perfect." I felt if I'm going to lose, I'm not going to lose that much. But I knew, I was positive that I was going to make it.

So, she says, "Do you mind if I ask you what you're going to do?" And I says, "I'm going to put a sandwich shop in here. It's a kind of sandwich, and drinks." And she says, "Well you know, there's two other restaurants in here." I says, "That doesn't make any difference. Nobody has ever had what I'm going to introduce to the market." She says, "Well, what kind of a sandwich are you going to introduce?" And I said, "It's an Italian sandwich. You've never heard of it." By that time she says, "Oh, you mean a calzone?"

And I said, "Yeah, how did you know?" And she says, "Well, I was with my boyfriend for six months in Italy last year and that's all we ate. That's all we could afford. We'd pay five cents, you know, whatever a nickel was there, for one calzone. We lived on them for six months and we thought wouldn't this be great to start something like this back in the States?" They both had the same idea! She says, "You mean you're going do that?" And I said, "Yes." I says, "I've perfected this calzone, I've changed it to Americanize it a bit, it's my recipe." Oh, she thought it was fantastic. So, I thought, well, here's two people in one day, I started thinking, here's two people that are encouraging me, instead of putting me the other way. So that's why I says I had to do it today.

I said, "Who do I talk to?" and she says, "Well, do you want to come back tomorrow?" She said, "I don't know if the owner of the building is here today." I says, "No, I want you to do it today. I can't wait until tomorrow." I just felt that if I went home, and talked about it or thought about it, I was just going to forget it again. So, she thought, "Well you know, just a moment," she says, "I'll go down the hall and make a phone call and see if Mr. Kinkoff is in his office." And I says, "Thank you. I'll appreciate it." So she went down the hall, she calls and comes back and she says, "Mr. Kinkoff is across the street at his office." I says, "Okay. Let's go right now." So she took her little iron box, or whatever she had her money in and we went across the street to this Mr. Kinkoff.

I knew him too, through my husband's business. So I walk in and he says, "Well, Mrs. Radkey, how are you? And how's Mr. Radkey?" And I says, "Fine, thank you sir," And thought to myself, Oh God, here is my first strike out. And he says, "What can I do for you?" And right away the young lady, she was about nineteen years old, pops up and says, "Oh, this lady wants to rent my space and that way I won't lose my six months' rent that you still have," 'cuz she was going to get married. So anyway, he looks at me and he says, "You're going to sell shoes, Mrs. Radkey?" I said, "No, Mr. Kinkoff, I'm not going to sell shoes. I have an idea for a calzone that I would like to introduce to the Columbus area." And right away his secretary pops up and she says, "Oh, Gerry," that's his first name, "we have enough restaurants in the market. We don't need anything else." And, so he says, "What type of food are you going to put in?" and I says, "Well, it's an Italian sandwich, but I've Americanized it." And he says, "Well, what type is it, Mrs. Radkey?" So, I told him, "Meat, and vegetables on homemade bread." Ah, the girl, the secretary, again, she says, "Gerry, that sounds disgusting. That's horrible. She'll never make it and let's not put her in the market." I turned around to her and I said, "I don't think you're very nice. I don't know who you are and at this point I don't care who you are, but," I says, "I don't think you're very nice and you're not very fair. You've never had my calzone so how can you be a judge of my calzone?" Mr. Kinkoff turns around to me and he says, "Mrs. Radkey, you've got the space." He says, "With that

attitude, I know you can make it." I says, "I'll be back in a half-hour. I'll
bring you three months' rent in advance, have the lease drawn up for me."
I went home, I had a little cache, you know, and I came back, and I brought
him cash, and I signed the lease and thanked Mr. Kinkoff and I says, "I'll
be back with you Monday to talk about this."

Thinking Back
"When you kids get a little older, Mama's going
to start a little restaurant."

So I went home. I started getting my dinner ready, everything was all set,
my son walks in—at that time he had finished, this was another reason why
I wanted to do it, because both of my sons had finished school. My daughter,
in the meantime, got married to a very nice boy from Italy and moved to
Philadelphia, and that was another thing that hit me with all my other
problems, my baby, the first guy she went out with, moved to Philadelphia
and he was going to the university there. And I thought, oh my God, you
know, that was another one of my traumas. But anyway, so I just had the
two boys at home, so, and they didn't want to go to college, and this was
another reason why my husband was so mad at me, 'cuz every time I'd
bring this idea up, the kids would be excited, but not my husband. He'd
say, "Those kids should go to school and become engineers like me." I says,
"I grant you, Tom, that's true, however, you can't force the kids to do it." I
mean I would talk to him, in private, I'd say, "You can't force those kids to
go to college and become engineers if they don't want to." He says, "Well,
it's your fault that they are not doing it," and we used to argue.

Twenty-five years ago, so this is going back, I took my three children—I
wanted them to learn Italian—and I told my husband, "I'm leaving. If you
want to come for a year with me, you are welcome but I want the kids to
learn Italian. I want them to learn about their heritage, their grandparents,
the country and everything," and he says, "No, if you want to go, take the
kids and go." So I took my children when they were little. My daughter was
only sixteen, Tommy was ten, and Guido (that's Kenny's real name) was
eight years old. So, I took them and I lived there for a year. And this is
another reason why my kids loved my idea. I'd want to take them to a nice
Italian restaurant, and all they wanted to eat was this. So that encouraged
me so much, to go ahead and do it someday when these kids grow up.

So it's twenty-five years ago. And I kept thinking of this idea and kept
thinking of it. So I had it. The only relatives I had were an aunt and uncle who
lived down the hill from the apartment where I was renting for a year. So I
used to go down to Uncle Stefano almost every day. So, this morning after the
children left for school and the bus picked them up, I had my breakfast and I
went down to see my aunt and uncle. I couldn't sleep that night, I kept
thinking, and thinking and I says, "You know, Uncle Stefano," and of course

all this is in Italian, I says, "the more I think of it, the more I want to do this." And he says, "What is it, my dear?" And I told him, "I says, I would like to buy a machine from here, in Italy and when I go back to the States," 'cuz we went on the boat, I says, "I can bring the machine back on the boat, back to Ohio," and I says, "When the kids grow up, Uncle Stefano, I would like to start a calzone place in where we live." And he says, "They have nothing like that there?" I says, "Nothing like that. All we have is hot dogs and hamburgers." And he says, "Mama mia. If I can help you, you let me know." I says, "Tell me tomorrow where I can go to buy the machine." He wrote down the address, that night when the kids came home for dinner I told them. I says, "Guess what Mama's going to do. I'm going to buy a machine tomorrow and when we go back home, we're going take it on the boat with us," and I says, "When you kids get a little older, Mama's going to start a little restaurant like that." Oh, they got so excited and they were so happy.

So the next day I get in a cab and I go to this address where my uncle told me to go. And I had cash with me. I walk in and I told, I speak Italian, and I told the gentleman that I wanted this machine, and he says, "Okay." And so, all of a sudden, I hear somebody from the back, on the other side, and he's saying, "Don't sell her a machine." He's hollering in Italian, you know. "Don't sell her a machine." And the guy in front of me says, "Why not, she's Italian. Let her have a machine." And he comes running over and he says, "No, I don't want her to buy a machine, because . . ." And I thought, what is going on here? They're arguing back and forth. He says, "She's going to take and copy our idea and she's going to open a store back in America." And I turned around and I said, "Yes I am." And I told him in Italian, I says, "What difference does it make? I'm going to pay you. You're going to get your money. So I'm going to be the first one to start it back in the States, so what?" I says, "Look how far we are." I said, "What are you worried about?" He refused. He more or less told me, very politely, to get out of there. Well, that upset me.

So, I go back. The kids said, "Did you get it Mama? did you get it?" And I says, "Oh, no I had a little problem, honey. Don't worry, Mama's not giving up. Don't worry." So after we had dinner we walked down to Uncle Stefano's again, and Uncle Stefano says, "How did it go? Did you get it?" And I told him "No," and I told him the story. Well, he just said one little swear word, you know, a real nice word. And he says, "You give me the money and I'll go tomorrow." He says, "Don't worry, they're that way. They are anti-America sometimes, but don't you worry." So I gave my uncle the money and he went down the next day. No problem. He asked them to put it in a wooden crate and he had it shipped to his house. His address. So then, when I left, it went on the boat. The machine came with us.

In the meantime, all these years, I was experimenting, it had taken over three years to come up with the recipe of the bread. And a lot of times on Sunday, I would invite friends to our house and I would make this. I would make this calzone, with Tommy, my son, and give it to them to try. I had more people saying, "Oh, it's all right, but I don't think you'll ever make it with the American people." I mean, you know, I had so many people—it just seemed that every time they said something, about this, I was put down. But it was meant to be. And God was on my side. That's the only thing I can think of. I don't know the words to say, but I guess, in my lifetime this had to be for me. Because I think if it was anybody else, they wouldn't be as determined as I was. They would have just thrown in the towel, especially when your husband is your number one obstacle. And by the way, it's going to be forty years that we've been married. And we're still married. It's just that we've had our ups and downs.

Initiation
"Tommy, we're in business . . . (and)
I want you to be my partner."

So, in comes my son. He was working at a Saab dealership. He loved cars. He'd come home greasy and so forth. He walks in and I said, "Hi, partner." And he looks at me and he says, "What do you mean 'partner'? What are you talking about?" I says, "I did it Tommy." He says, "You did what?" I says, "Go take your shower and come downstairs, and I'll tell you what I did." So Tommy comes downstairs in the kitchen, he says, "Well what happened, Ma?" I says, "Tommy, we're in business." He says, "What are you talking about?" I says, "I did it." I said, "We're going to open up, and I want you to be my partner." He says, "Ma you know I haven't got any money." "Hey Tommy," I says, "I don't either." I says, "I don't know where I'm going to get some money to get started, but, I know Dad's not going to give it to me. So, don't worry about it. All I'm saying is I want you to be my partner. I want you to help me, Tommy, because I cannot do it by myself. I need some, you know, support from a man." And at that time he was 19. So, he says, "All right Ma, fine." He says, "You know, I've been wanting to do this for years. I just don't want to go to college. I don't want to become an engineer, I'd rather do this with you."

So, he says, "Okay, but where did you get a place? Where are we going to rent? And what are we going to tell Dad?" I says, "I'm not, you're going to." He says, "What do you mean? I have to do the dirty work?" I says, "Yeah, Tommy. This is the only way it's going to work. You're going to tell your father you found the place. I know it's not nice for you to say a little lie, but once in a while in life, we have to. You're going to tell Dad you found the spot and that you're opening and that I'm just going to make the dough and prepare the ingredients. I'll just help in the back." He says, "Ma, Dad's never going to go for that." I says, "That's okay. I'll cross that bridge when I have to." He says, "Well, what should I tell him? Where are we going to open it?" I said, "The Eastland Market." He says, "Where?" He says, "Forget it, Ma. I've told you how long ago, never to go in there. That's no place to start a new business. Ma," he says, "we're never going to make it." I says, "Tommy, you just have faith in me. I promise, we're not going to fail. We're going to make it." He says, "But Ma, the place has a bad reputation. All you're going to get in there is young kids from school." I says, "Don't worry about it." He says, "What are you going to charge for it?" You know, with that sound. "What are you going to charge for it?" I said, "I don't know. A dollar, seventy-five cents." He says, "No, start fifty cents Ma, 'cuz you're only going to get kids." I says, "Tommy, let's not argue now. "First of all we're going to have to pay rent. We're going to have to pay these bills by ourselves, so we have to make some money." So I said, "Al right, I'll compromise. Seventy-five cents a calzone it's going to go for." And that's how we started the seventy-five cents of the original calzone.

Anyway, so husband Tom comes home. After dinner, Tommy says, "Dad, I want to talk to you." He says, "Sure Tommy, what's up?" Well, he told him. He said, "I know your mother's behind this. I know your mother started this. I know your mother put you up to this. It's not going to happen, Tommy, forget it. You're not going to open up." And all this and that. "Well I says, Tommy, don't worry about it. Let's not discuss it anymore." He's a nice guy, but he gives me a hard time. But anyway, I went ahead and started on Monday.

Getting Things Set Up
"So, that's how we started."

I went to the City Hall, asked what I had to do, because I asked my husband, and he says, "I said I'm not helping you." So I did something that wasn't very nice. I went to one of his architect friends—a real nice guy—and he says, "How are you Mrs. Radkey? And how's Mr. Radkey?" I says, "Fine. I'd like to ask a favor, but only if I can pay for this favor." And he says, "Sure anything for you Mrs. Radkey. What can I do for you?" I says, "I need a small sketch, the place is eleven by ten, all I want is a sketch where I can put a grill, a 220 outlet, a little bar, and a counter, so I can have a sink and a counter on top." And he says, "You know, what are you doing?" And I says, "I'm going to open up a little calzone shop down the street here in the Eastland Market." "Oh, great idea," he says, "what's a calzone?" And I told him. He happens to be Jewish, by the way, he says, "Wow, does that sound good!" You know, they love their food! And I says, "Well, thank you, Cal." And he says, "But why are you here?" he says, "I don't mind, you know, but why are you here?" And I says, "Well, I don't want you to feel bad, but Tom isn't for this idea of mine, and he won't draw up the little sketch. And I went to the City Hall and they told me that I have to have a little drawing." And he says, "Oh gosh, Mrs. Radkey, I don't know if I should do that." I says, "Well, I still appreciate it, . . . look, there are not going to be any hard feelings. He's probably not going to even ask me where I got it from." Well, anyway, he did it for me. Drew a little sketch for me, and I took it to the City Hall.

Now, how am I going to buy equipment? So I went to the landlord, Mr. Kinkoff. And I said, "Mr. Kinkoff, this is my first time. I have no idea, I don't even know where to go to buy restaurant equipment or anything." And he says, "What do you need, Mrs. Radkey?" And I told him just what I needed. And he says, "Well you know, we had a restaurant that went out of business here, and I had to take some of the equipment because they didn't pay the rent. Do you want to come and look at it at the warehouse?" I said, "Sure." So I went, and I picked out whatever I needed and he gave me a good deal. I says, "I'll be back with some money." He says, "Okay." And I thought, Now where am I going to get the money to give Mr. Kinkoff for the equipment? I got to open up. I couldn't sleep that night. I thought, Geez, now what am I going to do?

Got up the next morning, did my chores, got dressed, and I went to the bank, right up here at Columbia which used to be the Columbus Bank and Trust. So, I go up to Mrs. Rorke who is the president of the bank, and she says, "Good morning, Mrs. Radkey." I says, "Good morning, Mrs. Rorke. May I have a few minutes with you?" And she said, "Yes." And I said, "I would like to borrow three thousand dollars," and before I could say anything she said, "Oh, no problem, Mrs. Radkey. Here you are dear, take this application home, have Mr. Radkey fill it out and bring it back to me. There's no problem. We've known you for years. And you've been here in Columbus thirty-five years." So I says, "Oh, I'm sorry, but there is a problem." She says, "What's the problem?" And I says, "Well, Mrs. Rorke," I says, "I am doing this venture on my own," and I said, "I would like to borrow the money myself. Mr. Radkey, is sort of against this, and I have to do it by myself." And she says, "Oh, Mrs. Radkey. I'm sorry, you're a woman"—at that time, the women's lib hadn't started either. It was the beginning of 1970, and it was in '71 when all that happened. So she says, "I'm sorry. There is no way. We can't give a woman money." She says, "You're married, you know, he has to sign." She says, "You sign, but he has to sign." I says, "Please," and my eyes filled with tears. "Please, you don't know what this is going to do for me. It's very important to me. I promise this money is going to come back to you." And I described the calzone to her and she says, "Well, it sounds very, very good." I says, "Well, please have faith in me and give it to me." Well, she went over the rules of the bank and she gave me the three thousand dollars with my signature, alone. I was the first woman to get money from the bank in 1970 with only her signature. So I did that. And I just kept praying and thanking God for all these things that were happening, you know, for me. So I got the money and I went and paid Mr. Kinkoff.

So, I got the money and we got started. By the time they did the electrical work I had to pay cash every time I had something done. By the time we got all the permits, and everything all in order, it was about two months later when we finally opened. I didn't have enough money. They wanted a deposit for the phone, I didn't have it, I couldn't put a phone in. So, what we used to do—across the hall, was a liquor store and we were right across from the liquor store and one of Tommy's friends, Joel, used to work in the liquor store. So, I went to his manager, and I said, "Look, right now I'm just opening this place, across the hall from here and I can't afford to get a phone with a deposit and all that. Do you mind if I give your number, and have people call in for orders and then we'll have them ready when they come? Do you mind?" "No, no problem, Mrs. Radkey." Everybody was starting to be very nice. So, that's how we started. I didn't even have a phone, nothing at all. And the aisle was so narrow that we couldn't put a bench there, we couldn't put a table with chairs, nothing, I had nothing, all I had was an eleven-by-ten counter and a garbage can on each side of my counter that people would lean on and eat their calzone. And that's the story of the beginning of June's.

First Days in Business
"Young lady . . . you've got a winner here."

It was about two, two and a half months of preparation and our first day was so hard! People would come, you know, a few people would walk through, from offices and they would walk in and they would see the product there. When I first started, it was all beef, strictly beef. And they'd say, "What's that?" And I'd say, "Oh it's delicious, it's beef and vegetables." But they'd walk away. A woman would come up and say, "What's that?" and I'd go through telling them, you know. My son, he says, "Ma, we're never going to make it." I says, "Tommy, don't give up. It's our first day. Don't worry about it." He says, "Mama, what are we going to do?" I says, "Tommy, will you be quiet. Don't upset me." I'd be at the front of the counter, trying, and he'd be in the back slicing the meat and tomatoes or whatever, and I'd be talking to the customer. Every time someone would walk by I'd say, "Come here. Do you want to try a delicious calzone?" They'd never seen that before.

So then this woman, this Jewish lady comes in and she's got two little kids. And by then I sold a few of them—you know, actually, most of them I was giving away. I just wanted people to try them, I felt that's what was important. I felt once they tried it, they would come back again. So this woman comes in. She's got these two little kids and she's looking at all this. And I says, "May I help you?" And she says, "Oh, this is new! How long have you been here?" I says, "Today's my first day." And she says, "Oh," she's looking at the calzones there and she says, "What's that?" And I says,

"Oh, that's a calzone." She says, "Oh, I *hate* meat." And I says, "Oh, this is delicious" and I went on you know, but her two little sons kept saying, "Mom let's go, I want a hot dog, I don't want this, I don't want this." You know, I thought, oh, those little brats, to myself. So, I says, "Could you wait, just one moment ma'am?" I says, "I'll be right back." Peter, who I used to get all my meat, my fish, every week, he was about two doors down from me. So Tommy says in Italian, "Where are you going, Ma? Don't leave me here by myself!" I says, "Tommy, I'll be right back." He was so scared. I says, "Keep talking to this lady." So, he started a conversation with the woman, started telling her about the calzone, and I go to Peter, and I said, "Peter, give me a pound of sausages." He looks at me and he says, "What do you want with the hot dogs? You're buying meat from me." I says, "Give me a pound of sausages and I'll pay you later." I took the sausages and I threw them on the grill. My son says to me, "Ma, what are you doing?" I says, "Be quiet, Tommy, leave me alone." I mean he was so scared he was driving me crazy. I says, "You make the bread Tommy." He heated up the bread. I take it hot, and those two sausages and I put vegetables on it and gave them to the kids. I put just mustard and ketchup on the sausage with the bread. They went out of their mind. That's all they needed.

And by the way, this woman says, "I don't know what this is but it's delicious, and I'm going to tell you something. I'm bringing my husband in this Saturday." And he did come in the following Saturday, he came in, and he ate three calzones, two of the sausages and one of the beef, and he says, he goes like this to me, he says, "Young lady," he says, "you've got a winner here." And they were Jewish people. And he says, "I'm going to tell you something. You're not ready yet, but when I feel you're ready—I'm going to be coming in here every Saturday. And when I feel that you're ready," he says, "I'm going to bring the right people to you." And do you know, that he did. Bless his heart. He is gone now. He died of a heart attack. But Maury did bring my people in, that I went with, ten years later.

Growing Pains
"I've never catered before . . . we were still green."

About a month later the owner of the Buckeye and his wife heard about me. This was a month after I opened up. And they came in. She came, the woman came in and she says, "Are you Mrs. Radkey?" I says, "Yes I am." She says, "Well, I was just told about your little shop, and I'd like to try your calzone." And I said, "Sure." And I says, "Tommy, fix a calzone for the lady." And so, we fed her and she fell in love with it. She says, "I'm having a press party at my home, could you make these calzones for me?" And she says, "There are going to be three hundred people." Three hundred people! This is a month after I opened. I mean, you know, we were still green. And, I says, "Oh, I don't know, I've never catered before." And she says, "Well, I'm going to tell you, this would be very good publicity for you." "Well," I says, "May I have your card or your name? And I'll get back with you." "Well, thank you."

Didn't sleep. Another sleepless night. I thought, Oh my God, how in the world am I going to make three hundred calzones? And I started to think, Gee what am I going to do? I can't make the calzones here, and take them there. They'd get cold. So anyway, I came up with an idea, I remembered how people do these pancakes, you know, we went a couple times where they have little portable heaters and they make pancakes. You know pancake supper, whatever they call it. And I thought, well, I'll check tomorrow. Maybe I can rent a heater. And the main thing is, as long as I have the meat all cooked, I'll make the bread in front of the people. Roll it out. 'Cuz I had no machines, nothing. I did it with a rolling pin. And we'll put it on the heater, right in front the people. It will smell good, and we'll have the meat cooked from here, from the shop and then just assemble the calzone. And I thought, maybe that will work. 'Cuz I didn't know. I mean I had no experience, I just didn't know about restaurants. I didn't know nothing. "So, I solved, I think I solved that problem, so I finally fell asleep.

So the next day, I called the woman. And, oh, before I called, I called my daughter in Philadelphia, I says, "Ally, hi, and how's everything?" "Fine, Mama," and she says, "How's it going?" and I said, "Oh, pretty good." I says, "I'm happy because the same customers are coming back. Almost every day. So that means one thing. They like it. And they are telling other people. So we're getting a little busier. But, I got a problem now." And she says, "What is it Mom?" And I said, "This woman from the Buckeye wants me to cater the calzone, a piece of pastry, a salad and a drink." And I said, "I don't know how I'm going to do it, but can you kids come on the weekend? I'll pay for your fare, just you and Mario"—he is my son-in-law. "Come for the weekend so you can help me." I says, "There is no way Tommy and I are going to be able to do this by ourselves, and Guido"—my younger son. So she says, "No problem, Ma. Find out what weekend it is. The day that they want it." I says, "I know it's on a Saturday." She says, "Find out, Mother. And don't worry about it, Mario and I will fly up and we'll spend the weekend with you, and go back on Monday." I says, "Good." At least I got some help. And I asked my sister to come in and help me, and she says, "Fine."

So, I called the woman and I said, "Okay. What's the date?" She gave me the date and I says, "Fine, we'll do it." So then I told my son Tommy, "We got to find a place where we can rent a grill, so we can make the bread." He says, "Mama, we'll never," you know, again he was scared to do this. I says, "Tommy, don't worry about it. Alice and Mario are coming, and we're going to make it, don't worry." "All right, Ma. Okay." We did it. I never dreamed that this was going to happen.

So that day, we're there from six o'clock in the morning. My son is pounding out the dough, fixing it you know, and slicing the meat, and customers were coming by. "We'll take three, June. We'll take four," they're all hollering like this. I said, "I'm sorry." "What do you mean? What do you mean, you're sorry?" I says, "I can't give you any." "What do you mean you can't give us any?" I says, "We're doing a big party tonight. We're so scared. We're making the meat. I can't, I can't waste the dough. I can't give you any meat. Please, I'm sorry." "You mean we came all the way over here . . ." and they're, you know, this is a couple months after I opened. Less than two months after I opened. And I thought, "Oh, my God, they like it." So I mean, it made me feel real good. But I couldn't sell any calzones whatsoever that day. All we did was, I kept making the dough and Tommy kept preparing the bread, I mean the meat, so it would be ready for the big party. Well, we did it. Thank God, it turned out nice. And then the Buckeye put an article, a beautiful article, about us in the *Columbus Times*. And then it just blossomed, it started blossoming.

Stu Young came about five, six months later to interview me on TV on Channel 2 and then it just kept going. Then, in 1971, I think it was, when *The Godfather* came out. It just exploded, because see, at that time, it was an Italian theme. My place was all decorated in Italian. I had the Italian and American flag, and I had all Roman statues, and stuff like that, and I had *The Godfather* theme playing real loud and the people just loved it. And like I say, right after *The Godfather*, I mean, Italian was in. And that helped me too. It just seemed that God was behind this whole thing. Everything was just happening. I wished that I did some things different. I mean we could have taken pictures of certain things that was happening, but I still remember them, so it's the same thing. You know, this place is open now, and customers would come. "Oh, give us three, June. Do this. Do that." They start calling me June. No more Mrs. Radkey. Everything was June.

Making a Fortune, Remaking the Family
"Just name it June's."

Actually, the name goes back, before I opened up, to my attorney when we were making out the papers for the partnership. Mr. Haines says to me, "What are you going to name your restaurant, your little calzone shop?" I said, "I don't know." And he asked my son Tommy, and he says, "I don't know." And he says, "Well, you have to have a name." And I said, "All right." So Tommy says, "Hey, Mama, it's your idea, you're the one in charge of this, after all you invented the bread and all this and that," and he says, "Just name it June's." And I said, "Oh, forget it." I said, "I've hated my name all my life," I did. This is the God's truth. The kids used to make fun of June, that's a very rare name anyway, I says, "I'm not calling it June's." And the attorney says, "You know something? That's a great name. If you want my advice, if you're starting out something new, you never know, it might catch on," and he says, "The shorter the name, the better the gimmick." I thought, "All right," so we named it June's. After me.

Then I did two parties for this Mr. Maury. I did two parties at his home. And what we'd do, is, I would get an Italian band, and I would do the same thing, rent the heater, make the stuff right in front of people, do the meat ahead of time, and have it all prepared, just put them in ovens and heat them, in the customer's home, you know, and that's how I solved my problem. And these two gentlemen that went in with me ten years ago didn't happen to come to these parties that I did for Maury. They were out of town.

And then, eleven years ago, I did a big party for another Jewish lady, over three hundred people. Had the band, the whole shot, it was beautiful. This family was there. But nothing was said to me at all, Maury didn't say anything. I guess he didn't want to excite me or say anything to me. The following Saturday, he comes over to me. That family was there every Saturday with their two boys. And they brought me so many customers. He comes over and the place is jammed. People just standing in line. The kids, school kids, would sit on the floor, on the cement floor. This is a nice building. But the old one was so unique and so quaint, and so charming, as old as it was, it was very charming. And Maury comes to me and the place is jammed. He comes to me and he says, "Come here, June. Do you remember what I told you the second Saturday that I came in here, with Irma?" I says, "Yeah." He says, "Well, in the next fifteen minutes, he goes like this, he says, "this family is going to come in here, and try it, and I want you to remember one thing," he says, "they're going to make you famous. More famous than what you are." I says, "Oh, Maury!" He says, "Just mark my word." He says, "I negotiated the whole thing." And I says, "Well, who are they?" And he says, "Well, they were very impressed at Mrs. Edson's party that you did last week." And I says, "Were they there?" He says, "Yes." I says, "Why didn't you introduce me?" He says, "Because it wasn't time, but they were very impressed. So they're coming today, his whole family, to try your calzone." I said, "Oh geez!"

So anyway, at this time, my son-in-law and my daughter were with us. Because we started getting so busy, he finished school and they moved back to Columbus from Philadelphia. So, on Fridays and Saturdays we were so jammed that I had all my kids working for me. I mean, my son-in-law, my daughter, and my two boys, and I had to hire help, too, then. I was in the original place for two years. And after the two years, on this side of the market, there was a bakery on the other side, called Freedman's Bakery. And they were going out of business. So Mr. Kinkoff was so proud of me, because, when I started, this market was not so busy. And they all told me, and I knew myself, and I don't mean to sound like I'm conceited, but I saw it with my own eyes. Women would come in there with their fur coats and this and that and I mean, you know, a lot of wealthy people were coming in this market to eat my calzone. And with that, they were shopping at the other shops. And by the way, a year after I opened up, the Market was the hangout for all the teenagers and all this stuff that was going on. But when Mr. Kinkoff saw the type of people that were coming into his market through me, he didn't renew the lease for the jean place and they were out.

So two years later we bought Freedman's and we expanded and—so, that's where this guy was going to come to meet me. And still all I had there was two little ice cream tables. And eight chairs. The place would be jammed. Kids sitting on the floor, in the summertime they'd sit out on the sidewalk. I tried to get tables in Columbus. They wouldn't allow it. Now they allow everything. So, in comes the gentleman whose name I cannot disclose because that's the way he wants it, with his family. And he had three teenage girls. Well, that was it. They went out of their mind. So, Maury gets me back in the kitchen and he says, "Now listen, these people are very interested. And they want to talk to you right away." I says, "Okay, what am I supposed to do?" He says, "Well, just go outside there now and sit at the table, and this gentleman is going to talk to you." I says, "Okay."

So I went and I sat down and he says, "We'd like to meet tomorrow with you." And I said, "Tomorrow is Sunday, sir, and I always go to church on Sunday with my family." And he says, "Well I'm leaving for Chicago, and I want to make a decision. I'd like to buy you out. You've got a great idea. I want the recipes, and blah, blah, blah." I said, "Wait a minute. I can't commit myself. I can't say anything right now. Can we meet when you get back?" He says, "I'm going to Chicago." Because he has other business. And he said, "No, you have to meet with me tomorrow." "Alright, I'll meet with you." So we met at the Pancake House at ten o'clock the next morning. Oh, so I took my son-in-law with me. And we talked and I says, "Look, I'm going to tell you one thing right now, without talking with an attorney. I am not interested in being bought out right now. Maybe down the road, we can work something out. But even if you buy me out, there's got to be a clause in there, that I will be involved as far as doing the promotion and the PR, because I feel I can do that job and I know that the customer appreciates that personality coming up to them and overseeing everything, and I want that personal touch and I want it to stay with my name." And he says, "Okay, we'll work something out. When I get back from Chicago," he says, "we'll sit down with attorneys." So six months later, we did that.

They didn't buy me out at the beginning. The buy-out just started two years ago. And it's a ten year buy-out. And, like I say, I'm still involved and I just do all the traveling, I'm not part owner, I have sold out. I have sold those rights now and they own the stores. The parent company owns all the stores and then, all the new ones that are opening now are all franchises. So, it's just been a year and they sold about eight franchise stores. However, I was worried about selling out. I thought, well, maybe this is going to be just like another franchise store and they're not going to care. But it's been ten years. It's going on eleven years, at Christmas will be eleven years that I went with this party and in those eleven years they have opened thirty-nine and next month will be the fortieth, forty stores in Illinois. That's going to be number forty. And I can honestly say that I'm still proud when I go into any of the June's.

The Restoration
"A shot in the arm."

When it does go to the stock market, I'll be able to own some of the stock. But the money is good. It could have been better if I had stayed in, but I felt at my age, the fact that I did this, and I succeeded, with God's help and with their help, because I could not have done this by myself. And the worst thing was, I just didn't have my husband behind me. That was very hard. Though he did get behind me, I mean, indirectly. And now, I mean, he's a great guy and all that, but I don't know what it was, I don't know if it was just his ego or what it was or the fact that, well, I know up until today, and I feel for him, he is very sorry that neither one of his sons became engineers. And I can understand that feeling. And I respect that feeling. But by the same token, I was down here and I had to lift myself up. I was very insecure. Very. And I had my problems. And this is a shot in the arm every time I go into one of the June's. I don't mean it as being conceited or anything, but it's a wonderful feeling. It's absolutely a wonderful feeling. For three people that started this—that helped me in the beginning. The company has over three thousand employees now.

All this happened even before women's liberation was all out in the open. Before the liberation of women and all this and that. I didn't do it for that reason. I didn't want to show up my husband. I didn't do it for the money either, I mean we were financially fine, I mean I didn't do it for that. I just felt, and like the doctor told me, "You have to do something for June, for Mrs. Radkey. You *have* to, to save your sanity." And I thought, he goes on his trips. I was involved with my family and, Alice moved and got married and I thought, geez, before you know it Tommy and Kenny are going to be out of the house. What's going to happen to me? And I thought, I've got to do this even if I'm going against his wishes. Oh, I know he's proud. You know he says now, that stinker, when we're at a function or you know, people come up and, you know, they naturally are complimenting me. And they say, "Oh Tom, that's wonderful what your wife has done and blah, blah," and he says, "Yeah, boy, I hung in there. If I didn't, if I wasn't as stubborn as I was and every time I told her she couldn't do it—that's what encouraged her to do it." I just listen, and I just smile very nicely and I say, only God above knows what I went through. And me.

Now I just want my family to be healthy and be good citizens. There's nothing else really that I want. I'm still doing the PR for the company. And I get a very nice salary once a year. That's paid separately. That has nothing to do with the buy-out price at all. We own a lot of property in the Columbus area and the buy-out money has helped. Although, as long as I have my health I consider myself wealthy. Like I say, I think that's important. Because you can have all, I have seen it. You can have all the money in the world but if you don't have your health, and happiness. Health is number one, happiness you can get around, but if you don't have your health forget it. Ah, then as far as financially? Ah, I think we're all right.

Another thing is, I share the money with my children. I feel, if I can help my children while we're still alive, I'd rather do it now, not when I'm six feet under. So, in other words, whatever I've got coming, I give a share to my kids. And, of course, my son Tommy gets more, because we were, my word was steady, I said, "Tommy you're my partner" and that's how we did it when I broke up the partnership and sold out. Again, I says, "Tommy, do you want to stay in the company? Do you want to work for the company?" He says, "No, Ma." So my children get their share now. In other words it's a trust for them, they get a certain amount every month. The attorney has got that all set up. The issue of trusts for the grandchildren, that's for their parents. And, I've only got the two from my daughter. My two sons are still single. . . . I would say, if you put everything together, I've got, I don't even know if I'm right, five to ten million. Also I've helped, in charity. I give away I'd say about twenty thousand per year: at least five to church, about ten more to charities, and about a thousand to ethnic clubs. My son, Tommy, volunteers at a soup kitchen where he goes every Thursday and I give clothes and money there. And I've talked on a couple of occasions for the women's, you know, for women's lib or whatever. I mean, on how I became successful. The same thing like I'm doing right now. And I've been on about three women's TV programs and I've talked. That's it. I seem bubbly, but I am shy, I am very shy.

The Aftermath
"Don't worry honey, Papa knows."

All three of my children are good kids. That's what I mean. That's what makes me feel that I'm wealthy, to have good kids. And, of course, what I did, I mean you know. I only have one regret. I shouldn't say a regret because my mother is ninety-six years old and a lot of times we'll sit and talk. And when I first opened up I used to stand at the corner, at the end of the thing and I used to just say, "If my dad could only be here he would be so proud," and then Mama will say to me, "Don't worry honey, Papa knows. He knows that you did this." But, really, down deep in my heart, he would have been so proud of me. And I was happy that my brother, at least, witnessed a year of it, when he had come home from his therapy from the hospital. Every day when he'd finished, he would say, "I want to go see my baby sister." I was his baby sister. And he'd come from chemotherapy. Because he was so proud I had started something. And a year later after I opened up, he passed away. But I was happy that at least, Marco you know, was able to see me. That's the only thing that I wish, that my dad could have seen me. He would have been so proud.

Why I wanted my dad to live to see this, is because everybody told him he was crazy too. He bought an old slaughterhouse in Akron for a thousand dollars, a slaughterhouse! This goes back forty-five years ago. And he took this slaughterhouse, and I remember, us kids had to help him. You know what a slaughterhouse is, it's full of that real thick cork. And we had to go with sledgehammers with my dad. We had to take all that cork off of that building and then my dad said, "I'm going to open up a little family bar in here, just a shot-and-a-beer-type of thing." And my dad had that, and it was during the war and my brother and my brother-in-law, my sister's husband, had to go to the service, and my sister and I used to help out with my mother and father in the bar, but anyway this is very interesting. My mother is ninety-six but, when she was younger, man, she ran that bar! She sure did. So they all thought Dad was crazy to put a bar there. But he did and it became successful.

Then my Dad was thinking about the Akron dump, where everybody would go and just throw all their trash and everything. So, my father kept thinking ahead, could hardly read, he came from the old country with no education. He could speak English, but broken English, but he had a terrific sense of mind. He went to five businessmen in Akron and he says, "I want to buy the city dump, will you people help me? And we'll open up a race track." They thought he was crazy. They says, "You've got to be out of your mind, Kenny"—they used to call him Kenny. Well, he convinced these five people so my dad put money in it too and my father was the original owner of the Akron Race Track. That's why I wanted my father living, to see what I did. But at least Mama is still alive, God bless her.

Of course my mother had no schooling at all. I just went to high school and graduated from high school. When my Dad put my mother behind the bar he says, "Now, Sophia, you've got to be real careful so you don't make a mistake in the cash register." She says, "Well, I don't know how much money to give back." "Now, look," he got these black beans and he had them in a drawer. He says, "You're going to count how many beans. If the drink is ten cents a glass, the beer, and he gives you a dollar, you count ten beans and you give him the rest back." That's how he taught my mother to give change back.

This has been a major change in my life like my son, my youngest son, says, "Mama," he's into filming and music and so forth, he says, "I want to do a story on you some day." And I said, "Well, a lot of the truth won't come

out." There was some things that, I mean not with the business or that. . . .
Anyway, he wants to write a book about me someday, but I don't know if
that will ever happen.

10

Thomas Cooke: The Moral Career of Patrician Wealth

Born to a family of old wealth, the sixty-seven-year-old Presbyterian sought to prove himself worthy of his received advantages by making a career in financial institutions. Brought up in an environment steeped in philanthropic values, he administers the family foundation and has made philanthropy a second career.

Thomas Cooke, heir of an illustrious family of old wealth, recounts a life story marked by a recurrent theme of industrious virtue. From the opening statements of the narrative, we hear an account of a moral career, where early schooling is conceived as its initial steps. "I went to public schools from the first six years of my career." Cooke was the only child in his family not to receive his entire education in the sheltered environment of private schools. After college, he joined the marines, and considered himself lucky to have survived his perilous service during World War II. Upon his return, feeling that he lost important time, Cooke chose employment over graduate school. But, in spite of working in the bank, where his father was president, he would start his career at an entry position. At one point, Cooke would admit that his job offered a sense of security, however, to him, security was contingent on performance only. "As long as you worked hard and did a good job you didn't get fired."

Wealth did not pave the way to easy life for Cooke. Instead, the sense of vulnerability, brought on by circumstances of his upbringing and his own decisions, lessened the advantages of wealth and rendered life as a series of challenges to be overcome. Thus, his own sense of self-conception as a moral person is the outcome of his career in proving himself in the arenas of life: in public schools, students are not pampered; in the army, soldiers are treated equally; at war, the enemy does not recognize one's social standing; at work, despite his background, he starts at "the stockroom"; and later, when engaging in philanthropy, he will not simply give money but also dedicate his time.

According to Cooke, success is the fruit of effort and determination, and as such, is also the source of pride and self-satisfaction. "I was lieutenant colonel when I finally got out. Went in as a captain," he says, referring to his army tenure; and describes his business ascent tersely by saying, "Eventually, I worked my way up to vice president." Thus, Cooke downplays the importance of his inheritance and his entry to privileged circles; and emphasizes the necessity of his work in order to take care of his family and the community. On this account, he sees himself at variance with many inherited wealthy: "I think, we all should earn wealth ourselves. I think, it's a disgrace that people, who have a lot of wealth, don't pull their weight in society."

Unlike self-made wealthy and most inherited wealthy, for Thomas Cooke, contributing to the community is never something routine but a legacy spanning almost hundred-fifty years of family history. Ushered, early in his life, into a philanthropic sense of stewardship, he was groomed by his father to become his successor as the trustee of the self-perpetuating family foundation. In this position, besides his own philanthropic endeavor, he was given the opportunity and obligation to disperse a large part of the accrued interest to specified causes. "I'm operating under the original will of this gentleman," he says, referring to the distant relative who established the foundation. However, when the original instructions feel like a straitjacket, Cooke seeks, by court order, to expand the will. And significantly, recasts this task as another challenge to be overcome by effort and determination. He says characteristically, "I don't associate myself with any organization to which I don't feel that I can make a contribution. And I do make a contribution. I don't just put my name on something and that's the end of it."

Thus, Cooke turns his trusteeship into a vocation. "I think one of the things that makes it a fascinating job is to always be in a position where you can be doing something new." And he is preoccupied with carrying it out efficiently. "You want to stretch the dollar as far as you can." However, in his personal philanthropy he manifests the religious underpinnings of his entire orientation toward life and wealth. A devout Presbyterian, he says, "I'm trying to be a Christian and that takes a lot of doing and you have to work at it every day of the week. I think it puts a hell of a burden on somebody if you have a lot of money." The level of his own giving is also inspired by tradition. "We tithe to charity ten percent of our income," he says. Moreover, such financial generosity is to be complemented by personal effort. "I contribute time and money. You really can't separate the two."

Though philanthropy is absolutely essential for the community, Cooke thinks, philanthropy cannot resolve the underlying issue of poverty. The latter is the consequence of the differential motivation of people. After all, he says, "That's where the Rockefellers come from." It is also why poverty will always exist."I don't think that the government is going to be able to eradicate that, no matter how much they extract from the wealthy people." Philanthropy or government assistance beyond a certain point is counterproductive because it undercuts effort. Philanthropy can undo some of the imbalances of opportunity that society naturally produces. However, he is resigned to the fact that "the poor are always with you."

BIOGRAPHICAL NARRATIVE

Apprenticeship of an Heir
"You always start in the stockroom."

Well, I was born in St. Louis, grew up in University City, and went to public schools for the first six years of my career. I really wasn't cognizant of growing up wealthy. I was really the oldest in the family. My older sister died at a relatively young age. And I was the one who went to a public school and I think that made a bit of a difference. Public school where everybody's equal, so to speak. It's not like being in a private school. The rest of my family went to private schools. Then, I went to private school in St. Louis, Knight Academy. And I went to Washington University in St. Louis. While at Washington, I was in the ROTC program and I headed up a marine unit. And so, when I graduated, I got a commission for three and a half years. And that was a pretty good experience. The Mediterranean, North Africa, Angio Beach in Italy, and the invasion of southern France. Then finally out in the Pacific, the landings in Japan. I stayed in the Reserves, I was lieutenant colonel when I finally got out. Went in as a captain.

That three and a half years during World War II was not exactly business experience, but it, sure as heck, was an experience of sorts. So, that's where I started, and then, I went into the banking business. Worked at the Saint Louis International Trust Company for twenty-five years and worked up to vice chairman of the board. When I completed twenty-five years, I came over here to Burns and Tucker as a partner. I have been here for fourteen years. So that's 39 years, plus my years in the Marines. That's my career since I graduated from college in 1942. I didn't go to graduate school. I got home from the war a little late. I can't say that I went through hell during the war, but it was no picnic. And just to be back home and safe in one piece and reunited with my wife and family, I've just got a lot to be thankful for. I would have missed a whole year of grad school, so, I started to work. I figured it was time to earn an honest living anyway.

I went into my father's bank, and I'm not sure that that was the best place to be. He put a lot of pressure on me. I think it's awfully hard for a person to be his own self when he's really working for his father in an organization like that. Oh, you always start in the stockroom, you always do that. Eventually, I worked my way up to vice-president. But people always say, "Oh, he's getting up there because he's who he is," that sort of thing. I wouldn't do it again. And the least satisfying part of working in a bank was that the internal politics unfortunately deteriorated after my father died, so that people were being fired left and right for no apparent reason and other people were stabbing each other in the back. And you didn't feel that you were working on a team, so to speak. I got caught in the middle of that very much, because the person who succeeded my father as head of the institution never should have been put in charge of managing people. He wasn't in the war, and he just had a psychology that he was out to get people, and he did. Sooner or later he got about everybody who was around him. So that was most unfortunate.

But anyway, I went ahead when I had the opportunity to come over here in 1971. It's just wonderful, nothing like working for a partnership. It's the difference between day and night coming into a place like this. There are nine partners here. We all work hard and we all work together and our customers come first. We're a small organization, trying to stay small. We're trying to do a good job for our clients and in doing that we've been very successful for ourselves.

I suppose a person has a sort of financial security when he goes to work for a banking institution because, in those days anyway, they didn't fire people left and right. As long as you worked hard and did a good job you didn't get fired. And so there was a certain amount of security there. And that means being able to put bread on the table every night and have roof over your head and to be able to do things that you want to do and not really have to worry about where the next paycheck's coming from. To have a good steady job. From that point of view I don't have any financial pressure.

Vocation of Trusteeship
"I'm operating under the original will of this gentleman."

Now, the Cooke Institute was established by one of my forebears, in his will back in 1853, as a private foundation. He left half his worldly goods to establish that because his whole family had been tragically wiped out, his wife and then two daughters by a typhoid epidemic three or four years before he himself died. He died relatively a young man. He established this foundation to fund medical research. And he appointed his first cousin by the name of Beauregard Cooke as the first trustee. He stipulated that there should always be a male member of the Cooke family as sole trustee. Now the trustee was given pretty broad latitude on how to fulfill his mission. Initially the capital of the fund was $250,000, and I think it's now approaching $12 million. And the annual income is approaching $600,000. So the trustee has a pretty fair-sized job of determining how to spend that money.

Among other things, the Institute has provided the seed money to establish KSTL, our public television station here in St. Louis, of which my father was the original chairman and I am chairman of the trustees of the station. That's a nonpaying position. And we have established a night school at Saint Louis University and we underwrite the Extension Program there, which is a rather large program. And then we fund research at any number of places. So, I'm operating under the original will of this gentleman. Recently, we've been to the probate court to get them to liberalize the provisions of the will a little bit, because we had been branching outside of St. Louis and we just wanted to get that legalized. So the court liberalized the geographic area to include all of the Missouri River Valley, and they also liberalized the terms so that I can fund lectures as well as research. But we're not supposed to charge anything for these lectures, they're supposed to be free public lectures. So that is the major charitable thrust that's come down through the family, going back to 1853.

There's only one trustee of the Cooke Institute and I have named my successor. And the trustees of the Saint Louis Consortium really look over my shoulder and review what I do. I'm answerable to them, that was provided in the original will. And I appoint my successor with a letter to them, which they keep sealed and nobody knows who it's supposed to be. Although, I've notified my successor, because I don't want to create any friction in the family. It's supposed to be a male member of the family. And fortunately we've been able to—now Cornelius C. Cooke, who was president of Washington U, was the trustee and then he appointed my father 'cause he didn't have any children. He appointed my father, Everett Cooke, and my father appointed me. So that's the way. I think there have been five trustees over the last hundred and thirty-three years. There's no provision for what I would call a co-trustee. I think that's one fallacy, I mean if I get doddery and so forth. . . . But I will do what my father did. He brought me in as sort of his righthand man. And I worked with him over the last ten years of his life. And I intend to do that too. And of course I've got my secretary, who really is the administrator. She holds things together. She's the staff [laughter].

I really work through the institutions that conduct the research. They come up with ideas of what they want to do and my basic philosophy is to try to leverage the Institute's funds for the maximum benefits of, we'll say, Mercy Hospital, Washington University Clinic, and St. Louis City Hospital. And so really, to help them with their programs; since these are known medical research centers, they attract other people and institutions that will support them.

In theory, I have a veto power over the grants that would be given to these institutions, but I've never exercised it. And, obviously I can't fund everything that they come up with, but I generally go along with them. Hopefully most of these institutions will present a balanced program. On the lecture side of funding, we underwrite the Ludlum House Forum, and I guess that tends to be a little bit on the liberal side, but they do balance it off pretty well. On that specific one, it's been suggested, and I'm going to go along this year, that a certain portion of their program be specifically underwritten by the Cooke Institute. So, I will know the speakers and the subjects ahead of time. Then the Chelsea Forum, which we underwrite along with a church group, I think that tends to be rather liberal too, but heavens, now I really don't want to get into censorship. As long as the lectures are good in quality and if they're well attended then I'm satisfied. I don't try to inject my own political philosophy at all. However, I think that it's a question of degree. If one institution is getting a little bit off the beam—that is, too far away from what I would consider to be reasonable, let me put it that way, I guess you'd say politically—I won't increase their funding from year to year and . . . that's easy to say. You just say, "The budget is full up this year" and so forth. I wish I could do more, because I think one of the things that makes it a fascinating job is to always be in a position where you can be doing something new. And if you're sewed into a, well, let's take the Republic Seminars in St. Louis, if you're sewed into those things then you don't have much choice year to year or many options on doing something new. Which I think you always should be able to.

Most of my arrangements with these institutions are renewable annually. Now, I have made a pledge of $25,000 a year for five years at the Botanical Gardens, so, they can put on some programs and give them a little lead time. And one of $50,000 a year at the St. Louis Planetarium to underwrite their computer program. They have a program down there which is de-signed to train teachers from the inner city on how to use computers and how to teach astronomy through computers in the classroom. That was my thought, that this is a way to reach an awful lot of people through the teachers. And, again, leveraging the funds to do this as best I could. That program is $50,000 a year for five years.

I think you want to stretch the dollar as far as you can. And I think you want to kill two birds with one stone, really. In providing for research and free public lectures, obviously I'm doing everything that's required of me under the terms of the original will. But, I also want to benefit the museums and the cultural institutions around town, social agencies around town; and if you can, by using this as seed money to attract other funds you're accomplishing a lot more than if you're just going off on your own so to speak.

Noblesse Oblige
"We tithe to charity ten percent of our income."

I think I inherited about $100,000 which as inherited wealth goes, is not very much. I inherited that from my grandmother because my father's firm went bankrupt in 1929, so from that point he was really starting from scratch. And when someone died, my wife inherited about the same amount of money on her side of the family. It's mostly what I've been able to make, but I don't aspire to wealth quite frankly, and if I had more money I'd give it away gladly because that's what I want to do. It probably sounds silly, but, well, it's my Christian belief, really. I believe that I was put on this earth to be useful and help other people. And once I've taken care of my life and my family, my efforts are always going to be for somebody else.

I have some deeply held religious convictions, and I think that I'm probably different from a lot of folks in that regard. My Catholic friends all go to church on Sundays. I never miss a Sunday, and I guess for a Protestant that makes me a little bit unusual. But my wife's the same way. Well, I was Presbyterian, she was a Methodist, and now we go to a sort of a community Congregational church. But, the church is a very, very important part of our life. And I think that, that makes a big, big difference in one's outlook. I mean, I'm trying to be a Christian and that takes a lot of doing and you have to work at it every day of the week. It really does. I think it puts a hell of a burden on somebody if you have a lot of money. What does the Bible say? How difficult is it for a rich man to go through the eye of a needle? Well, that's true. And, I must say, I look around at some of my wealthy friends and I see how they spend their money and how unhappy they are and so forth. And I just feel sorry for them, and I don't want any part of their kind of life. I really don't.

We lead a very modest existence. And we're not in the social whirl. And we love gardening and sailing and tennis and those simple little pleasures and that's about it.

We contribute ten percent to our church's budget, just automatically. Whatever the budget is we, my wife and I, contribute ten percent. And we really, I guess I should say, tithe to charity ten percent of our income. We must give to a hundred different organizations, on the order of $35,000. It's not all that much. Of course, if you're on the board of something— For instance, St. Louis University, having been a trustee, I contribute annually there and Grange College where I've been a trustee for a great many years. I have been giving to Mercy Hospital at which I've been president, I feel obligated to continue to do that, and the Museum of Fine Arts where I'm a trustee, the Museum of Science, the Botanical Gardens. I am not a musician so the Symphony's not one that— The Conservatory, I contribute to that. Well, and of course Washington U I contribute to. And the Buckingham School was founded by my wife's aunt, so, we contribute to the Buckingham School. Well, most of those charitable organizations are listed, and the Gaudette School for the Deaf and East St. Louis Mission House, those are just things that I've got some interest in. The Cancer Society and things that I have become interested in over the years. Not to say there aren't a great many other very, very worthwhile things. But when you get involved in managing and directing them, then you just feel that you've got to help them out.

Of course, from time to time certain things catch my eye. Project Love is something I've become interested in over the years. Very, very wonderful organization. I've always been interested in the Troeltsch Mission which helps people in the Ozarks. I worked for the mission a couple of summers in college, and I've been a director of the organization for a great many years. And I get down there every now and then. And those people are pretty destitute and Rev. Troeltsch established this around the turn of the century and he went into the Ozarks and started building hospitals and nursing stations, up and down the range, because there weren't any medical or social services available to the people. And he raised a lot of money in this country and interested a lot of people. And he interested my father among others. And interested me, and I served on the supply truck for a couple of summers. We were taking food and medical supplies around to the nursing stations and hospitals. And I've kept up an interest in that, all my life. I don't know, I guess it's just happenstance; you can't support everything that comes along. You try to do a little bit. My wife is a trustee of the Missouri Dental Clinic, and I've been president of Mercy Hospital. And I've been interested in and supported East St. Louis Mission House for a long, long time. That's a settlement house with a black clientele now. And I've found that a very, very rewarding experience and those folks certainly need all the help they can get. And the Cancer Society is something that I've become interested in, and, as I say, schools, colleges, hospitals.

I contribute time and money. You really can't separate the two. I've got more time to give than I have money, but when you get involved time-wise and you see the financial needs, then you just have to sort of, well, you just have to pinch a few pennies and give it. I think the largest donation I made was to the campaign for Washington University, that was ten thousand dollars a couple of years ago. That was a pledge. But it all adds up because, as I say, we must give to, gosh, almost a hundred different organizations. They probably think that I've inherited a lot of money and that I'm able to give a lot of money. But I'm not in that position, and so my contribution is mostly in time and whatever I can bring to help them run their affairs.

My guideline is ten percent of my income. In recent years I've been able to do that. Got the mortgage paid off and things of that nature. When the mortgage got paid off that was a big feature, psychologically. I mean, there was your house; you owned it; it's yours, you did it; the bank didn't own it. That was important. And then I think when the kids got through college, that was another milestone, and those things pretty much coincided.

More than Money
"I don't just put my name on something and that's the end of it."

I'm a very fortunate person because my wife looks at things the same way I do. I don't try to talk her into it. We don't aspire to great wealth. We just feel that we have a marvelous life, and we want to share it. And if we get more, we gamble and give more. 'Cause God knows there are an awful lot of deserving causes and people around the world. I see a good deal of this in the East St. Louis Mission House, where the folks are desperately poor and need a lot of help. You're trying to get some of them off welfare which means a daycare center for their kids so that they can go to work and you're trying to get people who are down on their luck off the booze and back onto a job. And that's right here in a disadvantaged neighborhood. Then, of course, I mean, we look at Africa and the drought over there and the horrible things that those people are having to endure. And you get an appeal from CARE and certainly you want to write them a check now and then. I'm impressed with CARE. They've been at it a long time. I'm very impressed with the Salvation Army. I've supported them for years. I think the dollar goes pretty far in that organization. There's not much overhead there. Those fellows are right out in the street helping people that need it. Some of these organizations have pretty high overhead but the Salvation Army has expendable wealth and I think they stretch the buck about as far as you can stretch it.

Of course I'm very proud of our hospital, Mercy Hospital, marvelous hospital, the safest place to have a baby, I guess, in the world. And I'm very proud of that. I've been a trustee of that institution for, oh, thirty years. And I was president and then chairman and then we merged with the Maxwell Center of Dodge Hospital. I'm proud of that. It plays a valuable role because bringing healthy babies into this world is a very worthwhile accomplishment. They set a standard. We actually get women dropped off on our doorstep, either they or their babies are in desperate straits but we don't turn anybody away. I contribute to the hospital, and that helps to cover some of the free care that they're providing. If we run the hospital the way we should and if we charge those people who can pay what they should, assuming we are not regulated, then I think there's ample room for providing a certain amount of free care. And really I suppose that's one of the reasons I've been involved with that hospital. I'm not particularly interested in helping wealthy people have their babies. I mean, I was born at home and a lot of people could be. It's the ones that need the special attention and care and so forth that we're trying to take care of.

Again, I don't have all that much money. I mean we have five children that we put through college. And what you have to earn before taxes in order to do that is a tidy piece of change. And now we have six grandchildren coming along and we've been picking up the bill for two of those, so that it's really endless. Actually, that means prep school, for them, because I think that's important. I went to public school, the first six years, and then some of my own kids went to public school the first few years. But, I think once the kids get into junior high and high school, private school education is superior. I hate to say that, because I've been chairman of our local school committee and I'm a firm believer in public schools. But it's been my observation that there's quite a divergence when you get up to that level.

I'll tell you honestly, and I don't mean to toot my own horn, but I don't associate myself with any organization to which I don't feel that I can make a contribution. And I do make a contribution. I don't just put my name on something and that's the end of it. If there are meetings you'll find me there. Believe me, you'll find me there and if I'm not at a meeting there's a damn good reason why I'm not. I really feel that I put a lot of time and effort into it and that's a contribution that I can make. I'm not the wealthiest guy in the world, but I like to think that I bring on a certain degree of common sense to these deliberations. I'm not a brilliant person, gosh, I just barely got through college. Fortunately some of my kids are smarter than I was. But I'm conscientious. And when I say I'll do something, I do it. And when I say I'll go on a board, I'll go to the meetings. I'll participate. And then, during the course of my forty years in business I've made a lot friends, I know a lot of people around town. I guess I know all the bank presidents, most of the insurance executives. And I don't know too many politicians, but that doesn't disappoint me much. I know all the college presidents because they're all trustees of KSTL. And so I just get asked to do things and I try to do them the best way I can.

The Heritage of Hard Work and Motivation
"That's where the Rockefellers come from."

There are poor people because they never have a chance. They are born into poverty. I'm a great believer in birth control and family planning and I think there are too many unfortunate kids born into poor families that never have a chance. They don't have the education, they don't have any skills. So they get frustrated. They drop out of school. They're on the street. They get into trouble. And the cycle just goes on and on and on. Why? Well, I guess the Bible says the poor are always with you and I'm afraid that's true. I don't see how we're going to eradicate that. And I don't think the government is going to be able to eradicate that no matter how much they extract from the wealthy people. It's an unsolvable problem as far as I'm concerned. But if I were to wave my magic wand I think I'd be inclined to do something like what they're attempting to do in China, and say, "Two or three kids, four max, is all you should have." And then I think that the families would at least be able to give them a little more by way of education and a little more tender loving care as individuals than they get now. I don't know. Lack of opportunity, I think that's partly it. Yet we've seen some perfectly fabulous success stories and then we see these Mexicans and Puerto Ricans and people from all over the world clamoring to get into this country. Working their tails off when they get here and getting up the economic scale. They can do it. I wish I could say there was room for everyone to make money, but I just don't know.

It's just my personal philosophy, but I think a man has a real responsibility to the community in which he lives. And as I've said, I've been chairman of the school committee and I've been on the city council, so that's the way I've tried to fulfill that responsibility. I can't see these people who go to work and then come home and shut the door and don't do anything in their community. Maybe I could have made a lot more money if I didn't put in all that time, I don't know, but I wouldn't be half as happy, I'll tell you that.

There are wealthy people because somewhere along the line somebody was motivated to work a little bit harder than the next guy. Either work a little bit harder or was a little smarter, invented something, had the greater incentive, and so was able to accumulate a little bit more than the next guy. So that's where the Rockefellers come from. Now, a lot of that wealth has been passed down through families and squandered. There is a lot of that and I think that is a disgrace really. 'Cause I don't think wealth should be allowed to perpetuate itself. I think we all should earn it ourselves. I think it's a disgrace that people who have a lot of wealth don't pull their weight in society, a disgrace. I think they should be utilizing their talents for the benefits of their fellow man, rather than running around on their yachts and so forth.

Is there a connection between the making of wealth and the creation of poverty? That is a theory. I guess the other side of that would be, if this guy hadn't worked his tail off and got up here, everybody would be down here. I believe in incentive and I believe in rewards very strongly. And I believe in our system very strongly. And I think the standard of living in this country, even among the poor, and even among those who are defined as below the poverty level, is so much better than almost any other country I can think of. I got to say it. I think this is the best system that's yet been devised. It certainly isn't perfect.

I definitely think the government has a role in alleviating social problems. I think a partnership between private and public is good. But I think the private sector and private philanthropy can manage things an awful lot better than the public sector seems to. I don't know why that should be. But I just have that feeling. And I also have the feeling that the further things get removed from the community, the more uncontrollable they become. I think it's sort of a question of neighbor helping neighbor. The neighborhood knows what goes on in the neighborhood, rather than a bureaucrat in government trying to tell you how things should be run.

I think the community sort of takes its lead from the St. Louis Foundation, which is far and away the largest pool of philanthropic funds. I think that's about a hundred and thirty million now. That is their capital. They're just giving away the income on that, in annual distributions. But they have a good staff and they research all of these requests very carefully. They do an excellent job. They know what they are doing; they have their finger on the pulse of who needs what. And they will concentrate on areas that they feel need the most attention—like the inner city recently. And they are trying to improve the school system in town and so forth. Besides two more large foundations, the banks and the insurance companies are very, very generous and they get into some very worthy endeavors as well—the kinds of things that really improve the quality of life in the city.

I guess the agenda in this community, among the wealthy, is to be useful; and I would hope, also, to stretch the philanthropic dollar just as far as you possibly can. And to leave some seed money for innovative approaches to get to the bottom of some of these intractable problems. What I do doesn't have anything to do with politics. I couldn't care less. I'm not a politician. Politics never really influences any of my charitable giving at all. I mean, you know, why was I on the board at Saint Louis University, why do I give to Saint Louis University? I'm a Protestant and a Washington U man. I just get wrapped up in it and I just love those people. The Jesuits are marvelous people. And so, I mean, hell, we're all members of the human race. And politics, I couldn't care less. And I think that would be an unfair characterization of the St. Louis philanthropic community to say that they care about politics. You ought to look at the board of directors of the St. Louis Foundation, and the boards of directors of these other foundations. I don't think those folks are seeking any power for themselves. I really honestly think that they're doing it altruistically, most of them, purely altruistically.

11

Camile Russo: "What It's Really Like to Be Born Rich"

Russo, twenty-six, articulates the advantages and difficulties of being born into wealth. She enjoys privilege but recounts such challenges as the pressures of working in her father's corporation, negotiating courtships with men, and carving an individual niche for herself.

"For my position now, I never had any public relations training . . . but I do well in my job because I'm very knowledgeable in the company and I have a practical sense." Unlike inherited women of the previous generation, Camile Russo is a wealthy young woman, who is given the opportunity and is expected to succeed in the family business. Though well educated, she emphasizes the value of her early exposure to business matters at the dinner table, and her learning on the job. For Camile, life is a series of challenges and she feels confident that she will always rise to the occasion. Referring to her siblings and a small circle of friends she says, "We were all leaders as kids growing up. . . . We're all very forward and do what it takes to get the job done."

Family is the source of Camile's psychological empowerment as well as worldly opportunities. The difference, in her case, is not that her family's company is the third largest in the teenager apparel industry—and growing—as much as that her parents taught all their eight children, boys and girls, about their business by allowing them to participate in creating wealth. "So, we don't have taboos about talking about money in the family, not too much." As a result, when discussing her parents' business and family values, she says, "I don't feel different from them at all." If anything, as director of public relations, she would like to seek more public recognition for her father's philanthropic generosity, something he is content to keep quiet about. To her, "It's a matter of taking a positive thing and making it more positive." It turns out that philanthropy is another occasion for her parents to provide freely the relevant attitudes and skills. Referring to her family's strong consensus about philanthropy, she says, "99 percent of the time ask any person in our family the same question, you'll get the same answer."

Despite all this involvement and training, she is not completely liberated from troubling questions. Unknown to her entrepreneurial parents, her concerns revolve around issues of autonomy and the expression of envy and resentment by her peers in business and social life. Thus, amidst a generally confident demeanor, Camile also recounts a saga of emotional confusion and pain, as she attempts to carve out her own direction amid the strong currents of familial, business, and social expectations. Ultimately, these are problems arising from identification with, not alienation from, the opportunities of wealth. "It's a pressure of wanting to be apart, yet wanting to contribute."

"I realize that all these things I've been given, some people work years for and still never get," says Camile, explaining how the excitement of having opportunities and responding to such a challenge is tempered by feelings of guilt and a sense of obligation. "If I don't succeed, I'm a fool. How can I fail? I have to succeed." In a manner characteristic of many inherited wealthy, Camile meets these "inside pressures to succeed" with hard work and perseverance. However, the process of "paying back" for what she received is also the process of building an independent moral identity. She insists on clear boundaries between family and business relations. For instance, when her mother calls on a Sunday morning about business, she angrily responds, "I work nine to five," refusing to carry business in off-hours. Typically, she confronts these pressures with determination to succeed on her own, personally and professionally. "One day I'm going to write a book and call it 'What It's Really Like to Be Born Rich'—a book whose chapters will recount the personal dilemmas of a wealthy young woman and her efforts to overcome them." She is also determined to pursue her own lights: "There is something inside me that I want to do. In about five years, I'm probably going to be a teacher."

These dilemmas of wealth follow her into her workplace. "I take unnecessary abuse because of where I'm working, because of who I am." As a young, female executive in the family-owned corporation, Camile's competence and ambition collide with her peers' and subordinates' resentments about her status. Though she feels unprepared by her parents to face such prejudice, she refrains from blaming them. They are after all "post-Depression babies" who could not anticipate the professional and social challenges facing their offspring. The difference is that "[my father] didn't grow up wealthy, we did. We didn't grow up poor, he did." Besides the work problems, she is constantly perplexed by the problem of having to find friends and a potential mate who are neither put off nor enticed by her wealth. As she says, "Most men are blown away by my name: what it means, the status, the privileges, and the way other people treat me." To deal with these problems, Camile adopts a patient strategy. She says, at work, "I look at prejudice as an advantage," while in her social life she sometimesrefuses to tell potential suitors her true name, "to see if they like me for me."

True to her insight that guilt and self-doubt will subside "after you prove yourself in the marketplace," Camile's identity is changing. "Little by little I'm getting better," she says, referring to becoming more comfortable with her destiny. In the meantime, while she awaits her inheritance, she exercises financial responsibility by meeting payments for her apartment and her credit cards. Thus, at age twenty-six, Camile has come a long way, but realizes there are more transitions ahead. "I hope I'll be financially secure in five years, because I feel in five years I'll be married. . . . I also think my life will be less confused and more directed. I'll see a very good direction."

BIOGRAPHICAL NARRATIVE

Early Lessons
"Growing up in a family business."

I was born in St. Louis. I grew up in Parkton, then we moved to Gray Woods. I went to high school at Kingsley. Then I went to college at the University of Missouri in Columbia, graduated from U of M in 1983. I'm still connected with Kingsley now. I'm an alumna and we do a lot of work for them through Next Generation. We participate in their programs. For example, my family is responsible for the football field. They were the major contributors for that as well as other things that happen in Kingsley that we support. In terms of my family I'm child number four. Out of eight, I'm daughter number two. I'm 25, I'll be 26 in another month. I don't live at home now, but I'm not married.

In college I majored in, it was a general studies degree and my concentrations were in political science and history. I started out in business, but one of the reasons I didn't continue in business was that my Mom and I argued with the professors. That's really the truth. I had a tough time in business, accepting what I was being taught, accepting certain things as rules. A good example is in marketing class. One of the professors tells how important it is that we memorize marketing terms because in the real world that is how it works. I was working full-time the last two years of college, or year and a half. I was in charge of Kids Stuff. We had 10, we had 12 at the time, we were franchising and I was responsible for all the marketing. So I was working when we were opening new stores and finishing college at the same time. Prior to that, I worked every summer since I was ten years old. I knew the business quite well. I had a hard time at school studying and learning things there. I just, I didn't agree with the institutionalized teaching. Then I transferred from Columbia to Bryar Academy, which is a free enterprise business school which I liked a lot. They had practical professors, who had worked in the field, teaching the class. So for instance, I took an advertising class and my professor came from PepsiCo. So they were very practical and taught street sense as opposed to big business theory.

From there, I then came home for the summer. My father told me about Kids Stuff, an opening there, so I picked up and started doing it. And I didn't want to stop. Kids Stuff is, well, the corporate company has since gone bankrupt, but it was founded by Eric Efstratios. And it was built up. And the headquarters are in New York. So we became franchisees. We weren't the franchisers. Next Generation is a franchiser. So it was like a little security. So I did that, and I finished up my degree at the University of Missouri—in St. Louis. When I came back from Bryar, I got two associate degrees—one in banking and finance and one in accounting. I had no problem with business classes there. When I came back to Missouri, I didn't particularly care for Columbia, I didn't agree with them about their curve. They marked on the curve. I had like a 97 percent in a calculus class and that was a B+ on the curve. I'd have a 3.3 in economics and it would be a C on the curve. So I had a really difficult time. The logic was that when you get in the real world it's very competitive. Well, I didn't agree with that. So anyway, when I came back to U of M—in St. Louis it was a lot different. I finished up my degree here, and decided to stay away from business courses, because I had such a problem. So I took things to make me more well rounded. History I wanted to learn. It was actually nicer. I liked it a lot better.

Looking back, there is definitely a more important turning point, in my life, than my experience at Bryar—growing up in a family business. I think my father's the type of person that never demanded anything. He never asked us to work for him, he never expected us to work for him, although we all do. I think as a young person growing up, just dinner talk and being around the family business, being around people who are very high achievers, something is instilled in you that thinking skills become very practical. And I find myself today, I'm in a position, for instance my position now, I never had any public relations training, I never took one writing class, I've never taken any communications, but I do well in my job because I'm very knowledgeable in the company and I have practical sense. So I'm a good director, but I wouldn't be a good specialist in a field. I'd be much better on a broader scale. Some decisions I make, I don't know where I've even heard it sometimes before, but just subconsciously, growing up, there are just certain things I know about our business that would take years to learn, just from the nature of being around.

I am now the Director of Corporate Communications. Basically, I handle all the media. We do all the news releases. We do all the major promotions, the charity work. For instance, our one time event, we work with the Red Cross, and do the telethons and do runs and we're doing the US Open, all types of things like that. And then there's another division which is a publications division which handles all corporate correspondence. We put out a monthly newsletter, and a couple of other publications that we write. Another part of our department is a consumer information center, which works if customers complain.

What Her Parents Could Not Teach Her
"I don't think they raised us understanding . . . how wealthy we are (and) what does it mean."

I first realized that I was wealthy, I guess, when I was young. I guess from being in private school. I was placed in a private school at age, well, second grade. And I think at that point I saw the difference. I think that's when I realized it. I had no idea where the family came from. We never talked about it at home. It never was an issue, it never mattered. I think that's the first time I ever heard a figure or a fact on our company. And I remember my brother and I both looked at each other like, oh my goodness, John, let's go ask for a raise on our allowance now! It was never an issue. We never talked about how much. At school, you know, kids would talk about it, looking at clothes and . . . but it never really was an issue.

Well, I think I went to high school with very spoiled children. With the exception of public school in between my two private schools, but even at the public school that was an occasional issue. Yet, I considered it a fortunate opportunity to be taken out of my Utopia. Because my brothers were in basketball and traveled to all kinds of suburbs of St. Louis playing. And I would meet friends from that area, and I would go out with them, people like that. And to this day, the guys that I date are very nonclassified. They weren't even classified as "not wealthy." And I think I've had a good mix. A lot of the kids that I went to school with never have seen that. They were very, very sheltered. They were very much into status, they were very much into how wealthy they were. I find a large percentage of wealthy people born into wealth, inherited wealth . . . there's definitely a difference.

There's for sure a difference between second and third generation wealth. No question. My father, I have direct contact with his being poor, being born very poor and now being very rich. I can feel that. He can touch me with that. One of my best friends is third-generation, and is so far removed from that. She's so much more into status, and I don't mean to speak negatively, not that it makes her any less of a person. I think it's just a matter of how you gear yourself. That and how you are raised, as far as how humble you are. My father and mother are very, very humble. You'll never hear them talk about themselves. They're just real low-key. They never forget where they've come from. They always remind us. They always tell us, "Don't ever brag. We could be broken up." I think they raised us with really important values.

But at the same time, I don't think they raised us understanding enough about wealth, as far as how wealthy we are, what does it mean. My father didn't prepare me for what I'm seeing now in the business world or in my social life. Wealth doesn't matter when you're in school. You are kind of on allowance, and Daddy owns, or whatever. But when you become an adult working in a business, it's real life almost and you're planning your future. You're making friends, definitely people will be your friends and hang around you because your father's wealthy, whether they want, for whatever reason, they like to be near you. You're a celebrity in the sense that they like to be close to you, they like your opinion, they like favors, they like to get you to do things for them. I think it's human nature but I didn't realize how extensive it is.

When I say he didn't prepare me for being wealthy, I must say I don't know how he could have prepared me. I don't know the answer to that, I guess. I don't know and I know he doesn't know. It's very difficult for him to even train us in the business, because he's never done it before. He didn't grow. There's one thing he can't understand and we [kids] can't understand. And we butt heads on it sometimes, and that is he didn't grow up wealthy, we did. We didn't grow up poor, he did. So there's always that fine line of, "We don't always quite understand." We don't have that value for a dollar like he wants us to have. His position is, his philosophy is provide for people a good product. Try and give them the best value you can, instead of charging a lot for the product and making the most money. If you have the best product, then you have the best value for it. And you develop loyalty that way. I might go out and spend 40 bucks and think no big deal, where he's more sensitive to what that 40 dollars represents even though he has a lot. So what's a lot of money to me, and what's a lot of money to him, that's two different things. And he's not, my mother's the one who really watches the books and stuff. So she's really, she'll go out and she does some pretty nutty things. Like she'll go spend x amount on one thing and then she'll say, "Well, I'm not going to spend 20 bucks for a pair of sunglasses." They're in that era. They're after-Depression babies, you know, so, really Depression babies. So they really felt that. And they remember, and that becomes apparent.

I've thought a lot about this, because it's a concern of mine at especially this time in my life. It's probably one of the most critical, from the standpoint of I'm not, I always say this, it's really terrible, but I consider myself a middle-class person. I was raised as a middle-class person in a rich world. My values, my thinking, my personality, my friends, everything around me is very middle-class, but I was raised in a society of wealth. I'm used to having lots of nice things around me. But I wasn't raised with the more negative things that go with it, as were many of my friends, more than many, it's amazing to me to this day. You watch people and their careers, and you see money change them. And I always laugh, and think, well, at least I don't have to worry about that. I was born with it, so I'm already changed.

Money changes them—your usual standard stereotypes. "I'm better than you because I have a nicer car. I can't talk to you because you're not at this country club." Very snobby. Very yuppie. You know there are a lot of people like that, very many people. But what's interesting is, I think the really, really successful ones, the owners, the chairmen of the board, top vice presidents are very, very humble as people. So I think when the kids grow up it's interesting for me to see where they're at in their careers. In ten years, it'll be real interesting to see if their logic in school works in business. If they can be bratty in business and get what they want, like they were in school. My guess is no. Especially when you work for the family business. Employees will do what you say because you're the boss and you're a family member, but they won't stay very long no matter how great it is because I think you need to be a nice person.

People told me as a youngster, "It matters, your social background matters. It matters how you were raised. It matters what community you're from. Were you raised rich, were you raised poor? Were you raised ethnic?" Whatever. It does matter. I disputed that for a long, long time. "No, it doesn't matter. Look at my friends. No, it doesn't matter, it doesn't matter." I'm back to my original . . . they were right, it *does* matter. It matters very much. Not to me, so much. But it matters to the perception of people like me. And I found, for most people, their income and smarts, success and ambition go hand-in-hand. The smart people make money. Business people do well and make money for it. So, there is a correlation and it does matter. I never used to believe that.

The Book I Will Write
"What It's Really Like to Be Born Rich."

I consider myself independent of and dependent on my family. Independent in that I physically live away from them. Very dependent in that they still determine my destiny. I think many, many people, many kids that I grew up with, all of whom were wealthy, all the car people, went to school with all of them, and I think for the most part it's probably one of the most difficult things. If someone were to ask me what's it like to work for a family business. It's not that it's, there are so many, so many positives, but there are an awful lot of negatives. One day I'm going to write a book and call it "What It's Really Like to Be Born Rich." You hear about it and you read about it, but it really puts an unnecessary pressure on you to either over-achieve or achieve the level of your parents, really impossible in my case. Yet, you feel that inner-family pressure. It's not a pressure that comes from my parents because they're very easygoing. It's a pressure of wanting to be apart, yet wanting to contribute. Almost a guilt of, I've been given all of these things in my life, and when I'm an adult I realize that all these things I've been given, some people work years for and still never get. I can spend the same amount of money that people spend on a family of four in two months and it would be commonplace for me, and I know I'm no better.

So, I think dependency is very difficult as far as making a decision in your life. Yes, I want to help and work in the family business, but no, I don't want to be your little girl forever! No, I don't want you to control all my trust funds. I don't want you to have control of my checkbook. I need to have my own. I need to establish my own finances, by myself, independent, by myself. Founded on the fruits of my labor because I was born a leader type, very energetic and very ambitious. I'll never be satisfied with my salary. So if I didn't work here, in the family business, I know I would work somewhere else, owning my own business or working to achieve a very high level. And I think it's very, very difficult to break those ties. Because my parents as employers have a very difficult time forgetting that I'm their daughter, me as an employee, can use that to my advantage on Sunday afternoons to get business questions answered. I don't think that's always the healthiest way. And in a lot of cases, I find with my friends as well, not really being able to control your own life, both monetarily and in learning to cope.

When it comes down to it, things can be colder at home. And I think that's an insecurity. That is, if I get mad at you because you borrowed my car without asking, I'm not going to meet with you on business the next day. It's like the reward system when you were a kid. If you're good you get this, if you're bad you get this. But now you're an adult and it affects your career and it affects everything around you. It's a lot more difficult to handle when you're an adult than when you're a child. "You were late to school today, so I don't think you can go out tonight." You're relating school to fun activities. In business, you did something, you borrowed my whatever without asking, so I'm going to be mad at you at work. I'm still mad at you when I get to work. This is all siblings, this isn't just parents, it's all siblings and the whole bit. Just in general terms, you are different as an employee, you know that. You have to know that.

This leads up to my family, as far as working together. I think it's very important that the same rules apply with coworkers as they do with family members. You have to respect them. You have to never deface them in public, or in front of everyone. Or ever tell them they're wrong, or ever embarrass them. Especially so with family members. I feel that it's true in general, no matter who the other person is. But it becomes a very sensitive issue. You must always try to separate that you're my sister and my coworker. It's very difficult. I think that one thing that helps is that each child has his or her own area of expertise, own department, own area of business. Although we intermingle, we don't overlap in decision-making. If you don't have respect for your sister or brother, then you'll never be able to work with them, never, it won't work. My sister and I, you know, we're always asking each other's opinions. At the present, there are four of us kids in the business.

The fact that there are so many of us in the business makes me particularly sensitive to relationships. And also you can't have friends at work. You can't. I can't. I could, I wouldn't. I can't really explain it, it's from a lot of things. Because they don't want you there, they don't want you over them. I'm very perceptive. Also there are only certain places I can go socially. My father's very well-known in this city. There are very few places I can go. And if I do anything, I have to say to myself, Would it be okay in the headlines? If I go to a party or if I go to a bar or if I go wherever, I have to be very sensible. What am I doing? Did I have too much to drink? What time is it? You know, it's a very, very protective . . . paranoia almost. I think there is a point where you refuse to succumb to a lot of it, but you have to, you know, if you believe in a certain goal and that's to be respected, then. . . .

When I first started I was twenty-two. And I still am really young in the business world. I was in Kids Stuff when it wasn't really a company yet. I pretty much was in charge of it, and I had no background, so my dad always said he was crazy. Nobody would do that, but I learned so much by that. I think at first I used to feel guilty for what my father had and for what he stood for, and how was I ever going to make myself worthy of this position he had placed me in. And when I see others having to work their way up. Then I learned, I think, the reality of meeting people, and it's not really the background as much as how you perform. And I became confident in my skill, and saw it wasn't that difficult. It's just basic common sense mostly and also that my father worked very, very hard to get where he is. And my family worked very hard. So, I think those feelings go away after you prove yourself in the marketplace.

The Pressure to Succeed
"I started to realize what a head start I had on life."

I think the biggest chapter in my book would be "Fallacies: The Wrongs and Perceptions about Rich Kids." Rich kids are perceived as spoiled. Spoiled is the biggest one. Not nice, very terrified that you're not nicer. Everything's handed to you. You don't work. Laziness. You only got the job because your dad owns the business. I always say, "True." Those are the biggest ones I think. Just the perception that you don't work. But the opposite can be a problem too. Why are you working? You're so rich, you don't have to. Why don't you just stay home? Why do you work? You have so much money, you don't even have to work. Why do you work so hard? You have enough money. Why do you need to work? Lot of people *need* to work for money. Those perceptions. People have said these things to me. Friends. People I meet in general. Even business people have said it to me. People are very envious, very jealous of wealth. It's what everybody strives for. The dynasties, and that definitely makes it worse. It's a measure of success in our society, in all societies. It started with the kings and queens. If you were a king, there were only two types of people, kings and peasants. You were either in royalty or you're a peasant. You're either rich or poor. I think it started way, way back then, when wealthy people became established. The sad part is, it's mostly true. I think the stereotypes are very much true. And I think, what is it, 2, 3 percent of our population is considered very wealthy. Probably over half the people who fall into that category live up to their stereotypes at least initially. I think they are humble when they grow up because people don't put up with it.

I don't like the way spoiled people act. I just don't believe in this way of doing anything. I believe in asking people, "What is your opinion? Would you object to this?" don't believe in "Do this, do that!" don't like people who are pushy, who demand things because they are of a certain economic status, or in a certain position. Maybe that's why I always like being kind of my own boss. I have to have a lot of leeway in my job because of that. Just in general, I never appreciated it when I was young going out with my friends, I don't appreciate it now. I use my name to my advantage when I need it, when I really need it, because I know it will work. But nine times out of ten, I don't at all. I don't rely on my name. However, I think I am spoiled in a lot of respects. I think I am some of those stereotypes. I think one of the areas is . . . I determined in my life that I can't live under a certain economic level. I could, but I wouldn't choose to. I always hold to that. Give me a dollar, put me in a merger account. I believe I'm a survivor, but I also am not going to sacrifice. Because I'm going to be successful, and income goes along with that, I want the same things I was used to when I was younger. I'm starting to try to learn. I'm not doing too well but that's another thing I'm having a hard time with. What's a lot of money? You know, a salary, a year. You know, you break down how much. I never had to pay bills before. I never knew how much they were.

I think what else I would have in the book would be, "The Pressure to Succeed." Something to the effect of, you have no choice but to conform to something inside you, that you just have to achieve a certain level, inside and outside. One chapter would be on the outside. One chapter would be on the inside. From your peers you are looked at as a loser, as non-successful if you don't have a career like a lawyer or a doctor or a whatever of the status that you were born into. So, I think I would talk about that. I would talk about the family problems, working with your brothers and sisters, mother and father. How to overcome those difficulties. And then, I would talk especially about women, wealthy women and how you date. How difficult it is to date normal guys with a normal job, it's very difficult. As a wealthy son, it's easier. There are all kinds of great deals. But as a woman, it's very much different, both in your business and social life. So, I would bring a being-a-woman aspect into it, and then being young.

"The Pressure to Succeed." That's a big one. Again, I don't think it's the family pressure, although it is, because you strive. You want to make your family proud. How do you do that? Well, yes, you can pick any occupation you want. You feel comfortable with it when those around you are working in the business, getting their own stores, doing all kinds of things. I think there's this inner pressure that makes you want to, my parents never say it, but there's something inside of one that always says, You're going to disappoint them if you don't do this, if you're the director of the department and don't make it the best. You're going to disappoint them if you don't get your own business. Although it was never said, it was something I always felt obligated to do. Because of all these things I had watched. I felt like it was time for me to pay back what I'd been given. And only did I start to feel that when I started to realize really how fortunate, and what a head start I had on life because I was born wealthy. It was such a head start. For instance, many people I meet, in fact my boyfriend now, given my position, born into my family, and having private schooling, which I highly believe in, he would be in a completely different life, completely different career, completely different mental attitude, completely different situation. You can study all the facts and figures, the wealthier the family, the smarter the kids. That's just the way it is. Scholastically, but not street sense, not street smart.

I look back to the opportunities that I was given and I say, Geez, I was so fortunate to have all these opportunities. If I don't succeed, I'm a fool. How can I fail? I have to succeed. I've been given all these wonderful things. Can't go and be a, which I'm going to do, one of the things I want to be in my life is, junior high school teacher. But I can't go and do that, I was raised in this family, I went to these fine schools. I really should be a. . . . Really there is a pressure that I feel. Luckily I have an ambition that goes hand-in-hand with that. I want, there is something inside me that I want to do. I'm probably going to be a teacher. I hope to do both. And I'll probably start graduate school next year. I want to get a graduate degree and a teaching certificate.

So, the "inside pressures" are—we were all such high achievers. We were all leaders as kids growing up. You know, your little group you hang out with, we were all very, very social, lots of parties, lots of friends, very outgoing, because we strive for the same things. We all have to be our own bosses because we have a difficult time holding back. We're all very forward and do what it takes to get the job done. If we were in a structured situation, where someone said, this is all you can do today, here's your job, perform these duties, and then come to me when you need more, we'd go nuts. We're self-starters. It's in us and I think it's in us from our parents. And also, your brothers and sisters, just like, you could never be in a bad mood around them. If you were in a bad mood, your brothers and sisters bothered you so much, you had to get out of your bad mood into a good mood because you couldn't take them giving you a hard time. The same way when you grow up. They could say, "Why are you always doing this? Why aren't you getting A's in school when you know you could be?"

The "outside pressures" are again those pressures of others perceiving you as, "You're Mario's daughter, o! my God!" Right away there's an image marked down. I have people, who have been in this business 20, 30 years, who are experts in their field, nervous, I made them nervous when I was 10 years old and walking by people's doors. It's their perceptions and they result in pressure when they say things like, Why aren't you wearing the most expensive dress to this party? How come your jewelry doesn't reflect your wealth? Why are you dating a guy that makes $18,000 a year? Why are you only manager of a store? Why aren't you vice president yet? All of these things, all of these perceptions, all of them. I find myself very bitter at times. It gets better as I get older. But I get very angry sometimes at people because of that. I don't think it's fair. I don't think a lot of it's fair; I take unnecessary abuse because of where I'm working, because of who I am. It's all related to dollars. How much do you make a year. You just have to make a lot of money. Where do you live. But on the other hand, it's also not very fair to take advantage of it, so it really balances itself out. As mad as I can get, as happy as I can get. But I think it's very difficult to overcome those perceptions. For me, it is. My friends, some of them could care less. They say, "You don't like it, fine."

Sometimes, I just look at myself and I say, why can't I be normal? By normal, I mean normal in my situation in how I was raised. Low on money. I'm way on the side. My sisters are a little different than me. I'm way the other way. I'm trying to learn. As far as things I attend, little by little I'm getting better. I was very much a tomboy when I was young. Like I said, I didn't hang around very many rich kids. I'm getting better because professionally I think it's important. In my career, I've seen it's very important that I present myself to achieve the things I want to achieve. How to dress for success. Many vice presidents, many people all agree. Your parents have a lot to do with it. Not only of others' perceptions, but of making yourself feel better. And I do feel better, no question about it. I'll find a happy medium. I don't think I'll ever be one way. I don't think I'll ever be real snotty, uppity or whatever.

Dilemmas of Wealth and Gender
"Most men are blown away by my name: what it means, the status, the privileges, the way other people treat me."

I think, there's a book I read, it's a very good book, written by men. I's called "Smart Women, Foolish Choices." It has a chapter in there on marrying up and marrying down. And I, again, that's another one of my pet peeves, especially at my age now. Probably the biggest problem, I think, is going out with a fairly wealthy woman who's smart, it's very, very intimidating. You know, I'm reading about women and changing society, but I don't believe it. It's not really changing as quickly as one thinks. Do a survey and ask people, versus what the trends are. Most men will still answer, most men, the majority of men, I feel, still want a woman that's subordinate. Even though they want her to work and have her own career. They don't want her to be smarter. They don't want her to be richer. They want her at home. They want her to know how to take care of the kids. I think that tradition in families still exists very much. I think just because women are working doesn't make things different. And I think the percentage of change would be very, very small. Wealthy and smart women, again smart usually goes hand in hand with wealthy. Now put another thing there, "Born Wealthy, and Succeeding Father." For my husband to look at my father and say, "I could never outdo him, I could never do better."

Most people are blown away. Most men are blown away by my name: what it means, the status, the privileges, the way other people treat me. They say, "No way could I ever keep up." But I'm not tempted to become a dumb blonde! What I do a lot though, is I don't tell people who I am. I don't talk about my job. I don't initially. I do a lot of that, to see if they like me for me. That works pretty well. But I never, never act dumb—because the older I get, the less patience I have for dumb people. My new joke is, "education is for grown-ups," but I don't like that too much. I just tend to really, really downplay my position. I don't tell you my last name. Sometimes, my girlfriends and I switch names. Like we'll go to a bar and switch names, but that's fun. In business I always use my last name.

My boyfriends are crazy. I take 'em to this dinner. He's all nerves, he's acting really strange, like how do I act and how do I sit at the table? Didn't quite know how, he didn't feel comfortable. I could tell that. He wasn't with, he was just with people of course. But he knew that these were people that were more successful than he and he was with me, and it was really uncomfortable for him. The whole bit, you know. So we were sitting there and I noticed that and I talk to him and I say, "Why are you nervous?" "No, no, I'm not nervous." He's all worried about what forks he uses. So without anyone looking I was . . . , "Why did you do that?" "I got to show you that you don't have to be prim and proper. Just be yourself and you'll be fine." And after that he was. My message to him was, "They all put on this act for you in front of other people."

The difference from the way my brothers' experience this is . . . and it's so funny because my dad now always says, "Don't overlook your girls." My sister and I are here, and my brothers live out in Miami, and they run stores out there. But my sister and I are really involved. It's just the old stereotype: men are supposed to be better, they're supposed to be smarter, they're supposed to be richer. Their problem is different. Even though I hear that guys will marry women for money, I don't think quite as much as vice versa. I think guys have a little more pride, in general. Yeah, there's always the gigolos and others, but I think, in general, it's pretty tough to find someone who really thinks they're going to marry me for my money, because I'm a woman. On the other hand, my brothers, definitely, many, many women look at them for that reason. No question.

So, it's not as complex from the standpoint of finding a true love mate. It's a different problem. My problem is, how do you keep them? They get scared of me and go away. You have to be a very, very strong individual to go out with me. Very strong. You have to be self-confident, and take a lot of abuse. People do, they say some nasty things. "Well, we know you're going out with her because. . . . Will you do this for me because she's your girlfriend?" You know, a lot of social pressures. Most of them are my age and I think a lot of them are self-confident and that's what boils down to: how confident are you? It's very difficult to be a judge of character in this situation. My sister says, "The reason I married my husband is because he was the first guy I ever met of all the guys I dated who could handle my name." That's a large part of it.

At work, I had many terrible incidents when I first started working. Being female and being young, people would perceive me differently. And I really learned the trick of the trade, what I do now is I respond to individuals the way they respond to me. I walk into a meeting, and I can tell they're looking at me like I'm young and innocent and whatever. That's okay, I'll play a young and innocent part. I always try to be aware of how I'm being perceived so that I can adjust my personality accordingly. What matters is to be businesslike regardless of what they think of me as a person. I always try to be nice. I always try to be fair. And usually it works out. I think that goes away when you start gaining their respect as an individual or as a family member. People in general are not nice. They can be real mean. That's always going to be there. You know, the politics of "I'm not going to like you because you're a family member, whether you're nice or not." So that exists, no question about it, but I think I'm in control of how bad or good it is.

I think as a woman, you have to be able to handle the prejudice. It bothers a lot of women, though. Boy, they hate it, like my sister, she'd answer the phone and they'd say, "You're the attorney?" Or, "We'd like to talk to the attorney, not the secretary." Things like that, really bother her. They don't bother me at all. Or people want to talk to my brother before me. Or they assume I'm not smart. They assume I don't know as much. They assume they don't have to treat me a certain way because I'm a woman. That's bad. But I look at it as an advantage. I think, again, Look at me how you will, you can perceive me how you will, and I'll adjust accordingly so that we can get our business done. It doesn't bother me at all. Being a woman in business doesn't affect me because I never pay attention to that. Only if they use it against me. But I've never had that, only once a reporter said that if I went to this party, "I'm going to write a bad article." And I obviously didn't go to the party. But that was really bad. So a lot of women have dealt with it.

Another aspect is being young. They look at that in two ways. They either trust me immediately because I'm young, or they think I'm stupid because I don't have experience. It's a matter of perception. Being young to some means energy and trustworthiness to them. "You can trust her." To other people, most of the time, I even have trouble with people that work under me. Lot of problems, as a matter of fact. At first, not respecting me because of my age. Or thinking they were smarter because they had been in the business for twenty years, and I had only been there for two. But there are ways to get at that, I do things to reverse that. It doesn't bother me too much, but I feel it's there. I'll do something like, for instance if someone's working for me, trying to establish, let's say, a radio station, I'll come up with a comment like, "Oh, by the way, why don't I call so-and-so?" "How do you know so-and-so? I thought I knew everyone." You know, little things letting them know that I'm the director for the reason I am qualified. In little ways, as opposed to saying, "You have to respect me. Age doesn't matter." Never say that. It usually goes away the first five minutes if I say the right thing appropriately.

Wealth and the Meaning of Life
"Financially, I feel secure and not secure at the same time."

There are different kinds of wealthy people. There are very wealthy, real wealthy, and those who think they're wealthy. The very wealthy people don't have time to tell people how wealthy they are because they're too busy working, getting wealthier. The ones who think they're wealthy are the ones who haven't quite made the level that they want although they're comfortable. Their kids still debate with the kids down the block who has this and that, living like the Joneses. And then there are those who, I know this is going to sound real strange, but I really believe there are many people, who are living in our society, that are very happy the way they are. Very happy in their life because they have very happy family lives. They're very, very content with themselves. They have a wife or husband that they love. Children that they love. They are doing enough in their life to make them happy. Then I think there are those who are never going to be happy, never have enough.

Financially, I feel secure and not secure at the same time. I feel secure from the standpoint of inheritance. When my parents die, I know I will have a lot of money. But I also don't feel secure because I don't have control of my money; a trust is there, but I don't have control of it. I don't know much about my finances. And my salary, no, I'm not making enough to be where

I want to be. I don't consider myself to be financially secure on my salary. I discuss this with my father. Everybody does everything differently. I have no complaint at all. I know we have a lot of money. I know I can have it any time and if I wanted to do an endeavor I know that I can. But I can't independently run my lifestyle on a lot of money, right now. I hope I'll be financially secure in five years, because I feel in five years I'll be married. Marriage brings about a certain set of, for me, I think it will make me more serious about life. Not that I'm not serious, but I'll have achieved my short-term goal, I'll be vice-president, and I think I'll be making good money. What I consider a real good salary, though, keeps changing. The older I get, it keeps getting higher. Probably anywhere from $60,000 to $100,000 a year. I also think my life will be less confused and more directed. I'll see a very good direction.

As far as my personal expenses, I think the first most important thing to me is to establish my own personal credit, and to own something. I have a company car. I don't own one. So I bought a condo. So that was really important to me. Credit cards. Again, establishing credit is very important. On my own. I don't spend my money on too many things. I spend it mostly on the condo, payments, bills, living bills. Clothes are a big one. Dinners, that's a big one. I go out to eat a lot. And things for my condo, furniture, the kitchen, I like to cook. I don't really have any major things. I have a really pretty simple life as far as what I spend money on. I don't want to spend a lot. I spent more when I was a kid. I think it's just because of my lifestyle. I work. What I do, I travel sometimes. I spend money on trips. But I don't really have, I live a single life. I don't really have a lot of things that I'm too concerned with.

I'm saving but I'm also not saving [laughter]. I'm saving in the sense that I have a balance I always want to maintain in my savings account. I want to make sure it never gets below that. I'm a big one on "Don't ever have more debt than you have in the bank!" Don't like that. It makes me nervous. But I don't really save, and that makes me feel like a spoiled brat. If I try really hard I might be able to save five grand a year, you know. And I look at that amount of money and I say, So what? So that's really spoiled but it's true. I need to have a purpose for saving. That's why I say marriage will give me that purpose for saving, or more so. If I really wanted something, which I don't, I'm not very materialistic at all. I don't see things and have to have them. I do in business, but not in private. There's nothing in life I want, I can tell you honestly. If there were, like if I wanted a fur coat or something, if I wanted a boat, I would save for it. I'm talking about big ticket items. Most anything I want I can buy. I can't go and buy a diamond ring for $15,000. But I don't want that. So there's nothing really I want.

Directing the Company's Charity
"Me, being promotion-minded, I'm going to make sure that Next Generation's name is in the credits."

I handle all the charitable giving by our company. The percentages probably range from one to ten percent. In actual dollars it is close to a million that we give away. We handle that per request. We get probably a hundred calls a week wanting something. Money, usually money. We evaluate it according to our demographics and our target markets. Our favorite projects involve kids in sports. We give mostly to sports and kids. We try not to play favorites with the big time organizations: Red Cross, American Cancer Society. We try and spread that out. Personal friends working on projects. Mayors working on projects. People that we deal with in the business. Business associates working on projects. There are a lot of different criteria we have. It's fun, I love it. But, for the time being, they are more in my head. They will be written. We're just not organized enough. My father taught them to me. I have a staff that implements it, but I make all the decisions. Sometimes I'll ask my father or my sister, I'll say, "I'm not sure on this one." And they may say, "Oh, go ahead."

I don't think my philosophy differs a whole lot from my father's, because his values are instilled in his corporate values. Our corporate philosophy is really founded, strongly founded, and we're really committed to them. So, as a seller of a company especially, I think my philosophy is the same. The only difference is I think I'm a little tougher than my father. Seeing people take advantage of him and seeing some of the unfortunate experiences he's been through, I think I'm tougher. I don't think I'm quite as nice. He's really nice. He's helped many, many people in his lifetime. I do the same. I'm nice, but I'm a little more cautious than he, I think. I'm a little more outspoken. I will tell someone if I think they are trying to use us, way before he would. He would just never do that. So, I think a little bit that way maybe our personalities are different. I'm a little more protective of the company than he is, because I want to secure our whole . . . I feel very, very strongly about making our company bigger and better. The day that we can watch them retire will be the happiest day of our lives because we've seen them work 16 to 18 hours a day for 20-some years. We've seen it and we've lived with it. I think that if someone were to ask me what's my goal in life, that would be it. I don't have any career goals. If someone says to me, What do you want to do in five years? I skip jobs. I've done everything. I've worked in a store. I've traveled. I've been in many departments in our company. I learn about wherever I'm needed; I don't have a normal career goal. So, if I have to answer that question I'd say it's to watch our company grow successfully, and to see my mother and father retire.

I don't feel different from them at all. I think it's extremely important that you take very much notice of the customer and treat your employees very well, that you are nice to them. That I agree with. The parts I don't agree with are the people who misjudge my father and expect certain things. I expect you to donate $5,000 to my group. I expect you to do this. I expect you to have a difficult time saying no. *Never* has he asked for anything in return. He never does. Me being promotion-minded, I'll say, "Okay, we'd love to give you $5,000 for your tournament," but I'm going to make sure that Next Generation's name is in the credits as a sponsor. Whereas he'd never do that. So it's a matter of taking a positive thing and making it more positive. He would just write that check and say, "Here you go." I talked to him about that, but he always tells me to calm down. He's really shy. He never wants to brag, never wants, he doesn't even like to do media interviews. He's really a shy guy and he just really wants to keep his customers and his people happy. That's his thing in life. His customers and his employees and his family. And so, he lets me go and do my thing, but he's always saying, "Don't go overboard." So we compromise.

We never say no; we use the word "pass." Instead of writing a letter, "I'm sorry, we cannot," we say, "because our budget strictly adheres to youth and sports." We use all real positive words. Like we'll say, "We are doing this exclusively," instead of saying, "No, I'm sorry, we can't." I don't like those words. Because we're not really sorry. We're sorry, but we're not. If we were that sorry, why didn't we help them? That's how I look at it. I think when I was a kid, asking for things on yearbook staff, and ads, it used to make me mad. First of all, no one ever wrote me back. I strongly want everybody who writes our company to get a letter back. And the second thing is that I think you owe it to people to write them back, just like you owe it to call them back. And, the third thing is, I used to feel bad if people did write me a letter and said, "We're sorry we can't do this because of . . . ," and I didn't believe in the excuse. So I always make sure to tell the truth. And to use nice words.

We also have some regular contributions and some big ones, like Red Cross, United Way, most of the bigger organizations. Tournaments we sponsor. Like we have a cancer tournament—American Cancer Society— it's a tennis tournament. We do that every year. Various leagues, basketball, softball, baseball leagues. We do that every year. You know, there are different programs. And, we like to help the city out a lot. We like to help *all* our cities. Parades, community centers, things like that. We try to make fair contributions around and not to play favorites. We are expanding across the country, 38 states. We're the third largest in number and the world's largest outlet.

I discuss these things formally with my dad many times. But, I don't talk to him, each kid has their own way of dealing with him. I treat him much just like a boss. I write memos. I ask permission. I schedule a meeting. Not all of us do that. Some of us just walk in. I bop in when I have to, interrupt when I have to, but I would do that with any boss. In business, it's very important to me, I don't call him at home, I try not to. I get very angry when they do it to me. One incident we had, my mother called me on a Sunday morning at eight, asking me where I had spent a certain amount of money. I was so angry, I said, "I work nine to five." I refused to get into it. I don't think it's fair to cross over unless you want, unless both parties agree. Yes, we're going to do business on Saturday, fine. Let's do business. I'm very strong-willed about that, because it only leads to bad decisions. So I always try and treat it very firmly.

We talk about money within the family more or less openly. He gives me leeway. I have a budget for certain things. And he gives me leeway on it. But anything over $10,000 I check, just because I feel I should. Tournaments like we run, I know how to run 'em, I know how to do 'em, it's no big deal. Ninety-nine percent of the time ask any person in our family the same question, you'll get the same answer. Now, we can know amounts just because we're working in the business. So, we don't have taboos about talking about money in the family, not too much. We don't have too many. In fact, I don't think we have any money arguments. We can get whatever we want. Show logic and reason. Just like any other company. Go into any boss or any chairman of the board and tell them you need a hundred thousand dollars, and why, and if it makes sense they're going to give it to you.

Also, I solicit money for charities, all the time. For our tennis tournament we had to find people to donate. So we do a lot of these projects, we're in charge of soliciting people to give money. My father's in charge of a $13 million campaign to light the city of St. Louis. He's the chairman of that. We're trying to get donations from all kinds of corporate people and all kinds of individuals. That's a five year project. I work a lot on projects that my father is the chairman of. Every time we open a store we give a couple hundred dollars, or however much, to charity. It's part of our family philosophy. It's not written or staged for the franchisees either. But they do it. It's something we've always done. Give something to some organization in your community when you open a store. We opened our thousandth store. I was looking for someone to give it to. So I did. I went and found programs in the city I thought were good, and decided that. Personally, I give to the paramedics. But I don't really look for more. It usually crosses me in the mail. I see myself doing much more in the future. Giving your time is very, very difficult. And I know it's an excuse. I don't think it's an excuse in that it is an answer given by many, but it's a very realistic answer. I feel you always have time for at least one big project. Red Cross is mine. I'm a board member. So I think, you know, as many things as you can do for charity, it all comes back to you.

Following in the Footsteps
"I give to the areas that my family
and the company give."

I'm also personally giving constantly. I give away a lot. I've often thought about giving it all away to see what it's like. But I give a lot to my schools. I like to give as much in proportion to my salary, you know, I can't give thousands of dollars, like my parents. But I can give a couple of hundred dollars, or a hundred dollars, or whatever every time they ask for something. I give to my high school. I give to my college. I give a lot to Red Cross of which I'm a board member. I give a lot of my time. I work on a lot of charity projects. I work on a lot of community projects. I love giving money. I've given some friends' brothers and sisters, to help them go through school, given them tuition. Friends of mine. People I know that can't get loans and need help getting through school. I never loan people money except for school or if their life depended on it.

I give more than money. I also give my time. Probably, on the average like ten hours in a month. Not a whole lot. It depends. Like some months are busier. Like now the summer is busier. We have a lot going on. A lot of things we'll even sponsor that I don't need to be at. It's a company philosophy. If we take on a project we want to make sure it's successful, so we get involved in all aspects. Instead of giving Red Cross a thousand dollars to do an event, we'll give that thousand dollars and all our time to make sure that event is successful. So I work a lot of weekends like that, a lot of weekends.

I wasn't told to do that. I do it because I feel that it's important to make it successful for the cause. Charity is great PR, that's true, I won't deny that. But I don't think you can ever lose sight of what you're doing. I don't think you can ever understand, until you spend time watching. If you want to "humblize" your students about poverty, take your next sociology class to a soup kitchen. Some of them will walk away saying, "Those bums. . . ." And some of them will walk away so shocked. I was that way when I went away to the Caribbean. It blew my mind. When I went to Red Cross and I saw the people and learned about their suffering, I became very attached. And my father's very much the same way. He's always giving things in order to give, and never for PR. That's why he gets mad at me since I try to take recognition. He doesn't like that. I think it's so important to find out why you are doing this. What's the real reason. I think you have to ask that of yourself and company, there's so many companies that just do things for PR.

My father is saying, "Be careful that you keep . . . your reasons are our reasons." He's always just been like that. He's always given from his heart. Our medical truck, the Good Samaritan, traveled around and treated 70,000 people. He provides medical treatment, visits hospitals. Been in 22 states. Given care away free. And asked why he did it, he says, "Because I wanted to. I want to give back. Society has been good to me. People have helped me succeed. I haven't done it alone. My customers have helped me." I definitely feel that too. I'm the type of person that if I had a quarter and you needed it more than I did, I'd give it to you, because I just believe in that kind of stuff. I do crazy things. Like I'm in a restaurant and see somebody or one lady was telling me she had a hard life, two kids, and the salary she makes. So I'll give her some . . . but I'll do something for her just be nice to people. . . .

I give to the areas that my family and the company give. That's all where it is. I have one area, but my whole personality, my values, everything I think, it all comes from my family. In fact, I've been accused many times of being a daddy's girl. The guys I go out with can't stand it. "You do whatever your parents say. You're still . . . can't you grow up? Why don't you dismiss yourself from them and have a mind of your own?" I very much have an opinion and mind of my own. Because I work for him, work with him, see him, love him, it's very difficult to dismiss him. Very difficult to separate the two, very hard. I like him, I value their opinion highly.

My area is ambulatory personnel—paramedics. I was in an automobile accident, I'm very nervous about cars. I was on the Interstate, May 22, I had a broken leg and I was trapped. I was under the steering wheel. I was trapped for 45 minutes. I fell asleep at the wheel, woke up trapped, couldn't breathe, couldn't move. A paramedic came in and saved me through the door, cut open the door. The paramedic who saved me was in intensive care because my car caught fire. I gave nearly all the money I got. Once I read an article in *People* magazine about a paramedic who had major, major burns all over his face. I sent him, I think it was like a hundred dollars. Then I had the nicest note back from him—those are brave people.

I give away, personally, about $5,000 per year. Though, the more I make, the more I give. I give as much as I feel is appropriate for my income level. I base it all on that. I also have plans about charitable work. One of the things is I want to build a nursing home. I want to build a nursing home that's— they have some now I've been reading about—a real cool place. They have music. An exciting nursing home that allows people to feel alive. My grandmother was in a nursing home. I visited her every day. Every single day I went to see her for two years when I was young. And it was a mile from our house, and she had lots of visitors, but it was such a decrepit old place. I hated it. When I'm older, if I can afford it, I'm going to build a nursing home that's really fun, that has swimming pools, and is just like a country club, and has beautiful rooms. Like a room in your house instead of hospital rooms. A nice place to live. To be used by whoever needs to stay there. I'd have to charge, I'm sure, because otherwise I couldn't run the business. But I definitely would have those that couldn't afford it be there. I wouldn't make it a home for the elite. Depending on finances, and how much it would cost, and what I could afford, my dream would be to make it a social service type thing. Like an adoption home for those that couldn't afford it.

I'd like to blow them away with wealth. Never in their life would they have experienced it. I like that. I like exposing people to wealthiness, like taking them in their first limo, taking them to their first state dinner, taking them to their first head table. Because what they learn is that it's no big deal. And they learn that they're not, they aren't less better because they're less wealthy. They learn that and I really get a high on seeing that. I like them to see my life as I see it. And they do. Given that they're intimidated at first.

There are so many times in my life I've had friends that were less fortunate, they didn't have what I have: my clothes, my cars, my education, my everything. And I don't want to keep 'em. Take whatever. I know one day I'm going to give all that, just keep giving back, you know. I always used to say, "If I had this amount of money, I'd give it to such-and-such." But I don't. But I know one day when I do, I'll do that. I love to be among people and help them. My mother would die if she knew the places I go, like you know rough areas. It doesn't bother me. Unless my life's in danger obviously. But most common people I love . . . and I dress down. Individuals at a certain income level that I know would be jealous of my wealth. I won't wear watches or things. I won't do certain things. Being sensitive to that. Some people call that phony; I call it smart business. Why intimidate someone because of your wealth and status?

Pieces of the Larger Picture
"If it weren't for corporations and wealthy people we'd have a Soviet Union."

In terms of larger issues, I think poverty relates to where you were born, I know I'm not using the right term, your environment, I guess both monetarily and socially. The social environment has everything to do with it. There are a few exceptions, not many. As our standard of living as a country increases, I feel our poverty level will decrease. There won't be as many poor people. I really believe that poor people are born poor. When you look at the statistics of education and you look at what some companies do to poor people in quite a few places in the cities, and you really study and analyze why are those people poor. . . . Do these companies really think about it, do they really, who wants to be poor? Think about it logically. It's just like if you have somebody you don't like as a boss, nobody likes him, do you think they really want to be disliked? Do you think they really look at themselves and say, "I want to do bad in my job?" Everybody wants to succeed, know that they do a job well. They all want recognition. They all want to be complimented. And they sure as heck don't want to be poor. I won't buy that for a minute.

I think direction is an important word. Which direction do I go. I went to high school in St. Louis, where 43 percent, I was reading yesterday, of the kids, can pass the math test. That's 43 percent, *less than half*. That tells me less than half of those kids are taught to think, whether it's math or any subject that lets your brain be utilized. And a lot of it is environment: the friends you hang around with; the way you were brought up; what's important; what's not; drugs, alcohol, pregnancies. I mean the list goes on and on and on of things you have against you. I think it's very hard. It's also a simple life from the standpoint that, if you can take advantage of all the social services, you don't have to do a heck of a lot. You get lazy.

But, I don't think that the wealth of some is based on the poverty of others in society. No, not at all, and I'll fight that one. If you look at statistics, do your survey, you'll find out. How much do rich people give? How much do corporations give to people, to charities, to poverty? Unbelievable, way more than the government. Look at the numbers. I guess I'm really a Republican, and I believe in encouraging corporations to give. I do. Our company does, every chance we get. Through our Good Samaritan Treatment on Wheels. Through other things that we do. I'm always encouraging corporations to sponsor, to give, to help. If it weren't for corporations and wealthy people, we'd have a Soviet Union or royalty. Where there's rich or there's poor and there's no in-between, no middle class.

I think the role of philanthropy in society is awareness. You never feel it until it happens to you. That's true in almost anything, a fire, accident, a heart attack, your child suddenly has leukemia. I found in my little surveys and studies that I've done, 90 percent of the time, you're involved with a charity because it touches you, closely touches you. Except, in my case, I don't know why I got involved in the Red Cross. I don't know any handicapped people at all, or people that have major diseases. But the people I work with at Red Cross, the people I work with through Next Generation are in sponsorships and charity work, those heads, the chairmen of those organizations have a sister who has MD, have a brother that died of leukemia, have a retarded child, whatever. There always seems to be a hook. Those that don't give usually have never had anything like that or they are just selfish. There are so many selfish people.

I believe in total freedom. I believe that our private corporate sector supports organizations like Hands Across America, and US Aid for Africa. The private sector might not keep a program going for ten years, but the governing bodies who work for charities and nonprofit organizations are used to soliciting funds. It's hard. They have to solicit funds anyway, even with government help. No program is independently set without private funds. And I truly believe our corporations would take a greater interest and show a greater responsibility for poor people if the government didn't intervene so much and stuck more to providing direction.

I think we are getting very socialistic. I don't believe the government has had, the people in the government—I don't know, I have a bad attitude. I don't think the people who work for governmental institutions in most situations like social services. I think they should be better educated. I think that and law enforcement are my two pet peeves. If you don't know anything about business, why are you telling me how to regulate my ability? You never ran a business. How do you know where the effort should go? I'm very bitter towards that, the government, because usually the people that get those jobs are the ones that couldn't make it in the private sector. They couldn't get jobs at GM, so they're going to be fire marshal, or they're going to tell somebody, a career placement that the government supports. Train your people. Let them have their own career and then let them be a career personnel. Don't send them to school on careers and then tell them to decide somebody's destiny. You want a social service to provide services to people who have problems, then train them, teach them. Send them to a professional psychiatric whatever. So I think we have a problem. The teachers are the one exception, teachers that get paid by the government but I think they're qualified. Teaching, education. . . .

I think taxes and government should still be there. But, it's a matter of you have to. You have a right to this and a right—I don't think so, even in a wealthy society. Because, it's like I'm really against the seat belt law. I mean that infringes on your liberties. If somebody told me I had to give my money to someone. I think you have a right to choose what you want to give to. And I hold, most people do, that there is niceness and kindness that individuals possess as human beings. The percentage of bad people is less than two percent of the people. There are very few people that can see a picture of a soup kitchen and don't want to give to it, or visit that soup kitchen. If there was a way, and I don't know of a practical way, I'm speaking theoretically, that I could choose, I would give more than my tax, probably. If you told me, "I'm going to tax you 50 bucks a week to give to food." And I pay more than $5,000 in taxes every year, but it doesn't all go to things I think it should go to. Give a choice, even if they said, "Your tax this year is $5,000, where would you like it to go, x, y, or z?" Give me a choice. I didn't realize that half of the taxes go to the military. Okay, give me that choice. Where do you want to put your money? I think the child that's hungry has a right to be fed. Definitely he does. Actually, I don't think it's a right as much as a concern, from a humanistic perspective. I think it's a humanistic question. You have to be a pretty nasty person not to say that child has a right. But, I've seen so much going on. There's so much waste because they don't know how, because they are not in business for profit, they don't pay attention to cost. When you don't have to make a profit, boy oh boy, it's a different story. I've seen so many, I've seen them waste time, I've seen them waste money because they don't have to make a profit. Though, I've seen that in the private sector, too.

12

David Stephanov: "Them with the Gold Makes the Rules"

Calling entrepreneurship his "sport," David Stephanov, the son of Polish immigrants, has built an empire in real estate, pension management, and philanthropy wherein he wields power autocratically—and with enormous pride. Getting rich quick breeds a bravado which spills over into his philanthropy.

The fifty-three-year-old Detroit entrepreneur made his initial fortune by designing actuarial plans, then increased it through investments and (a favorite hobby of his) real estate. "I won't let anybody count it up," he says in reference to his net worth, which a conservative estimate might still place at well over $10 million. A substantial, though dissatisfied, philanthropist and strategic political contributor, he directs most gifts to his major "cause": his children.

"When you're young and you don't have a phone in your house, or a car, and you see a brand new Oldsmobile and the only privilege is to look inside the window, there's greed. I wanted some of that." And he got it and talks proudly about it. Thus, David Stephanov offers a self-portrait in worldly empowerment.

"In American history, there are old rich, nouveau riche, and swift rich. I'm swift rich." This son of a longshoreman and a cleaning woman rose rapidly in the business world, his meteoric flight deriving largely from the management of other people's money. Since only "one-quarter of one percent of America knows what to do with money that their companies don't need," he has learned to exploit his superior knowledge over most of the business world by buying real estate, making excellent investments, and designing innovative investment vehicles for others. One key to success was the resolve to work for himself. "There are four ways to get wealth," Stephanov explains. "You inherit it, you work for it, you borrow it, or you steal it. I thought you could do it by working. I'm a workaholic. And then after about two or three years I recognized that [working for others] wasn't the way to do it." So, like Brendan Dwyer, Stephanov capitalized on his own math talents and his courage to strike out onto his own. He continued to work for his wealth, but found working for himself a "swifter" plan.

Being in the right place at the right time, with the right product, helped too. "Everybody was looking for somebody who could design [a pension plan], get it approved by the government, and administer the plan for them." Subsequently, one door opens on another: "What I did is I had an opportunity, because I sat in on literally hundreds of meetings every year, with companies relative to money. . . . I started investing my money as a person with tax plans. Then I bought into Burger King hamburgers. At one time, I owned more Burger Kings than anybody. Then I bought manufacturing plants; and then I bought a number of insurance companies, banks. I never promoted, I did it all myself. . . . I was going to build an empire."

Stephanov throws himself into competition at every opportunity. Competing allows him to satisfy an incessant hunger for preeminence. "A man is, we're like nature. Make a couple of mistakes and we'll eat you up." The CEOs of the nation's major companies (whose earnings are published) are his rivals; and he enjoys beating them—just as he enjoys whipping an adversary in his other sport, squash. "You know, there's no difference in learning to practice and play the piano or a violin, or in playing squash, or in being an entrepreneur. I've never had a vacancy in twenty-two fucking years in the state of Michigan. And I mean that's—the banks go crazy. That's why they come and see me, and I don't go over asking them for nothing. You know, when you're good at a sport the good players search you out even the ones that are just playing. It's a good feeling. . . . That's really where it's at.

Stephanov reigns proudly from the center of his *principality*. His "game" or "sport," to use his own metaphor, is for power—in all spheres: business, politics, philanthropy.

He plays hardball at the workplace, where he refuses to tolerate unions. "I decertify them," he asserts. He plays a broker's game with politicians ("whores" he calls them) and bankers, who seek him out for favors. "When I want something, they come here and meet me for breakfast, and I tell them what I want. When I have to convey a message to the governor, he comes here, or he'll have one of his top two or three aides come down, and I'll tell them what I think should be done. And then we go from there."

His philanthropy reveals a somewhat softer side, but even here Stephanov proves a demanding master. "When a swift rich first starts to accumulate money and he's got enough, he recognizes that one of his ways to overcome some of his insecurities is to become a little bit benevolent." Stephanov puts youngsters from backgrounds similarly underprivileged to his own through school. Yet he abandons this beneficence when the kids he has helped fail to express their gratitude by helping others. From this he claims to have learned a clear and bitter lesson: "I think the kinder you are sometimes to people, the worse they have it and the worse you have it."

But his own children are a different story. They are the primary targets of his prodding and benevolence. They are his "cause," free to do and have what they want within a fairly liberal set of rules: no Rolls Royces and the obligation to get good marks. Shaping his children's future is Stephanov's favorite endeavor. He purchases companies for them, keeping everyone (kids included) in the dark as to which child will receive a particular corporate portfolio. But Stephanov would create children only partly in his own image. In the end, he is pleased to offer his children what his own father, poor and often ill, could not give him. "I gave them twenty-some years. I traveled with them. I raised a nice family. That was my cause. . . . So, I ended up being a special dad for them. And it turned out to be good. I'm really going to provide for them. Why shouldn't I? Even though it didn't happen for me."

The ability to redress past wrongs may well be the greatest indicator of Stephanov's empowerment—unless his power to rewrite history is outflashed by the language in which he rewrites, or rather, *redeclares it.* Tossing out expletives as the stereotypical tycoon bestows dollar bills; charging his language with spatial metaphors reminiscent of "the mountain coming to Mohammed" ("the good players search you out," "the governor . . . comes here"), the macho metaphors comparing business to sport or sexual conquest, the vignettes punctuated by laughter ("I even bought a bank just to find out how bankers think!), the boasts, quotes of astronomical figures, the putdowns—these words and phrases are symbols of dominance in that they *are* what they point to: other objects appropriated by Stephanov. *Vide* his tailored version of the golden rule "Them with the gold makes the rules."

BIOGRAPHICAL NARRATIVE

The Good Fortune of Education
"I didn't know how I could lose."

I came from a poor family on the east side of Detroit. I went to a parochial school, that would have been St. Isaac's Parish, for three years because they couldn't teach me English in the public school. But afterwards, I ended up going to public schools. My Dad got sick when I was about four-and-a-half and was in the hospital. So, I remember him mainly ill when I was growing up. Very small family with a good work ethic, that's all it takes. I was clean, always warm, always well-fed. My mother was a cleaning woman at the Owen Building. She went to the third grade, my Dad thinks he went to the fourth.

I went to West Tech. I didn't see that as an opportunity at the time, despite the fact that it was a high school for a select group of students. It was by accident. I went to high school a block away from my home. For some reason, our teachers selected about five or ten of us. And so we went, you know, for the test. About two days later they said, "You have an opportunity to go to West Tech." And I thought to myself, I've got to be crazy to do that. I lived one block away, I could walk to school, it didn't make sense. And then somebody told me, "You'll get a better education there." I thought I would try it. So, once I got there, I liked it. So I was getting a much better education compared to my friends. I sort of tried to encourage them, but they couldn't figure it out. I realized I was getting some kind of an advantage. I didn't know how I could lose.

And then I ended up at Michigan, went to law school there. I got an early discharge from the military, and ended up at the University of Detroit working on a law degree. In reality, I was a draft dodger. Who's kidding who? I mean, I got a scholarship, and I didn't take it until one of the boys across the street from where I lived was wounded and came over to see me. When I saw him, I ran right up to U of D with my transcript and I said, "I want to get into med school," because it was four years. They told me I didn't have enough science courses. But I had the grades and I ran over to the dental school, same morning. They told me I needed another biology and another chemistry course. But the guy told me, "You can get into law school." He knew what I was doing. He knew I was just trying to avoid the draft. We used to take tests during the Korean War, and if you stayed within the upper percentile you were not drafted. You had the privilege to get your degree, if you were admitted to any graduate school, you know, on that stupid testing thing they had. And so, I took advantage of all of that.

So I went my one year, and I was worn out, I was broke, and I was 21 years old. I had nothing but debts. Never had any relief, you know, we never had student loans or nothing. So I borrowed money from one of my uncles. I got tired of owing money. You can't be 21 or 22 years old and not even have a car, for Christ's sake. You know, kids out of high school went to work in factories and would be married at twenty, would buy a house, and would get a car. Probably all on payments, good ole America. So I was frustrated. I was a very frustrated young man. I had material goals. I think I had them all the time. When you're young and you don't have a phone in your house or a car, and you see a brand new Oldsmobile and the only privilege is to look inside the window, there's greed. I wanted some of that. The only way I was going to get it was to work for it.

The Fast Track to Wealth
"And what I did was I had an opportunity."

There are four ways to get wealth. You inherit it, you work for it, you borrow it, or you steal it. I thought you could do it by working. I'm a workaholic. And then after about two or three years, I recognized that wasn't the way to do it.

I was working as an actuary, 'cause I have a degree in math. When I got out of the service, I went back to law school, and I took my first job. I was working for an actuarial department of a trust company and going to night school. And I lasted about 18 months, I think it was. And then I saw a potential, so I went into business for myself doing actuarial work. I had a business at the right time, good luck, and I made some money. Implementing plans, and administrative ventures, that's what this office does. I don't do any personal financial plans for anybody. I just do the administration of retirement trusts. But I don't recommend, I am not a financial consultant. I would not permit my people to be financial consultants.

This company, Republic Associates, got about ninety some people. And I felt it as my moral obligation that when these people get to be senior citizens, that when they leave, I owe them more than just Social Security. So I started to put money in a trust fund. I put money into the trust every year. And as a result of a defined formula these people know that when they get to be 60, 61, 62, 63, they're permitted to leave and I give them a big cash check, or they can take their money monthly. Either way, I prefer them to take their cash and get out of my hair. So I handle about 1,100 of those of other companies' plans. I don't do anything with the money. I just, every year, make studies and tell them how much they have to put in to accomplish this end result. There's a lot of government filing forms, and we do all of that here. And I get a fee.

The company has 3,000 people, the one that I'm going to have to work on in the next two days. And they don't want a union. They know the way not to have a union is to provide fringe benefits. They must always pay a decent wage scale. So they say, "If I were to get a union, which union would I get?" They'd say, "Retail Clerks Union, it's a food outlet." "What does an average employee who is under a collective bargaining agreement in the food industry, what does he usually get as a retirement?" Nine hundred dollars a month by age 57 or age 58. This company says, "Holy smokes, what does that cost?" Well, they'll hire a firm like ours. So we take all their employees, all their ages, when they start and everything else, and we design a plan, and we say, you're going to have to contribute to this plan, $3,300 a year per employee, no matter what their ages are, and then there's terminations, firings, there's deaths, and various things before any quinquenial group finally reaches the point of retirement. And we're the ones that say this year, you got to put a million nine in, and next year, you made the extra interest on your money, you'll only have to put a million three in. Some years you put two million one in. We are the ones that do the work which the government accepts; we have to sign these statements.

What we do are defined benefit plans, not retirement plans. That's just money purchased by what you've got. You contribute to it when you purchase. It's a simple plan. I won't even handle that. I used to handle those, but I can teach a high school student how to do that, and I usually tell a client, "You know, wouldn't you like to spend $5,000 with me, here's the set-up." Or if they have computers, I'll just say, "Here, here's the software, have your girls punch this junk in and if you need any consulting advice to do more or something, use us, but that's a simple plan that you want."

Back in 1960, it was the era where your major Fortune 500s and your unions all had pension plans, but your remaining four million corporations did not. And everybody was looking for somebody who could design one, get it approved by the government, and administer the plan for them. Pension reform laws came in '74. I've got two men that have been with me for 25 years. So as a team we're pretty tough. We do the things we want to do. I'm the oldest independent in the industry; and one thing I don't do is I don't swindle my clients by going into their money. I think it's horrible. What has happened in this business is terrible, because all the thieves got into the business. The suede-shoe boys who try to get into these funds and try to make investments for them, you know, and tell them, "Buy this, or buy these mutual funds or bonds, or this," or you know, "invest in that."

And I learned something from an old man I was representing one time. A couple of Jewish fellows had a plan. What they wanted to do was, they wanted to sell their company to three of their employees. The employees didn't have any money, but the corporation had tremendous cash. I mean, back then it had about $2 million in cash, liquid cash. This was 1959, 60. And it had already been taxed. So now the point was to get maybe $3 million into a fund before taxes. That's pretty hard to do, unless you know what you're doing. So I put together a plan, I took this $3 million before taxes, took $2 million that was already taxed and could revert into a trust under 401 of the Internal Revenue codes, and gave the corporation deductibility for that money. And then that money was used to buy these boys out, and turn the stock over. It was very nice; two Jewish fellows sold the company to three Christian boys. I was very impressed with this old man. I learned a lot.

One day, we were sitting there, he's telling me something about the millions, and he says, "What would you do with them?" I said, "I'd go into real estate." He said, "What kind?" And I mentioned what I thought was good because I'd seen other companies doing that. And he said, "Good, when you make a million dollars, come back and I'll pay you for advice like that." And I said, "It'll be a hell of a long time before I'll be back." But I learned something from that: most people who know how to accumulate money in their various professions are pretty bare outside of their business. There are very few professional entrepreneurs in this country. Outside of their business. Very few people. I'd say that ¼ of 1 percent of America knows what to do with money that their companies don't need.

And what I did is I had an opportunity, because I sat in on literally hundreds of meetings every year. I watched all these Goldman Sachs and Charley Allens, you know, I had nine offices in New York, and I realized that very few people knew what the hell they were doing. So I was making money. I started investing my money as a person with tax plans. Then I bought into Burger King hamburgers. I was at one time the largest Burger King owner: I owned more Burger King stores than anybody. Then, I bought manufacturing plants; and then I bought a number of insurance companies, banks. I never promoted, I did it all myself. And then, around 1966, 1967 when I was about five years, six years in the business, I really started to wonder what I wanted.

Dropping the Drudgery
"For maybe ten years, it's been nothing but fun."

Then I was going to move to New York. I was going to build an empire. But you have to sacrifice, and I have four lovely children, and they're happy kids, and they turned out real nice. They're my friends. One's at Princeton, one's at Georgetown, two just graduated from Trinity, and they're all in law schools or graduate schools. You can't usually get both in life. I saw that in a lot of my clients that were worth $3, $5, $10 million, and more. Ray Crock is an example. And I saw that they lost some things in life. And so I made a decision. The only way to grow was to have gone public at that time. And I bought a public company; and I saw all the headaches that were involved in a public company. It was pretty hard to raise capital from within. You must do it by issuing stocks—borrow from the public. You don't do it normal; you leverage. And I decided I was not going to put my money on people. I was going to make my passive investments on a simple basis 'cause any one day I could get killed if I had private planes flying me all over the country. I would be exposing myself to such risks. The children were very young, and I was sick and tired of buying millions of dollars in life insurance. I felt that if I was going to leave them anything, I was going to leave them swift rich.

In American history, there are old rich, nouveau riche, and swift rich. I'm swift rich. And I had 6,000 people working for me at one time, in my operating companies. If you don't think that's a headache, let me tell you, my friend, *that is* a headache. And I realized I had the unions coming on me. I'd buy companies, and I'd buy union contracts when I acquired a company, so now, stuck with them, I'd decertify them. That is, I'd throw the union out [laughter]. Convince them I'd pay them better. Give them good working conditions and then if they still complain give them fringe benefits. You know, booklets. I was an artist at that. I made a lot of money doing that.

And then I decided, about fifteen years ago, that I like real estate. That building over there—I built that eleven years ago. Power Computer Company is in there. They pay me about $154,000 a year and I don't do anything. See what I mean? And they pay all the taxes and insurances. I've got 520 of those. I put together quality set-ups. And I never promote or lower myself.

I built these buildings. I've got twenty-one of 'em going up right now. When I die, my kids are going to do exactly what they want with them. But right now, I'm building them for tax reasons. Every tenant has to do his own bidding: General Motors, RCA, NCR.

I'm on top of the world, financially. I'm not big, but you must understand something—I'm not big, but I'm not leveraged, you understand that? I'm insecure, very insecure. I've probably got forty-eight buildings that have new mortgages; I think that's my Polish ethnic background. I don't let the fucking union make the interest. But what happened to me is that I got more than I wanted. I reached my goal at about 39, 40 years of age, which was to have some substantial money, tremendous income. I didn't have to work for it anymore. And building's what I enjoy doing. I really get a kick out of it. And I still keep this company here because it's a place for me to come, and I have good people here. I got people that have been with me a long time, this is a twenty-six-year-old company.

My goals have changed. I mentioned that I did not want a labor intensive business, I didn't want to be part of a big business. I'm very comfortable, and I guess I solved my insecurity with the tools that I was able to accumulate. 'Cause from here on in, and it has been for maybe ten years, it's been nothing but fun. Yeah. Actually, fun. My kids do whatever they want—up to my rules. They must study. I don't need the things that I've seen. When I owned a bank, I only sat on a committee, my mortgage committee. That's the only committee I sat in on. I controlled that. And I would see people that I used to think were big shots in the community, you know, socially and prestige-wise. My God, they'd submit for a loan, I'd see their statement and I used to always say, oh my God, I've got to talk to these people. They're crazy. They're living over their means. What are they doing? Half-a-million-dollar house with a $400,000 mortgage, they're nuts! All they are is showtime. This is a fictitious society. Believe me, it is. You would die if you ever sat in on a bank board meeting and saw the statements of about 92 percent of this so-called middle-class society, the upper crust. Phony.

It's OK to mortgage a house. But I don't think America was built by mortgaged houses. I think there's a tremendous amount of stress and insecurity there. I think people got to live within means. You got to be a little more realistic, you know. As you get into your golden years, when you get to your 50's, 60's, you should be able to sit back, take a deep breath, and say, I've done it. I'm comfortable, I'm not dependent on anybody. Financially, I'm not beholden to anybody. My family is educated, as much as I could educate them—you can't force every child into education. But I fulfilled all those requirements.

Then I just got through going to Europe, and got back two days ago, and as I was driving through southern France and Italy, I saw these beautiful farms out there. Big four-hundred-year-old barns and homes are something to see. Those people don't live under stress. The old farm that was given to them, you know, by their great grandfather, when Polacks were allowed to own land, is in real good shape. They have nice homes. They're not communists of course, they're private farmers. There's no stress. They're happy. Everything's owned, you don't borrow money. It's within the society. And then I've been reading about the plight of the farmers in our country. And I own substantial land, it covers a lot of miles, I'm comfortable with it. And I think that maybe it was wrong what has happened to maybe twelve percent of the farmers. And I love the farmer. Without him and the shoemaker, man, I got no food or shoes. Then, something cruel happened. Well, nothing cruel happened. You know, if your father leaves you a house, and you go out and mortgage it, don't you think that's going backwards? I don't think there is any reason to do this. Whatever they may say is bullshit. If you need money, banks will give you all the money in the world. You don't have to put up your house for anything. If it's a business investment, tell them, explain the business investment to them, tell them what your objectives are, give them a performer, they'll give you all the money in the world.

I get all the money I want. And I'm talking eight digits, and I don't personally sign. See all these complexes? I don't sign for them. I go to the bank and tell them, "I'm building ten buildings. I need $7 million. I'm going to put a million and a half into the deal and I don't want to sign that mortgage. If it goes bad you own the building, not me." Not many people can do that. A man is like nature. Make a couple of mistakes and we'll eat you up. In the business world, it's the same thing. That's why I never negotiate with somebody who's down and out. I watch them and make the good deals but, I got to have fun. And I have fun.

As I said, I feel financially secure now. I started feeling that way, I'd say, when I sold out one of the Burger King chain operations, in '78 or '79. I got a whole lot of cash at one time, and got rid of 5,000 employees where every year I used to have to put another two or three million into the business. So my security became a reality. What a man normally does when he's 60, 65 years old, you know, I was able to do that at a younger age. Financial security for me means that in the event I become disabled I'm not going to be in the poor house, back on the East Side. That I'll still maintain the same standard of living that I've been used to, whatever the economic circumstances. The chain was a very minor part of my portfolio, but it was liquid. It was a chance to get checks in the eight digits, unencumbered. The second year I was in the business, I started having an income of about $200,000 a year.

The Sport of Making Big Money
"I don't like to lose. Do you?"

I don't put my name on any company that I own and I own forty of them. I usually get a kick out of reading what the chairmen of the board of the major three companies make in this country. You know how they publish that. Nobody would ever put my name in there. Only last year did some son of a bitch beat me. But I had a year bigger than that, of course, six years ago [laughter]. So I get a kick, it becomes a game, an absolute game. You don't watch it until at the end of the year when they tell you. That's all, it's a game. I play racquetball. I was pretty good. I was second in 1961 in doubles, nationally. You know, there's no difference in learning to practice the piano, or in playing racquetball, or in being an entrepreneur. I've never had a vacancy in twenty-two fucking years in the state of Michigan. And I mean, the banks go crazy. That's why they come and see me, and I don't go over asking them for nothing. You know, when you're good at a sport the good players search you out, even the ones that are just playing. It's a good feeling. And I have come to the opinion that there are very few people that really understand what free enterprise is about. And they really don't know how to invest money. I represent 1,000 people, and I watch the bad advice financial consultants give to people like them. Oh, it's a shame.

I have a young man who's president of one of my companies, he was the head man of the Wisconsin Bank's Commercial Loan Department. And he came to me after he left. He said, "I've watched you, you're a master, you made a tremendous amount of money." And he says, "I don't know where you're going, you sort of stopped." I said, "I'm tired." He said, "I've got my profit-sharing money and I'll give it to you. I'd like to go in business with you." Forty-year-old man. And, I thought about it. What do I want more headaches for? But I took him on. I said, "I'll make you a millionaire." I made a lot of people millionaires, not the phony kind but really there. And kiddingly, about four months after he was here working hard, I said, "I'll tell you, you'll be a millionaire within fifteen to eighteen months." And about two months later he said, "I'm ashamed to admit this, I made a million dollars already." I said, "It was easy wasn't it?" He said, "I've worked hard, but I'm going to tell you it was fun." He said, "I've never had so much fun in my life." That was worth me doing it.

I look at probably eight deals every week and I might say no to eight. Because you don't take a deal unless it's a good deal. And with me, it's like sports. I don't like to lose. Do you? It wouldn't be good if you learned to lose. And the only problem I ever had is I made one mistake, one financial mistake that cost me a third of a million. They were kidding me about it, we were sitting having coffee this morning, and they said, "That was amazing." But after thirty years, the banks still look upon me and say, "My God, don't even question him. Give him anything he wants." And that's really where it's at [laughter]. I sit back and think, Christ, I got to make a mistake, I didn't get all A's in college, right? So how am I going to get all A's in business? True? I'm already about a B plus—I choked once! But it's like saying, I'm going into that shopping center that I'm building in the city. I'm going into Southfield, bucking one of the most stringent economic periods we've had in real estate. I've got to be crazy to go into Southfield. I'm going in where all the promoters and thieves and concession makers, all the shadies are. I'm gonna go right up their ass [laughter]. That's really like winning. And I want to do that, because I know what I'm doing. I'm going there to build some buildings. I'm not over my head.

It's a game. You're looking at an opponent. Like playing for big money. I just played for five grand a game in racquetball [laughter]. This guy came in from New York. I watched him, how he walked, studied every move he made, oh, he doesn't look that coordinated and the most important thing was how he served that ball. And I knew right then I could beat the son of a bitch, and [laughter], I've played for as much as thirty grand. A kid came into town and wanted a piece of me [laughter]. I was scared. I didn't want to lose the thirty. I was watching him put on his shoes, I was watching him in that locker room like a hawk. As soon as he served and the ball landed, I had his ass. I let him get seven points in the first game, and I shut the son of a bitch out in the second game. He was seven or eight years younger than I was then. I was smarter than he was. Do you realize that there are probably 3,000 syndicators that are going to be out there promoting business deals and everything else, with other people's money? I do it with my own. It's a game [laughter], it's no more than a game, that's all it is.

Winning is when you put it together and they lease it up and the bank walks in and just raves about what a great thing you just did, and says "Do you want more?" That's all it is. No more than a game. What else can it be? There is a thrill in it, hell yeah! There's the anxiety, there's the anxiety before. Like playing in a tournament. Winning in my business is having no vacancies. I'm proud of that! Fucking A, I am! You don't know how hard you got to think that out, my boy. You got to think that out well.

You got to know another thing, I never advertise. I never use my own name. I have substantial wealth, but I won't let anybody count it up. My personal financial statement is five years old, and they have to accept what's on it. If the banks want to make some changes, they make them. *They* make them, not me. When they want to put some numbers down, it cannot be in any file that's attributed to me, because all they do is create state tax problems for me. So I make no adjustments. And I don't personally sign. A game. It's all a game, I even bought a bank just to find out how bankers think [laughter]! Kalamazoo Federal. Just for study. I didn't have time to go and study banking at Harvard or some graduate school. I thought I had better do it on my own. I learned that they're human beings, they just wear three-button suits, and that they're just normal, ordinary prudent people. And then I found out how they really take loans and turn down loans. Which is really what banking is all about. It's not the passbook savings system.

When Power Runs Its Course
"You start to become a little bit benevolent."

You know, I'm good for my percentiles. I give to the schools, churches—
not as much to churches, they got too much money. On an average year, 35
to $40,000. Some years a lot more. As an example of a major gift, there's a
seminary, Orchard Lake Seminary and last year we wanted to put up
something in a very confidential manner. The other man, on this, wanted
publicity and I wouldn't take it. And they were building an auditorium,
with a display on it, so I gave I guess $25,000. Last year I gave maybe $35,000
or $40,000. I also gave to a hospital. They came to me like Orchard Lake.
They know who the suckers are. You're on a list. And then my father-in-law
passed away, and they were opening up a wing up here, a couple miles
away. That's Kramer Hospital. So I built them a kitchen. I didn't want to do
that, but my wife wanted to do something. And I give the normal, I give to
the schools and all that nonsense. Now I'm on the alumni committee. The
kids are all away at school, so you got to give there. If their school sends it
to me, they're good for a grand. It says 25, 50, 100, 500, 1,000, and 5,000.
Well, I just want to see what's going on. I'll send them $1,000.

These days, I have a lot of decisions to make about how to allocate my
money. When a swift rich first starts to accumulate money and he's got
enough, you start to become a little bit benevolent. What I did is I put a lot
of kids through school. I set up a little trust for any boy or girl in Michigan,
primarily in Michigan, who is without mother or father. I put them through
school. Then I finally put a doctor through medical school—a girl. I used to
have congregational ministers find them for me. I put through 42 kids, then
I quit. Because my only condition was that they help somebody else, and
not one of the bastards helped anybody else. Even the doctor let me down
tremendously.

So, I felt that my system was only satisfying me, and it wasn't a good
system. So then I started giving to various schools. We have a chair at the
University of Michigan, this is confidential, but it's registered, you know, it's
registered. We just gave them about ¾ of a million dollars about five years
ago. Just to the university. We didn't want anything. No publicity and no
hands-on, just gave it. I knew what chair they established, but I didn't want
publicity over it. I didn't want to attend any of the ceremonies or functions.
That's not good for you to do, for the family, or for the neighborhood.

It's OK to do when you're older, take a little publicity, but not when
you're younger. It creates jealousy, it creates a lot of jealousy. Money's a bad
thing. Money's a terrible burden. All the luxuries that we have are a burden
also, the homes we live in, our toys, boats, airplanes, anything else available
to the rich in society today. And it sparks tremendous jealousy. It's a disease
in our country. That's terrible. And I've been through it for twenty-six years.
I've had a lot of fun and I'm real lucky, really am. Like Napoleon said one

time. He was getting ready for battle and he asked one of his generals, he said, "Who is leading my attack today?" And the general answered, "Philip." He said, "Is he lucky?" He didn't ask if he was good or if he was educated or is he a military graduate or what. "Is he lucky?" It meant a lot to the guy, it meant an awful lot to the guy.

My daughter's at Georgetown, she's getting out early. And everybody after their third year has to move off campus. They don't have the facilities. So now she's only got one semester to go, 'cause she could have got out in three years, but instead she wanted to stay one semester more just to have some fun. So I couldn't sign a rental lease, you had to sign for a year, so she says, "Come on, call, Dad, call." She'd told somebody else who said, "My God, all your dad has to do is call up Father somebody." And I didn't like doing that. But I finally called. And the golden rule came into effect: Them with the gold makes the rules. She gets a call and she's now got it. The guy in the housing office told me, "You've been fair." Well, that's wrong. I do not like that. I do not like the golden rule. The golden rule's a cruel rule. So the golden rule is not always right. There's a lot of cruel people with money that do strange things, you know.

Probably it's clear by now that I don't give a lot. I'll tell you why. Oh yeah, I was called just a while ago, the University of Detroit was having a drive for more student money. I guess I was going to go maybe fifty, a hundred thousand, but when I heard the way they were going to disperse the money, I didn't like it. And I decided not to give. Then when I went back and thought over the people that I helped, I wasn't happy, I wasn't satisfied. You would think that some of those kids would, over the years, help somebody else out. And so I just felt that I wasn't getting enough satisfaction out of it.Then I felt I've paid my debt back, you know, to the Kellogg Foundation for helping me with my undergraduate work. I had to wait on tables and I played my horn, but I went through very easily. My mother gave me seven dollars when I got out. A hell of an education. And I felt that maybe the kinder you are sometimes to people, the worse they have it and the worse you have it. And I sort of feel that the universities are not doing as quality a job in student control as I really wanted. So I decided not to give to them any more.

As far as other than educational needs, I'm good for it. I'm good for the typical gift. One thing that frustrates me is that when you live in a community like Birmingham, you know, with all the phony stuff that goes on in my class. The church comes down, and they say, "We got a drive," and they raise $75,000. And I sit there and I say, well, what are some of these older, you know, third generations and fifth generations, what are they giving, I wonder. So finally I agree and say, "Well, I'll give $5,000." I give $5,000 and there'll be a meeting called five weeks later, saying, "We're having problems on this drive. We've only collected $17,000." And I say, shit, they've only collected twelve, not including myself. Well, when you finally realize that there are lists, you look at the lists and say to yourself, this is a joke. Everywhere I go, I am a substantial contributor. That's not right. That's not right. When the Pope, the Polish Pope was appointed, a whole lot of businessmen hurried up, made a quick meeting, and decided to buy him a limousine. The huge limousines were tops, and bullet proof and all that stuff. And I said, "OK, count me in on it." One of them, named Czarnicki, knew Henry Ford and he called him up and he told him, "We got one from Cadillac and one from you." And Ford said, "We want that Pope in that Lincoln very bad."

There's an organization called Youth for Christ. And they had a place up here for young boys. Some woman donated some land, about eighty acres. And they put up these little homes. There were about ten young men living in those homes without parents, kids that got in trouble, not serious trouble. So I busted my back and I helped build one of the homes. Those are things I've enjoyed doing. I'm not going to be that much of a benevolent type of a contributor. It's not my bag. If I ever did lose my family, I'd give all my money to a medical foundation. I'd probably set it up to put kids through medical school. But I'd make them pay back. I'd set it up differently. I think the kinder you are either to children or to anybody else, the worse they're gonna have it and the worse you have it. If you don't set up good, strong rules, it's bad.

I'm in a period of my life where I'm not that happy with my giving. And I'm 52 years old. And I sort of feel that I've done my share, I know I've done a lot more than my share when it comes to community contribution. My son was an all-state football player. And in his senior year—this is very confidential. Only one other person knows this. There was this young boy from Pontiac, Michigan, and he was a great athlete. And Pontiac shut their athletic program and music program down. I thought Ford, who owns a lot of Pontiac, wouldn't let that happen. But Ford did. And then I actually thought that we'd get called, you know, twenty-five guys would get called on and told, "Okay we can't let this happen to a black community where we really need to keep these kids occupied." And that we would pick up the tab. But that didn't happen either. Instead, the young black boy who was a senior, and my son's greatest threat, I paid the $2,400 to send him to Birmingham so he could play in high school in his senior year. And he beat my kid out. Would you have done that? I did it. That little black boy managed to get a scholarship and he's finishing at Ohio State. That was more important to me. I did not want my son to be a jock anyway. Even though he was a star in lacrosse and football and all that. But he was also a hell of a student. He came out with a 3.6. That's all I asked. As long as my kids get a 3.5, they get anything they want: airplanes, boats, travel, anything they want. But they got to get those grades first.

Envisioning the Legacy
"I'm going to share with them what my sport is:
being an entrepreneur."

I didn't seek to have more control over how the gifts are used because I was thinking a lot tax-wise. But, give away ¾ of a million dollars when you're only 45 years old, you do not want any planned attachments. There ain't too many you're going to pass up on the highway that have done that. And I've done that for Michigan. And I sort of feel it's somebody else's turn now. Most guys that do set foundations up are flattering their wives. If I do something with excess funds, I'll give it to the kids because I've got no objections to leaving what I've earned in the family partnerships.

I sort of decided that I wanted to see my children when I'm alive with good money, you know, substantial incomes, for their academic use. But also, I just didn't want for them to have to wait until I die to get it. So I started setting up family partnerships about seven, eight years ago in their own names. So I have more fun, like right now my question is I'm building for Chrysler in Flint and everybody's waiting and thinking, "Is he going to give it to his family?" The kids own a lot of land and a lot of my estate, as a vehicle, a tax vehicle. And when is there enough? I don't know. And I guess that my kids might as well erode the money, as well as what I've given away out of benevolence. So let them get rid of it 'cause that's all anybody else is doing.

I don't have any particular causes. If I ever have a cause, it'll be primarily medicine. If I set up a foundation, it'll be a medical foundation. But, primarily, what I want to do with my money is give it to my kids. I got no hard objections if they turn out bad. It's nothing that I did 'cause I already gave as much as I could. I gave them twenty-some years. I traveled with them. I raised a nice family. That was my cause. 'Cause I didn't have a dad. When I grew up, my dad was in the hospital. So, I ended up being a special dad for them. And it turned out to be good. I'm really going to provide for them. Why shouldn't I? Even though it didn't happen for me. My daughter flies, rides the boats, does everything as well as the boys. She hunts with me, good shot.

What my kids need now is to finish their educations, establish some work habits and decide what they want to do. They worked here this summer. One's in Europe. And I'm going to share with them what my sport is: being an entrepreneur. That's all this is. This is a game. It's a big game. Putting up a shopping center, 300 more apartment units, a bunch of office buildings or an industrial plant. It's a game, like squash, like racquetball, like skiing. That's all it is. That's all it is. That's all it is. You find a piece of land, you think about it, you look at seven pieces of land, you say I'll take that piece, and put up 120,000 square feet. We'll resell it in six months and we'll make nothing but money on it.

I also have a network of friends that I confide in. I have a number of nice friends. We have a lot in common; we've raised our families together. I like boating, skiing, fishing, hunting, and I've done it mostly with my children. The only shock I had was when they finally all went away to school [laughter]. I didn't have any more of them. But I've got partners. I have an oil company, and my partner there and I have been together for 17 years. We hunt together a lot, we see each other quite often and we share our thoughts. He's in the construction business also, doesn't do any building for me, 'cause he's in the middle of the state. And I have a partner in the western side of the state, and then I've got some close friends in the neighborhood, there are about three of them only. We don't socialize a lot. But I do contribute to the Symphony crowd. I just went to that, the big to-do they had for the top boys here. You always have to show up to that stuff. I don't think they got from me more than, whatever the thing cost to have that status, $1,500 or something. So, more or less, I give ten of these gifts away a year. But there is a lot of phonyism in that. Lots of phonyism. It's a social clique. And I don't want that because I think it reflects on my children.

I have beautiful homes. I've got our nice homes: one here where I live, and one in Albuquerque, Palm Beach, Chicago. And I was going to put a Rolls Royce down on Palm Beach and I said to myself, what am I doing with those children? That would be terrible to do. That's the reason I didn't put a Rolls Royce down there. I know most people would flip if they even had the privilege to do something like that. I had it, but I called back my dealer who sells me all my cars, and said, "I can't let my kids drive that car around Palm Beach. It'll distort them, screw them up more than maybe they're screwed up already." So that's the reason I didn't buy it. And then I didn't want those people to see me driving around in a Rolls Royce. Once they find out you got a little money, you're on every sucker's list in town. It's terrible. And I know it because, fuck, I'm on it! You get on everybody's, everybody's, you know. You can't imagine. Everybody solicits money.

Turning Wealth into Influence
"I tell them what I want . . . and then we go from there."

I also get involved in politics. I know everybody. If I want to call a federal senator right now, I just pick up the phone and he'll fucking take my call 'cause I give them money. 'Cause they're whores [laughter], they're whores. I'm on the top part of the computer list, $5,000-plus. You have to contribute to every campaign. I got a lobbyist that works for me. 'Cause I can do a lot, I do a lot, whatever the law permits. I will not do anything that will ever get me into trouble. When the IRS came in to audit me, I threw one out physically, right out of my door. 'Cause I have never skimmed, I've played it right, as legitimately as I possibly could.

I give to the senators in Michigan. Just in Michigan. They can help you because now and then you run into some problems. I have a client who's got a small problem now. The bureaucracy is giving him some headaches, but I'll just make a phone call, we'll fly to Washington that day and resolve this matter. The lawyers ain't going to book him for $150,000. 'Cause it's pure bureaucracy. We're not doing anything illegal. I give to the congressmen too. You got to give money to everybody. Like I told you, I'm on a sucker's list. I give to both Democrat and Republican. I've picked every winner.

I used to be on business committees. Then I found out they're just not so constructive according to the way I want to lead my life. I do not go to any political or business meetings. Instead, now, when I want something they come here and meet me for breakfast, and I tell them what I want. When I have to convey a message to the governor, he comes here, or he'll have one of his top two or three aides come down, and I'll tell them what I think should be done—and then we go from there. There's always a need to do that when you're as strung out as I am. I'm a pretty substantial taxpayer and personal property owner in the community. I know the local officials, too. But I don't play politics. I do my homework, I know what I'm allowed to do, and I do it.

Yeah, we've got people to help us. We assign a project, we look at the outline, and after twenty-some years in the business, you know what the rules are and who the actors are. And I challenge them. I'll take them out, sue 'em at the drop of a hat. Sue whoever's getting in my way [laughter]. If I think they're wrong, I don't want to push them, but they will not push me. When I tell them this is what I'm going to do, they'd better say yes. 'Cause I don't make too many mistakes before I go. I'm prepared. It's not a joke with me. It's just like a student who's not prepared for a final exam, versus one prepared for his final exam. That's the way life is. You've got to get a good game going, you got to get physically prepared, and play four or five times that week for a good match on Friday or Saturday. And that's the way business is. Business is the same way; life is the same way.

Afterword: Truth and Falsehood in Gospels of Wealth

Paul G. Schervish

The preceding narratives confirm that the wealthy are well aware of their special power and that most take special steps to be careful about its effects. But such concern provides no guarantee that the effects will be salutary. Hyperagency presents a formidable temptation to manipulation. When coupled to self-conceived responsibility, empowerment may become an ominous danger—to the fate of others as well as to the souls of the rich.

Given the consequential nature of hyperagency, it would of course be convenient if we could easily discern which wealthy individuals lack true responsibility. But when it comes to autobiographical statements, especially when proffered as gospels of wealth, evaluating responsibility becomes extremely complex. In 130 interviews with millionaires we have never found an account that is not presented as gospel of wealth. Narrators never leave their stories with a failure unattended, if not solved. We hear about separations, mistakes, sins, and abuses. But then we immediately hear about reunions, corrections, reconciliations, and remedies. The wealthy by their own accounts have often been confused and venal. But they have not remained such. "I once was lost, but now am found; was blind, but now I see" is the epigraph of every gospel. All wealthy individuals admit to an empowered agency, while at the same time testifying to life-long efforts to attend to their problems, reform their lives, and care for others.

How then are we to evaluate the gospels of the wealthy? Just because we invariably find the convergence of power and responsibility, is every gospel equally valid, equally inspired, equally to be emulated? Are not at least some gospels, as intelligible as they may be as literary forms, really apologetic stories of legimation and justification? In responding to such questions we need to make two cautions about the disposition of the critic and two methodological points about interpreting the truth of autobiographical accounts.

The first cautionary note is that any criterion of judgment applied to gospels of wealth (including Carnegie's) must in all integrity be applied with equal diligence to the gospel that each of us purports to live. The second thing to say is that the object of any criticism is the content of the person's gospel, not the person. The greatest temptation in regard to evaluating the wealthy is to end up either adulating or attacking them. If much popular culture such as Robin Leach's "Life Styles of the Rich and Famous" succumbs to undiscriminating acclaim, much sociology succumbs to the temptation of zealous denunciation. Because no account admits to ultimate irresponsibility, any criticism must be leveled against the array of responsibilities voiced by particular individuals. It will never do to declare there is no gospel. For unless we have good reason to suspect intentional deception, what the respondents present to us as narrative truth is almost always what they have previously presented to themselves as emotional truth. What we may legitimately argue, however, is that a particular gospel is misguided, incomplete, or base. But even then we must proceed to make our case not by denying the presence of moral responsibility or dismissing normative declarations as hypocritical legitimation. Instead, we must evaluate the content of the responsibility by demonstrating its shortcomings and hurtful implications. The primary object of judgment is the gospel, not the person.

As to interpretation, the first point is that the biographies are moral because the wealthy formulate self-justifications and self-criticisms within a framework of culturally determined normative sentiments of what is right to do and what ought to be done.[1] What they recount publicly reflects the fact that they have learned to experience wealth in terms of dedication, obligation, responsibility, and merit. Their biographies are moral not because we find what is to us an acceptable ethical understanding of dedication, obligation, responsibility, and merit. They are moral because the wealthy experience and interpret their dealings with wealth, as meeting normative commands rather than simply meeting personal desires. For this reason, their accounts contain expressions of duty and social concern as much as they contain legitimations and self-justifications. Like the rest of us, they forge an intelligible myth out of their lives. Despite temptations to the contrary, then, a crucial first methodological principle is to avoid conspiracy-type analyses.

Conspiracy analyses are "structural" criticisms derived from an often well-meaning yet too facile attempt to uncover the "true" motivations and purposes which the wealthy are said to hide beneath a veil of self-serving testimony. The logic of conspiracy analysis is akin to the following: "The wealthy say they are contributing to economic well-being through their business activity and to social welfare through their philanthropy; however, *what they are really doing* is to line their own pockets, assuage their guilt, and preserve the semblances of the social order." The problem here, of course, is not claiming that the wealthy are unaware of or unforthcoming about their self-interests; indeed their gospels may in fact be all too suspiciously silent about their stakes. Questioning such silences in gospel is always appropriate. What is not appropriate, however, is to begin and end an analysis with an implicit, if not explicit, accusation of dissimulation. Unfortunately for such a critic, but fortunately for the long-term health of social science, conspiracy analysis is self-limiting. For once a researcher initiates a conspiracy analysis, the very same mode of inquiry may be mobilized against the critic—namely, that the critic is also tied to self-interest and prone to dissimulation. Beginning with the much more complex task of excavating and evaluating the array of moral duties to which the wealthy feel themselves obligated emancipates us from repeatedly orbiting around a circuit of recrimination and counter-recrimination.

The second issue of interpretation concerns the problem of truth and falsehood in self-reported life histories. It might seem that it is crucial to figure out when people are telling the truth and when they are being deceptive. Yet, it is not only impossible but largely unnecessary to discern authorial intentions or distinguish whether words are objectively true or false. James Olney is persuasive in saying that "When it comes to autobiography, the truth of falsehood is a deeper and truer concern than the falsification of truth."[2] I also agree with Timothy Dow Adams who writes:

All autobiographers are unreliable narrators, all humans are liars, and yet . . . to be a successful liar in one's own life story is especially difficult. Because what we choose to misrepresent is as telling as what really happened, because the shape of our lives often distorts who we really are, and because, as Roy Pascal reminds us, "consistent misrepresentation of oneself is not easy," even those autobiographers with the most problematic approach to lying should be valued to be telling the truth of their lives.[3]

I interpret Olney's and Dow Adams's statements to mean that it is not the "veracity" of what the wealthy say but how, in making a case for what it means to be rich and good in America, they have calibrated their words to their emotional recollections. It is usually suggested that we need to establish the veracity of biographical narratives in order to establish underlying social reality. The goal is to discover how what has been said can be used to disclose objective social processes. The object of analysis is not the internal emotional sentiments but the external social processes that mobilize the personal dynamics of an individual life. For this purpose, I concede, searching for veracity is a legitimate, even if an ultimately futile, task. But in any case, to obtain information about objective historical processes other methods than examining oral histories must be used. Here, the work of Domhoff is especially valuable. For instead of simply making claims about objective dynamics, he actually documents the social processes by which wealthy individuals translate their interests and desires into particular social practices and outcomes.⁴ For what, then, are autobiographical accounts instructive? In what way is Olney correct that "the truth of falsehood is a deeper and truer concern than the falsification of truth"?

The major significance of autobiographical accounts resides in what they reveal about the motivational forces that shape a person's life. If institutional analysis is better at documenting historical forces, biographical analysis is better at documenting what influences agency. Certainly, as Giddens rightly insists, there can be no real separation between institutional analysis and the analysis of strategic conduct.⁵ The two research strategies must always remain united. Nevertheless it is often useful to "bracket" one strategy in order to pursue the other more fully. In taking the moral biographies of the wealthy as valid representations of motivational dynamics, what we lose in documenting historical processes we gain in documenting emotional dynamics. For instance, institutional analysis may show that successful entrepreneurs receive a level of income from their enterprise that far surpasses the income of its employees.

While it may be correct to conclude that receiving such disproportionate income *may be* the central motivation of the entrepreneur, it would be incorrect to conclude that it *is* in fact the motivating principle. On the other hand, if from autobiographical narratives we learn from entrepreneurs that fulfilling their dreams and providing employment for others is their chief motivation, it would be correct to conclude that these are indeed motivating principles. It would be incorrect, however to conclude that these are the only motivations. In this instance, to say that even falsehood is truth means the following: that even if disproportionate income may be an objective institutional factor, the entrepreneur's failure to mention it and alternate emphasis on fulfilling dreams and providing social benefit reveals an important subjective dynamic regardless of what we might also learn from institutional analysis. Even though institutional analysis can uncover objective causal forces, we cannot jump to the conclusion that these objective forces are necessarily also an individual's real subjective motivation and that the failure to mention the objective factors is evidence of self-serving deception. At the same time, of course, we cannot conclude from the biographical analysis that receiving disproportionate income is not a factor.

To put the point another way, objective analysis may reveal historical forces, but it cannot demonstrate that these historical forces are in fact the moral sentiments that drive any particular individual. On the other hand, biographical analysis reveals the mobilizing moral sentiments of an individual, even if we have evidence that in general such factors are at most only incidentally important. Put bluntly, the problem of truth and falsehood in biographical narrative comes down to this. On the one hand, an objectively general factor may be "true" but, unless it is also cited by an individual, it is impossible to conclude that it is a mobilizing factor in the life of that individual. On the other hand, a factor cited by an individual is personally important, even if it is objectively "false," and must at least be taken among the set of "true" moral sentiments that motivate the individual. We are back to that crucial distinction between truth and significance. Something may be true, but unless it is also subjectively true, then it may not in fact be a significant causal factor. In contrast, something may be "false," but if it is subjectively cited, it must be considered a mobilizing "truth." To give another example, if an entrepreneur reports that early childhood encounters with an adult model of entrepreneurship are largely responsible for the former's entrepreneurial career, it will not do to dismiss this mobilizing memory even if, upon extensive research, no evidence is found to support the claim that a significant adult even tried, much less succeeded, in starting a business venture.

In view of the foregoing arguments, the fundamental interpretive principle is that moral discourse is a lens onto underlying moral sentiments and that moral sentiments motivate behavior. Even those who readily admit they have taken advantage of others or lived decadently at times in their life describe these events within a normative discourse. The "shadow side" of their lives is interpreted as morally as are periods of moral rectitude. Even episodes of failing manifest the authority of a normative consciousness. "Novelists spin stories aimed at the penetration (by writer and reader alike) of the many layers of truth," says Robert Coles, "whereas liars spin stories meant to deceive, mislead, trouble, harm."[6] In telling their stories, the rich are more novelist than liar. They may spin lofty tales, but they do so to make meaning rather than to mislead.

NOTES

1. In this and the following paragraphs I have drawn in part on my analysis of issues of interpretation in biographical narratives in Paul G. Schervish, "The Moral Biographies of the Wealthy and the Cultural Scripture of Wealth," in Paul G. Schervish, editor, *Wealth in Western Thought: The Case for and Against the Rich* (Westport, Conn.: Praeger, 1994).

2. James Olney, "Autos*Bios*Graphein: The Study of Autobiographical Literature," *South Atlantic Quarterly 77* (Winter 1978), 118.

3. Timothy Dow Adams, *Telling Lies in Modern American Autobiography* (Chapel Hill: University of North Carolina Press, 1990, p. ix; the quote from Pascal is from Roy Pascal, *Design and Truth in Autobiography* (Cambridge: Harvard University Press, 1960), p. 189.

4. Domhoff avoids falling into conspiracy theory by taking special pains to distinguish between the kinds of life-style analyses he carries out in *The Higher Circles: The Governing Class in America* (New York: Vintage Books, 1971) and *The Bohemian Grove and Other Retreats: A Study in Ruling-Class Cohesiveness* (New York: Harper & Row, 1974), and the power elite analysis he presents in *Who Rules America Now?: A View for the 80s* (Englewood Cliffs, N.J.: Prentice-Hall, 1983) and *The Power Elite and the State: How Policy Is Made in America* (New York: Aldine DeGruyter, 1990).

    5. Anthony Giddens, *The Constitution of Society* (Berkeley: University of California Press, 1984).
    6. Robert Coles, *The Spiritual Life of Children* (Boston: Houghton Mifflin, 1990), 21.

Biographical Sketches

Thomas Cooke: 67 years old, Protestant, native of St. Louis where he presently resides; married, five children; inherited, member of distinguished moneyed family; financier; approximate net worth: $5 million; approximate annual income: $500,000–$650,000; prominent constituent of St. Louis philanthropic community, administrator of family trust.

Gretchen Dowell: 41 years old, Protestant, native of San Diego, raised in Philadelphia, now lives in Columbia, South Carolina; married, two stepchildren; heiress to wealth on mother's side, and stepdaughter in a nationally prominent family; aid to stepfather who served as governor of South Carolina; former director of state agency; approximate net worth: $5–$10 million; approximate annual income: $250,000–$400,000; significantly engaged politically and philanthropically.

Brendan Dwyer: 57 years old, devout Catholic, native of Worcester, MA, resident of Birmingham, MI; married, four children; entrepreneur, made wealth by insuring state employees; owner of successful Christian book distributorship; approximate net worth: over $10 million; approximate annual income: over $500,000; active in philanthropy.

Benjamin Ellman: 53 years old, Jewish, native of Chicago where he still resides; widowed, remarried, seven children; entrepreneur, mass-produces light fixtures, holds contracts with national hotel chains; approximate net worth: $5–$10 million; approximate annual income: over $500,000; active in Chicago Jewish community.

Ross and Beverly Geiger: mid-60s, Evangelical Christians, lived in metropolitan New York area until retired to Miami; two daughters, grandchildren;

self-made fortune in banking and real estate; approximate net worth: over $10 million; approximate annual income: over $500,000; founders of two charitable trusts dedicated to the propagation of the gospel, significant givers of time as well as money.

Rebecca Jacobs: 47 years old, Jewish, native of Chicago, resides in Chicago; twice divorced, remarried, five children; entrepreneur, largest franchise-holder of chain of makeover salons; approximate net worth: over $20 million; approximate annual income: $500,000-$1 million; heavily involved in Jewish philanthropies and civic causes.

Dale Jayson: 43 years old, African-American, Protestant, native of Texarkana, AR, resides in St. Louis; married, two sons; former NFL All-Pro with St. Louis Cardinals turned entrepreneur upon retirement from football; owner of appliance distributorship; approximate net worth: close to $6.5 million; approximate annual income: over $1 million; concerned with socioeconomic advancement of African-Americans.

Laura Madison: 63 years old, raised Catholic but practices Buddhism; Chicago native, resident of New York City; widowed, four children; heiress in old-line wealthy elite family, also married into wealth; approximate net worth: $5 million; approximate annual income: $400,000-$500,000; extensively involved in progressive and New Age philanthropic causes.

June Radkey: 60 years old, Catholic, emigrated from Italy at a very young age, resident of Columbus, OH; married, three children; founded ethnic restaurant eventually sold to franchisor; approximate net worth: $5-$10 million; estimated annual income: $650,000-$1.3 million; gives to ethnic, Church, and local causes.

Camile Russo: 26 years old, Catholic, native and resident of St. Louis; single, daughter of apparel mogul, director of public relations in family company; approximate net worth: over $500,000 (prior to receiving inheritance); approximate annual income: $130,000-$250,000; extensive involvement in family-related charities.

David Stephanov: 53 years old, Catholic, Polish background, native of Detroit where he still resides; married, four children; entrepreneur, made wealth in insurance, afterward in real estate development; owns numerous companies; approximate net worth: $10 million; approximate annual income: over $500,000; substantial political funder, moderately active in philanthropy.

Norman Stryker: 59 years old, Jewish, Houston native now resides in New York City; divorced, remarried, four children; scion to an industrial fortune, noted writer on national policy issues, formerly on the staff of *Baltimore Sun Times*; approximate net worth: $5–$10 million; approximate annual income: over $500,000; substantial charitable giver to progressive organizations, administrator of family foundation.

NOTES

All names and identifying information are changed. Where real institutions are alluded to, they are representative of the type rather than the particular institution.

All annual incomes and net worth are reported in 1992 dollars and represent approximate amounts.

Selected Bibliography

Aldrich, Nelson W., Jr. *Old Money: The Mythology of America's Upper Class.* New York: Alfred A. Knopf, 1988.

Allen, Michael Patrick. *The Founding Fortunes. A New Anatomy of the Super-Rich Families in America.* New York: E. P. Dutton, 1987.

Amis, Martin. *Money: A Suicide Note.* New York: Penguin Books, 1986.

Atwood, Albert W.M.A. *The Mind of the Millionaire.* New York: Harper & Brothers, 1926.

Baltzell, E. Digby. *The Protestant Establishment: Aristocracy & Caste in America.* New York: Random House, 1964.

————. *Philadelphia Gentlemen: The Making of a National Upper Class.* Chicago: Quadrangle Books, 1971.

Berger, Peter L. *The Capitalist Revolution: Fifty Propositions about Prosperity, Equality, and Liberty.* New York: Basic Books, 1968.

————, ed. *The Capitalist Spirit: Toward a Religious Ethic of Wealth Creation.* San Francisco, Calif.: ICS Press, 1990.

Bingham, Sallie. *Passion and Prejudice: A Family Memoir.* New York: Alfred A. Knopf, 1989.

Burlingame, Dwight F., ed. *The Responsibilities of Wealth.* Bloomington, Ind.: Indiana University Press, 1992.

Carnegie, Andrew. *The Gospel of Wealth and Other Timely Essays,* edited by Edward C. Kirkland. Cambridge, Mass.: Harvard University Press, 1962.

Coles, Robert, M.D. *Privileged Ones: The Well-off and the Rich in America.* Boston: Little, Brown and Company, 1977.

Dahl, Robert A. *Who Governs? Democracy and Power in an American City.* New Haven: Yale University Press, 1961.

Domhoff, William G. *The Higher Circles: The Governing Class in America.* New York: Vintage Books, 1971.

————. *The Bohemian Grove and Other Retreats: A Study in Ruling-Class Cohesiveness.* New York: Harper & Row, 1974.

_____. *Who Rules America Now?: A View for the 80s*. Englewood Cliffs, N.J.: Prentice-Hall, 1983.

_____. *The Power Elite and the State: How Policy Is Made in America*. New York: Aldine DeGruyter, 1990.

Domini, Amy L. with Dennis Pearne and Sharon L. Rich. *The Challenges of Wealth: Mastering the Personal and Financial Conflicts*. Homewood, Ill.: Dow Jones-Irwin, 1988.

Ewen, Stuart. *Captains of Consciousness: Advertising and the Social Roots of the Consumer Culture*. New York: McGraw-Hill, 1976.

_____ and Elizabeth Ewen. *Channels of Desire: Mass Images and the Shaping of American Consciousness*. Minneapolis: University of Minnesota Press, 1992.

Haughey, John C., S.J. *The Holy Use Of Money: Personal Finance in Light of Christian Faith*. Garden City, N.Y.: Doubleday & Company, 1986.

Heilbroner, Robert L. *The Quest for Wealth: A Study of Acquisitive Man*. New York: Simon and Schuster, 1956.

Heller, Robert. *The Age Of The Common Millionaire*. New York: Talley Books, Dutton, 1988.

Hunter, Floyd. *The Big Rich and the Little Rich*. Garden City, N.Y.: Doubleday & Company, 1965.

Inhaber, Herbert and Sidney Carroll. *How Rich Is Too Rich?: Income and Wealth in America*. New York: Praeger, 1992.

Jaher, Frederic Cople, ed. *The Rich, the Well Born, and the Powerful: Elites and Upper Classes in History*. Champaign: University of Illinois Press, 1973.

Kirstein, George G. *The Rich: Are They Different?* Boston: Houghton Mifflin Company, 1968.

Krueger, David W., ed. *The Last Taboo: Money as Symbol and Reality in Psychotherapy and Psychoanalysis*. New York: Brunner/Mazel, 1986.

Lamont, Michèle. *Money, Morals, & Manners: The Culture of the French and the American Upper-Middle Class*. Chicago: The University of Chicago Press, 1992.

Lenzner, Robert. *The Great Getty: The Life and Loves of J. Paul Getty—Richest Man in the World*. New York: Crown Publishers, 1985.

Lundberg, Ferdinand. *The Rich and the Super-Rich: A Study in the Power of Money Today*. New York: Bantam Books, 1968.

Marx, Karl. *Capital: A Critique of Political Economy, Volume I: The Process of Capitalist Production*, edited by Frederick Engels. New York: International Publishers, 1967. [Originally published in 1867.]

_____. *Manifesto of the Communist Party*. In *Karl Marx and Frederick Engels, Selected Works*, Volume One. Moscow: Progress Publishers, 1969. [Originally published in 1848.]

Marcus, George E. with Peter Dobkin Hall. *Lives in Trust: The Fortunes of Dynastic Families in Late Twentieth-Century America*. Boulder, Colo.: Westview Press, 1992.

Mellon, Paul with John Baskett. *Reflections in a Silver Spoon: A Memoir*. New York: William Morrow and Company, 1992.

Millman, Marcia. *Warm Hearts & Cold Cash: The Intimate Dynamics of Families and Money*. New York: The Free Press, 1991.

Mills, C. Wright. *The Power Elite*. Oxford: Oxford University Press, 1956.

Mintz, Morton, and Jerry S. Cohen, ed. *America, Inc.: Who Owns and Operates the United States*. New York: Dell Publishing, 1971.

Mogil, Christopher and Anne Slepian with Peter Woodrow. *We Gave Away a Fortune: Stories of People Who Have Devoted Themselves and Their Wealth to Peace, Justice and the Environment*. Philadelphia: New Society Publishers, 1992.

Myers, Gustavus. *History of the Great American Fortunes*. New York: The Modern Library, 1936.

Needleman, Jacob. *Money and the Meaning of Life*. New York: Doubleday, 1991.

Neuhaus, Richard John. *Doing Well and Doing Good: The Challenge to the Christian Capitalist*. New York: Doubleday, 1992.

Nickerson, Hoffman. *The American Rich*. Garden City, N.Y.: Doubleday, Doran & Company, 1930.

Novak, Michael. *This Hemisphere of Liberty: A Philosophy of the Americas*. Washington, D.C.: The AEI Press, 1990.

———. *The Catholic Ethic and the Spirit of Capitalism*. New York: Free Press, 1993.

Odendahl, Teresa. *Charity Begins at Home: Generosity and Self-Interest Among the Philanthropic Elite*. New York: Basic Books, 1990.

Ostrander, Susan A. *Women of the Upper Class*. Philadelphia: Temple University Press, 1984.

Packard, Vance. *The Ultra Rich: How Much Is Too Much? Boston: Little, Brown and Company, 1989*.

Phillips, Kevin. *The Politics of Rich and Poor: Wealth and the American Electorate in the Reagan Aftermath*. New York: Random House, 1990.

Rubinstein, W. D., ed. *Wealth and the Wealthy in the Modern World*. New York: St. Martin's Press, 1980.

Sampson, Anthony. *The Midas Touch: Understanding the Dynamic New Money Societies Around Us*. New York: Truman Talley Books, Dutton, 1989.

Schervish, Paul G. and Andrew Herman. *Empowerment and Beneficence: Strategies of Living and Giving Among the Wealthy*. Final Report of the Study on Wealth and Philanthropy: Final Report. Chestnut Hill, Mass.: The Social Welfare Research Institute at Boston College, 1988.

Schervish, Paul G. "Wealth and the Spiritual Secret of Money." In Robert Wuthnow and Virginia A. Hodgkinson, eds., *Faith and Philanthropy in America: Exploring the Role of Religion in America's Voluntary Sector*. San Francisco: Jossey-Bass, 1990.

——— and Obie Benz, Peggy Dulany, Thomas B. Murphy, and Stanley Salett. *Taking Giving Seriously*. Indianapolis: Indiana University Center on Philanthropy, 1993.

———. "The Moral Biographies of the Wealthy and the Cultural Scripture of Wealth," in Paul G. Schervish, ed., *Wealth in Western Thought: The Case for and Against the Rich*. Westport, Conn.: Praeger, 1994.

Simmel, Georg. *The Philosophy of Money*, 2nd edition, enlarged. Edited by David Frisby. Translated by Tom Bottomore and David Frisby. London: Routledge, 1990. [Reprint of 1907 edition.]

Slater, Philip. *Wealth Addiction*. New York: Dutton, 1983.

Smith, Adam. *An Inquiry into the Nature and Cause of the Wealth of Nations.* Edited by
       Edwin Connan. New York: The Modern Library, 1937. [Originally pub-
       lished in 1776.]
Tebbel, John. *The Inheritors: A Study of America's Great Fortunes and What Happened
       to Them.* New York: G. P. Putnam's Sons, 1962.
Train, John. *The Money Masters.* New York: Harper & Row, 1980.
Veblen, Thorstein. *The Theory of the Leisure Class.* New Brunswick, N.J.: Transaction
       Publishers, 1992. [Reprint of 1889 edition.]
Wachtel, Paul. *The Poverty of Affluence: A Psychological Portrait of the American Way
       of Life.* Philadelphia: New Society Publishers, 1989.
Weber, Max. *The Protestant Ethic and the Spirit of Capitalism.* Translated by Talcott
       Parsons. New York: Macmillan, 1958. [Weber's essays originally ap-
       peared in German in 1904–05.]

Index of Biographical Narratives

General Index

Adams, Timothy Dow, 269
Autobiographical narratives, 10; issues of interpretation, 3, 267–71. *See also* Biographical analysis; Critique; Gospel of wealth; Moral biography

Base of command, 5. *See also* Empowerment, spatial
Biographical analysis, 12–13, 270. *See also* Autobiographical narratives; Moral biography

Carnegie, Andrew, 2, 15, 268
Class trait, 3, 14–15. *See also* Hyperagency
Coles, Robert, 271
Conspiracy analysis, 268–69
Consumption theories, 14
Critique, 3, 14–16. *See also* Consumption theories; Cultural leadership theories; Marxist class theory; Power elite theories; Stewardship
Cultural leadership theories, 3

Dialectic: of alignment to the rules of money, 2; of fortune and virtue, 3, 11, 13, 15–16, 20, 79, 111–13, 175
Domhoff, William, 269

Empowerment, 2–3, 8, 13–16, 267; psychological, 2, 6–7, 9, 14, 193, 225 (*see also* Individuality); spatial, 2, 4–5, 8–9 (*see also* Principality); temporal, 2–3, 8–9, 251 (*see also* Principality)
Entrepreneur, 2, 6–7, 9–11, 19–21, 35–36, 59–60, 147–48, 176, 193, 249–50, 270–71

Freedom, 2–3; to choose, 3, 14, 19, 112; from necessity, 3, 14
Frisby, David, 1

Giddens, Anthony, 270
Gospel of wealth, 14–14, 267

Holiness, 7
Hyperagency, 2–3, 8, 14–15, 60, 112, 267. *See also* Class trait

Identity, 8–9, 128; financial, 2; philanthropic, 78; transformations of, 11–12, 128, 193–94 (*see also* Liminality); troubles of, 77–78, 127, 226. *See also* Socialization
Individuality, 3, 8–10, 14, 20, 35, 60, 176–77. *See also* Empowerment, psychological